Praise for
History of Greed

"David Sarna has written an important, readable, erudite, and compelling book that delves into all of the dark corners of the financial markets in a way that only one who is a knowledgeable intellectual like David and who has seen, as David has, the inner workings of the markets can do."

—Andrew Malick
Chairman, Needham & Co.

"David Sarna has provided a close-up, insider's view of some of the shenanigans going on in and around the financial capitals of the world. It is very readable, entertaining, and almost funny until you realize all the lives that have been hurt by the combination of at best amoral and more correctly criminal acts aimed at investors of all stripes who foolishly expected and chased outsized returns. Sarna describes all this against a backdrop of regulatory complacency, along with overgenerous bonuses and salaries for the titans of finance and industry who added little if anything to the quality of life for those who did not ride the gravy train with them."

—Jonathan Harris, CPA
Retired Senior Partner, Big Four accounting firm

"David Sarna is a visionary technologist. He is also a sophisticated investor and financier. He has written a readable, comprehensive, fascinating, and well-researched book that explores troublesome aspects of the financial system in a way only an experienced insider could."

—Jay N. Goldberg
Senior Managing Director, Hudson Ventures

"A comprehensive review of what has happened to us in our financial markets over and over and over and over again. It's an important history, written with wit and delivered with wisdom. Undoubtedly, *History of Greed* will become required reading by anyone serious about understanding the capital markets."

—Frederick L. Gorsetman
Founder and Managing Member, Oxbridge Financial Group LLC

"Fascinating! I did not think the trading of securities and reading about it could be that absorbing."

— Carl Nisser
Counsel, McGuire Woods
Former Judge at Svea Court of Appeal, Stockholm

"*History of Greed* is right on the money and quite timely. I found a lot of information and much I did not know, and I have been around the industry for a while. It made me feel like a dunce once I saw how the manipulative trading on the over-the-counter (OTC) stock market really works."

—Philip Fox
Insurance Executive and Former Broker

History of Greed

Financial Fraud from Tulip Mania to Bernie Madoff

David E. Y. Sarna

WILEY

John Wiley & Sons, Inc.

Published by John Wiley & Sons, Inc., Hoboken, New Jersey.

Published simultaneously in Canada.

For general information on our other products and services or for technical support, please
contact our Customer Care Department within the United States at (800) 762-2974,
outside the United States at (317) 572-3993 or fax (317) 572-4002.

Wiley also publishes its books in a variety of electronic formats. Some content that appears
in print may not be available in electronic books. For more information about Wiley
products, visit our web site at www.wiley.com.

Library of Congress Cataloging-in-Publication Data:

Sarna, David E. Y.
  History of greed : financial fraud from tulip mania to Bernie Madoff / David E. Y.
Sarna ; [foreword by] Andrew Malik.
     p.   cm.
  Includes bibliographical references and index.
  ISBN 978-0-470-60180-8 (hardback); ISBN 978-0-470-87769-2 (ebk);
  ISBN 978-0-470-87742-5 (ebk); ISBN 978-0-470-87770-8 (ebk)
  1. Fraud—Case studies.   2. Commercial crimes—Case studies.   3. Avarice—
Case studies.   I.   Title.
  HV6691.S27   2010
  364.16'3—dc22
                                                              2010010929

Printed in the United States of America
10 9 8 7 6 5 4 3 2 1

For my family,
with all my love

Contents

Foreword

In my more than 40 years on Wall Street, I've had the opportunity to participate in more than 1,000 transactions, but I have written very few Forewords to books. However, when David asked me to write the Foreword to *History of Greed*, I couldn't say no. David Sarna has written an important, readable, erudite, and compelling book that delves into all of the dark corners of the financial markets in a way that only one who is a knowledgeable intellectual like David, and who has seen, as David has, the inner workings of the markets, can do.

Ever since the Dutch invented shares and limited liability companies as we know them around the year 1602, capital markets have fueled the growth of countless companies, created millions and millions of jobs, and produced great wealth for nations, entrepreneurs, and investors.

I've had the good fortune to be associated with some of the most successful capital raises of all time, through initial public offerings of such technology companies as Intel, Cray Computing, Tandem, Lotus Development, and Qualcomm. I have also lost money on many start-ups that didn't make it. That is okay. Win some, lose some. It's the price we pay for free markets; and in the long run, the winners have more than made up for the losers.

Unfortunately, some are not content to merely compete in free markets; they seek to rig the game through fraud and deception, casting a pall on the entire financial industry. As early as 1609, the governors of the Dutch stock exchange imposed limits on unfettered naked shorting to keep the markets fair and open to all.

Training a spotlight on the market's dark corners, illuminating wrongdoing for all to see, does a service to honest investors. As the late Sy Syms said since 1959 until his passing in 2009, "An educated consumer is our best customer." By explaining what's going on in clear language understandable to laypersons, but with detail sufficient to satisfy the consummate professional, David shows the various ways that crooked individuals have corruptly sought to gain an unfair advantage through deception or outright theft, serving as a warning that what looks too good to be true usually is.

In 1817, Chief Justice John Marshall of the Supreme Court, writing for the majority in *Laidlaw v. Organ*, made *caveat emptor* (let the buyer beware) the supreme law of the land in the United States. *Caveat emptor* is an implied warning to a buyer that the goods he or she is buying are "as is," or subject to any defects. Some use the rule as justification to mislead or cheat. This is wrong. It is not a rule designed to shield sellers who engage in fraud or bad-faith dealing by making false or misleading representations about the quality or condition of a particular product or offering. It merely summarizes the concept that a purchaser must examine, judge, and test a product before buying it.

The excesses discussed in this book highlight the need for competent regulation to ensure that the principles of transparency, equitable handling, and adequacy of disclosure are observed, together with fair and even-handed enforcement to deter and punish wrongdoers. Only then can integrity be restored to the markets, to the benefit of all of us.

History of Greed serves as a warning of what can go wrong when these simple principles are forgotten. It is required reading for anyone trying to understand how financial markets really work.

ANDREW MALIK
Chairman, Needham & Co.

Acknowledgments

I'd like to acknowledge with thanks the unwitting contributors to this book: all of the gullible and greedy retail investors; naive and/or larcenous entrepreneurs; avaricious PIPE writers; dishonest stockbrokers and placement agents; willfully blind lawyers, accountants, stockbrokers, and investment bankers; the army of jaded and crooked promoters; and all of the money-loving service providers who have, over the years, given this author an expensive education in all the ways in which they cheat, lie, and steal. They all know who they are, and they are consigned to anonymity as partial penance for their many misdeeds. Without them, there would be no securities fraud cases to write about.

Many people helped in the preparation of this book—too many to enumerate them all. Thanks are due to my editor, Debby Englander; to Kelly O'Connor, development editor; to my publisher, Joan L. O'Neil; to Adrianna Johnson; Tiffany Charbonier; Claire Wesley, Production Editor; and to all the other nice folks at John Wiley & Sons who strived behind the scenes to make this book the best possible; to Jen Westmoreland Bouchard, principal of Lucidité Writing, LLC (www.luciditewriting.com), who edited, prepared the bibliography, and kept it all in accordance with the *Chicago Manual of Style*; to my agent, Bill Gladstone of Waterside Literary Agency, who believed in me from the first e-mail; to Scott-Martin Kosofsky, who introduced me to Bill; to Cape Cod Compositors for the index; and Michael Freeland for the cover design.

Heartfelt gratitude to my rabbi and teacher of more than 50 years, Rabbi Dr. Haskel Lookstein for always being there for me and for my family. Heartfelt thanks also to my brother, Professor Jonathan D. Sarna, who read the manuscript more than once, made many very valuable suggestions and has been supportive in many ways. Many thanks to Jonathan Harris, CPA, and to Carl Nisser, Esq., who also read the entire manuscript and gave me much helpful feedback. My sincere thanks to my longtime counsel and friend Melvin Weinberg, Esq.; to Andrew Ceresney, Esq.; and Sean Hecker, Esq.; to David Jaroslawicz, Esq.; and Elizabeth Eilender, Esq.; to Jay N. Goldberg, and to Frederick L. Gorsetman. My gratitude to Hillel Weinberger, Nathan Low, and Marilyn Adler for their generosity. Thanks also to A. Charles Lubash and Philip Fox for their unrelenting support.

My deepest thanks go to my very devoted and loyal friends, too many to list, who supported me and helped me through some hard times and celebrated the good times with me and my family. Most of all, words are inadequate to express my thanks, gratitude, and love to my wife and children for their unconditional love, loyalty, and support through thick and thin, for putting up with all my meshigas for these many years, and who were extremely helpful to me in so many ways.

May the Almighty reward you all for your many good deeds.

Thanks to my parents, of blessed memory for bringing me up with love for the written word and whom I trust are smiling down on us from the Yeshiva on High.

Introduction

A lexander the Great, King of Macedonia, visited Jerusalem in the year 332 BCE, as recounted by Flavius Josephus in *Antiquities of the Jews*. The Talmud records that he asked for a souvenir of his visit. The rabbis presented him with an orb (an eyeball). Alexander weighed it against all his gold and silver, but the orb was not outweighed.[2]

"What is this?" Alexander asked.

They said, "It is the orb of an eye of a flesh and blood man, that is never satisfied with any riches."

[Alexander] said to them, "What proof is there that this is so?"

"Take a little bit of dirt and cover [the eye], so it can no longer see," they said. "It will be outweighed immediately."

It was.[1]

Commenting on this story, Rabbi Judah Loew, known as the Maharal of Prague (1525–1609), explains that an unceasingly hungry eye was the defining characteristic of Alexander. Even after he was an emperor of historic stature, even after he was "the Great," he was not satisfied and sought to conquer new frontiers. Following his desire to reach the "ends of the world and the Great Outer Sea," he invaded India, but was eventually forced to turn back by the near-mutiny of his troops, who had tired of war. Alexander died in Babylon in 323 BCE, before having the chance to realize a series of planned campaigns, beginning with an invasion of Arabia. In the years following Alexander's death, his empire was torn apart in a series of civil wars, which resulted in the formation of a number of states ruled by Macedonian nobility.

As the rabbis warned, greed eventually did him in.

In contrast, on April 12, 1955, Dr. Jonas Salk made public the success of his vaccine against polio. The late Edward R. Murrow asked him, "Who owns the patent on this vaccine?"

Salk famously replied, "Well, the people, I would say. There is no patent. Could you patent the sun?"[3]

Obviously, that was selfless behavior.

So one must wonder: What is greed, and where does it come from if not all people are greedy?

Greed (also called avarice) is an excessive desire to acquire or possess more than what one needs or deserves, especially with respect to material wealth.[4]

That is what this book is about: greed, which leads to fraud and dishonesty.

In Christian theology, greed is one of the seven mortal sins, unpardonable sins entailing a total loss of grace. In the past few years, we've all been reading an awful lot about it, specifically the greedy financial crime that has become widely prevalent, and is commonly blamed for the financial crash of 2008, among other ills. One might also wonder why financial crime seems to be so much on the rise.

In my opinion, it's because, as the saying goes, a rising tide lifts all boats, an aphorism said to have been coined by Seán Lemass, the Irish Taoiseach (prime minister) from 1959 to 1966. Many frauds have come to light only recently, even though, as we shall see, securities fraud, dishonesty, and greed have a long and storied history. When times are good, less fraud comes to light, because even dubious schemes make money; and Ponzi schemes keep rolling on, with new investors' funds going to pay out redemptions, thus keeping the fraud going. With no public outcry, oversight tends to become lax.

"People aren't bothered when boom times are rolling, but when they need their money again, that's what catches out the crooks," Terence Gourvish, director of the London School of Economics business history group, told Tom Cahill of Bloomberg.com.[5] "They get away with it for quite a long time if there's a boom because no one needs the money. They just leave it there."

When times turn bad, that's when the cockroaches start crawling out of the woodwork. Times have become very bad, indeed, as unemployment has exceeded 10 percent, and the amount of fraud coming to light has reached epic proportions.

The meltdown of 2008 has affected us all, and we are justifiably angry. But was the worst economic crisis in decades caused by blatant illegal acts or by some terrible, but noncriminal, combination of greed, naïveté, blunders, and just plain stupidity? After all, neither stupidity nor naïveté is a crime, and, in and of itself, neither is greed. As we will see, however, the problems go well beyond simple greed, for there is no shortage of manifest criminality, which is *illegal*, as opposed to simply *immoral* greed.

History of Greed does not purport to be an exhaustive catalog of financial misdeeds. Unfortunately, such a catalog would fill an encyclopedia of many, many volumes. Rather, I have selected cases that are illustrative and representative of various kinds of financial fraud, as well as some cases that are particularly noteworthy for their size, duration, mechanics, or notoriety. In my focus on recent events, I remain aware that financial fraud is by no means an invention of the twentieth century.

As Goldwin Smith, a nineteenth-century American historian, journalist, and lawyer, observed, "If anyone supposes that there was no commercial fraud in the Middle Ages, let him study the commercial legislation of England for that period, and his mind will be satisfied, if he has a mind to be satisfied and not only a fancy to run away with him."[6]

Even Phaedrus, the Roman poet (15 BCE–50 CE), observed, "Whoever is detected in a shameful fraud is ever after not believed even if they speak the truth."[7] With over two thousand years of experience to learn from, modern financial fraudsters are more sophisticated and entrap more people for greater sums than ever before.

In this book, we take a close look at the different kinds of fraud, greed, and dishonesty that pervade the securities industry, in good times and in bad, and examine what can be done so we can protect ourselves as much as possible against the inevitable.

Chapter 1

Selling Air

WHY NOW?

U nless you have been living in a cave and have been completely cut off from outside society, you know that in the space of a few months, at least $11,000,000,000,000 ($11 trillion) was lost from the U.S. economy in 2008, and that the world was turned upside down and plunged into a deep recession, if not depression.[1]

What happened?

Fraud and greed had a lot to do with it.

In general, pundits, seeking simple answers, blamed it all on subprime mortgages, or on credit default swaps, or on auction-rate securities, or whatever, but these answers are unsatisfying. They are at once both too complex and far too simplistic. For the real explanation of what happened, however, we need to look to the experts, to history, to literature, and even to my Grandma Rachel.

My Grandma Rachel

Grandma Rachel Leah Horowitz, born on Christmas Day in 1893 at the end of the nineteenth century, was a very wise lady who lived to the age of 92. Her husband, Reb Alte Elisha Horowitz, a merchant who

1

was also a noted Talmudic scholar, had died young of esophageal cancer in London, where they then lived, when she was only 39. He left her with nine children and a run-down liquor store in London's East End. Overcoming many obstacles, she raised these nine children well, and built up the store into a very successful enterprise where she bought and sold wine, whiskey, liquors, and schnapps. She liked the business, she said, because the bottles were real. You could hold them, smell them, drink from them, and enjoy them.

There were other businesses in London that didn't make anything or sell anything but just traded paper, which turned into more paper. "This is not a real business!" she used to say. "It is *luftgescheft*," which in German and in Yiddish means "air business" or "ethereal business." Someone who engaged in *luftgescheften* she called a *luftmensch* (an air person or schemer), and she would have nothing to do with such *luftmenschen*. My beloved Grandma Rachel Leah lived through the Great Depression, and survived her home being bombed by the Nazis during the Blitz.

Little did she know back then how amazingly prophetic her words would prove to be for the twenty-first century. What happened in the United States of America was essentially the result of all the *luftgescheften* run by financial wizard *luftmenschen* who turned money into paper and then supposedly back into even more money, siphoning off outrageous profits in the process. When the music stopped, the entire house of cards suddenly collapsed, and all that was left, of course, was *luft* (air) and worthless paper.

Tevye the Dairyman

In her dislike of *luftgescheften*, my grandmother, who was steeped in Yiddish literature, was (at least subconsciously) influenced by the Yiddish literary giant Sholem Aleichem (the literary pen name of Sholem Rabinovitsh, 1859–1916). He, unforgettably, wrote about *luftmenschen* in his novel *Tevye der Milkhiker* (*Tevye the Dairyman*).[2] First published in 1894, *Tevye der Milkhiker* is known throughout the world partly because of its adaptation into a play by Arnold Perl called *Tevye and His Daughters*, which became the famous Broadway musical and film *Fiddler on the Roof*.

Menachem-Mendl, a distant relative of Tevye, the (impoverished) dairyman, is a *luftmensch sans pareil*. He begins talking to Tevye, who made a little bit of money helping out a wealthy lady, about stocks and options in a way that Tevye, a simple man, can't possibly understand. Then he gets to his point. Menachem-Mendl promises Tevye that he can turn 100 rubles into 1,000, and Tevye would be a fool to forfeit the opportunity. Tevye agrees to give Menachem-Mendl his last hundred rubles in order to enter into a *shutfus*, or partnership, with him— "I put in the money, and Menachem-Mendl put in the brains"—with the two of them splitting the profits (and thereby neatly sidestepping the age-old Jewish prohibition against lending with interest).

You know what happens. It was all lost. Sholem Aleichem also describes in detail Menachem-Mendl's ultimate failure at various other ethereal (*luft*) moneymaking schemes—such as his attempt at selling "Londons," an apparent reference to a currency speculation, which Menachem-Mendl describes to his wife as "a very refined substance" in that "you can't see it" (classic *luft*).

So, as it says in Kohelet, "There is nothing new under the sun." *Luftmenschen* have been around for ages, if not for millennia.[3]

Luftgescheften Then and Now

One of the early documented examples of *luftgescheften*, which presages many other episodes, was recounted by Joseph de la Vega, a Portuguese-Jewish trader who emigrated to Amsterdam to avoid persecution from the Spanish Inquisition. He famously wrote in 1688: "This year too was a year of confusion for many unlucky speculators declared in one voice that the present crisis was a labyrinth of labyrinths, the terror of terrors, the confusion of confusions."[4] He could just as well have been speaking about the state of the national and global economy in 2008.

Trillions of value were erased from the nation's housing stock in 2008 as foreclosures flooded the market, an oversupply of homes built on speculation remained unsold, and real estate prices everywhere plummeted. Martin Feldstein, the noted economist, estimated that overall $11 trillion to $12 trillion of value disappeared.

The value of global financial assets, including stocks, bonds, and currencies, probably fell by more than $50 trillion in 2008, equivalent to a year of world gross domestic product (GDP), according to an Asian Development Bank (ADB) report written by Claudio Loser, a former International Monetary Fund (IMF) director.[5] "This crisis is the first truly universal one in the history of humanity," former IMF Managing Director Michel Camdessus said at an ADB forum in Manila.[6] "No country escapes from it. It has not yet bottomed out."

Stephen Schwarzman, CEO of the private equity company Blackstone Group, said to an audience at the Japan Society, "Between 40 and 45 percent of the world's wealth has been destroyed in little less than a year and a half." He added, "This is absolutely unprecedented in our lifetime."

Savvy investor George Soros said in mid-February 2009 that the world financial system has effectively disintegrated, and that there is as yet no prospect of a near-term resolution to the crisis. Soros said the turbulence is actually more severe than during the Great Depression, comparing the current situation to the demise of the Soviet Union. He said the bankruptcy of Lehman Brothers in September marked a turning point in the functioning of the market system.

"We witnessed the collapse of the financial system," Soros said at a Columbia University dinner.[8] "It was placed on life support, and it's still on life support. There's no sign that we are anywhere near a bottom."

Who knows what other unthinkable turbulence is yet to come?

As we can see, the economy collapsed from greed-driven *luft* in the form of frauds, derivatives, strips, collateral debt obligations, credit default swaps, auction-rate securities, and all manner of exotic financial instruments that dominated the financial markets beginning in the 1980s in a feeding frenzy that reached its apex during the two terms of the hands-off administration of George W. Bush, the 43rd president of the United States. What happened was yet another chapter in the sad but recurrent story of greed gone wild. Greedy financial promoters, investment bankers, and their cohorts and all-too-willing accomplices were all allowed to run unchecked by a complacent government.

In April 2010, the Securities and Exchange Commission (SEC) charged Goldman Sachs and one of its vice presidents for defrauding investors by misstating and omitting key facts about a financial product (ABACUS) tied to subprime mortgages. The SEC alleged that Goldman Sachs structured and marketed a synthetic collateralized debt obligation (CDO) that hinged on the performance of subprime residential mortgage-backed securities (RMBS). The SEC alleged that Goldman Sachs failed to disclose to investors vital information about the CDO, in particular the role that a major hedge fund played in the portfolio selection process and the fact the hedge fund had taken a short position against the CDO.

"Synthetic CDOs like ABACUS 2007-AC1 contributed to the recent financial crisis by magnifying losses associated with the downturn in the United States housing market," the SEC said in its press release.[9]

"The product was new and complex but the deception and conflicts are old and simple," said Robert Khuzami, Director of the Division of Enforcement. "Goldman wrongly permitted a client that was betting against the mortgage market to heavily influence which mortgage securities to include in an investment portfolio, while telling other investors that the securities were selected by an independent, objective third party." The SEC alleged "that undisclosed in the marketing materials and unbeknownst to investors, the Paulson & Co. hedge fund, which was poised to benefit if the RMBS defaulted, played a significant role in selecting which RMBS should make up the portfolio. Investors in the liabilities of ABACUS are alleged to have lost more than $1 billion."

Society apparently forgot the famous words of Hank Rearden, the hero in *Atlas Shrugged*, the great novel by Ayn Rand (1957), "I work for nothing but my own profit—which I make by selling a product they need to men who are willing and able to buy it."[10] Instead of making and selling products people need, we in the United States mostly imported other people's products and we sold *luft*. Now, we all must pay the price.

Selling *luft* honestly is bad enough. Selling it dishonestly just makes things worse. As the anonymous blogger who calls himself 1boringoldman wrote, "Piracy made lots of money. Slave trading made plenty of money. The robber barons made money. The problem is that it's somebody else's money—taken, not made."[11]

The Bezzle Is Shrinking

As the *Financial Times* remembered, the famous economist John Kenneth Galbraith once proposed a measure of the economic cycle called the "bezzle." It is a measure of the inventory that has been purloined from investors.[12] In fat years, the bezzle grows as auditors relax. In the lean years, it shrinks as investors become cautious. The allegations against Bernard Madoff, and now Sir Allen Stanford, suggest the bezzle is large—but shrinking.[13]

This is the story of how *luft*, wizardry, dishonesty, and fraud were used to take other people's money, ignoring the lessons of history. My Grandma Rachel would have seen it all coming; may her soul rest in peace.

Chapter 2

Crash Postmortem

How Greed, Hubris, and Lack of Supervision Did Investors In

In Chapter 1, I blamed greed, hubris, and lack of supervision for the crash of 2008. In this chapter, we'll try to put the events in historical perspective.

The year 2008 is destined to go down in history as a disastrous year for the world's economy, and a near miss for plunging the world into deep depression. It disrupted the lives of many millions of people, and caused enormous pain and suffering to many.

In this chapter, we look at the major factors that that gave rise to this sad state of affairs, and tackle the obvious questions: Why was the disaster not foreseen? Why was nothing done to prevent it?

Is It Something That Started in the 1980s?

The cataclysmic events of 2008, when markets seized up, the government stepped in with a bailout of $85 trillion and ended up owning huge chunks of the private sector, and the stock markets collapsed, did not come about overnight, even though their effects became apparent in just a short period of time. The excesses that became obvious to all by the end of 2008 had already begun in the 1980s.

In *Liar's Poker* (W.W. Norton, 1989), Michael Lewis humorously chronicled the excesses and greed that he saw in his three years as a bond salesman at investment bank Salomon Brothers during its heyday in the late 1980s. (Salomon Brothers was, until recently, a part of Smith Barney, a division of Citigroup Global Capital Markets Inc.; it was unloaded to Occidental at roughly its net asset value, at the urging of the government, which now owns a huge stake in Citibank and calls many of the shots). In this book, Lewis provided a first-person account of how bond traders and salesmen truly work, their personalities, and their culture. He accurately captured a period in the history of Wall Street that, as we shall see, was eerily like what was to happen again, with even more intensity, two decades later.

Other books that captured that period of excess were *Barbarians at the Gate* by Bryan Burrough and John Helyar (Harper & Row, 1990) about the leveraged buyout (LBO) of RJR Nabisco, and the fictional *The Bonfire of the Vanities* by Tom Wolfe (Farrar Straus Giroux, 1987). These, too, foreshadowed what was to happen later.

Still, with the events of the 1980s chronicled so clearly, one must wonder why experts didn't see the crash of 2008 as inevitable. Or, more accurately, if they did see it coming, why didn't anyone do anything to stop it?

Professor Nouriel Roubini of New York University believes the answer to this question lies in the way in which the media treat Wall Street. He said:

> The problem is that in the bubble years, everyone becomes a cheerleader, including the media. This is the time when journalists should be asking tough questions, and I think there was a failure there. The Masters of the Universe were always on the cover, or the front page—the hedge-fund guys, the imperial CEO, private equity. I wish there had been more financial and business journalists, in the good years, who'd said, "Wait a moment, if this man, or this firm, is making a 100% return a year, how do they do it?"[1]

But we can't simply blame it on the media. After all, some media outlets were brightly shining a negative light on Wall Street, and some journalists did ask the right questions. The problem was that people didn't listen. After all, people believe what they want to believe, and the naysayers were largely ignored.

Don't Markets Always Fluctuate?

Some might say that the vicissitudes of the market are inevitable. So for example, when J. P. Morgan (1837–1913) was once asked by someone what the market would do that day, Morgan reportedly replied, "It will fluctuate, young man. It will fluctuate."[2] On Black Monday, October 19, 1987, when the market dropped 25 percent, a reporter asked John M. Templeton to comment. "Stocks fluctuate. Next question," he answered.[3]

So in a perfect world, markets fluctuate exclusively on the basis of honest variations in supply and demand and reflect perfect information. Everyone has access to exactly the same information.

Unfortunately, the world is not perfect. Seekers of easy money try to gain an unfair advantage by:

- Manipulating supply and demand to their benefit.
- Taking advantage of information unavailable to the market and then using this secret information to profit so long as the market supply and demand have not yet reflected their inside information

Ordinary folks, who are just following the herd or who put aside money for their retirement in supposedly safe and prudently managed funds and neither manipulate the market nor have access to inside information, get hurt badly once the music stops, the bubble bursts, and the markets crash.

Was It the Junk Bonds or the Subprime Mortgages?

Some sought an explanation for what happened in 2008 by blaming it all on so-called junk bonds, high-interest bonds issued by less than totally blue-chip companies that had been popularized and peddled in the 1980s by the likes of Drexel Burnham Lambert (which collapsed in 1990).[4]

Andrew Ross Sorkin (2009), an award-winning financial journalist for the *New York Times* and founder and editor of DealBook, quotes Martin Lipton, the superlawyer who co-founded Wachtell, Lipton, Rosen & Katz, as one who espoused the "blame it all on Drexel Burnham" explanation for what happened. Lipton said derisively at a conference in November 2008: "The financial crisis we're in today stems from the invention by Drexel Burnham Lambert of the junk bond. . . . You can draw a straight line from Drexel Burnham to the financial world today."[5]

I think a better analysis was offered by Michael Milken, the man who essentially invented the junk bond while at Drexel Burnham Lambert: "Critics who compare the subprime debacle to the bubble in high-yield, high-risk corporate bonds that Drexel helped inflate in 1980s are people who don't understand markets very well," said Milken. He believes that junk bonds, or those rated below investment grade, "have little in common with mispriced subprime mortgages," which he argues are the real culprits.[6]

"Having financed several of America's largest home builders, I know a few things about the housing industry," Milken said. "What happened to housing was not a failure of securitization, but rather a disastrous lowering of underwriting standards and other unfortunate practices."

As Sorkin rightly noted in the *New York Times* on April 29, 2008, Milken's detractors are misinformed.[7] Did he invent the junk bond? Yes. Did he help make securitization popular? Yes. Did he have anything to do with the current mess? Absolutely not. "Blaming Milken for today's credit crisis is like blaming the inventor of paper money [for money laundering]," says Sorkin.[8]

No—It's All Fraud, Alchemy, and Greed

So, if the crisis was not caused by the media, is not the result of ordinary market fluctuations, and was not caused by junk bonds, then what did cause it?

I argue that the real underlying causes are fraud, alchemy, and greed.

In its suit against Goldman Sachs, discussed in the previous chapter and filed as we go to press, the SEC appears to agree, although so far only civil fraud charges have been filed.

The recently disclosed frauds of Marc S. Dreier, Bernard L. Madoff, and Allen Stanford were all carefully concealed frauds, aided and abetted by willing and greedy investors. But their special trick was to snooker people by appealing not just to investors' greedy instincts, but also to their egos. They, the "lucky ones," Dreier, Madoff, and Stanford told their marks, were being offered an opportunity for profit not available to the hoi polloi. As we shall see, these types of frauds have occurred before, and more than likely will occur again.

The common denominator of making this easy money—whether it be through frauds or by selling subprime mortgages—is that they are all forms of alchemy, ways to turn worthless paper (what my grandma called *luft*) into money by relying on the "greater fool" theory of economics— a theory that suggests it is possible to make money by buying securities (pieces of paper), whether overvalued or not, and later selling them at a profit because there will always be someone (a bigger or greater fool) who is willing to pay the higher price. Inevitably, there comes a time when there is no greater fool to be found, at which time . . . pop! The bubble inevitably bursts, and you're the fool.

Investors Suffer Huge Losses

Simply put, the folks taken in by major frauds—frauds committed by Marc Dreier, Bernie Madoff, and Allen Stanford as well as other, smaller frauds—had all succumbed to greed and hubris. Dreier was hawking performing notes from solvent real estate companies at a 40 percent discount to value on the ruse that the sellers he represented were hedge funds forced to sell at a loss, and he was offering the hedge funds that still had liquidity a huge bargain. Come on now—40 percent below the market on performing loans? Greed and hubris caused a suspension of disbelief.

The same went for Madoff's clients. His ruse was to offer "can't lose" returns year in and year out, and in an old gambit he played hard to get. So people's egos got in the way of their good sense. No one has ever consistently produced returns like Madoff claimed to have produced over an 18-year period. This doesn't happen in the real world.

But greed suspends disbelief. We are all guilty of being greedy. As Evan Newmark wrote in the *New York Times*, "The belief that one can beat the market is the core operating principle of Wall Street. It is the philosophical grease that keeps all the machines of Wall Street humming."[9]

Indeed, most of the problems in the economy have their roots in greed, hubris, and lack of supervision.

To Be Criminal

Since every investor wants to beat the market, and every investor believes he or she has an edge, the question then becomes, "When does smart investing cross the line into criminal behavior?"

In her article entitled "On Madoff: The Scholar, the Regulator, and the Trader" in *Condé Nast Portfolio*, Megan Barnett asked the question, "Were the occupants of the executive suites of Lehman Brothers, Bear Stearns, or Merrill Lynch criminals?"[10] The question was answered in the affirmative. "The short seller Jim Chanos thinks so. And so does former SEC chairman Harvey Pitt."[11]

> Chanos, whose investment firm, Kynikos Associates, is one of the largest short-sellers on the Street, and Pitt, who now runs the consulting firm Kalorama Partners, joined Holocaust survivor and professor Elie Wiesel at a breakfast sponsored by *Condé Nast Portfolio* . . . in New York. The topic at hand was Madoff, but the conversation turned to the widespread problems on Wall Street.
>
> "I believe there was criminality in the executive suites of these firms," Chanos said, after explaining how Lehman's "hole" in its balance sheet was twice that of Enron's. "I believe they materially misrepresented the financial shape of their companies." He added later that, while Merrill Lynch may not have known what its financial position was, "it always knew its bonus pool."
>
> Pitt was equally as harsh. "I agree there was criminality at a lot of these firms, but where it resided, I'm not sure," he said. He pointed out that banks took multiple marks on the same

assets, and gave them higher or lower marks, depending on what they were calculating. The assets were "worth" the most when calculating fees they were collecting; they were "worth" the least when calculating margin calls for clients.

"That reflects more than carelessness," he said. "It reflects criminality."[12]

Or Not to Be Criminal?

Others would forcefully disagree that the major financial firms engaged in criminal fraud. In one famous case, a federal jury in Brooklyn acquitted Ralph Cioffi and Michael Tannin, two former Bear Stearns hedge fund managers accused by the government in a nine-count indictment of lying to investors to cover up the 2007 meltdown of two funds widely viewed as the start of the financial crisis. The two had faced multiple charges, including securities fraud and wire fraud.

Megan Barnett continues in her report on the *Portfolio* breakfast meeting:

> As for Madoff, there was no debate about criminality. Pitt, who was at the helm of the SEC [Securities and Exchange Commission] during the post-Enron years of 2001 to 2003, while Madoff was perpetuating his fraud, chalked up the regulatory breakdown to human failure. More regulation wouldn't have stopped or prevented the fraud, he said, because his scheme should have been easy to determine.[13]

All in all, the events leading up to the crash of 2008 had their roots in the the early 1980s. So long as the markets were rising, no one looked at the rotting foundations, and naysayers were ignored as anticapitalist, anti-American, or worse. Quite a lot of clearly criminal behavior is chronicled in this book, which discusses but a small sampling of the criminal cases brought each year.

Chapter 3

Why We Do It

BUBBLES AND FRAUD

Henry Blodget was voted the number one Internet/e-commerce analyst on Wall Street by *Institutional Investor,* Greenwich Associates, and TheStreet.com in 2000.[1] In 2002, then New York State Attorney General Eliot Spitzer published Merrill Lynch e-mails in which Blodget gave private assessments about stocks that conflicted with what he said publicly. In 2003, he was charged by the Securities and Exchange Commission (SEC) with civil securities fraud, charges that he ultimately settled without admitting or denying the allegations. However, he consented to and paid a $2 million fine and $2 million in disgorgement and was subsequently banned from the securities industry for life.

Since then, Blodget has made a living doing writing and analysis. Shortly after the crash of 2008, he wrote a long article for the *Atlantic* called "Why Wall Street Always Blows It" in which he tried to explain what happened in 2008, based on what was known at the time he wrote the article. Our views generally agree that greed and lack of government oversight had a lot to do with it. "The SEC fell asleep at the switch . . . we got greedy; we went nuts; we heard what we wanted to hear," he writes in his article.

However, he also believes that bubbles are inevitable in the capitalist system. He says: "Most bubbles are the product of more than just bad faith, or incompetence, or rank stupidity; the interaction of human psychology with a market economy practically ensures that they will form. In this sense, bubbles are perfectly rational—or at least they're a rational and unavoidable by-product of capitalism."[2]

Greed: Nature or Nurture?

In Blodget's view, greed is an innate part of human nature. In this, he follows Sigmund Freud, who wrote, "Culture has to call up every possible reinforcement in order to erect barriers against the aggressive instincts of men. . . . Its ideal command to love one's neighbor as oneself is really justified by the fact that nothing is so completely at variance with original human nature as this."[3]

However, Blodget also concludes that the human animal is naturally greedy and also arrogant. We think we are smarter than everyone else, and we take unfair advantage, so long as we think we can get away with it. In this same issue of the *Atlantic*, Virginia Postrel writes, in "Pop Psychology," basing her argument on experimental economics research by Vernon Smith and Charles Noussair, that if you put people in front of a market that is behaving a certain way, you are inevitably going to get a bubble.[4] "People are just wired to create asset price bubbles," she says. In stating this, Postrel seems to subscribe to the literal understanding of the Biblical verse found in Genesis, "for the inclination in man is evil from his youth."[5] Blodget appears to agree with her.

In *The Social Contract*, the famous French philosopher Jean-Jacques Rousseau (1712–1778) wrote that he believed that man was born innately good but that it was society that corrupted him.

Don Isaac Abarbanel, a fifteenth-century Jewish exegete, understood the verse in Genesis differently, and takes an intermediate view between these two positions: "When the Torah says that 'for the inclination in man is evil from his youth,' it is not referring to individual people, but to humanity. . . . Childhood is a turbulent time, a chance to experiment with reckless immaturity; adolescence is marked by rebellion and self-assertiveness. But with adulthood comes sensibility, settling down, and stability."[6]

Abarbanel said, "The flood had a sobering effect on mankind; God slapped humanity's face, demanding that they cut out the nonsense and just grow up! Well, after that, the lesson has been learned. Future generations will look back on the story with the pain we all feel about certain events of our teen years, and keep themselves in check. Thus, future catastrophes will be avoided."[7]

Capitalism: You Can't Live with It or without It

Although I agree with Abarbanel's view that future catastrophes can be avoided, I also know that greed drives Wall Street, and always has; in pursuit of easy money, rules are sometimes bent or broken.

Adam Smith, in *Inquiry into the Nature and Causes of the Wealth of Nations* (1776), described the origin of capitalism. He came up with the concept of "the invisible hand," whereby "the private interests and passions of men" are led in the direction "which is most agreeable to the interest of the whole society." As Robert Heilbroner said,

> Self-interest is only half the picture. It drives men to action. Something else must prevent the pushing of profit hungry individuals from holding society up to exorbitant ransom. This regulator is competition, the conflict of the self-interested actors on the marketplace. A man who permits his self-interest to run away with him will find that competitors have slipped in to take his trade away. Thus the selfish motives of men are transmuted by interaction to yield the most unexpected of results: social harmony.[8]

In other words, competition acts as a brake on greed.

Capitalism is not about stealing, swindling, or screwing the little guy. On the contrary, capitalism is about the creation and exchange of value: It is about the individual improving his or her own situation by producing something of worth that improves the lives of others. True capitalism increases the good of the whole by creating an incentive for the individual to increase his or her own good.

Capitalism, as Winston Churchill told the British House of Commons, "is the worst economic system in the world except for all the others that have been tried."[9]

Convicted felon Sam Antar (now reformed), whom we will read about in Chapter 6, said it well:

> The main pillar of our capitalist free market economic system, which is a cornerstone of our democracy, is the integrity of financial information. Without reliable financial information, capitalism cannot survive. The integrity of financial information can only be achieved through building blocks such as sound internal controls and independently verifiable financial information. The well educated, skilled, and experienced accountant is the first line of defense for the capitalist system.[10]

Fraud and swindling disrupt the markets by compromising the integrity of financial information. This comes about when fraudsters and swindlers believe that they can get away with it.

The economic historian Charles Kindleberger believed that "swindling is demand-determined, following Keynes's law that demand determines its own supply, rather than Say's law that supply creates its own demand. In a boom, fortunes are made, individuals wax greedy, and swindlers come forward to exploit that greed."[11] Kindleberger seems to me to be right on target.

Capitalism for Smaller-Company Stocks

Fraud and small public companies go together like bees and honey. A thoroughly disproportionate number of prosecutions involve smaller companies. The smaller stock fraud game, which we discuss at some length, is a play in several acts, with good guys and bad guys, winners and losers. It is part drama, part suspense thriller, part comedy, and, inevitably, several parts tragedy.

Like all plays, it has actors. Some, like the CEO of a company, play starring roles. Others, like accountants and lawyers, have important supporting roles. Promoters sometimes play the part of the jesters, but more often they play the role of the villains, and in some cases they play a starring role. The overall theme of the play is greed. Tremendous amounts of money are being made (and lost) every day in the markets for the low-priced, thinly capitalized stocks known as small caps, microcaps, or nanocaps depending on their size, and collectively as smaller caps.

We don't know exactly how much is made by actors in the small-cap markets. However, hundreds of millions of dollars are conservatively estimated to be spent every day by investors (buyers) of low-priced stocks (those with a market capitalization, which is the share price times number of shares) of under $500 million. And remember, for every buyer there is a more-than-willing seller, so the gross annual profit for purveyors of penny stocks (which are the most easily manipulated but make up only a small portion of the overall market in manipulated securities) reaches into the hundreds of millions of dollars or even more, perhaps much more.

Them's the Crooks, Not Me

Now, be honest. If you have ever bought a stock, why did you buy it and not one of 10,000 others? Of course, you expected the price to go up. But why did you expect that the price would move up? Did you receive a hot tip from your brother-in-law? Did your broker want to reward you as a (supposedly) favored customer? Did you read something in an obscure place?

Whatever your reason, somehow you thought that you had the inside track on that stock, and that you knew something the market didn't. You thought you had an edge, and you wanted to take advantage of your special knowledge. So then you too have a bit (or a lot) of larceny in your heart, and you too want your unfair share of the market. You and I then have something in common; we're human.

While one can certainly debate whether man is inherently good or inherently bad, history, at least since the industrial revolution, has amply demonstrated that capitalism and a free-market economy create wealth and a high standard of living. Capitalism is compromised when there is inadequate competition, when information is not freely disseminated, or when fraudulent information is allowed to be passed off as genuine. That said, each of us hopes that we have (legal) access to information that others don't have, or that we have superior tools (better analysis, better judgment, and/or better intuition) so we can profit by buying when others are selling or selling when others rush to buy.

Inevitably, then, in capitalism there are winners and losers, but in a fair (swindle-free) system, we all have equal opportunity to become winners. Also inevitably, however, some will seek to load the dice, tip the scales, or unfairly influence the results. And that's when greed becomes criminal.

Chapter 4

Securities Fraud

Its Long and Storied Past

For centuries, if not for millennia, businesspeople have sought to make outrageous returns on investments by:

- Cutting corners (or worse).
- Artificially creating imbalances between supply and demand and then capitalizing on the imbalance by unloading their cheaply acquired supply into artificially created demand.
- Magically (or fraudulently) attempting to turn worthless base metal into gold.

While this book focuses on recent events, as George Santayana famously wrote in *The Life of Reason*, "Those who cannot remember the past are condemned to repeat it."[1] William Shakespeare had Antonio say in *The Tempest* that "what's past is prologue" (act 2, scene 1).

Accordingly, the following are some of the major financial frauds from centuries past.

Dutch East India Company

The United East Indies Company (in Dutch, Vereenigde Oost-Indische Compagnie or VOC), which became known as the Dutch

East India Company, was the first company to issue shares to the public, and was the world's first multinational. It was granted a government monopoly over the Asian trade. The charter of the new company empowered it to build forts, maintain armies, and conclude treaties with Asian rulers. This provided for a venture that would continue for 21 years, with a financial accounting only at the end of each decade.

The VOC had two types of shareholders: the *participanten*, who could be seen as nonmanaging partners, and the 76 *bewindheb-bers* (later reduced to 60), who acted as managing partners. This was the usual setup for Dutch joint-stock companies at the time. The innovation in the case of the VOC was that the liability of not just the *participanten* but also of the *bewindhebbers* was limited to the paid-in capital (usually *bewindhebbers* had unlimited liability). The VOC, therefore, was a limited liability company. Also, the capital would be permanent during the lifetime of the company. As a consequence, investors who wished to liquidate their interests in the interim could do this only by selling their shares to others on the Amsterdam Stock Exchange, which was the first stock exchange.

First Stock Exchange

The Amsterdam Stock Exchange, or bourse, was founded in September 1602 within six months of the company's formation and was an integral component to its success; the exchange grew to an organization of 50,000 civilian employees, with a private army of 40 warships, 20,000 sailors, and 10,000 soldiers and a mind-blowing dividend flow. The whole of Holland was revitalized. With a market for its stocks and bonds, the Dutch East India Company became probably the most powerful business in the history of the world. It became, for all intents and purposes, a state within a state.

The Dutch East India Company remained an important trading concern for almost two centuries, paying an 18 percent annual dividend for almost 200 years. In its declining years in the late eighteenth century, it was referred to derisively as Vergaan Onder Corruptie, which translates as "Perished by Corruption." The VOC became bankrupt and was formally dissolved in 1800. Soon after the founding of the Amsterdam Stock Exchange, other companies began to raise money on it and to list their shares for trading. Market manipulation and stock fraud began to appear not long afterward. The first recorded stock fraud involved Isaac Le Maire, the first naked short seller.

Isaac Le Maire

Isaac Le Maire was a large investor in the VOC (80,000 guilders). He also was the key figure in the storm of controversy that characterized the early trade in VOC shares. By 1609, the VOC still was not paying a dividend, and Le Maire's ships on the Baltic routes were under constant threat of attack by English ships due to trading conflicts. Le Maire was concerned about these threats, so he cashed in by selling more shares than he had, making him the first naked short seller. Short selling is a legitimate investment technique where an investor sells borrowed shares (borrowed for a fee) in the expectation that the price will fall. At a future date the investor then goes into the market and buys the shares, replacing the shares borrowed. If the investor has guessed right, the shares bought in the market cost less and the investor profits from the difference. If the investor has guessed wrong and the price goes up, he needs to pay more to replace the borrowed shares and will suffer a loss. Le Maire, however, sold shares he didn't borrow. This is known as a naked short, and, as we discuss in detail in Chapters 9 and 10, it's inherently unfair, because it puts pressure on a stock, and carried to the extreme it can be a self-fulfilling prophesy, driving the stock to zero, because a potentially infinite amount of stock can be sold short at ever lower prices.

The Dutch stock exchange did not approve of Le Maire's actions and temporarily banned short selling. Later, during the Dutch depression of the 1630s, speculators saw short selling as a means to profit from the economic downturn. The English reacted by banning short selling completely at the time.

Tulip Bulb Scandal

The tulip bulb scandal in 1636 and 1637 followed as the first well-documented securities manipulation fraud, but of course it was by no means the last. Essentially, the rapid expansion of commerce in the Netherlands brought about gambling on profit speculation.

Now and again, speculation intensified into a frenzy of what the Dutch called *windhandel*, literally "trading in the wind," that is, buying or selling in futures without actual possession of goods. Maybe this is the origin of the German and Yiddish term *luftgescheft*, "air business," and if you recall, one who engages in *luftgescheften* my grandma derisively called a *luftmensch*.

According to Herbert H. Rowan, during the tulip bulb scandal,

. . . the bulbs of tulips and hyacinths . . . had become the modish flowers of the day in their myriad new varieties. Rapidly escalating prices spurred the gambling instincts of all sorts of people, especially in the district of Haarlem. In 1637, after prices had soared to fantastic heights, the speculative castle in the sky collapsed suddenly. For those who lost fortunes, there was tragedy.[2]

Geoffrey Cotterell writes:

Bulbs were bought and sold and resold dozens of times. They were bought and sold unseen. . . . One Amsterdamer made 60,000 guilders in four months, when his annual salary as a burgomaster [mayor] was only 500. . . . The fever kept on getting wilder and wilder until suddenly at the beginning of 1637, the market cracked. In a few days hundreds were ruined. The losses were such that the whole credit system, not merely for tulips, was endangered.[3]

(Jonathan Friedland narrated this interesting tale for the BBC; you can listen to it at http://www.bbc.com.uk/radio4.)

Mississippi Company Scandal of France

Somewhat closer in its characteristics to a modern securities fraud was the Mississippi Company scandal. In August 1717, Scottish businessman

John Law, a mathematical genius and reckless gambler, acquired a controlling interest in the then derelict Mississippi Company (what we would today call "buying control of a publicly traded shell"), and he renamed it the Compagnie d'Occident (or Compagnie du Mississippi), just as today shell owners rename the shell to conceal its troubled past. The initial goal was to trade and do business with the French colonies in North America, which included much of the Mississippi River drainage basin, and the French colony of Louisiana.

As John Law bought control of the company, he was granted a 25-year monopoly by the French government on trade with the West Indies and North America. In 1719, the company acquired the Compagnie des Indes Orientales, the Compagnie de Chine, and other French trading companies, and became the Compagnie des Indes (or Compagnie Perpétuelle des Indes).

Buying hard assets with inflated stock ("useless paper") is, as we see from these transactions, an old trick, but as Jean Baptiste Alphonse Karr wrote in his journal, Les Guêpes, in 1849, about 120 years after the Mississippi Company scandal, *"plus ça change, plus c'est la même chose"*[4] ("the more things change, the more they stay the same"). Shareholders of Time Warner Inc. painfully relearned this lesson about 280 years after the Mississippi Company scandal when Time Warner agreed to merge its solid but old economy business with price-inflated America Online Inc. (AOL) in 2000, at the height of the dot-com boom. AOL paid for the purchase mostly with *luft*, "useless paper" securities that promptly lost most of their value (ultimately $99 billion was written off from AOL–Time Warner's books, making it the largest write-off in history). Ted Turner, who had earlier sold CNN to Time Warner, personally lost $8 billion from the ill-fated merger.

Nonetheless, in 1720 the Mississippi Company acquired the Banque Royale, which had been founded by John Law as Banque Générale in 1716. Today we call this "self-dealing" or "related party transactions"; they must be disclosed under the securities laws. Law exaggerated the wealth of Louisiana with an effective marketing scheme (similar to what crooked promoters do today with a promotional campaign), which led to wild speculation in the shares of the company in 1719.

Shares rose from 500 to 15,000 livres (the "pump" part of a classic pump-and-dump scheme), but by the summer of 1720 there was a sudden decline in confidence, and the price dropped back to 500 livres in 1721, after the inevitable "dump" (£1.00 was worth 23 livres, 3 sous, 6 deniers back then, and one livre equaled 10 pence and 1.4 farthings).

By the end of 1720, the Regent Philippe II of Orléans had dismissed Law, who then fled France, leaving a massive trail of losses behind him. Speculators and investors took to the streets and stormed the Bank of France.

South Sea Bubble of England

A similar fraud, which became known as the South Sea Bubble, occurred in England at about the same time (1720). The South Sea Company proposed a scheme by which it would buy more than half the national debt of Britain (£30,981,712, equivalent to £6.1 billion in today's money based on average earnings), and would issue new shares, along with a promise to the government that the debt would be converted to a lower interest rate, 5 percent until 1727 and 4 percent per year thereafter.

The purpose of this conversion was to offer liquidity in return for a lower interest rate. It would allow a conversion of high-interest but difficult-to-trade debt into low-interest, readily marketable debt/shares of the South Sea Company. All parties could supposedly gain. This sounds suspiciously like some of the securitizations, swaps, and restructurings that were engineered during the first decade of the twenty-first century, and contributed to the market crash of 2008, proving once again the validity of Karr's observation that "*plus ça change, plus c'est la même chose.*"

The South Sea Company then set to talking up its stock with "the most extravagant rumours" of the value of its potential trade in the New World, which was followed by a wave of "speculating frenzy" (today we would call that an "intense promotional campaign" as part of a "pump-and-dump operation"). The share price had risen from the time the scheme was proposed, from £128 in January 1720 to £175 in February, £330 in March, and, following the scheme's acceptance by the Bank of England, to £550 at the end of May. The price finally reached £1,000 in early August (at the height of the "pump" phase), but then the level of selling was such that the price started to fall, and dropped back down to £100 per share before the year was out, after the "dump" phase. Altogether, it's a classic pump-and-dump scheme.

In the South Sea Bubble, well-known members of society were fleeced. The noted bluestocking Lady Mary Wortley Montagu invested in the hope of using the profits to pay off a blackmailer with whom she had had an indiscreet romantic correspondence. Poets, bishops, Sir Isaac Newton, and King George I were all drawn into the euphoria. This was the first of many Ponzi schemes, which are primarily equal-opportunity scams.

Rothschild and Insider Trading

One of the all-time largest cases of rumormongering and trading on inside information was pulled off in 1815, when London financier Nathan Rothschild led British investors to believe that the Duke of Wellington had lost to Napoleon at the Battle of Waterloo. In a matter of hours, British government bond prices plummeted. Rothschild, who had advance information of Napoleon's loss at the hand of the Duke of Wellington, swiftly bought up the entire market in government bonds, thereby acquiring a dominant holding in England's debt for pennies on the pound. Over the course of the nineteenth century, N. M. Rothschild & Sons would become the biggest bank in the world, and the five Rothschild brothers would come to control most of the foreign-loan business of Europe.

"Let me issue and control a nation's money," Nathan Rothschild boasted in 1838, "and I care not who writes its laws."[5] In 1875, N. M. Rothschild & Sons funded the Suez purchase. Today, N. M. Rothschild & Sons Ltd, usually called simply Rothschild, has offices worldwide, from Abu Dhabi to Zurich, and enjoys an AAA credit rating, even after the turbulence that decimated other banks.

The great House of Rothschild was essentially built through massive trading on inside information. Similar claims of illegality have been made against the Rockefellers, Joseph Kennedy, and others. As Honoré de Balzac said, "Behind every fortune there is a crime."[6]

John Sadleir

John Sadleir (1813–1856) was an Irish crook who inspired at least three novels. He served as the original inspiration of Dickens's Mr. Merdle in *Little Dorrit*. He also inspired *Davenport Dunn* by Charles Lever, and *John Needham's Double* by Joseph Hatton. John Sadleir was the son of a Dublin solicitor whose practice he at first managed. Within a year of moving to London, he became chairman of the London and County Joint Stock Banking Company, which eventually became part of National Westminster Bank, acquired by Royal Bank of Scotland Group Plc in 2000.

Sadleir became a junior lord of the U.K. Treasury, a railroad promoter who served as chairman of the Royal Swedish Railway Company, the Rome & Frascati Railway, and France's Grand Junction Railway, and led the Carson's Creek Consolidated Mining Company in California. He was a Member of Parliament (MP) for Carlow. In addition, he established the *Telegraph* in Dublin in 1851 as an organ of the Catholic Defense Association chaired by Archbishop Cullen, and supported Duffy's Tenant League. He accepted the post of junior lord of the U.K. Treasury under William Gladstone in 1852. He was well liked and well trusted and took advantage of it by robbing everybody he could lay his hands on. He got in trouble when he forged title deeds as collateral for loans on London banks.

Sadleir committed suicide in February 1856 by lying down under a bush on London's Hampstead Heath and sipping poison (prussic acid) from a silver jug upon the failure of his brother's bank (Tipperary Joint-Stock Bank, established in 1827), which had assets worth only one-tenth of its deposits. John Sadleir had overdrawn his own account by £200,000 (equivalent to £16 million adjusted to the consumer price index, according to Lawrence H. Officer, "Purchasing Power of British pound from 1264 to 2007," http://www.MeasuringWorth.com) to purchase votes and maintain the Telegraph; the banking loss fell heavily on Tipperary's small depositors. The *Nation* described him as

"a sallow-faced man with multifarious intrigue, cold, callous, cunning";
there was an unfounded rumor that he was not dead but escaped to
America.[7]

Less than a year after Sadleir's death, two more bank frauds came to
light, one of which also ended in suicide, according to George Robb,
a professor at William Patterson University in Wayne, New Jersey, and
the author of *White-Collar Crime in Modern England: Financial Fraud
and Business Morality 1845–1929*.[8]

The scams helped accelerate the banking crisis of 1857, a panic
that started in the United States and spread to England (prompting one
of the last bank runs in Britain prior to Northern Rock Plc, the U.K.
bank nationalized in 2008). Within a decade, the United Kingdom had
another panic, the commercial crisis of 1866, blamed in part on the
limited liability rules.

Tom Cahill of Bloomberg has compared John Sadleir to Bernie
Madoff because both were agreeable and hurt many small investors.
A detailed biography of Sadleir is *Prince of Swindlers: John Sadleir, M.P.,
1813–1856*, by James O'Shea.[9]

Charles Ponzi

Charles Ponzi (1882–1949) did not invent the fraudulent pyramid
scheme that bears his name. Charles Dickens's 1844 novel, *The Life and
Adventures of Martin Chuzzlewit*, described a Ponzi-like scheme decades
before Ponzi was born. However, Ponzi was such a flashy operator
that *Ponzi scheme* is the name often applied to any fraudulent financial
scheme that uses money from a steady stream of new investors to pay
off old investors seeking to redeem their investments. Of course, when
no assets are really purchased, but dividends are paid out, the scheme
inevitably collapses whenever redemptions outstrip new investments,
and the whole deck of cards comes crashing down.[10]

By the time Ponzi concocted the fraud that bears his name, he
already had two prior fraud convictions and had already spent years
in prison. Ostensibly, he was running an arbitrage scheme, based on
international reply coupons (IRCs), a way for someone to prepay reply
postage internationally. The key to the scheme was that IRCs were sold

at the postage rate charged in the purchasing country and could be redeemed for stamps at the rate in effect in the correspondent's country.

At the time, there was a huge difference between the low postage rate in effect in Italy and the high rate in effect in the United States. Theoretically, one could purchase an IRC in Italy, send it to the United States, and redeem it for postage worth four times as much. At one time, Ponzi was taking in $250,000 a day in 1920 dollars, worth about $2.6 million in today's dollars. Arbitrage is not illegal; however, while Ponzi collected huge sums from investors, but he didn't actually buy the IRCs. Clarence W. Barron, founder of *Barron's*, determined that to cover the investments made with Ponzi's firm, the Securities Exchange Company, 160 million postal reply coupons would have to be in circulation. However, only about 27,000 such coupons were actually circulating.

The United States Post Office stated that postal reply coupons were not being bought in quantity at home or abroad. When this became known, the scheme collapsed. A government raid disclosed only a handful of IRCs in the vaults. Ponzi was arrested in August 1920, 200 years to the month after the collapse of the South Sea Bubble.[11] He was charged with 86 counts of mail fraud.

At the urging of his wife, on November 1, 1920, Ponzi pleaded guilty to a single count before Judge Clarence Hale, who declared before sentencing, "Here was a man with all the duties of seeking large money. He concocted a scheme which, on his counsel's admission, did defraud men and women. It will not do to have the world understand that such a scheme as that can be carried out . . . without receiving substantial punishment."[12] He was sentenced to five years in federal prison and later to an additional seven years on state charges, after a landmark Supreme Court decision—*Ponzi v. Fessenden*, 258 U.S. 254 (1922)—determined that the additional state charges did not violate the double jeopardy provisions of the Constitution. After serving the second sentence, Ponzi was deported to Italy, but died a pauper in Rio de Janeiro in 1949.

William "520 Percent" Miller

In 1899, before Ponzi started his scheme, William "520 Percent" Miller opened for business as the Franklin Syndicate in Brooklyn,

New York. Miller promised interest of 10 percent a week and exploited some of the main features that keep Ponzi schemes going, such as customers reinvesting the interest they made. He defrauded buyers out of $1 million (worth more than 20 times that in today's money) and was sentenced to jail for 10 years. His sentence was commuted after he served five years of imprisonment in return for his help in convicting his accomplices.

After he was pardoned, he opened a grocery store on Long Island. During the Ponzi investigation, Miller was interviewed by the *Boston Post* to compare his scheme to Ponzi's. The interviewer found them remarkably similar, but Ponzi's became more famous, on account of his taking in seven times as much money.

These late-nineteenth-century and early-twentieth-century frauds, large as they were and even after adjusting for inflation, pale and become almost insignificant in comparison to the magnitude of today's frauds. But as noted, the past is only prologue. The most massive frauds of all belong to the late twentieth and early twenty-first centuries.

Chapter 5

The Perils of Greed

IT'S ALL FOR THE EASY MONEY

Many of today's securities frauds go one step beyond the frauds that we briefly discussed in the preceding chapter. After all, fraudsters have had nearly 400 years to polish their skills. By turning paper into stock certificates or debentures that they print and then give to themselves and their friends, who turn them into money, stock operators are fulfilling the dream that had eluded man for over 2,500 years.

Ever since the ancient Mesopotamians, Egyptians, Persians, Indians, Japanese, Koreans, Chinese, and classical Greeks and Romans first tried, unsuccessfully, to turn worthless base metal into gold (efforts that continued until well into the nineteenth century), people have tried to turn nothing into something. Now, this feat of alchemy is accomplished every day by entrepreneurs and promoters as well as by investment bankers. It's done legally or not, as the case may be. And very often, there are no bright lines to distinguish one from the other.[1]

In the previous chapter, we've noted that securities fraud has a long history. In this chapter, we look at the huge penalties meted out to fraudsters, and consider why, notwithstanding all the lessons of history, we still see so much fraud.

The Lure and the Risks

The lure of easy money is great. So are the risks. Turning an unlimited supply of worthless paper into money can create theoretically infinite wealth, but the risks can be equally impressive. According to the *Sourcebook of Criminal Justice Statistics*,[2] sentences of incarceration were imposed in 62.5 percent of the fraud cases where the sentencing guidelines were applied (and they nearly always are). In financial crimes, the monetary amount of the fraud is almost always the major component in determining the length of the sentence.

One financial fraudster, Sholam Weiss,[3] absconded and was sentenced in absentia to 845 years, in addition to restitution, fines, and penalties of $133,900,000. He was captured and incarcerated. His projected release date is November 23, 2754, and in the meantime he is inmate 32610-054 in United States Penitentiary–Canaan, where he is rumored to be dying of cancer. You can check on his progress, if you like, by going to www.bop.gov. Click on "Locate Inmate" and then enter his inmate number. Another fraudster, Norman Schmidt, was sentenced to 330 years of prison for taking "tens of millions of dollars from hundreds of investors," and using the money for personal gain. His scheduled release date is September 12, 2291.

By way of comparison, the punishment for murder can be as little as 10 years in some jurisdictions.[4] For innocent but greedy investors, who buy and sell shares in the market, or who buy into "too good to be true" schemes but are unconnected in any way, the risks are usually limited to the amount of their investment (unless they are illegally short selling). This means that they may lose all their hard-earned cash and be left holding worthless paper. If they were leveraged (borrowed money to make the investment) they may end up in debt, or even bankrupt.

For those who gave Bernard L. Madoff Investment Securities, LLC their money to invest, the worthless paper caused them to suffer enormous losses, up to $7.5 billion for some funds and up to $545 million for trusting individual investors, in what added up to the largest financial scam in history. More than a few retirees needed to go back to work in order to put bread on their tables. Many lost their homes. But for the crooked entrepreneurs, and for all of their service providers (including, as we will see, the lawyers), the risks can be even greater, causing them not only the loss of their accumulated wealth but their liberty as well—and for a long time.

While Sholam Weiss's 845-year sentence and Norman Schmidt's 330-year sentence[5] are exceptionally long, many others are increasingly sent away for a very long time for nonviolent, white-collar crimes. In October 2009, Richard Monroe Harkless, 65, was sentenced by United States District Judge Virginia A. Phillips in federal court to 100 years in prison.[6] He was the mastermind of a California-based Ponzi scheme that collected well over $60 million from hundreds of investors—and caused more than $39 million in losses. Others I write about in this book received sentences of up to 150 years of imprisonment.

There are other pitfalls to fraud beyond incarceration. Sometimes even a small misstep can kill the entrepreneur's company and trash the market value of the company's stock, in addition to potentially landing a company's executives in jail to serve sentences of 10 to 20 years or more, as well as saddling them with huge liabilities for fines and restitution, which means that investors who lost money must be made whole. For example, in the case of Computer Associates, executives accused of accounting fraud that inflated the stock price (a tale discussed in Chapter 31) were ordered to pay restitution of nearly $800 million,[7] many times more than they personally benefited from the fraud.

Martha Stewart and Dr. Samuel D. Waksal

Sometimes, people can go to jail for breaking the securities laws even when the company itself has real value. Martha Stewart allegedly told her broker, Merrill Lynch's Peter Bacanovic, to sell about $228,000 worth of the stock of ImClone Systems at $60 back on December 27, 2001, just ahead of news that ImClone's cancer drug, Erbitux, would not be approved by the Food and Drug Administration (FDA). She ended up being indicted, going to trial, and being found guilty by a jury on all four counts charging her with obstructing justice and lying to investigators about her well-timed stock sale. She famously was sent to jail. Stewart received a split sentence of six months in jail and six months of house arrest. She also was barred from ever serving as an officer or director of a public company (including her eponymous one).

The fellow who tipped her, ImClone's then CEO, Dr. Samuel D. Waksal, was released from prison in February 2009 after having served about five years of his seven-year sentence in federal prison camps (he got time off for successfully completing a drug treatment program as well as the standard allowance for good behavior of about 15 percent). The former ImClone Systems chief executive received his sentence of 87 months in prison and a $3 million fine after being charged for securities fraud, bank fraud, obstruction of justice, and perjury related to his attempts to sell stock, as well as scheming to avoid paying sales tax on art he purchased, by having it supposedly delivered out of state when in fact it wasn't.[8]

The irony here is that the FDA ultimately did approve Erbitux, and it has saved many lives. Indeed, had Waksal and Stewart just waited a few years, they could have sold the stock legally at an even higher price. In early 2008, ImClone's partner, Bristol-Myers Squibb, made a bid for all of the 83.4 percent of ImClone's stock that it did not already own, which kicked off a bidding war. Its offer of $60 a share was topped by Eli Lilly & Company, and ImClone was ultimately sold to Lilly for $70 a share, for a total consideration of over $6.5 billion.[9]

Why Take the Risk?

So, given the inherent risks such as we have just seen—to the entrepreneur, broker, investor, trader, or any other player—why would anyone in his right mind (or hers, for that matter, but overwhelmingly stock fraud is perpetrated by males, except for the public relations folks, who are generally female) want to tread in such treacherous waters? The answer, in one word, is greed. Or, in two words: easy money. Everyone playing the stock game—no matter what they may say—is in it for easy money.

The entrepreneur hopes to raise money from the public at a better valuation than what he can get raising it privately. He also secretly hopes—in the future, so he says—to cash in some of his chips by selling his stock into the market (usually, though, he means in the *very near* future, just as soon as he can). The investors are looking for huge gains on their money (threebaggers or fourbaggers, they call them—that is, to sell their stock for three or four times what they paid for it), and just as soon as possible.

The brokers are looking for spreads, commissions, and fees that are several times what they can charge for executing orders for large-cap, boring stocks like IBM or Microsoft, where commissions run to just a few pennies per share. Ditto the market makers and traders. Promoters and service providers (who try to get paid in stock) look to dump the stock into the market just as soon as they can, and charge fees far in excess of what they might earn offering similar services to others in a conventional cash fee-for-service transaction.

While companies of all sizes have been involved with stock fraud, and there have been some well-publicized frauds in large-cap stocks with a market capitalization in the billions (Enron being the poster child), most garden-variety stock fraud takes place in stocks with low prices and smaller market capitalizations, as these are the most easily manipulated.

It's Not Blackjack

Blackjack is a unique game of chance, in which the odds that favor the house (at least in some casinos) can be as small as 0.02 percent (under the Lisboa Rules in Macau, for example[10]); in most other games of chance, the odds strongly favor the house. In the small stock game, most of the participants are on the house's side and only the retail investors are the players; the odds overwhelmingly favor the house. And to help nature along even more, the dice are often loaded and the cards marked.

However, just as gamblers are drawn to casinos or to lotteries by the lure of winning the jackpot, so too are investors inexorably drawn—like moths to a flame—to invest in nanocap, microcap, and small-cap stocks in hopes of securing quick and enormous returns.

Chapter 6

The Elements of Financial Fraud

A CASE STUDY WITH "CRAZY EDDIE" ANTAR

U.S. Attorney Michael Chertoff (later the second United States Secretary of Homeland Security) called him the "Darth Vader of capitalism." Judge Harold A. Ackerman in his opinion issued in the civil case *Securities and Exchange Commission vs. Sam M. Antar et al.* (93–3988) wrote, "There is perhaps no more insidious drain on the overall welfare of society than greed unchecked. The saga of the Antar family and their operation of a major retail consumer electronics business is but a manifestation of that tenet."[1]

To best understand the major elements of financial fraud, we'll take a look at the drama that was Crazy Eddie and the Antar family.

Poster Child of Financial Fraud

While smaller in size ($120 million) than some of today's frauds, Crazy Eddie serves as a great introduction to modern financial fraud because of its lengthy time span (18 years) and its use of multiple methods, including:

- Skimming (not recording cash sales).
- Underreporting of income (tax fraud) prior to going public.
- Overstatement of income (securities fraud) after going public.
- Laundering money.
- Recording of fictitious revenue. (For example, a sale of $200,000 to another retailer called "trans shipping" was counted as a retail sale and included in "same store sales.")
- Fraudulently overvaluing asset valuations. (There was $80 million in overvaluation. Rather than climb over boxes in the warehouse, the auditors asked employees to assist them. Crooked employees volunteered. An employee would stand on top of a stack of television sets, for example, and call down the count to the auditors. If there were 10 sets, the worker would claim there were 25. Repeated many times, this clever trick helped to greatly increase the inventory count.)
- Improperly recording timing differences. (Taking advantage of the accounting cutoff period to boost sales and/or reduce liabilities and expenses, Antar routinely told his stores to hold the books open past the end of an accounting period to falsely inflate sales revenues.)
- Concealing liabilities and expenses. (The liabilities for any given period were normally not recorded until the next period; Sam E. Antar, the CFO (and Eddie's nephew), regularly stashed unpaid bills in his desk. The liabilities would be either entered after the year-end or held for long periods without being recorded. As a result, Crazy Eddie's never did know what it really owed, and neither did the auditors.)
- Making improper, misleading and incomplete financial statement disclosures Among other things, in one year, the footnotes stated that certain income was recognized when received (cash basis). The following year, Sam removed "received" and substituted earned (accrual basis) without pointing out the change.
- Illegally short selling.

Crazy Eddie

Eddie and Sam M. Antar founded Crazy Eddie as ERS Electronics in 1971, named after Eddie, his cousin Ronnie (Ronnie Gindi, a partner), and his father Sam. The chain rose to prominence throughout the tri-state region as much for its prices as for its memorable radio and television commercials featuring a frenetic, crazy character played by radio DJ Jerry Carroll saying, "Our prices are insane." Although the *New York Times* and others decided that Carroll copied most of his shtick from used car and electronics salesman Earl "Madman" Muntz, an early TV commercial pioneer, Larry Weiss, a Long Islander who helped create the original Crazy Eddie commercials and is now a life coach, denies it.

Weiss wrote in a personal e-mail:

> I had never heard of Mad Man Muntz until some columnist concocted a connection in some article somewhere some years back, which obviously served as a source for other articles and essays—even the *New York Times* (which tells you how stuff you read in multiple sources can still be convoluted). If we lifted anything, it was some inspiration from JGE [an appliance store whose ads had the tag line] (". . . that's the story").[2]

(Thanks to my friend Walter Reisman for fact checking with Larry Weiss.)

In any event, long after the memory of those commercials would fade, the fraud perpetrated by Eddie and Sam Antar would be remembered for its sheer audaciousness and brazenness and some of the unprecedented methods used by its conspirators in executing their crimes. At its peak, Crazy Eddie had 43 stores in four states, and earned more than $300 million in sales.

From the outset, Crazy Eddie was a criminal enterprise. In its early years (1969 to 1983), the company was privately held, and its main crimes were skimming and underreporting of income on a large scale. As it grew and became public, the volume and types of fraud increased.

Why did the Antars commit such massive fraud? According to Sam E. Antar,

> We committed crime simply because we could. Criminologists like to analyze white collar crime in terms of the "fraud triangle"—incentive, opportunity, and rationalization. We had no rationalization. Simply put, the incentive and opportunity [were] there, but the morality and excuses were lacking. We

never had one conversation about morality during the 18 years that the fraud was going on.[3]

Invoking the Statute of Limitations

Skimmed funds were deposited in secret Antar family bank accounts in Israel during the middle years of Crazy Eddie. Initially denying the existence of the skimming early in the investigation, certain family members, when confronted with the evidence, changed their stories and admitted to lying. They claimed, however, that the skimming had stopped many years earlier in 1976 (to reduce their criminal exposure due to the statute of limitations). In *Frankensteins of Fraud*, by Joseph T. Wells (Obsidian Publishing, 2000), Sam M. Antar, father of Eddie Antar, is quoted as having declared in court, "You are 1,000 percent right. You can show me 29 books of depositions. I did lie, I did lie," adding with vehemence and balled fists, "But I am not lying now." Sam M. Antar testified that he'd skimmed millions of dollars in five decades of business, but never took one cent from Crazy Eddie after 1976, so that he could "take the family legit."[4] However much he'd sinned in the past, Sam swore he was clean now. "I lied, I lied, I lied, I lied, I lied, I lied. But then I rescinded the lies and told them the truth. That is all I did."[5]

Eddie Antar's cousin Sam, the former CFO of Crazy Eddie, wrote on his web site that in 1986 they wanted to sell more stock and of course make millions more. "I was asked, and I willfully participated in creating fictitious sales initially to boost Crazy Eddie's reported comparable store sales and later to boost earnings and earnings growth."[6]

Beginning in 1986, Crazy Eddie's fiscal year ended on the first Sunday in March each year instead of May 31. Crazy Eddie's same-store sales, which were ahead up until Christmas 1985 at a rate of 20 percent, were running ahead only 4 percent for January and February of 1986. Eddie and his father wanted to sell over $30 million in stock by the first week of March 1986, at the highest possible price. They transferred or "maybe" advanced $1,500,000 to Crazy Eddie from their secret bank accounts in Israel, which contained the previously skimmed funds, by first wiring such funds to another bank secrecy jurisdiction in Panama.

Once the funds were in Panama, another family member withdrew funds from Bank Leumi in the form of drafts, so he would not violate laws regulating movement of funds into the country, and brought the funds into Crazy Eddie's offices in Brooklyn, New York.

As Sam Antar wrote on his web site:

> I later took these drafts, which were in amounts ranging from $50,000 to $100,000, and caused all $1,500,000 of them to be deposited into stores that were opened in both fiscal years. They were deposited after the last day of the fiscal year, which was March 3, 1986, and no invoice was generated. However, because the drafts were dated before the last day of the fiscal year, the deposit was entered as if it occurred and the sale happened before fiscal year end. The auditors never noticed anything since they did not do a sales cutoff test at year end in the 1986 audit.[7]

In all, same-store sales were artificially increased in total by $2,200,000 for the fiscal year 1986 and more specifically during the last week of that year, all of which went to the bottom line (i.e., was reported as pure profit), greatly (but falsely) increasing margins also. Sam Antar says,

> On March 7, 1986 Eddie and his father sold over $30 million of stock and I was a hero. I helped Eddie, his father and others plan and execute the misstatements of inventories and accounts payable that taken together with the sales fraud initial[ly] over-stated net income by approximately $15–$18 million.[8]

The two-word change in accounting policy for purchase discounts and allowances "gave us the opportunity to generate $20 million in phony debit memos and $8 million in legitimate debit memos to offset almost $78 million in accounts payable," Antar stated.[9]

Antar was able to get away with skimming and falsifying margin increases for many years. But eventually, the Crazy Eddie fraud collapsed. Antar wrote:

> The collapse of the Antar family's control over Crazy Eddie was due to infighting, rivalries, and jealousy among Eddie Antar and his family. . . . We never cared [about morality]. In the

early days when we were skimming the attitude was that the government was not entitled to tax our earnings. The government was considered an adversary. Customers were considered adversaries. Anyone outside the interests of the Antar clan ruling Crazy Eddie was an adversary.[10]

How Did the Government Find Eddie Antar?

In February 1987, the United States Attorney's Office for the District of New Jersey commenced a federal grand jury investigation into the warranty billing practices of Crazy Eddie. The Securities and Exchange Commission (SEC) began seriously investigating financial statement fraud at Crazy Eddie when Arnold Spindler (a former employee) tipped them off about the fraud in July 1987, four months before a hostile takeover of the company by a group led by Victor H. Palmieri and Elias Zinn.

In September 1987, the SEC initiated a formal investigation into alleged violations of federal securities laws by certain Crazy Eddie officers and employees. Eddie Antar and others were also eventually charged with a series of crimes. Eddie Antar fled to Israel in February 1990, but was returned to the United States in January 1993 to stand trial.

When Eddie Antar fled the United States, he carried at least a dozen phony passports, and all of his money had been shifted to bank accounts in what are known as foreign bank secrecy jurisdictions. His accounts were mainly accessible through secret passwords and code names. In order to conceal those accounts, Eddie routinely transferred money from one account to another and then deposited the money into new accounts.

It was during the course of these transfers that the SEC and the court-appointed receiver picked up his trail. The SEC froze an account in Switzerland containing over $30 million. Eddie attempted to get the money unfrozen by appearing at the bank under one of his false identities. The government then tracked Eddie to Israel.

Documents seized from Eddie Antar's apartment revealed that he controlled over 30 offshore bank accounts in 10 different countries. Nearly all of those accounts were in the names of Eddie Antar's nominees, one or another of Eddie Antar's false identities, or Liberian and Gibraltarian shell entities controlled by Eddie Antar under one or another of his assumed names. Deborah Ehrlich (Eddie's second wife) was identified as the signatory or as having power of attorney over at least three overseas accounts Eddie Antar controlled.

Trial and Its Aftermath

On July 20, 1993, the criminal trial resulted in the conviction of Eddie Antar and his brother, Mitchell Antar. Allen Antar was acquitted. The 1993 conviction of Eddie and Mitchell Antar was overturned on appeal, but eventually both pleaded guilty in 1996. In 1997, Eddie Antar was sentenced to eight years in prison and Mitchell Antar to two years. They were also held liable to the SEC for $15,087,000 in disgorgement plus $42,423,642 in prejudgment interest, for a total of $57,510,642. The government and various civil litigants have recovered over $75 million from Eddie and $2 million from Mitchell.

Sam Antar cooperated with the government and received a sentence of probation. He now serves as an expert on white-collar crime, and also talks to college students and other groups without charge. Eddie and Mitchell Antar, who didn't cooperate and served hard time in prison, aren't on speaking terms with Sam.

We've seen how the Antars committed, on a relatively small scale, nearly every kind of financial fraud: accounting fraud, securities fraud, money laundering, and tax fraud. We'll also see how others specialized in a particular fraud, and took it to impressively extreme limits.

Chapter 7

"Other People's Money"

THE O.P.M. LEASING FRAUD

O.P.M. Leasing perpetrated a major fraud in computer leasing. The computer leasing industry was founded by Saul Steinberg in 1961, when he started Leasco Data Processing Equipment Corporation, a leasing company. Leasco would purchase equipment (primarily mainframe computers) from a manufacturer, preferably on terms not requiring payment for 60 days. Leasco would then lease the equipment under a "hell or high water" lease to a creditworthy customer. (The term *hell or high water* refers to an obligation to pay come hell or high water—i.e., under all circumstances.)

The equipment lease would serve as collateral for a loan that Leasco would take out and use to pay the cost of the equipment. The loan proceeds would then be applied to pay the cost of the equipment before the vendor had to pay the manufacturer out of pocket. The equipment would often then be sold to investors who desired the investment tax credits and depreciation benefits of ownership.

Leasco Prospers under IBM's Pricing Umbrella

Steinberg grew Leasco into a profitable business that essentially took advantage of the fact that IBM's own leasing rates assumed very low residual values for equipment after the lease was up, and were offered for short terms. Leasco was a bit less conservative, and succeeded in undercutting IBM by locking customers in for longer periods and assuming somewhat larger residual values. Steinberg grew Leasco rapidly, and eventually acquired Reliance Insurance, a 150-year-old business, when he was only 29. He then used Reliance as a base to acquire other companies. Steinberg, who ran an honest business, epitomized the operation of the "invisible hand" of Adam Smith, where by competing with IBM he was able to build a hugely profitable business for himself while driving down costs for IBM's customers, who no longer had to deal with monopoly pricing when leasing computers.

Unlike Leasco, an innovator that operated successfully under IBM's huge price umbrella, O.P.M. Leasing entered an already crowded market with many competitors and where price was the only differentiator. The only way it could compete with Leasco was by resorting to dishonesty.

Steinberg Was Mordecai Weissman's Idol in Starting O.P.M.

Ignoring the changed market conditions and looking only at Steinberg's success, Mordecai Weissman saw Steinberg as the man to emulate. He started O.P.M. Leasing (OPM is an acronym for "other people's money") in 1970, in a small office on Church Avenue in Brooklyn, with $10,000 borrowed from his parents. The company name was based on a biography of Aristotle Onassis.[2]

As children, Weissman and Myron Goodman went to the same yeshiva in Brooklyn. They also attended Brooklyn College together. In 1969, Goodman married Lydia Ganz, whose sister had recently married Weissman. The two men become business partners, and Goodman joined Weissman in the Leasco business a few months later.

Weissman handled the marketing end, while Goodman was the inside man in charge of finances; they each owned half of the business. By the late 1970s, O.P.M. had become one of the nation's five largest computer-leasing companies, with 250 employees in 11 offices across the country, including plush headquarters on Broadway in Manhattan.

O.P.M. was buying multimillion-dollar computers from manufacturers like IBM and leasing them to such major corporations as AT&T, American Express, RCA, General Motors, Revlon, and Polaroid. Prestigious banks, insurance companies, and other financial institutions were glad to lend O.P.M. money, secured as it was by the obligations of the lessees to make lease payments and by the value of the computers themselves. Many of these lenders were recruited by Lehman Brothers, the company's investment banker. O.P.M. also raised more cash by selling legal title to the computers to individual investors seeking tax shelters.

O.P.M. Bet Wrong on Resale Values and Became a Ponzi Scheme

Although in those days the computer leasing business was reasonably profitable for many firms, O.P.M. tried to buy business by paying expensive (and illegal) kickbacks to have business steered its way, while also undercutting competitors by offering lower rates. To do this and still have a shot at making money, the company needed to assume that the resale value of the equipment at the end of the lease (the residual value) would be higher than its competitors assumed. O.P.M. turned out to be very wrong, as IBM came out with a new line of equipment that quickly rendered the old equipment that they owned obsolete.

To make matters worse, some leases, ostensibly written for long terms (seven years), had secret side letters that allowed the customer to return the equipment after three years without penalty. These side letters were never disclosed to the funding banks or to O.P.M.'s accountants. As the new generation of equipment came onstream, customers in droves began to exercise their termination rights under the side letters and returned the equipment to O.P.M., even though it remained liable to its banks for the remaining loan payments. To avoid insolvency, O.P.M. began to fraudulently finance the same equipment multiple times with different banks.

O.P.M., which had never been solely on the straight and narrow, became a Ponzi scheme. It used the proceeds from the new (fraudulent) leases to make payments on the older, underwater leases. No one (among

the investment banks, commercial banks, and investors) checked to
ascertain whether:

- Collateral existed or existed in a particular location.
- Serial numbers identifying the equipment matched the serial numbers marked on a sales invoice or the serial numbers etched on the
  collateral.
- The equipment user or lessee had, in fact, signed a lease.

On the few occasions in which a lender sought independent
confirmation of the existence of a lease, no one bothered to determine if the representative of the equipment user or lessee doing the
attestation was, in fact, such a representative. Instead, a representative of
O.P.M. would provide a fraudulent estoppel certificate (estoppel protects
a party who would suffer detriment if a second party has done or said
something to induce an expectation, the first party reasonably relied on
the expectation, and the first party would suffer a loss if that expectation
were not met).

A Ponzi Scheme That Was a $200 Million Fraud

Between 1978 and 1981, O.P.M. obtained more than $196 million
in loans from 19 banks, pension funds, and other lenders secured by
phony Rockwell International leases. These new loans went to meet
payments on old loans until the company finally came crashing down
in March 1981. The fraud came to light after Rockwell discovered, in
response to a lender's inquiry, that it was making lease payments to
O.P.M. under two leases for which Rockwell lacked documentation.
Rockwell notified the United States Attorney. Indictments of the principals of O.P.M. followed, as did bankruptcy for O.P.M. Losses to
defrauded lenders exceeded $200 million over a 10-year period.

Tearful pleas for mercy were to no avail, and Goodman and
Weissman were sentenced in 1982 to 12 and 10 years' imprisonment,
respectively. Several minor players drew shorter sentences. Goodman
was released from prison in January 1989 after having served just under
seven years, and Weissman was released in May 1987 after four years
and four months. This was back in the days before parole was abolished
in the federal system.

Greed Is Rarely Undetected but Mostly Unspoken Of

One of the interesting aspects of the O.P.M. fraud is the role of the company's outside counsel. Apparently, the lawyers for the company became aware of the fraudulent leases, and needed to figure out what to do about it. Ultimately, it became a landmark case.[1]

After much deliberation, the lawyers did not, in the end, turn in their client. Partly as a result, Singer Hunter (O.P.M.'s main law firm) and four co-defendants, including Rockwell and Lehman Brothers, became the targets of a spate of multimillion-dollar lawsuits brought by lenders. The civil suits accused the law firm of being an accomplice in the O.P.M. crimes, on the grounds that the attorneys knew or should have known they were part of an ongoing fraud.

There is general agreement that although lawyers must do their utmost to protect their clients, they cannot be party to a fraud. Federal law (Sarbanes-Oxley), as well as a revised code of ethics for the American Bar Association members (partly based on the O.P.M. experience) have laid out the rules more clearly, and had they been in force at the time, Singer Hunter might well have reached a different conclusion on how the law firm must act. Perhaps due to the ambiguity at the time, a settlement was ultimately reached, and the five defendants paid $65 million; of this, Singer Hunter and its insurers had to pay $10 million (5 percent of the overall losses from the scam).

Like Crazy Eddie in the previous chapter, O.P.M. was a business that was never run honestly. Since its business practices included routinely paying bribes to attract business and routinely quoting below-market prices, it never had a viable business model. Operating under a patina of respectability conferred on it by major (and greedy) investment banks, accountants, and its law firm, which were all willfully blind to O.P.M.'s misdeeds, it operated for years as a Ponzi scheme until its misdeeds were ultimately detected by chance. Amazingly, we will see many of the same warning signs in even larger frauds perpetrated years later.

Chapter 8

Smaller-Company Fraud

THE "ISC" STORY

Whereas O.P.M. operated as a private company, many fraudsters seek profit from the market, making money by fleecing gullible investors. With small companies in their early stages, the name of the game is to get stock cheaply (very cheaply), create some value and awareness of the company, and then sell opportunistically.

The following tale chronicles how money is extracted from the market and describes a sophisticated operation that I witnessed up close. Nearly everything—every step of the way—was done legally, except for the fact that supposedly nonaffiliated investors were really secretly pulling the strings and controlling the company; the CEO was nothing more than a puppet.

"Tom Midas" Sought to Make Money

Tom Midas, as we will call him (it's not his real name), wanted to make money from the stock market—serious money. And not money made based on his clever stock-picking skills with all the attendant risks of being wrong. He wanted a sure thing. He wanted his own shell company (a public company with no significant assets or business operations).

He would put something into it, and then promote the hell out of it. He had once been involved with a public company that we'll call "Intergalactic Software Corporation" (ISC),[1] which had filed for bankruptcy protection.

ISC had filed under Chapter 7 of the bankruptcy code, which provides for shutting down the company, selling off all the assets, and giving the money to the creditors. One day, as someone who was himself a creditor of ISC, Tom received a notice in the mail about a plan to sell control of it (after all of the known assets had been sold off) and the guy was offering to pay $10,000. Did any creditor have a better offer? This was the kind of opportunity that Tom had been waiting for. Also, Tom knew two things, one of which the other bidder didn't know. Tom knew that ISC was still trading (anyone could see that), and therefore it had value as a shell, but Tom also knew that there was a note for $150,000 that "Larry Silvermountain," a friend of his, had lent to ISC and that note had never been repaid. Tom developed a strategy. He incorporated a limited liability company we'll call "Kansas Financial Acquisitions Company, LLC" (KFAC) and prepared an offer.

KFAC

KFAC offered to pay $20,000 in cash to the trustee, twice the price of the competing offer, for "the right to all the authorized but unissued stock of ISC." Notice what is being bought: only the *right* to all the *authorized but unissued* stock of ISC. The offer also specified that none of the other assets or liabilities was being purchased, *except*—and this was key—the liability to Larry Silvermountain, which would stay on the company's books. All the other assets (and related liabilities) would go to the trustee for the benefit of creditors, as they normally do in a Chapter 7 bankruptcy, which involves liquidation. As a special bonus for ISC's shareholders, the common shares of the bankrupt company, normally canceled, would stay on the books, and therefore would retain some value, unusual in a Chapter 7 bankruptcy filing.

Tom then called the bankruptcy attorney who had been appointed by the trustee and offered to retain him to represent KFAC down the road with a $20,000 retainer to be paid once the offer was successful.

This doesn't sound kosher, but it's legal; the bankruptcy system is riddled with such conflicts. The $20,000 to be paid for control of the authorized but unissued shares was a fair price, and for the trustee and bankruptcy attorney it was found money.

Here's why: The trustee is entitled to keep a portion of all recoveries "for the benefit of the general creditors," meaning creditors not having a perfected security interest (lien) on specific assets.[2] The trustee and the attorneys (the "duo") were also entitled under the code to various fees, but there were no funds in the company from which to pay them. Thus, in reality, all of the $20,000 being offered for control of the ISC shell would go to the duo, with none of it going to the general creditors. Furthermore, if any other assets were to be found, they would still be held by the trustee for the benefit of the duo and/ or creditors. So, bottom line, this was found money, as nothing tangible was being given up, and the proceeds would all go to the duo. The bankruptcy attorney also was essentially getting a success fee if KFAC's offer were to be accepted.

As required by law, all creditors were again advised of the new offer, and could have objected or trumped it had they wished. No one objected, and so the offer was accepted. The contract was prepared, signed off by the trustee and the various attorneys, and then, after a suitable Notice to the Creditors was mailed out to creditors (who had no grounds to object and didn't), it was then confirmed by the bankruptcy court. Eureka! A clean publicly trading shell had been created (one with no liabilities other than the one to Silvermountain); this liability, as we will see, was the major ingredient for some very special secret sauce. And Tom, through KFAC, now was in control.

Stop Reporting and Clean Up

ISC had been a fully reporting public company before it filed for bankruptcy. Postbankruptcy, it had stopped reporting, which is a very bad thing for a public company to do. Of course, as a broke, bankrupt company, ISC had no choice; it simply did not have the money to keep current on its reporting (it could not pay the accountants and lawyers who need to sign the reports). ISC had never withdrawn as a publicly reporting company, and hence it was considered deficient in its filings once it had stopped making them on time. Simply filing a one-page Form 15 with the SEC allowed it to voluntarily suspend its duty to file periodic reports, based on one of several available exemptions.

For ISC, the reason it was permitted to withdraw as a reporting company was a common one; it had fewer than 300 statutory shareholders of record (as do many public companies, since for most shareholders, the broker keeps the shares in "street address," which means they are held in the name of, for example, "Cede & Company," a subsidiary of "DTCC" for the benefit of the broker's customer ("the beneficial owner") and all shares held in street address are counted together as a single statutory shareholder. While Tom might have bought the right to authorized but unissued stock in ISC, there was a small problem: ISC no longer had a valid corporate existence, as its charter had been revoked for nonpayment of fees to the State of Delaware. However, this could be easily remedied for just a few dollars. File the appropriate request for reinstatement, pay the missing fees, and the records will show continuous existence.

In return for giving him some restricted stock in ISC that KFAC was now able to control (remember, it bought the rights to all unissued stock, up to the total amount authorized in its charter), KFAC caused "Dan Goodfellow," an "independent" friend, to be elected sole director and CEO. Tom now had a buddy in charge of things at ISC (this was the only aspect of this scheme that was of dubious legality; Dan was really Tom's puppet).

Since ISC had been broke before declaring bankruptcy, it owed the transfer agent money, and so the transfer agent had ceased providing service. In order to issue shares, transfer agent services needed to be restored. KFAC helpfully lent ISC some money, and Dan, ISC's new CEO, used the money to pay the transfer agent a portion of what was owed to it. (Remember, ISC had been bankrupt and its debts were canceled or uncollectible, so whatever the transfer agent got was found money.) Dan also agreed to enter into a new contract with the transfer agent, so the transfer agent was delighted to resume service. Now not only did Tom have the rights he had bought, but ISC had a valid existence and a transfer agent ready to issue share certificates. Warm up those printing presses.

Squeezing the Old Shareholders

While KFAC had the right to all the authorized but unissued shares, there were millions of shares already in public hands, and those remained outstanding. Once something of value was put into the shell, all the long-suffering shareholders would undoubtedly run to sell, trying to recoup whatever they could. It was time to effect a massive share consolidation (a reverse stock split, or reverse) and also to reset the number of shares that the company was authorized to issue. KFAC issued to itself and its friends enough new (restricted) shares for nominal value (after all, ISC had no assets or business) to ensure control, and at this point, since ISC was nonreporting, an action by consent of the majority of shareholders was sufficient to accomplish a one-for-20 share consolidation, leaving the prebankruptcy shareholders with very little ownership.

Had ISC been a reporting company, it would have been required to prepare a proxy statement, submit it to the Securities and Exchange Commission (SEC) for review, and then mail a copy to each shareholder. As a nonreporting company, ISC was able to skip this onerous step.

ISC not only effected a 1-for-20 share consolidation (1 new share for every 20 old [presplit] shares), but it also increased the number of shares it was authorized to issue to 50 million postsplit shares. At the same time, certain onerous antitakeover and "poison pill" provisions were eliminated. Finally, a name change was effected. Change its name and change its *mazal* or luck, the Talmud says.[3]

Getting a New CUSIP

Whenever there is a corporate action like a reverse split and new postsplit shares are issued, there needs to be a foolproof way to distinguish between old and new certificates. This control has been accomplished, for the past 40 years, by CUSIP Global Services, which is operated by the CUSIP Service Bureau (CSB). CSB is managed by the well-known and venerable Standard & Poor's on behalf of the American Bankers Association. Each security is assigned a unique Committee on Uniform Security Identification Procedures (CUSIP) number that must appear on the face of the certificate.[4]

So, the company filled out an application for a new CUSIP number and attached a stamped copy of the reverse split paperwork, as filed with Delaware, its state of incorporation. ISC was then issued a new CUSIP number, in anticipation of the reverse stock split. It then ordered new blank stock certificates with the new CUSIP number imprinted and had them sent to the transfer agent. A reverse split also requires notification of NASDAQ, which assigns a new trading symbol, again to distinguish the old shares from the new. The process takes a few weeks. But then it was done: new name, small number of outside shareholders, and brand-new share certificates, just waiting to be issued.

Acquiring the Note

Now that ISC had a legal existence and a new CUSIP number; Dan, the friendly CEO, was on board; and there was a functioning transfer agent, a small number of outstanding shares (following the reverse), and shareholder authorization to issue lots more, it was time to issue freely trading stock. To do this, KFAC needed to acquire the overdue and supposedly worthless Silvermountain note that, if you remember, had stayed on the company's books. Silvermountain had written off the unsecured note four years before, when ISC filed for Chapter 7 bankruptcy liquidation, and had long ago abandoned any hope of recovering anything. (Earlier, he had earned a huge return on other transactions he had done with ISC, so he was not too sore.) Silvermountain was very happy to accommodate Tom Midas and gifted him the note by endorsing it over to KFAC.

ISC's stock was trading at the minimum quoted price of $0.0001 per share when Tom, as the new owner of the note, went to Dan Goodfellow and demanded that it be repaid. "Tom, you know as well as I do that ISC has no assets," Dan said. "How can ISC possibly repay you?"

"Yes," answered Tom, "I understand. Tell you what. We can recharacterize the note [agree to a change in terms], and you can pay it off in stock from time to time."

Papers were drafted allowing ISC to repay KFAC a portion of the money it owed KFAC from time to time at the market price of $0.0001 per share (the conversion price) on the date of the recharacterization. The debt was more than two years old, and the recharacterization was deemed a change in terms, so was eligible for tacking. *Tacking* means that the original noteholder's acquisition date is tacked onto the acquirer's date, rather than forcing the acquirer to start a new holding period. Thus, shares issued to KFAC in exchange were free-trading.

Under the terms of the agreement between ISC and KFAC, no conversion could occur if the number of shares KFAC already owned *at the time of conversion*, plus the new shares it would obtain *from* the conversion, would together exceed 9.9 percent of the outstanding shares. This is known as a blocker provision and ensures that the shares received do not lose their free-trading status, which is what would happen if the holder owned 10 percent or more of the company. KFAC also had the right to sell pieces of the debt to others, provided that the acquirer of each such piece also agreed to the blocker provision with respect to the shares that he or she received, was unrelated to KFAC as seller, and acted independently.

Note that while ISC had agreed to the *terms* of the conversion, it was not contractually *obligated* to make additional conversions in the future. The decision to convert from time to time was the company's. This provision ensured that the potentially issuable shares would not be aggregated with those already issued, again rendering the shareholder a control person, and the shares statutorily restricted.

For KFAC, this restriction presented no problem at all, as Tom knew that Dan was in control of the company and would do his bidding, even if not legally obligated to do so. An opinion as to the legality of the conversion was easily obtained from a securities attorney, and the transfer agent was directed to issue the free-trading shares, which he was happy to do at the company's behest, and in reliance on the opinion that he had received. *Voilà*, free-trading shares had been issued.

Today, based on some recent changes made by the SEC to Rule 144, some of these mechanics just discussed might need to change because the new "shell exclusion rule" requires a one-year holding period when a shell merges with an operating company before the shares issued can be sold; in most other cases, the holding period is six months. You should ask your own attorney if you've got a mind to try it.

Getting a Return

KFAC was now out a lot of time and some $80,000 in cash payments at this point, including payments to the trustee, legal fees, as well as fees to the bankruptcy attorney, transfer agent, printer, and others. It had free-trading shares, and having reversed out the older shareholders, little competition for buyers—if they could be found. It was time to get the word out, but it had to be done carefully and truthfully, especially since the company was not reporting.

The company issued a short and truthful press release stating that it was back in business and was looking for an acquisition. A small piece of the note was sold to a friendly investor who then converted it into free-trading shares. ISC's share price rapidly increased to $0.05. KFAC slowly sold its shares into the market, and the price actually increased, as various early stage investors who troll for such opportunities rushed in to buy ahead of the crowd. Money had been coined. The alchemy had been successful.

Sell the Sizzle, Not the Steak

There is an old saying among salespeople, "Sell the sizzle, not the steak," wisdom attributed to Albert Lasker, the father of modern advertising at the Lord and Thomas advertising agency in Chicago, now part of Interpublic Group, and the inventor of the soap opera. It was popularized by supersalesman Elmer Wheeler in 1936.[5]

More even than in other markets, investors in smaller caps are greed-driven, and what you are selling them is the sizzle—hope. Therefore, ISC needed an acquisition that would provide an abundance of hope. In fact, I've found that the stock of many companies does better when the company is still presales; actual sales tend to bring in a dose of reality and to shatter dreams. KFAC introduced ISC to a potential acquisition, a technology company (let's call it "Picotech") that had no sales, several patents, lots of sizzle, no steak, and a burn rate (ongoing monthly operating costs) of $100,000 per month.

The consideration for the merger (the price) was payable in stock of ISC, the public company. This is what usually happens when a private company merges with a publicly traded shell company. Since ISC had been cleaned by the bankruptcy court, it traded well, and KFAC had undertaken to find financing to feed Picotech's monthly spending habit, the terms were generous for ISC.

Before the merger was completed, KFAC also introduced ISC to investors, who provided cash (in return for some stock and a note) to keep Picotech's doors open while the merger was being completed. In order not to confuse things, those shares (which were issued as restricted stock) were issued to a trust for the benefit of Tom's family, and the trust was administered by two lawyers. Thus shares of the trust would not be counted in figuring out the control issues, since Tom had no "dispositive power" over them, meaning he couldn't make a decision to sell them.

Between the time the merger was first proposed and until it closed, nearly nine months had elapsed. During all that time, the conversion printing press was rolling at high speed printing free-trading shares, as press releases detailed the letter of intent for the merger, progress along the way, and finally, that it had been completed—all completely truthful press releases. All the while, Ken (whom you'll read about in Chapter 14) was busy creating awareness, uncharitably referred to by some as "pumping" a stock, and Tom was indirectly selling by trading pieces of the note to others who sold into the pumped-up market (also known as "dumping").

In all, more than 100 million shares were issued. Some went to KFAC's friends and others who bought pieces of the Silvermountain note from KFAC and then asked ISC to convert them to free-trading shares that they sold into the market. Others were issued based on KFAC having sold pieces of the Silvermountain note cheaply to promoters, who also promptly converted the pieces into free-trading shares, which they sold as soon as they could, but they also did a very good job of getting the word out.

It Was a Fine Line

There is a fine line between "creating awareness" and "pumping" a stock, and Tom tried to stay on the legal side of that line. However, sometimes it's tough to rein in promoters, and this ultimately became a sore point with the new management of Picotech that took over ISC after the merger. Between KFAC and its friends and promoters, over $4 million was taken out of the market.

Ultimately, there was a falling-out between Picotech and KFAC, mostly because Picotech's original owners felt that KFAC and its friends were making too much money at their expense (that greed factor again) and concern that the awareness campaigns were really a pumping operation. Ultimately, the merger was undone, essentially returning control of the once again empty shell back to KFAC, with Picotech's assets being spun off to Picotech's original shareholders and the public shareholders, thereby creating another public company for them that KFAC's owners were not a part of. Picotech subsequently merged with another public company, also in need of its sizzle, and Picotech's shareholders walked away with a few million dollars. The ISC shell then reverted to the control of KFAC and was subsequently sold for $350,000 to a group of investors in a mining company. Total return: close to $7 million, split among quite a few players. Essentially, ISC returned over $1,000 for every $1 invested by Tom and his partners.

The new owners of ISC have continued to use the Silvermountain note as a way of issuing themselves additional shares at the expense of the public shareholders, so the game continues. It's particularly these kinds of returns that attract people to play the smaller-cap stock game.

The ISC story is interesting because it highlights many of the behind-the-scenes steps involved in operating a public company, shows how insiders can coin money, and demonstrates why—despite all the risks involved—many continue to seek their fortunes from playing stock games with smaller public companies.

Chapter 9

Selling Long and Short

BUT MOSTLY SHORT

Before continuing on to the next fraud, we need to say a few words about short selling, as an understanding of the topic is necessary to fully comprehend certain types of financial shenanigans.

Selling Long versus Selling Short

When you own shares and sell them, that is called "selling long," as you are "long" the underlying shares—you own them. If you sell shares that you *don't* own, then you are "selling short," and are "short" the number of shares that you sold. When you engage in long transactions, your maximum loss is what you originally paid for the shares.

An old Wall Street truism says, "Bulls make money and bears make money, but pigs get slaughtered." This aphorism first appeared in its original form in the 1923 book *Reminiscences of a Stock Operator* by Edwin Lefèvre, a fictionalized account of the life of the trader Jesse Livermore.[1]

The quote means that with the correct strategy, you can profit irrespective of the market's direction, as long as you call the direction correctly and you don't get greedy. Normally, if you think a stock is overpriced, you can sell it without owning it by borrowing the stock through a broker, who lends it to you for a modest fee. You ultimately cover your short position by later buying the stock in the market to close out the transaction. If you are correct, you pocket the difference between the price you received when you sold the borrowed stock and the lower price you bought it at later, less commission and borrowing fees. (Of course, if you've guessed wrong and you sell short, your losses are potentially unlimited, as the stock could take off and covering your short sale could prove to be disastrously expensive.)

Short selling is just a bet that a share's price will go down and not up. It is a legitimate investment strategy, and often brings balance to the market when done legally. But perhaps no topic related to investing generates more heated debate that the topic of short selling. So let's begin with the rules.

Regulation SHO

Short selling is governed by Regulation SHO.[2] The Securities and Exchange Commission (SEC)'s view on several situations governed by Regulation SHO follows:

> Selling stock short without having located stock for delivery at settlement. This activity would violate Regulation SHO, except for short sales by market makers engaged in bona fide market making. Market makers do not have to locate stock before selling short, because they need to be able to provide liquidity. However, market makers are not exempted from Regulation SHO's close-out and pre-borrow requirements.
>
> Selling stock short and failing to deliver shares at the time of settlement. This activity doesn't necessarily violate any rules. There are legitimate reasons why a seller may fail to deliver on the scheduled settlement date.
>
> Selling stock short and failing to deliver shares at the time of settlement with the purpose of driving down the security's price. This manipulative activity, in general, would violate various securities laws, including Rule 10b-5 under the Exchange Act. Regulation SHO does not address this issue.[3]

Personally, when I was running public companies, I often felt that our shareholders were preyed on by short sellers, in violation of Rule 10b-5, especially those affiliated with private investment in a public entity (PIPE) writers. (It never failed. A week before we were to close on a PIPE priced at some discount from the market price, the stock would drop 20 percent.)

Regulation M—Shorting Before an Offering

Rule 105 of Regulation M governs short sales immediately prior to offerings where the sales are covered with offering shares. Specifically, Rule 105 prevents people from covering short sales with offering securities purchased from an underwriter, broker, or dealer participating in the offering if the short sale took place during the Rule's restricted period, which is typically five days prior to pricing and ending with pricing. Its aim is to promote offering prices that are based on open market prices determined by supply and demand rather than artificial forces. In this way, Rule 105 safeguards the integrity of the capital-raising process.

While the SEC does not often bring charges for violation of Regulation M, a recent case serves as an alert that the regulation is alive and well, and that violations can be costly.[4] In the case in question, a hedge fund sold shares five days early, making a profit of $185,000, which it agreed to disgorge in addition to paying penalties and interest of over $97,000 and probably several times that in legal fees.

Penny Stocks Are Different

The rules are different with smaller-cap stocks. In general, these are often thinly traded, with small floats (shares in the market) and few market markers; thus, even small amounts of downward pressure (often stock sales of less than $1,000) can dramatically drive down a stock's price. So for penny stocks, regulators have tried to level the playing field by restricting short sales by adding a requirement for at least $2.50 of margin (collateral) for each share of a penny stock sold short, in addition to requiring that the shares actually be borrowed (and are not a so-called naked short), even when the share itself is priced at well under $2.50.

However, as we will see, these requirements are often circumvented (usually illegally) in many different ways, and illegal shorting is the bane of any public company's existence. In times of great market turbulence, as happened in October 2008, the SEC can take emergency action to curb short selling even in large-cap stocks, and when it does, as it did at the end of 2008 (Rule 204T), the restriction can inflict great pain on hedge funds whose complex strategies depend on shorting. Rule 204T sought to reduce the potential for abusive naked short selling in the securities market.

The new permanent rule Rule 204, adopted on July 27, 2009, amends Regulation SHO by requiring broker-dealers to promptly purchase or borrow securities to deliver on a short sale (the close-out requirement). The earlier temporary rule, approved by the SEC in the fall of 2008, had been set to expire on July 31. In addition, the SEC announced that the Commission and its staff are working with several self-regulatory organizations (SROs) to make short-sale volume and transaction data available through the SRO web sites. This effort will result in a substantial increase over the amount of information presently required by another temporary rule, known as Temporary 10a-3T. That rule, which expired on August 1, 2009, applied only to certain institutional money managers and did not require public disclosure.[5]

Apart from these measures, the SEC is continuing to actively consider proposals on a short-sale price test and circuit-breaker restrictions.

Uptick Rule for Short Selling

From 1938 until the SEC eliminated it in July 6, 2007, a period of nearly 70 years, an uptick rule was in place to control short selling. This rule required that a security must either be sold short at a price above the price of the immediately preceding sale, or at the last sale price if it is higher than the last different price. This rule was designed to be a circuit breaker that would prevent a succession of short sales from driving down a stock's price. In 2007, the SEC decided that the uptick rule "modestly reduce[s] liquidity and do[es] not appear necessary to prevent manipulation," so it was eliminated.[6]

The market crash of 2008 again fueled discussion on this topic, with many believing that the rescission of the uptick rule contributed to the crash. On October 6, 2008, Erik Sirri, director of the SEC's Division of Trading and Markets, said that the SEC is considering bringing back the uptick rule, stating, "It's something we have talked about and it may be something that we in fact do."[7] In an op-ed piece on December 9, 2008, entitled "Restore the Uptick Rule, Restore Confidence" in the *Wall Street Journal*, Charles Schwab (founder and chairman of the eponymous brokerage house) said, "For the sake of our children and grandchildren, and to avoid a needless future repeat of a bad situation, it is time to restore the uptick rule."[8]

The SEC is considering bringing back the uptick rule. The news, which became public after Representative Barney Frank (D-MA) told reporters of the SEC's plan, helped drive a broad market rally, with a surge in financial stocks. A SEC spokesman confirmed that the agency is taking up the issue. "The commission may conduct a public meeting . . . to consider whether to formally propose reinstatement of the uptick rule or consider other measures related to short sales," he said. The proposed rules are discussed in a SEC Release, but have not yet been voted on and have not taken effect as this book went to press.[9]

In any event, even when the rule was in effect, fraudsters often used to find ways to circumvent it (e.g., buy 100 shares in one account from one broker at an uptick, sell 10,000 shares short immediately thereafter through another broker), and, like many laws, this one merely keeps honest people honest.

Short selling is a controversial topic. Done properly, it's a legal investment technique. Naked short selling is not. Many suggest that short selling added fuel to the fires that caused the market crash of 2008, and additional regulation and improved transparency may be implemented to mitigate its harmful effects.

Chapter 10

Market Manipulation

F amiliarity with the abuses described in this chapter is key to understanding the market crash of 2008, as well as comprehending why investors in small stocks often get taken to the cleaners.

Perpetual Fails

Stocks bought or sold in the ordinary course of business settle three trading days after the trade date (known as "T+3"). This means that three days after a stock trade, the seller is required to deliver the stock to the buyer, and the buyer is required to deliver the cash. Nondelivery is termed a failure to deliver, or a "fail." The penalties for a fail are not great, but eventually (usually within 10 days, but many times up to 30 days) the nondelivery must be rectified. If the shares aren't delivered, the broker will "buy in" the shares by going into the market on behalf of the failed seller. Shares properly borrowed and delivered to the buyer do not involve a fail.

Traders sometimes deliberately fail (which is against the rules) and then allow themselves to be bought in at a lower price down the road, pocketing the difference. Failed trades in Bear Stearns soared more than 10,800 percent during the week of March 10, 2008, just before its forced sale, according to data released by the SEC, and many blame illegal shorting and rumormongering for the collapse of Bear Stearns.

A market maker can legally be short a stock up to 30 days (in some cases, however, only 13). Unscrupulous market makers who want to conceal short positions have been known to flip a short position to another market maker, parking the position with the other broker for 30 days (meaning the flipper hasn't truly relinquished control), and then buying it back; the process can continue indefinitely until the stock's price has fallen to the desired level, at which time the new cheaper stock is bought in the market, covering the short and yielding an illegal profit.

No-Parking Zone—Parking Is a Serious Crime

Parking violations in traffic court are not deemed criminal and involve small fines. Not so with the parking of securities. When stock is parked, one party holds stock that is actually controlled by another in order to conceal the ownership of the shares. The "seller" agrees to repurchase the parked shares at a prearranged time and price. Parking securities is considered a form of market manipulation and is a crime, one for which Ivan F. Boesky, a greedy arbitrageur, was prosecuted in 1986. Boesky famously said, "I think greed is healthy. You can be greedy and still feel good about yourself."[1]

As a result of a plea bargain in 1987 involving his extensive cooperation with the government to finger others, Boesky received a prison sentence of three and a half years and was fined $100 million in 1987 dollars—until then the largest fine ever levied (Michael Milken later paid $1.1 billion). Had Boesky not cooperated and implicated others, his sentence would have been much longer. Although he was released after serving only two years (those were the days when parole was still alive and well in the federal system), he was barred from ever working in the securities business. Now divorced and reportedly broke, he survives on an alimony he gets from his heiress ex-wife.

Boyd Jefferies, founder of Jefferies & Company, a large wholesale brokerage firm, who traded with Boesky and parked stock for him (to allow Boesky to obtain a tax deduction to which he otherwise would not be entitled), was also barred for life from the securities industry for ignoring rules related to parking, and on July 7, 1989, Jefferies was sentenced to five years' probation and fined $250,000. Despite the possibility of severe sanctions, parking rules are often ignored, mostly because it is not an easy charge to prove when there is no smoking gun; such agreements are often oral.

Short Interest

The short interest (the number of shares sold short or failed) in a company is now required by the Financial Industry Regulatory Authority (FINRA) to be publicly reported bimonthly, and it's a number that is avidly watched by professional investors. Sometimes the short interest is actually greater than the float outstanding, which is a red flag for fraudulent activity, as it means that the same shares have been lent more than once. New rules have been proposed to require more timely disclosure of the short interest.

PIPE writers are some of the worst short sellers, and we expose their misdeeds in Chapter 11. In brief, writers of convertible preferred shares sell short, drive the price down, and then convert to their profit once they have driven the price down.

Some believe that brokerage firms also may use short selling ahead of large sell orders by insiders (regarded as a strong negative sign); it's an unfair and illegal technique called front-running. This scheme takes advantage of knowing that a large customer sell order is coming, selling short ahead of it, and then covering the short by buying stock after the customer's sell order becomes public knowledge and has caused a price drop.

Naked Shorts

As we noted, in order to sell a stock short, an investor (or his or her broker) needs to borrow the stock to be sold, for which a fee is paid. If the bet is right, then when the price falls, the investor goes into the market and buys the shares at the lower price, and then uses the bought shares to replace the borrowed shares that were sold. A short sale without having borrowed the shares is called a naked short. Naked short sales, as we have seen in our discussion of Regulation SHO, are generally illegal, as they put unfair downward pressure on a stock's price, because when you don't have to borrow the shares you are really suspending the laws of supply and demand.

Naked short selling can turbocharge the "distort and short" schemes employed in bear raids, described later in this chapter. In a naked short, the usual process of short selling is circumvented, because the seller doesn't actually borrow the stock. For this reason, naked shorting can occur even when actual shares aren't available in the market. It allows manipulators to force prices down without regard to supply and demand.

The SEC issued new rules on September 17, 2008, to try to rein in abusive naked shorting.[2] As we will see in the next chapter, naked short selling is one of the major tools for unfairly profiting at the expense of other investors. Of course, a naked short seller must eventually borrow the stock, as the buyer ultimately needs to be credited with the shares.

Did the Big Guys Engage in Naked Shorting of Taser?

Many believe that short sellers are creepy old men operating out of their basements. But on May 28, 2008, the legal consortium of The O'Quinn Law Firm and Christian Smith & Jewell, both of Houston, Texas, and Bondurant, Mixson & Elmore, LLP of Atlanta, Georgia, filed a complaint in the State Court of Fulton County, Georgia, on behalf of certain shareholders of Taser International Inc. against eight of the largest Wall Street firms—Bank of America Securities LLC; Bear Stearns Securities Corp.; Credit Suisse USA Inc.; Deutsche Bank Securities, Inc.; Goldman Sachs Group, Inc.; Merrill Lynch, Pierce, Fenner & Smith, Inc.; Morgan Stanley & Co. Inc.; and UBS Securities LLC.

The complaint accuses the defendant firms of engaging in a conspiracy to manipulate the market for Taser, which makes stun guns, through naked short selling resulting in the creation, loan, and sale of counterfeit Taser shares. When a defendant firm short sells shares of Taser stock that it does not possess or intend to obtain, that sale can result in the creation of counterfeit shares because the short seller is, in effect, introducing additional shares into the market rather than engaging in a transaction using existing shares.

According to the 70-page complaint, the defendants' illegal naked short selling of Taser stock flooded the market with counterfeit Taser shares.[3] For example, although in 2005 Taser had authorized and issued only approximately 60 million shares of common stock, more than 80 million votes were cast at the company's annual meeting (you are credited for and can vote shares that you bought and paid for, even if they haven't been delivered to you).

The complaint accuses the defendant firms of violating Georgia's Racketeer Influenced and Corrupt Organizations (RICO) Act. "These are not isolated incidents: we believe the trading data evidences an ongoing and coordinated effort to violate securities and other laws," stated attorney Wes Christian.[4]

The complaint also describes various means the defendants have allegedly employed in an effort to conceal their unlawful conduct, including citing instances where the defendant firms have marked short sales as long positions, submitted inaccurate short interest reports, and inaccurately netted short interest positions against longs. The complaint also identifies specific instances in which defendant firms have been fined by securities regulators for this very conduct.

According to the complaint, by creating, lending, and selling counterfeit shares, the defendant firms have diluted Taser stock and artificially depressed its value, harming Taser shareholders. Attorney Christian promised: "We will work tirelessly to redress the wrongs that our clients have suffered."[5]

At this writing, the suit was far from settled, and is in the early stages of discovery, so we don't know all the facts. Gary Weiss, a contributing editor at the defunct *Condé Nast Portfolio* and the author of two books probing the underside of Wall Street,[6] has opined on his blog (http://garyweiss.blogspot.com) that the lawsuit is groundless, and cites the fact that Taser itself did not participate in the lawsuit (in fact, it later did join the lawsuit as a plaintiff, in June 2008).[7]

Weiss also claims that the "Texas law firm of John O'Quinn has filed a bunch of other junk lawsuits on the same subject and has yet to get a nickel from anybody. This is the same O'Quinn who told *Dateline NBC* that naked shorting has 'put as many as a thousand companies into bankruptcy' resulting in 'market losses of more than four hundred billion dollars,'" without naming any companies.[8]

The SEC investigated this claim and in 2006 closed its investigation without bringing any charges.

As we go to press, the judge has refused to dismiss the Taser case, and it is still pending.

Sleazy operators have so-called friends or associates in Canada, where regulations are different. They sell stocks short without the need for posting $2.50 per share in collateral. When a significant portion of a stock's ownership is nominally held by Clearing and Depository Services Inc. (CDS—Canada's national securities depository), then you'd best be on the lookout for short sellers. I discuss one such incident in the next chapter, on PIPEs.

Bogus Shorts

Be aware. Claims of short selling are often greatly exaggerated, especially in smaller stocks, in an attempt to conceal selling on the part of an insider or someone close to the company.

This game is played as follows: A major stockholder arranges with a promoter to give him some quantity of freely trading shares that were held by a supposed nonaffiliate (so that their free-trading status is not lost). The supposed nonaffiliate (usually a friend who received the stock at little or no cost) is paid for his troubles—usually in stock. The promoter promises to drum up retail buyers for the stock, usually on a four-for-one or five-for-one basis. So, for example, if 500,000 shares of buying are desired, the promoter may get 100,000 free-trading shares. The major shareholder paying for the promotion swears on his mother's grave that he is not selling any shares, that all the shares in the float are "tightly locked up," and that he knows where every share is.

His only interest in generating the buying, he proudly and piously proclaims, is to help the price of the stock by stimulating demand (volume), so the company can obtain financing on favorable terms and grow, minimizing shareholder dilution. Meanwhile, the major shareholder is secretly selling shares as fast as he can.

A few days later, the promoter is angrily on the phone. "As you saw, I bought 500,000 shares as promised," he says, meaning, "I bought zero shares and unloaded the 100,000 shares you gave me, but

I persuaded others to buy 250,000 shares in a way that makes it look as though 500,000 were bought." "I put my best people into it," he says. Meanwhile, the price has fallen 20 percent, rather than having gone up 40 percent as expected, and so "everyone is mad at me."

"Oh, it's those dastardly short sellers," the major shareholder replies. "They must be shorting it up in Canada where you can't see it," he continues, neglecting to add that he unloaded 300,000 of his own shares, just as he had planned to do all along.

Of course, with only 250,000 shares of real buying and 400,000 shares of selling, the stock was obviously pressured, so it's not surprising that its price has dropped 20 percent. And so it goes. In summary, while there is shorting going on, it's often an excuse for other nefarious acts that we expose in this book.

Investors Charge That Goldman Engaged in Naked Shorting of Loans

Naked short selling is not limited to stocks. Pierre Paulden and Caroline Salas of Bloomberg reported on November 17, 2008, that investors in the $591 billion high-yield, high-risk loan market are accusing Goldman Sachs Group, Inc. of naked short selling of loans to profit from record price declines.

At least two fund managers complained verbally to officials of the Loan Syndications and Trading Association (LSTA), saying they believe Goldman helped drive down prices by using the technique, according to people with knowledge of the objections, Bloomberg reports.[9] New York–based Goldman is acting against its clients by trying to profit at their expense, the investors are quoted as saying.

A $171 billion drop in the value of the loans in the past year is pitting banks against investing clients on assets once considered so safe they typically traded at par. The drop exposed flaws in an unregulated market where trades can take from several days to months to settle and banks may have information unavailable to investors. Like naked shorts in stocks, in a naked-short loan transaction a firm would sell debt it didn't already own, betting the price would fall before it would purchase the loan and deliver it to the buyer.

There is no rule preventing naked short selling of loans, even though the SEC banned the practice for 19 stocks from July 21 to August 12, 2008, as share prices plunged. The rules applicable to stocks were strengthened and were applied to all equities on September 17, 2008. The slump in loan prices during the global seizure of credit markets is causing particular disruption in the loan market because the debt typically trades at close to 100 cents on the dollar. Prices never were below 90 cents until February 2008. By October, they had fallen to a record low of 71 cents, according to data compiled by Standard & Poor's. The decline, which S&P said equated to losses of about $171 billion, helped drive the complaints from fund managers.

"Investors are shell-shocked" by the decline, said Christopher Garman, chief executive officer of debt-research firm Garman Research LLC in Orinda, California. "In many ways they're all but wiped out."[10] Because prices were so stable, short sales of loans used to be unheard-of. "No one ever shorted loans," said Elliot Ganz, general counsel of the LSTA.[11] "Prices never went down."

Trading in this market is so opaque that it would be impossible to tell if a firm was short selling. Jay Katz, managing director of Storm Networks LLC, saw an opportunity. His New York–based technology company, launched in October 2008 with backing from Bank of America Corporation, Credit Suisse Group AG, and Morgan Stanley, helps settle loan trades within three days. "A trade could be delayed for many reasons including not owning the debt," he said.[12] And some of those reasons just might not be kosher.

The bottom line is that we may never know who did what, but we do know to whom. Ordinary investors are feeling a lot of pain.

Investigating the Bear Raid on Bear

A bear raid is the illegal practice of attempting to push the price of a stock lower by taking large short positions and spreading unfavorable rumors about the target firm. In a bear raid, the manipulators profit on the difference between the original stock price and the lower (manipulated) price.

This was a popular practice in the early 1900s, and, unfortunately, it has become popular once again. Some recent cases discussed in this book demonstrate that bear raiders, if they are caught, can face lengthy prison time. But believing there was a bear raid and proving it is not the same thing.

Bryan Burrough, in a well-written August 2008 article in *Vanity Fair* titled "Bringing Down Bear Stearns," seems to be persuaded that the downfall of Bear Stearns in 2008 was the result of an improper bear raid initiated by a couple of hedge funds and assisted by Goldman Sachs.[13] All involved vigorously deny the charges, and Burrough acknowledges: "Maybe the SEC. will figure out whether Bear was murdered. But maybe it won't. Even those who believe the firm was the victim of a predatory raid have their doubts it can ever be proved."

"Even with subpoena power, I'm not sure the SEC will get to the bottom of this, because the standard of proof is just so difficult," says a vice-chairman at another major investment firm.[14] "But I hope they do. Because you can look at this as just another run on a bank or as a seminal point in the financial history of this country that could bring about a change, perhaps a drastic change, in the way we govern financial markets. If there is a solution to this kind of thing, it must be found in the roots of what happened at Bear Stearns. Because other-wise, I can guarantee you, it will happen again somewhere else."[15]

In July 2008 then SEC Chairman Christopher Cox told Congress that the agency is probing "whether illegal trading spurred the collapse of Bear Stearns and the 72 percent drop this year in Lehman Brothers Holdings Inc.'s market value."[16] (Shortly after Cox's testimony, in September 2008, Lehman filed for bankruptcy after the government refused to intervene to save the company, and Lehman's shareholders got totally wiped out. At over $600 billion, it's the largest bankruptcy of all time.) The inquiry, Cox said, focuses on investors suspected of seeking to profit by intentionally spreading false information about the companies (rumormongering).[17]

U.S. Attorney and State Attorney General Are Also Probing

In September 2008, Michael Garcia, then U.S. attorney for the Southern District of New York (which includes Manhattan), and Andrew Cuomo, the state attorney general for New York, reached an unusual agreement to jointly investigate the shadowy world of credit default swaps, the $55 trillion market in unregulated financial instruments at the center of the meltdown of 2008.

According to the *New York Times*, Garcia's office has said it is looking into whether federal laws were violated, while Cuomo, with a broader mandate as state attorney general, can seek industry reforms, legislation, civil settlements, and other remedies.[18]

Mary Jo White, who served as U.S. attorney for the Southern District of New York from 1993 to 2002 and is in private practice as head of the White Collar Crime practice at Debevoise & Plimpton, warned of intense public pressure "to put the scalps on the wall."[19] She cautioned, "You have to distinguish between arguably bad risk taking and someone who has actually violated the law."

It's my belief that, Ms. White's warnings notwithstanding, she and her fellow members of the white-collar bar will enjoy full employment for a very long time. Many of the ongoing investigations will result in numerous indictments being handed down, as the government feels that poster children of the rampant greed that was endemic to the financial industry will need to be prosecuted in order to assuage the anger of the many who have to pay for the sins of the greedy. Unfortunately, it's the public that pays the heaviest price—as taxpayers, as people who have lost their homes and livelihoods or have seen their incomes plummet, and as investors whose life savings have all but been wiped out.

Market Manipulation Affects Everyone

Market manipulation cuts to the heart of market integrity, the lifeblood of a market. When markets are manipulated by the professionals, it's the public that is the great loser. While it's easy to allege (Monday-morning quarterbacking has always been a popular sport), it's not so easy to prove. Public anger against greedy market manipulation by insiders will lead to even more regulation, for which we will all pay the price.

Chapter 11

PIPEs

Investing Unfairly

Investors in small companies can often do extremely well through private investments in public entities (PIPEs). They can make money even if the companies don't. Some, however, are not content with normal profits and seek to stack the deck unfairly, hurting the companies they invest in.

We take a look at the PIPE market and illustrate the misfortunes that can befall companies that take money from investors who abuse PIPEs. I begin by introducing us to a scenario.

"Peter"

Let's start with "Peter."

Peter was a proud, distinguished, elderly, and highly respected medical doctor who was chairman of a small medical device company that had no sales, some patents for a promising medical device, and a desperate need for money to take the device through the regulatory Food and Drug Administration (FDA) process, get it manufactured, and pay for marketing. Comfortably middle-class but not wealthy, he needed to raise that money from investors.

He tried various angels and venture capitalists (VCs), but was always rebuffed. Someone convinced him to merge with a publicly traded shell, and he was promised immediate funding in the form of a PIPE from a hedge fund if he would agree. As we will see, things didn't turn out exactly as planned, and in this chapter we discuss why.

Raising Cash from Investors

Few have the financial resources to develop a business from scratch, nurse it to profitability, and then grow it organically until it can be sold or become completely self-financing. Until a few years ago, funding nascent businesses typically began with a small, initial friends-and-family round, and then further funding was primarily within the purview of venture capitalists. Today, few start-up businesses are of interest to VCs, and few entrepreneurs seek funding from them.

What happened? The growth of pension funds and other institutional investors has brought so much money to VCs that they often won't bother with start-ups, preferring larger investments in already-proven companies (sometimes called mezzanine-stage companies). It is more trouble to nurse a $3 million investment in a rank start-up to an initial public offering than to make a $20 million investment in a more mature company.

Venture capitalists as a breed are greedy. There is a reason that they are often nicknamed "vulture capitalists." If possible, they dicker and delay until the entrepreneur has exhausted his or her own resources and then offer money at a very low valuation, often causing the entrepreneur to lose control of the company. They always seek large returns on their money (tenfold), and often invest using participatory preferred shares, which ensure them a return of two or three times their money before anyone else gets anything.

Often, as a condition of funding or shortly after funding has been secured, VCs install their own management, relegating the unhappy company founder to an honorary or advisory role. With more entrepreneurs chasing fewer sources who are willing to fund rank start-ups, the terms for the entrepreneur are not attractive, and entrepreneurs desperately seek to avoid VCs. In short, there is not much love lost between an entrepreneur and the VC community. Peter tried hard, but he couldn't strike a deal with any VCs.

IPO—RIP

In the good old days (or bad old days, depending on your perspective), a promising start-up could do a "firm commitment" initial public offering (IPO) when it was still presales and/or losing money like a sieve. Often within just months of its founding, the company could close on its IPO and get its money from an underwriter that would buy all the shares and easily redistribute them to eager investors, who were its own clients and clients of other brokers. The excesses of the dot-com era and restrictions imposed in its aftermath have pretty much killed off the market for small "firm commitment" IPOs. According to Lawrence Delevingne's article on *CNNMoney.com* entitled "IPO 2009: Testing the Waters," there were only 43 larger, underwritten IPOs in 2008.[1]

The best-efforts type of IPO, when an underwriter commits to sell x shares or none on an "all-or-nothing, best-efforts basis with no commitment," and the so-called mini-max best-efforts IPO (at least x shares but no more than y, but still with no commitment) are still around, but they are less fashionable, having been replaced for the most part by "fund and register" transactions. This is when the company is funded in a private transaction by issuing unregistered shares, and then files a registration statement to register the shares for resale.

Due to new, more lenient regulations, a public company can sell unregistered shares privately in a negotiated sale and the investor needs to hold them for just six months before being permitted to sell them into the market, and without the company needing to file a registration statement with the Securities and Exchange Commission (SEC). For its shares to trade publicly, the company still needs to become publicly reporting, typically by filing a Form 10 with the SEC, a disclosure document that goes through a careful vetting process.

Who Are These Other Funders?

Beyond family-and-friend investors, who may not be overly picky, most investors that are willing to fund small companies demand a clear exit strategy. By this they mean that they want to see a clear path to getting their money back and securing a healthy profit from their risky investment. These other funders take many forms, including: (1) licensed small business investment companies (SBICs), which essentially leverage their own money with that of the government (usually on a one-to-two or one-to-three basis); (2) hedge funds; (3) offshore or foreign investors of unknown provenance; and (4) various groups that call themselves capital companies, investment companies, and the like.

By Small Business Administration (SBA) regulation, an SBIC may not hedge or collar its investment. As such, they are an ideal value-added lead investor or co-investor for syndicated transactions, as selling short or otherwise hedging their bets would get them into serious trouble with the SBA. Many of the other players, however, are merely acting as conduits to squirt stock into the market, and they will often presell or otherwise hedge (legally or not) and dump shares just as fast as they can.

Liquidity

A company can achieve liquidity for its investors by selling out (i.e., by merging with another company). While there have been some spectacular successes involving sales of companies with little or no sales and no profits (think Mirabilis's sale to America Online (AOL) for $287 million—Mirabilis's only product, ICQ, had no revenue), such sales are the exception rather than the rule. More commonly, a company needs to grow for a few years before its value can be maximized.

For example, Broadcast.com, founded in 1995, had 330 employees and nearly $100 million in annual revenues by the time Yahoo! acquired it. It was purchased for $5.9 billion in Yahoo! stock in 1999, instantly making Mark Cuban a billionaire. Mark, by the way, told me that he immediately collared his stock (meaning he simultaneously sold puts and calls to shrewdly lock in the sale price, so, unlike many others, he was not hurt when Yahoo!'s stock price later plummeted).

Liquidity and PIPEs

Liquidity is the name of the game. Skittish investors often want a shorter time frame than several years for their exit, or at least their ability to exit. Greedy promoters too often call the shots, promising companies like Peter's ample funding, but only if the company agrees to become publicly traded, all too often by merging with a vehicle that they just happen to have available and that they (often secretly) control. Once the company is (or has incontrovertibly agreed to become) publicly traded, financing is much more available.

Today, a common method of investing is through private investment in a public entity (PIPE). In these transactions, an investor buys securities—often shares (sometimes a note and shares, and sometimes a note convertible into shares).

The investors often demand a commitment to become publicly traded and maybe also a commitment to register the securities they buy. This technique gives the investor more protection, as publicly traded securities are much more readily sold, at least at some price. In 2005, according to TheStreet.com, PIPEs were a $17 billion business; today the business is surely much larger.[2]

PIPE Investors Are Not Saints

I once attended an early-morning party called a *bris*, where an eight-day-old Jewish male is circumcised and then formally welcomed into the Jewish community. We were all waiting around for the *mohel* to perform the circumcision by surgically removing the baby's foreskin. This is a very minor operation that takes but a few seconds, but with today's concerns over AIDS and other blood-carried infections, this *mohel* approached the procedure with preparations worthy of open-heart surgery.

While standing around, I overheard the top deputy for "M.I. Financial,"[3] an investment company that specializes in PIPEs for microcap stocks. He was speaking in anxious tones to his boss: "We're supposed to close on 'Doral Medical'[4] tomorrow, and I've been shorting it all week. The price has been dropping nicely. But this morning, they put out a press release reporting on excellent results from the Phase II study of their new drug. I'm afraid the stock will go up today. What should I do?"

"How many shares are in the free float?" asked the boss.

"Fourteen million," the deputy answered.

"And how many have you shorted?"

"About a million and a half," answered the lieutenant.

"We're supposed to give 'em $2 million, right?"

"Yes."

"That's about four million shares at today's prices, isn't it?" asked the boss.

"Yes," replied the lieutenant, "and we sold at an average price of 73 cents."

"Call Jerry in Canada and have him short it more," ordered the boss.

"Okay," agreed the lieutenant.

The foregoing true vignette (names changed to protect the guilty) highlights the risks (to the issuer) inherent in PIPE financing for smaller-cap stocks. Large companies with an active market can absorb some degree of short selling without the price dropping much, if at all.

PIPE investors may be individuals, hedge funds, or other financial institutions. You won't often see the Goldman Sachses of the world or other gilt-edged Wall Street firms investing directly in the PIPEs of small companies, but they may well back the hedge funds that do invest.

The best of the PIPE investors will be content to do a "fund and register" transaction at a fixed price. This means that the company agrees to issue to the investor x shares, representing y percent of the company as unregistered shares (also sometimes called lettered stock), often on the condition that the company becomes publicly reporting, if it is not already, (by filing a Form 10 with the SEC) and that it agrees to:

- Register the shares by filing a registration statement with the SEC within z days of funding (typically 120 days), registering the shares bought for resale.
- Use commercially reasonable efforts to have the registration declared effective within some number of days (typically 60) or else compensate the investor for the delay by paying additional shares for each day or week of delay.

The company may also be asked to commit to working with a sponsoring broker-dealer so that a market for the securities is allowed to develop (i.e., that it trades). Before rushing to agree to such a proposal, companies must ensure that securities' counsel and auditors have bought into the time frames. An example of a company that was funded this way but came to grief was Smart Online, a fraud we profile in Chapter 31.

PIPE investing just got even easier. In an effort to encourage honest players to participate, recent changes in the securities laws have reduced the holding period for PIPE investors to six months in many circumstances; so often, if the company is already public, there is no longer a need to file a registration statement at all—the company merely signs a contract, gets its money, and then files the details of the transaction with the SEC on Form 8-K.

This change was done by relaxing the requirements of Rule 144 to:

- Permit nonaffiliates of an SEC-reporting company to resell restricted securities without regard to Rule 144 volume, reporting, or manner of sale limitations after a period of six months.
- Permit nonaffiliates of an SEC-reporting company to resell restricted securities without regard to any Rule 144 requirements, including the current information requirement, after a period of one year. (In the event that the company existed as a shell for a period of time, then the holding period for nonaffiliates for unregistered stock is one year.)

When the Share Price Is Not Firm

It is not easy to get an investor to agree to a share price that is fixed now but then hold on until the shares are eligible for resale at an essentially unknown future date at least six months into the future. To protect themselves, investors ask for floating discounts. For example, the investor agrees to invest $1 million by buying 1,000 shares of Series A preferred shares with a face value of $1,000 per share, bearing interest at 10 percent annually with each preferred share convertible into common shares at the rate of 70 percent of the average closing bid price for the common stock for the three days preceding conversion, times 1,000. So, if the common shares were originally valued at $1, then the 1,000 Series A 10 percent preferred shares issued would have a face value of $1 million.

If the average bid price per share dropped to 50 cents on the conversion date (based on the closing price for the three previous days), then 2,850 shares would be issuable for each preferred share converted. Savvy investors would typically employ a "sell and convert" strategy, whereby they would sell the shares all day, and then at the close of business, send a conversion notice covering the shares actually sold, essentially locking in their 30 percent profit.

The SEC has been frowning on these types of open-ended conversions, which were known in the trade as "death spiral preferreds" or "floorless conversions" because the more the price falls, the more shares are owed, so that the owner of the preferred shares has a really unfair advantage over common shareholders. Such death spiral preferreds are deemed toxic, and wise investors avoid any company that has issued them. (Mark Cuban's decision to dump his stock in a company planning to enter into a PIPE is what precipitated his fight with the SEC.)

The SEC prefers a floor price so that there is a clearly determinable maximum number of shares that can possibly be issuable from a conversion, and it wants this number to be disclosed. If funders agree to a floor, they usually also demand a ceiling (a maximum conversion price, no matter how high the share price rises). So heads, the investor wins; tails, the company loses. Clever minds have come up with many legal circumventions of the ban on floorless conversions. While the terms for a reporting company, at least, must be promptly disclosed in detail, along with a copy of the "material agreement" contract in a Form 8-K, which needs to be filed within two days, the language is often sufficiently arcane so that its implications cannot possibly be fathomed by the average shareholder (and often not by the company, either).

How a Company Can Be Hurt by PIPE Investors

While there is no shortage of examples, consider ICOA Corporation, a provider of wireless Internet services for public spaces such as hotels, airports, restaurants, and marinas (see www.icoacorp.com). As this book went to press, the common stock of ICOA was trading on the Pink Sheets at $0.0002 per share (down from as much as $0.125 in the past), which is 1/625 of its value a few years ago. What happened in the meantime? The company's sales grew several-fold, its losses dropped substantially, and it managed to acquire several smaller competitors with cash raised from a PIPE. However, it had accepted the PIPE investment from an aggressive PIPE writer who has been investigated by the SEC for illegal short selling. ICOA is now among the walking dead. At $0.0002 per share it can't raise money by selling equity, and the unconverted debt from the PIPE constitutes a priority lien, so it can't sell debt, either.

Hedging

Except for regulated SBICs, hedging transactions are often carried out by a funding investor in PIPEs or someone close to that investor to mitigate risk and increase profits, legally or otherwise. By selling short (ideally prior to funding and continuing on afterward), the investor has locked in the higher price. If the stock price then falls as a result of the selling pressure from the hedge, the investor is entitled to more shares. The investor closes out the short sale, profiting from the fall in the price, but then profits a second time because the fall in the price requires the company to issue him additional shares.

With these new shares, the investor is playing with the house's money, as he already locked in profit on the spread through the short sale. The investor can, therefore, incautiously hit the bid, selling on the bid rather than the offer, further driving down the share price.

How Hedged Sales and Adjustable Conversion Prices Benefit the PIPE Investor

Let's look at an example of a typical PIPE transaction with a floor and a ceiling. Let's say a company's stock is trading nicely (50,000 shares per day average volume) at a price of $1.50. The funder will reckon that he can sell 10 percent to 15 percent of that volume without hurting the price. At 50,000 shares and $1.50, that amounts to $75,000 of volume, so the funder can sell $7,500 to $11,250 worth of shares per day. At that rate, it would take at least 100 trading days to sell out of the initial position, assuming the same daily volume continues. Based on that projection, a binding letter of intent is signed with these terms:

- A $3 million funding, to be taken down in three tranches spaced three months apart.
- Issuance of convertible preferred shares, with a conversion price set at a discount of 20 percent (because discounts greater than 20 percent require shareholder approval).
- A floor of $0.60 and a ceiling of $1.60.

To sweeten the deal (as if it isn't sweet enough), a *commitment fee* of 6 percent on the entire amount of the commitment ($3 million) and placement agent fees of 10 percent plus 3 percent in unaccountable expenses are to be paid *in kind* in securities of *like tenor*.

What does all this jargon mean? First, the *commitment fee*, which is a fee paid for the commitment to fund, is paid on the entire $3 million, even though the take-down in the first tranche is $1 million. *In kind* means in stock, and *like tenor* means paid in the exact same securities as the investor gets. So up front, the fees are paid in preferred shares with a value of $180,000, in addition to preferred shares issuable for $1 million for the investment, even if the company (or the funder, under some circumstances) walks away after the first or second tranche.

There is also a $100,000 placement fee for the first tranche, and $30,000 in unaccountable expenses. Knowing he has the deal, the funder goes out and sells the company's stock short, driving the price down to $1.05. The average sale price is, say, $1.30, and let's assume that the funder manages to sell 200,000 shares short at that price.

Well, by this time, the company likely is in deep, has fallen behind on its bills, and has made commitments to others based on getting the first tranche of its money. Nice guy that he is, the funder agreeably goes forward with the deal, but insists that in view of the reduced market price, the ceiling be lowered to $0.95 and the floor to $0.50. The company reluctantly goes along, and the deal for the first tranche closes. The company gets its first $1 million, and the funder and the related placement agent now have 1,000 and 180 shares of Series A preferred, respectively, as well as 30 shares for the unaccountable expense allowance, 1,210 shares altogether.

Now the real fun begins. While the shares are being registered (typically a three-to-six-month process), or are merely waiting out the six months under the revised Rule 144, both funder and placement agent continue to sell short (usually the funder is prohibited by contract from engaging in short selling at this point, but the funder's alter ego, the placement agent, rarely is so restricted; nor is the brother-in-law in Canada).

The stock continues to fall in price to $0.80. Meanwhile they have sold short another 350,000 shares, for a total cumulative short sale of 550,000 shares, at an average sales price of $1.10, yielding total proceeds of $625,000. As soon as the offering is declared effective, the funder and placement agent convert $300,000 and $100,000 of Series A preferred, respectively. They are left with $700,000 and $110,000, respectively, in face value of their preferred shares.

They have converted at $0.64 per share ($0.80 less 20 percent). Each preferred share, therefore, converts into 1,562.50 shares of common stock, whereas at the time the deal was struck it was contemplated that only 833.33 shares would need to be issued. Altogether, they receive 625,000 shares (156,250 + 468,750) from the conversion. They deliver 550,000 of these shares to cover their short position, netting themselves $625,000. They still have $810,000 face value of preferred. (Assume that the dividend on the preferred offsets the carrying cost on the short sale, and ignore commissions.) Left over after this initial conversion and covering of the short position are 75,000 shares of common stock worth $60,000, for a value (so far) of $1,465,000 on their $1 million investment. They have liquidated only 20 percent of the preferred so far, but they have gotten back nearly 70 percent of their investment—a lot better than the nominal 20 percent discount in the term sheet.

It's even more lucrative, however. The $810,000 of still unconverted preferred will now convert based on a price of $0.64 (80 percent of $0.80), so in fact, on conversion, 218,750 shares are issuable, and at a $0.80 market price, that's worth $975,000.

A PIPE Investor's Total Value

So the total value is $625,000 already received plus $975,000 worth of preferred plus $60,000 in common marked to the market, or $1,660,000 in all. Best of all, $625,000 of the $1 million investment is already back in the bank, ready to be put into the next deal. In all likelihood, many of the remaining preferred shares will actually convert later on at the floor price of $0.50, so the funder may well double his money in just a few months. When you add in leverage (i.e., the broker is probably lending the funder half the sum at a low rate of interest called the broker call rate), the cash-on-cash return is doubled again. When you consider that the PIPE writer hedged most of the investment up front and therefore really assumed very little downside risk, it's a pretty good deal.

In recent cases, three different federal district courts dismissed the SEC's allegations that defendants violated Section 5 of the Securities Act of 1933 when they used restricted shares purchased in a PIPE transaction to cover a short position; unless the rules change, these PIPE deals may well be perfectly legal (as long as any short selling is done prior to the deal being signed). Nevertheless, lucrative as the deals are, some folks bend the rules to make even more money. For example, according to an indictment in the Eastern District of New York unsealed in October 2007, Martin E. Weisberg, a mergers and acquisitions partner in Baker & McKenzie's New York office, helped investors Zev Saltsman and Menachem Eitan gain access to hundreds of millions of discounted but restricted shares in two companies he represented. The pair allegedly evaded the restrictions on the shares by short selling the companies' stock, using the discounted shares to cover their positions. Prosecutors charge they also paid Weisberg and executives of the two companies millions of dollars in kickbacks. (In March 2010 Saltsman pleaded guilty to a superseding Information charging him with a single count, and he consented to a $5 million forfeiture. An information is a statement of charges that have not gone to a grand jury, and to which a defendant has agreed to plead guilty. In this case, following negotiations, the original Information was superseded by one carrying reduced charges, presumably as a result of Saltsman's cooperation. He is scheduled to be sentenced in July 2010. The case against the other defendants is not expected to come to trial before late 2010.)

As you can see, adjustment of the conversion price and preshorting minimize the risk to crooked PIPE writers. But they still have some risk. Their main risk is that by overselling, they kill the golden goose. A downward price slide drives away trading interest, so that the volume that averaged 50,000 shares per day dries up and may now be only 10,000 shares per day, on average. If that happens, they are stuck with shares but no market into which to sell them. Thus, the PIPE writer will be on the company's case for news and promotions (which the smart funder will offer to pay for)—anything to keep the stock trading so that the funder can sell out of the position. If the funder gets impatient and dumps shares at any price, then a situation such as befell poor ICOA can occur.

Reverse Splits—Golden Preferred

When too many shares were issued as a result of a toxic convertible, the market price can easily fall to $0.05 or less, and the shares become a debased currency, like what happened to countries with runaway inflation, such as occurred in Germany near the end of World War II, or in Italy, Brazil, and Argentina at different times. We saw that happen to poor ICOA.

The fix for debasement of shares is the same as for currencies. Companies revalue their share currency by doing massive share consolidations (called reverse splits), sometimes in a ratio of one new share for as many as 10,000 old shares. Of course, this essentially wipes out the holdings of existing common shareholders. But trust me on this; you need not feel sorry for management. They usually find ways to take care of themselves, often through the issuance of low-priced options.

A nefarious but probably legal trick (which can be used in combination with the issuance of low-priced options to management) is issuance of so-called golden preferred, sometimes called evergreen preferred, to insiders *before* the PIPE is done, when management still has control and doesn't need shareholder approval but can authorize it by consent of the majority of shareholders (e.g., by management). This preferred security usually has golden voting rights (i.e., 60 preferred shares are issued, each with voting power equal to 1 percent of the total authorized and outstanding shares.

In this case, the holders of the golden preferred have effective voting control of the company and common shareholders are virtually disenfranchised, no matter how many common shares are sold or are outstanding. Insiders may also gain actual equity by arranging an acquisition of some useless private entity that they control in exchange for shares of the public company, or they may receive a toxic note in return for forbearance on high but unpaid salaries. In this last case, the shares so issued may even be eligible to be instantly registered, using a Form S-8, and they may become free-trading without an SEC review. The funders still have their unconverted preferred stock, so they are not adversely affected by share consolidations or by the stock issuances to management. Only the investing public gets screwed.

Risks of Share Consolidation

The market hates share consolidations. The news of a pending reverse is posted in advance by the National Association of Securities Dealers (NASD) and may be reported by the company in a press release. Savvy investors short the hell out of such companies' stocks, which almost inevitably ensures that the price will immediately drop post reverse.

Consider this example: Company X did a toxic PIPE and as a result now has 600 million shares outstanding that trade at $0.005 (a half cent). Its market capitalization is therefore 600 million times $0.005 or $3 million, which likely understates its fair value.

It does a one-for-600 reverse split, so it will have only a million new shares outstanding post reverse, and its opening price will be $0.005 times 600 or $3. It still has the same market capitalization. However, short selling—probably illegal naked shorting—may drop the price down to $2, lopping off one-third of its already low market value. Company boards generally give the CEO a wide berth in fixing the date of the reverse, so a savvy CEO will try to combine the timing of the bad news of a reverse with strong good news as well as a major promotional campaign.

The combination of good news and a strong awareness campaign can create upward pressure, giving the company a rare victory over the shorts and forcing them to run for cover by buying the stock in the market, which can cause a run-up in price all by itself.

What Happened to Poor Peter?

At the beginning of this chapter, I discussed Peter, the elderly CEO looking for funding. Well, he did his deal with the shell, and the hedge fund that had promised to invest actually sent along the first couple of checks. In accordance with Rule 211, the company had prepared an updated Form 15c211 to ensure that there was accurate and timely information available to investors, and it had a beautiful, informative, and fully accurate web site. It had issued no press releases and authorized no promotion. Nevertheless, one fine day, the SEC issued an "emergency action" to halt trading in the company's stock because of "suspected manipulation," and the FBI paid the company a visit. What could possibly have caused this sad turn of events?

It turned out that the fellows the company had done the deal with (whom they knew pretty well) had partnered with some folks that they did not know well, and (unbeknownst to either the doctor or the fellows he dealt with directly), the FBI had been watching those characters for some time. What really had been going on was that these partners had been hyping the stock (especially abroad), totally without the knowledge of the company. They were selling off some of the supposedly free-trading shares that they had in the shell, and used other shares to pay for the hype that pumped up the market. Then on a monthly basis they transferred a small portion of those proceeds to an offshore hedge fund that they secretly controlled. In turn, the hedge fund invested those funds back into the company, an illegal technique known as a "gypsy swap."

Those partners were all subsequently arrested and pleaded guilty to a multiplicity of charges, including securities fraud, money laundering, and tax evasion. It turned out that these criminals were related to a lady named Beverlee Kamerling, a recidivist promoter in the Seattle area who had previously gotten herself into trouble in both the United States and Canada. She was charged, and insisted on going to trial. At sentencing, U.S. District Judge Richard Jones told her, "You just don't get it . . . you exhibit total contempt for the law and ethics. . . . While I don't believe you were the kingpin . . . you served as the adhesive for a house built on ill-gotten gain."[5]

To save their own skins, the other co-conspirators pleaded guilty and agreed to cooperate with the government against her. Kamerling was sentenced to 90 months of prison (seven and a half years); Joel Ramsden (who was the ringleader) was sentenced to six years in prison; and Kamerling's son, Nicholas J. Alexander, was sentenced to

41 months. Disbarred Bellevue lawyer Tolan S. Furusho (who gave the improper legal opinions that the stock was freely trading) was sentenced to 13 months in prison for his role in the scheme, and for failing to file federal income tax returns. Several other defendants were convicted of perjury for false statements they made to the grand jury in Seattle that was investigating the scheme, or for other efforts to obstruct justice. Seth Quinto was sentenced to 15 months; Jamie Goldstein was sentenced to five months; and his father, Donald Goldstein, received a three-month sentence. Frazer Ramsden, Joel's older brother, was sentenced to 41 months in prison. John E. Worthen pled guilty to conspiracy to obstruct justice, and was sentenced to 18 months' imprisonment. The defendants were also ordered to collectively make $2,471,784 in restitution payments to the 3,300 investors who lost money in the scheme.

So justice was served. Right?

But what about poor Peter? He had a really hard time of it and he still is struggling. It has been heartbreaking. Funding from the hedge fund stopped, of course. And no one else wanted to touch his now-toxic company because of the SEC's "manipulation" charge. He and the chief engineer took no salary for a long time, laid off staff, and pumped in nearly $500,000 of their own money to somehow keep the company minimally afloat. Now, nearly three years later, he is still unfunded, his dream has not been realized, and his inventions are not yet FDA approved and cannot save lives.

Bogus PIPE Ponzi Scheme

PIPEs enjoyed a reputation for being so profitable that some investors clamored to be let in. Of course, there are always fraudsters happy to oblige. Here's a typical example: On September 15, 2008, the Securities and Exchange Commission charged an Irvine, California, attorney and two other promoters for conducting a $52.7 million Ponzi scheme in which they sold investors bogus PIPE investments, promised unrealistic profits, and misappropriated more than $20 million of investors' funds to function as their own personal piggy bank.

The SEC's complaint alleges that attorney Jeanne M. Rowzee, along with James R. Halstead of Santa Ana, California, and Robert T.

Harvey of Prosper, Texas, told investors that Rowzee was an experienced securities attorney who personally screened and selected each PIPE investment after thorough due diligence.[6] Contrary to these representations, they did not place investor funds in PIPE investments. Rowzee, Halstead, and Harvey instead used new investor funds to pay principal and returns to earlier investors, and to finance their own personal endeavors such as trips to Las Vegas, property purchases, and alimony payments.

"Investors must be wary of promoters, even securities attorneys or other purported 'experts' who offer investment opportunities with high returns but fail to disclose complete and verifiable information about the investment they're touting," said Rosalind R. Tyson, regional director of the SEC Los Angeles Regional Office.[7] "In this case, as alleged in our complaint, the so-called PIPE investments did not exist. The defendants raised millions of dollars from unsuspecting investors and simply used it to enrich themselves."

The SEC's complaint, filed in federal court in Santa Ana, California, alleges that from at least March 2004 through December 2006, the defendants sold the purported PIPE investments to investors, promising returns of 19 to 54 percent within 12 to 16 weeks.

Halstead pleaded guilty and received a sentence of 10 years and one month (thereby making him ineligible for a prison camp). Rowzee, who was also charged criminally with securities fraud and conspiracy, struck a plea deal in 2008 and is free on bail while awaiting sentencing. She has since been charged with fraudulently applying for credit cards in her children's names and adding herself to the accounts as a second cardholder, as well as forging checks drawn on the account of a woman with whom she had a romantic relationship, 13 new felony charges in all. She, too, can look forward to a long term of imprisonment.

In a similar scheme, Richard Monroe Harkless ran a scheme through a company he called MX Factors from 2000 until late 2003. Investors were promised returns of up to 14 percent every two or three months, at which time investors could either receive their investments back or roll over their investments into the next investment period. The vast majority of MX Factors investors were "reloaded," meaning they were convinced to invest money more than once. The operation collapsed in March 2004, prompting an investigation by the Internal

Revenue Service, U.S. Postal Service, and FBI. When Richard Monroe Harkless learned of the criminal investigation, he shredded customer files and fled to Mexico, where he hid for three years, Eric Vandevelde, an assistant U.S. attorney based in Los Angeles, said. Harkless was arrested in 2007 after returning to the United States. He received a 100-year sentence (that's not a typo) for his role in defrauding approximately 600 investors of $35 million from 2000 to 2003. Harkless "has shown zero remorse throughout the entire process," the prosecutor said.[8] "It's an appropriate sentence, given the incredible amount of harm he caused." The statutory maximum sentence was 280 years of imprisonment. In addition, Judge Virginia A. Phillips ordered Harkless to pay $35,479,310 in restitution to the victims who lost money as a result of the scam.

Harkless was sentenced after being convicted in July 2009 of three counts of mail fraud. Three of his sales agents—Daniel Berardi, Thomas Hawkesworth, and Randall Harding—pleaded guilty and received sentences of up to six years in federal prison.

Too Good to Be True

Though venture capital is expensive and hard to get, other funders may insist on a public vehicle as a condition of investment, and then invest in a PIPE. In structuring a PIPE, it is vital to avoid toxic terms. Even so, the company's interests are adverse to the investor's. Issuing too much stock debases its value and renders it useless as a form of currency. Curing an overissuance by an aggressive reverse split can boomerang, giving short sellers a field day.

However, good news and an aggressive awareness campaign can sometimes send short sellers running for cover—to the company's great benefit. PIPEs, like any other investment offered to unsophisticated investors that sounds too good to be true, probably is.

Chapter 12

Promotion Fraud

PUMP AND DUMP

W hen we looked at PIPEs in the previous chapter, we noted that PIPE writers need volume into which they can sell their investment. They look to promoters to create the volume. Company founders sometimes also seek to hype the stock, either to make it easier and cheaper to raise funds, or to surreptitiously sell stock.

In this chapter, we take you behind the scenes to see how this promotion works.

A Conversation

A company I came across (we'll call it "Widget Medical" to protect the guilty) decided that it needed to raise cash. Also, some of its officers illegally sought liquidity for the shares surreptitiously held for their benefit in the name of an offshore trust. (They've not been caught yet, so they need to remain nameless.) They decided to engage *five* groups of promoters to stimulate awareness in their stock. They paid out a lot of money in the form of free-trading shares, obtained through a beneficial conversion of a two-year note held by the CEO's brother-in-law (similar to what Tom Midas did more legally, as we recounted earlier). The CEO cleverly did not tell any of the promoters about the others, so each supposedly would think that the promotion was totally on his shoulders. Volume did increase, and for a day or so the price did, too. Then the price fell, to below where it had been before the campaign started.

Widget Medical decided to have a conference call with all the groups of promoters on the line. The CEO had hired a facilitator to select the promoters and to manage the campaign. The facilitator started the teleconference by saying, "Let's go around the horn and hear what was bought last week." Each group reported in.

"We bought 50,000," the first reported.

"We bought 30,000," said the second.

"We bought 100,000," said the third, and so on.

"Well," said the facilitator, who was keeping tabs, "that adds up to 350,000 shares. But the total volume for the week was only 220,000 shares, and the DTCC [Depository Trust & Clearing Corporation] sheets show it mostly came from Ameritrade, which means it's probably all from a single buyer."

"Well, the problem," said one promoter, "is that there is no news. The story is getting tired. I told you up front that I needed a press release every other day." (The obvious question about the discrepancy between the shares purportedly bought and those actually bought remained unanswered.)

The CEO complained, "It's those damned shorts up in Canada. And also, I think you guys are dumping your shares into the market."

"I haven't sold a share," protested one promoter, "but I do need some news."

"Okay. Tell your guys to look for news on Monday morning," replied the CEO.

"What will it be?" asked another promoter.

"We'll announce a letter of intent for a large order," answered the CEO.

"Are you sure?" asked a third promoter.

"Absolutely," answered the CEO. "I've already got the letter in my hand."

"Well, in that case," said the promoter, "why don't you fax it over to me right away? I'll get my guys working immediately. We'll also set up fax blasts to start going out tonight to prime the pump."

See if you can count the number of problems with the foregoing call, which is based on actual events but a composite of many such conversations involving more than one company. The vignette is designed to illustrate the perils of promotion. It appears that the shares used to fund the promotion were issued pursuant to a beneficial conversion (a conversion at below the market price). The company cannot benefit. If it will help raise cash for the company, or to fund a company-sponsored promotion, then that's a problem.

If the CEO is selling free-trading shares nominally in one name but beneficially owned by the CEO, and it is a sale by an insider, it is subject to all of the provisions of Rule 144, including disclosure. The intent to disguise the sale probably constitutes fraud and certainly would not immunize the CEO from compliance with Rule 144.

Regulation FD was clearly violated. Inside information was selectively disseminated. The promoters knew the pending news before the public and seemed to be planning to selectively disseminate it to friends ("prime the pump"). Moreover, it's likely that the contemplated "fax blasts" would hint of promised news that general investors would not know is coming; that appears to be front-running because these early investors are buying with the knowledge of information not yet disseminated to the public. They will likely sell next week at a profit once the news is disseminated, which is classic fraud.

If the news is indeed material and the large order is in hand, why is it not promptly being disclosed?

The details of the DTCC sheets (ownership changes) were not publicly disclosed, and the disclosure of that information to the promoters likely makes all of them insiders who cannot be selling their shares. It is also likely that hiring five promoters and a facilitator is an attempt (what the SEC calls a scheme) to hype a stock, rather than to create awareness. Company insiders are selling while the public is being urged to buy, which is the hallmark of a stock fraud.

There are also other lessons to be learned from this conversation, including the truism that all stock promoters are liars. Each promoter took credit for volume he had nothing to do with, calling into question the axiom that there is honor among thieves.

A Not-So-Creative Pump and Dump:
Beverage Creations

The Securities and Exchange Commission (SEC) has long been after penny-stock promoters, especially those who engage in pump-and-dump activities. Its main weapons are (1) to temporarily suspend trading in a stock (which then forces the company to go through a full review by the National Association of Securities Dealers (NASD); (2) to file a civil suit, which often asks for disgorgement, seeks fines, and bars from serving as an officer or director and/or transacting in penny stocks; and (3) to make a referral to the Department of Justice for possible criminal prosecution. Here is one typical case:

Beverage Creations, Inc., trading as BVRG on the Pink Sheets (an electronic quote system for over-the-counter stocks), promised to develop the next generation of sports drink. The SEC alleged that it is no more than a shell for a pump-and-dump stock scheme involving a small group of investors hoping to get rich quick.

The company is the purported developer of bio^{2}Tonic, a sports water product containing "an inhalable shot of oxygen," according to a company news release issued January 30, 2008, when Beverage Creations began trading on the Pink Sheets.[1]

The SEC suspended the trading of the shares two months later, in March 2008, and filed a civil complaint in May 2008 against Beverage Creations and three Texas stock promoters. The complaint alleges that they attempted to sell shares at inflated prices and in violation of SEC disclosure laws.

"The promoters are engaged in a 'pump and dump' of [Beverage Creations] stock, hyping the stock through spam e-mails and advertising mailers filled with specious claims, while reselling millions of shares in their own accounts for substantial profits," the SEC complaint says.[2] "For its part, [Beverage Creations] is misleading investors by disclaiming its relationship to the stock promoters."

Throughout February, the company issued one upbeat news release after another. In one instance, Beverage Creations said it was in discussions with Coca-Cola for a distribution agreement. In another release, it said that it had entered into an agreement to acquire a 44,000-square-foot production and bottling facility, but did not say

where. The company also announced the appointment of a former
Dallas Cowboys football player to its board of directors, and said that it
had hired Kohnstamm Communications, a well-known St. Paul public
relations firm, to help with marketing. But it was all part of a ruse,
according to the SEC.

"The company has no revenue from operations, has not manufactured or produced any proprietary sports drink, and offers no other
products," the government complaint said. In December, the SEC said,
Beverage Creations had $14,500 in credit card debt and just $12,506
in its bank account. In the preceding three months, the company had
lost $43,760.

The Texas partners of Beverage Creations in the alleged stock-
pumping arrangement are Jason Wynn, described in the SEC complaint as a former used-car salesman; Wynn Industries, owned by Wynn;
Carlton Fleming, a onetime stockbroker with a record of abusive sales
tactics; Thomas Wade Investments, owned by Fleming; Ryan Reynolds, a
onetime stockbroker who was barred from the industry; and Bellatalia,
a limited partnership owned by Reynolds.[3]

The SEC said in the complaint that Beverage Creations sold
9,999,999 shares to the Texas interests for $199,000, or about 2 cents
a share, on December 17.[4] By hyping the company and engaging in
manipulative trading to create the appearance of demand for the stock,
the Texans generated more than $2.4 million in stock sales, accord-
ing to the SEC. The SEC said the promotional campaign pumped the
stock to a high of $1.83 a share.

On February 21, 2008, after Dow Jones News Service reported
that Wynn and Wynn Industries were promoting the company's shares,
Beverage Creations issued a news release denying any affiliation with
them. That news release was false, the SEC alleged in its complaint.

On December 22, 2008, the SEC amended its complaint to add
additional charges related not only to Beverage Creations, but also to
other stock promoted through similar pump-and-dump schemes, in a
five-count, 42-page complaint.[5] In a press release, the SEC notes:

In its amended complaint, the SEC alleges that Reynolds,
Wynn, Fleming, and additional companies under their control purchased stock from ConnectAJet.com, Inc., My Vintage

Baby, Inc. and Alchemy Creative, Inc. for pennies per share
and immediately began liquidating those shares in the public market at prices grossly inflated by their own promotional
activities. The amended complaint adds as defendants Lugano
Funds LLC, Wynn Holdings, LLC and Regus Investment
Group, LLC, which are companies owned or controlled by
Reynolds, Wynn and Fleming, respectively.

In addition, the SEC alleges that Jason Wynn and companies under his control created artificial demand for the stock of
ConnectAJet.com, Inc., My Vintage Baby, Inc. and Alchemy
Creative, Inc. through various ad campaigns, nationwide promotional mailers and spam emails. While the promotional mailers
disclosed that Wynn companies received the stock being touted,
they did not disclose that Wynn and his companies intended to
sell that stock into the artificially inflated market created by the
promotions.[6]

Curiously, although the criminal statutes applicable to the alleged
violations could result in lengthy prison terms, as of now the U.S.
attorney has not filed a parallel criminal complaint. This does not mean
that a complaint could not be forthcoming.

This was not Jason Wynn's only involvement with small-cap
stocks. Another venture was to create an online innovator of private
jet travel and charter. He launched a company called Connect-A-Jet
Inc., which attracted a lot of attention. The stock hit $2.74 a share
in September 2008 after the company ran a self-promoting campaign
advertising its concept on cable business channel CNBC.

But the business plan began to crumble soon after. Companies that
Connect-A-Jet claimed to be partnering with disavowed any connection. The company's flight search engine wasn't fully operational. Its
last announcement, dated October 22, 2008, said it just saw its biggest
booking with a $90,000 flight, it was still nearing completion of its
booking tool, and it had just passed 5,000 "flight requests."[7]

Those flight requests apparently come from the rudimentary travel
questionnaire on its web site that still stands in for the promised booking tool. The SEC's statement said Wynn calls himself the "former
founder" of Connect-A-Jet; he sold his stake in the company and now
serves as a consultant, the statement said.[8]

Mr. Wynn and Bill Gates

According to an article by Dow Jones Newswires, Wynn has been a shareholder of Alchemy Creative Inc. of Plano, Texas, an education company whose penny stock started trading in December 2007.[9] Investors include billionaires Bill and Melinda Gates, who have a family connection to the company. The Gateses' investment wasn't widely known—until someone mailed brochures in December highlighting the connection.

Without admitting or denying the allegations, Beverage Creations, Inc., Robert Wieden, former CEO, and Patrick Dado, former COO, settled the action by consenting to entry of a court order that permanently bars them from violating Section 5 of the Securities Act of 1933 and Section 10(b) of the Securities Exchange Act of 1934 and Rule 10b-5 thereunder. In addition, Wieden and Dado will pay civil penalties of $20,000 each. The SEC's action against the remaining defendants is ongoing.

Michael Paloma

Michael Saquella, aka Michael Paloma, did face criminal charges. He pleaded guilty to committing securities and electronic mail frauds, and was sentenced to 10 years in federal prison. He was also ordered to pay $7,806,303.58 in damages.

In 2004, Paloma, 47, and four colleagues hustled investors by convincing owners of 15 small corporations to turn over large chunks of those firms' penny stocks after promising that they could take the companies public.

They then e-mailed fraudulent press releases to drive interest in the companies' stocks, create artificial demand, and drive up share prices.

Once the stock price had been pumped up, the men dumped the shares they controlled, leaving duped investors holding the bag. The "scams netted more than $20 million in profits," said Alice Fisher, assistant attorney general of the Justice Department's criminal division.[10] The men kept the bulk of the proceeds, but some profits were turned over to the companies in question.

"What makes this case stand out is the intricacy of the scheme," said Cheryl Scarboro, associate director of the SEC's enforcement division, in a statement.[11] "These defendants were not only able to sneak these companies onto the public markets through the back door, they were able to manipulate those markets with old-fashioned pump-and-dump techniques."

Abraham Hochman

In January 2009, Spanish police arrested six people, among them Abraham Hochman, a former Mossad agent, on suspicion of involvement in a €450 million ($600 million) fraud on the London Stock Exchange. The *Daily Mail* reported that an Argentinian named Diego Magn Selva is also thought to be among the six arrested.[12]

Police did not name the company involved, but reports have identified it as Langbar International (formerly Crown Corporation Ltd), a cash-rich shell company formerly run by Monte Carlo–based entrepreneur Mariusz Rybak—also known as the Baltic Barracuda.[13] One of the people under arrest is suspected of organizing the fraudulent scheme involving shares in a British company called Langbar International between 2003 and 2005.

Police said the fraud began in 2003.[14] The investigation was launched in 2005 following the disclosure that Langbar may never have owned £365 million it claimed to have stashed away in Dutch and Brazilian banks. The company was delisted from London's Alternative Investment Market (AIM) in 2005, when the investigation began. The scheme was to create a bogus company, list it on the London Stock Exchange, use false documents and rumor to inflate the share price, and then sell shares at a profit. The company's market cap was $300 million when it was floated, and reached a peak of $600 million. Once the fraud was exposed and the shares delisted, investors lost everything.

Penalties

The lessons in this chapter are obvious. First, pump-and-dump hype can get not only the promoters into hot water, but also the company and its officers, and sometimes even its lawyers as well. Incomplete or misleading disclosure is akin to nondisclosure, and can be fraudulent. Also, use of Rule 504 (an exemption from registration requirements applicable to accredited investors) is not available to nonaccredited investors, or if the accredited investor is merely a conduit for a disguised offering to the general public.

While there may not always be a bright line to define illegal promotional activity, all involved should carefully consult competent securities counsel, as the penalties for missteps can be severe.

Chapter 13

Leaks, Front-Running, and Insider Trading

TEST YOURSELF

If you have gotten this far, you probably have a good idea of some of the perils CEOs face, but not perhaps the pressures that they face. You now have an opportunity to play CEO and consider how you would act in several situations. We then look at several real-life examples, and how the companies and their investors made out.

Three Problems

So, based on what you know, here are three problems for you to consider.

1. Pretend that you are the CEO of a publicly traded company. You are sitting on the hottest news in the company's history—you received a firm purchase order from Cisco Systems worth $40 million. Your PR guy and Cisco's are finalizing a joint press release to go out next week to be announced at a major industry conference. The phone rings. "It's Mary Poppins, the analyst from Credit Suisse First Boston," says your secretary. What are you going to say

to her when she says, "I've heard you folks are about to get your first really big order"?

"Easy question," you say? "You just piously issue a 'no comment.'"

2. Now try this one: You are still the CEO of the same company, but your stock is in the toilet, the main market maker has been calling to complain about how much money he has lost supporting your stock, and you have a PIPE in the works that you need to get done. The bills are piling up, and a higher stock price would dramatically reduce the cost of the PIPE as well as ensure that it gets done. "Tell me what's going on," says the market maker. "My boss wants me to stop making a market in your stock." What can you say to him? The temptation for you to let some good news slip is enormous.

3. Try an easier case: You have a golfing date with good old McKenzie, your fraternity brother from Pomona College. He says, "Gosh, your stock has really taken a beating lately. I bought it at the IPO. Tell me, good buddy, should I get out while I'm still comfortably ahead?" "Well," you say slyly, "why don't you hang in there for a bit? I think some really good news might be out real soon [wink, wink]. And how are Mabel and the kids doing?" "Really," answers McKenzie. "Should I double down, then?" Now you are really in a pickle. It's like answering the question "Have you stopped beating your wife yet?" Whatever you say will get you into more trouble.

From these three problems, you'll see that selective disclosure is a no-no. It violates Regulation FD. And trading on insider information before the news has been fully disseminated is a no-no. If a broker does it ahead of a customer order, it's called front-running. The penalties, at a minimum, are twice the gain, and can lead to a permanent bar from serving as an officer or director of a public company, or even, as Martha Stewart learned, to imprisonment if you lie about it.

Don't Leak News: Raj Rajaratnam and Danielle Chiesi

More recently, Raj Rajaratnam, Danielle Chiesi, and Roomy Khan were indicted by a federal grand jury (SDNY 1:09-cr-01184-RJH,

USA v. Rajaratnam et al.) on 17 counts of securities fraud and conspiracy. The indictment accused the billionaire founder of the Galleon Group, which managed $3 billion in assets, and also the former Bear Stearns hedge fund manager of operating at the center of a vast insider trading ring that profited from corporate secrets passed by an extensive network of informants that ensnared at least 18 people, including Robert Moffat, a former senior IBM executive, and Anil Kumar, formerly a partner at McKinsey & Company. Eleven lawyers, traders, and executives implicated in the case, including Khan, Moffat, Kumar, and Mark Kirkland have already pleaded guilty.

In short, no matter what the pressure or the temptation, don't leak news. The answer to all three questions is the same: "You know that it's illegal for me to answer that kind of question." Don't leak news. Don't trade ahead of the dissemination of news. If you are the tippee—the one to whom the news was leaked—don't trade on the information, and don't pass the tip along. You have been duly warned.

Mark Cuban Fought Back

There is an interesting footnote to the foregoing discussion. In a much publicized case, the SEC, on November 17, 2008, sued Mark Cuban, billionaire owner of the Dallas Mavericks and the founder of Broadcast.com. The charges stem from an allegation that he sold shares of Mamma.com prior to a private offering (3:08-cv-02050-D *Securities and Exchange Commission v. Cuban*).[1]

The SEC charged the outspoken owner of the Dallas Mavericks for allegedly dumping shares in Mamma.com upon learning it was raising money in a private offering.[2] The SEC alleged in a civil action that Cuban sold his entire 6 percent ownership stake on June 28, 2004, after learning that Mamma.com was raising money through a private investment in a public entity (PIPE). The next day, on June 29, the company announced the PIPE financing and shares of the company dropped by more than 10 percent. By selling his stake, the SEC alleged, Cuban avoided more than $750,000 in losses. Four years later, the SEC brought the charges.

Cuban and his lawyers denied that he was under any obligation not to trade on the information he received. Not one to take such things sitting down, Cuban fought back hard, and U.S. District Judge Sidney Fitzwater in Dallas agreed. He ruled that Cuban was not an insider and threw out the charges in a way that undercut the SEC's legal argument and could make it more difficult to prosecute similar cases.

The dismissal became final (with prejudice) on August 13, 2009. However, it remains clear that an insider still cannot trade on insider information.[3]

The SEC appealed (09-10996) the judge's order to dismiss to the Appellate Court of the Fifth Circuit (an atypical move on the SEC's part), so this case may ultimately reach the Supreme Court.

Meanwhile Cuban sued the SEC for his legal fees, on the grounds that persons at the SEC were conducting a vendetta against him and that the suit was not brought in good faith. He won an initial skirmish, in that the judge did not dismiss his motion, but permitted discovery. Of course, the government has vigorously opposed. The case in unlikely to come to trial until late in 2010.

Ads in Major Newspapers

While e-mail and fax blasts used to be the promotional tools of choice, an article in the *New York Times* entitled "Breathless Pitches for Penny Stocks, Now in Newspapers," by Lynnley Browning, published on September 5, 2007, highlighted a relatively new technique for promoting smaller company stocks: an explosion of advertisements in major newspapers.[4] For example, ads appeared, respectively, in the *New York Times* and *USA Today* touting the stocks of MitoPharm, which claimed to be selling a "true anti-aging drink," and Nano Chemical Systems Holdings, which said it "plans" to become a maker of biofuels.

Beverage Creations, discussed in Chapter 12, used similar techniques.

Like brochure campaigns, full-page ads in major newspapers are not cheap, and Nano Chemical acknowledged that GIA Consulting was paid $232,000 by a third party to prepare and place the ads.[5] You can be sure that if there is an explosion of ads, then they are profitable to the promoters. The ads that have appeared so far appear to have been carefully vetted by lawyers. They use terms like "ground floor" opportunity, and they ask rhetorical questions like "How much would you pay to slow or stop the aging process?"

More dubious are claims like "The buying frenzy is likely to continue" or "MTPM could be that hottest story to hit Wall Street this year!"—possible but not likely.[6] Even more blunt is the exhortation in the Nano Chemical ad: "Don't miss this incredible investment opportunity." The ads don't, however, make specific claims for appreciation in share price. Be aware that newspapers, according to Maria Terrell, a spokeswoman for the International Marketing Association, who was quoted in the *New York Times* article, do not have a "responsibility to verify the facts of an ad being placed."[7]

What Happened Afterward?

I followed up on the three companies featured in the *New York Times* article to see how they made out.

MitoPharm, which on a split-adjusted basis had traded as high as $350 when the ad ran, is now down to under $1 even after it effected a one-for-500 reverse split (share consolidation) in November 2007. Since June 12, 2007 (before the ads ran), MitoPharm has not been a reporting company. As of today, its web site, www.mitopharm.com, is not up. There is no information about it on www.pinksheets.com, the disclosure site for nonreporting companies traded on the Pink Sheets. Some disappointed investors reported that their holdings are worth only a thousandth of what they paid. On July 13, 2009, the SEC filed suit against MitoPharm, Seattle-based securities lawyer David Otto, and several others for conducting a fraudulent pump-and-dump scheme in which they secretly unloaded more than $1 million in penny stock of a company touting a nonexistent anti-aging product.[8]

The SEC complaint alleges that the scheme began in late 2006 when Otto, who was hired by MitoPharm CEO Peter Cheung, arranged to purchase a publicly traded shell company as a merger partner for MitoPharm.[9] Otto and Van Siclen drafted opinion letters to MitoPharm's transfer agent filled with false statements in order to secure supposedly freely tradable stock certificates for individuals and entities secretly controlled by Otto.[10]

The SEC's complaint alleges that Cheung hired Charles Bingham and his Houston-based company Wall Street PR, Inc., on Otto's recommendation, and they embarked on an aggressive public relations campaign that centered on the misleading promotion of two key products—Restorade and Stamina Solutions—that did not exist.[11] They developed promotional materials that falsely stated that both Restorade and Stamina Solutions are "[a]vailable as functional beverage or as a soft gel capsule."[12] To accompany the written text of MitoPharm's web site and other promotional materials, Cheung had a graphics artist create renderings of what the containers for MitoPharm's products could look like. Written materials and Web profiles created by Bingham and others were disseminated to investors with fake images and present-tense descriptions of the products.

The SEC further alleges that as the promotional campaign caused the stock price to rise above $2.30, Otto sold his shares for more than $1 million and Bingham netted an additional $300,000. The massive selling of the stock caused the price to fall to a nickel per share by November 2007. The case (2:09-cv-00960, *RAJ Securities and Exchange Commission v. Otto et al.*) is still pending in federal court in the Western District of Washington.

As for Nano Chemical Systems Holdings, it changed its name to PanGenix, has new management, and is in a new and unrelated business, which is to say it became a shell.

BioStem Was Something Special

Perhaps most noteworthy was the ad in *USA Today* for BioStem, Inc. (BTEM), which said it engages in stem cell storage.[13] BioStem was formerly known as WebViews Corporation, a dot-com, and before that as Cascade Mountain Mining Corporation, so it seems to be a serial shell company. BioStem had stated that Cryobanks International, Inc., a private company, was in the process of doing a reverse merger into BioStem.[14] Both the disclosures in the ad and the nondisclosures are interesting.

BioStem disclosed that it hired ATN Enterprises LLC to prepare the ad, and paid Discovery Stocks $37,500 to place it. ATN was hired by "third-party consultants" (what we term facilitators) and was "contracted" to receive one million shares of BTEM. The ad notes that Discovery Stocks can "trade in the shares."[15] Not mentioned, or disclosed by *USA Today*, is that Cryobanks was involved in a Ghana-based money laundering scheme, based on a complaint filed in Federal District Court in Brooklyn in 2004, and the defendants in that case settled with the SEC by paying $1.3 million.[16]

Those one million shares of Discovery Stocks may have been worth as much as $2 million based on BioStem's $2 share price while the pump-and-dump scheme was going on. BioStem, Inc. changed its name to Joytoto USA, Inc., but it is now known as Pollex, Inc.

The announced Cryobanks transaction never did close. The company did a 1-for-40 reverse split before merging with Joyon Entertainment, Inc. (JEI), a Delaware corporation, in exchange for 115,000,000 shares of (postsplit) common stock, thoroughly wiping out earlier shareholders. Pollex is a now majority-owned subsidiary of Joytoto Korea (an electronics company), and its trading symbol is now PLLX. On a split-adjusted basis, the stock traded as high as $35 during the period of the ad, and now trades for under $0.02. It reported no revenue and an accumulated deficit of $106,688,248 as of September 30, 2009.

Be Smart

Selective disclosure is unfair to investors. Tipping others or acting on tips can get you into trouble, and unless you have the resources of billionaire Mark Cuban you don't want to be fighting the SEC.

Bombastic ads touting stocks raise red flags. Common themes of these ads are:

- Comparison to major large-cap stocks like Microsoft and Intel that have been spectacularly successful.

- Comparison to household names like Coca-Cola (e.g., "a mature competitor was acquired by Coca-Cola").
- Use of breathless language touting "incredible" investment opportunities.

In short, not one of the companies that advertised and were discussed in the *New York Times* article is still around. None was successful. Promoters made a lot of money. To date, one of the groups has been charged. Lesson to prospective buyers: Caveat emptor.

Chapter 14

Fictitious Volume

A PUMP-AND-DUMP SCAM
WITH INTRIGUE

I n Chapter 12 we looked at promotion fraud and pump-and-dump scams, and in Chapter 13 we saw responsibilities of the CEO to guard against pump-and-dump fraud. In this chapter, we focus in detail on the mechanics of how the pump-and-dump promoters go about their nefarious activities.

A Story for Example

"Ken," a promoter, met up with "Jacob," who owned a day trading operation. They were jammed around a tiny table in a noisy room upstairs in the lounge of the tony Four Seasons Hotel on 57th Street in New York, where the right people on expense account budgets come and spend three times more on a drink than they would in a nice restaurant with less cachet. They can also mingle with overly made-up 50-something divorcees, high-class call girls, and businessmen hustling for business. In short, they can see and be seen.

"So tell me your problem," said Jacob, in between drinks.

"I've got this really good client," replied Ken. "'Dreck Minerals.' They are digging for oil in Turkey, right near the border with Iraq. They have already got their first producing well."

"How much is it producing?" asked Jacob.

"Right now, it's only $2,000 per day," said Ken, "but it really is more like a test bore. This can easily produce a million bucks a week at today's prices for crude."

Jacob continued with his due diligence. "And how many shares are out there?" he wanted to know.

"Well, there are a total of 500 million shares outstanding. But 450 million are owned by the founder and a few of his friends and they are all restricted," Ken answered. "And most of the rest of the shares are in friendly hands," he added.

"So what do you want from me?" Jacob asked.

"The stock is around 50 cents. They are fully reporting, but they need money to continue drilling. They have commitments, and if they don't meet them, they can lose the drilling rights. I have found them some investors who will give them money at a straight 30 percent discount, but the investors need to see volume. Right now, the price is stable, but it trades by appointment. They need to raise $3 million and it trades only 10,000 to 20,000 shares a day."

Jacob did a quick calculation. "Selling 15 percent of that, $1,500 a day, it would take the investor 2,000 trading days to get his money back," he said. "And that's if the price and volume hold up."

"Now you understand my problem," said Ken.

The Story Continues

"But," Jacob continued, "no way is that piece-of-junk company worth its $300 million market cap. This deal is way too rich for my blood."

"Listen, Jacob," argued Ken. "If the geologist's projections prove out, the company will be a bargain at 10 times its price."

"Hey, that's a really big if, and I wasn't born yesterday. I've been around the block a few times. Sorry, no can do. Do you know how much I'd have to buy of those 50 million free-trading shares? All of it, probably at least twice. Sorry, I love you, Ken, but this one is not for me," said Jacob with finality.

"Look," persisted Ken. "I promised them volume, but it doesn't have to all be real. You have day trading outfits. Just trade it around."

"Okay, now that's different. It will be expensive, but that I can get done," said Jacob. "Let's talk turkey."

"I need sustained volume of 150,000 to 200,000 shares per day," said Ken, "and the program needs to run for at least four weeks."

"That means trading four million shares altogether," said Jacob. "I'll need a million shares to run the program, and a half million for me."

"I don't have that much available," said Ken. "I think I could get you a million, but I'll have to push him real hard. He was looking to pay one share for each five or six shares bought," said Ken.

"I can't go under a million and a quarter," said Jacob. "I gotta pay my guys also."

"I'll try to get that done," said Ken.

"Remember," reminded Jacob, "this is only for trading it around—just so the schmuck can get financed."

"It's a deal," said Ken. "Jacob, you have an account over at First Nevada, right? I want to use them because my buddy there can LOA [letter of authorization] stuff."

"LOA, huh? Bet you remember him at Xmas," said Jacob.

"Xmas? I remember him all year 'round," said Ken. "Since 9/11, everything is a hassle and if you need something to get done quickly, you need to grease the skids pretty well."

The Problem in the Story Comes to Light

"Well, that's *your* problem," said Jacob. "Here are the coordinates for an account at First Nevada. It's in the name of the First Abyssinian Church of South Carolina, and its account number is 54-230-593."

"A black church. That's good thinking, Jacob. You're a pretty smart New Yorker," said Ken admiringly.

"Thanks, I have a buddy who is a Hasid. He called a buddy of his, a rabbi in South Carolina, and he spoke to the pastor, who made it happen for me in the spirit of ecumenism. Hey, I gotta run, buddy. Nice to see you again."

Ken's next step was the Prime Grill, a swanky kosher restaurant on 49th Street in Manhattan just west of Park Avenue, where

"Eli," the CEO of Dreck Minerals, was waiting, wearing his black velvet yarmulke.

"So what have you got for me?" asked Eli, getting right to the point.

"This was really hard," Ken told Eli. "I talked to all my people, and most of them turned me down. They said it was just too rich. But I have one source I have worked with for years and he owes me some favors. He's willing to do it. He needs two million shares. But that's for real buying. And I need half a million to manage the program."

"This is what I'll do: I'll give him the two million as he asked—half up front and half at the back end. And the same deal for you," said Eli.

"No way, José," said Ken. "First of all, my guy keeps a very low profile, and he doesn't even want to know from you. So the shares come to me. And second, he gets the job done, but he doesn't even extend credit to his mother. To get him, I had to call in all my favors and I still needed to twist his arm pretty good to get him to agree. So, if you don't want to do it, no problem, but that is what I've got for you. If you want to do the deal, you have to pay up front. It's the best I can do."

"You're absolutely sure this is real buying?" asked Eli.

"Oh yes. This guy has discretionary control over accounts of big players. He just tucks the stock into their accounts—a little here, a little there, and nobody notices. And tell you what. I'm confident enough that he'll perform that I'll take half of my shares on the come, even if he can't," Ken offered.

"Okay," said Eli, "I'm trusting you. Send me your coordinates and my cousin Boris in Israel will send you two and a quarter. Look for it to come to you out of Turks and Caicos. Can you start buying tomorrow?"

"No," said Ken. "I won't lie to you. These things take some time to set up, and it'll take a while for the shares to clear. I can't do anything till they clear. Today's the 10th. Here are my coordinates. If your relative speaks to his broker tomorrow and we get the shares by Monday, we should be able to get going by Thursday. But you know what? Friday in the summer is not good. Everyone is away. We'll start off the following Monday, on the 18th. And by the way, I'm going to need some press releases. Make sure you have a good one on the wire at 7:30 A.M. on Monday. This is a big program. You gotta give me real news. No BS," Ken added.

"Don't worry about that," said Eli. "I'll do my part. It's late in Israel. My cousin 'Boris' will call you from Israel tomorrow morning."

Ken next got on his special cell phone, a throwaway pay-as-you-go model that he bought at Wal-Mart for $25 and filled it up with $25 worth of local minutes bought in a different shop. He used the phone to call the local number in New York of some phone card company. He had bought the phone card from a newspaper vendor near the subway stop at 86th Street and Lexington Avenue, a stop he rarely used. The call was placed to Canada.

"Hello, 'Amos,'" said Ken. "How's the weather in Vancouver?" Without waiting for an answer, he continued: "Listen, I need you to nibble at Dreck Minerals (MMQC) tomorrow. I got a really sweet deal going, and I want to surprise 'em a bit to seal the deal."

"What's it all about?" asked Amos. "I see it trades by appointment."

"Yeah, some piece of overpriced garbage. But it's a great deal for us. As soon as I know when the shares have been transferred out, you can start to short it. I haven't told anyone else about the deal," promised Ken.

"Okay, buddy. Will do. Did you like how HEWZ turned out? We got an extra bite of the apple on that one," said Amos.

"Yup, that was a good one, but this will be even better," answered Ken. "Gotta go now. It's late back East and I'm getting hungry."

Ken then made three additional but substantially identical calls.

The next day, bright and early, he called Eli. "How ya doin'?" he asked. "Watch your ticker today. We're going to do a little work to give you a taste. Good things will happen."

Each of Ken's four friends made 10 trades that day, each trade for 1,000 shares. By 4:00 P.M., when the market closed, MMQC had traded 100,000 shares and the price had climbed to $0.65, a gain of 30 percent in one day, with 10 times the average volume.

At 4:01 P.M., immediately after the market closed, Eli was on the line. "I'm impressed," Eli said, neglecting to say that he himself had "lost" 50,000 shares in the market that day—half the volume—at an average price of $0.60, so he already had a nice return on his $250 dinner from the night before. "You certainly did what you promised."

"Ah, that was nothing," said Ken modestly. "I just wanted to give you a taste."

"Did my cousin call you?" asked Eli.

"Yeah, Boris and I had a nice chat, and he promised to do his homework. Seems like a stand-up guy. I'll let you know of any developments. And get that package ready to be delivered by 8:00 A.M. Monday," Ken reminded him. "Eli, I've got two calls waiting. I gotta run. See you."

Ken then dialed Jacob's number. "I saw what you did today," complained Jacob. "That just makes my job harder, you know. Now this complete piece of crap has a nearly $400 million market cap."

"Bull," said Ken, "and you know it. When a stock goes up, everyone runs to grab onto the gravy train. A rising tide floats all ships. Works every time. Anyway, my guy says he's sending the shares. I'll let you know when they arrive."

The Scam Undressed

Let's look at this scam more carefully. While Ken is the real villain in this drama, no one involved has clean hands. Ken has persuaded the company to give him 2.5 million shares—2.25 million up front. He is keeping a million for himself (just for making a few phone calls) and is giving 1.25 million to Jacob. Eli thinks Ken is getting only 250,000 for himself, up front. The shares themselves are probably secretly controlled by an insider and aren't free at all.

Ken also promised Eli "real buying," but he knows it is all just smoke and mirrors. Moreover, Ken knows that the stock price will eventually fall, so he is having four different guys up in Canada sell it short. Ken is going to profit on the way up and on the way down.

Jacob is laundering shares through a black church. He is going to get a million and a quarter shares ($625,000 worth) and he is planning to do a series of fake trades. One of his day traders will buy, another will sell, and so on. He will spend $100,000 in bribes to his day traders, keep $500,000 for himself, donate $25,000 to the rabbi in the South Carolina synagogue, and give another $25,000 to the black church.

Besides the back-and-forth trading, Jacob needs to unload his own 1.25 million shares. The day traders will do it for him, as the bribes insulate them from losses. You can be sure Ken will unload his million shares as fast as he can, too. So, the float will go up 5 to 10 percent really soon.

Eli is not only using his overseas cousin to secretly park shares to give to the promoters, but he is undoubtedly planning to have his cousin sell into the volume that he imagines that Ken will create, just as he did when Ken gave him a taste. He is also playing the PR game, rather than releasing news only as he has it.

Notice that Ken is no virgin. He'll do nothing until the shares clear, meaning that they are in his account, marked as "unrestricted" and put into street address. He still has to get Jacob's shares over to him, but he has a friendly broker he takes care of who will "LOA stuff" to third parties, meaning that the bribed broker will accept a letter of authorization to move shares already in street address from one account holder to another, something most brokers refuse to do.

Ken told each of four people they were the only guy he called. He also plans to sell while encouraging others to buy and seems to plan to goose up the price as much as possible, sell his shares short at the higher price and then as soon as he gets free-trading shares delivered he will cover his short, locking in the profit.

He knows that Eli is going to sell as much as he can into the volume that Jacob will create, so he knows the price must fall. By shorting up front, he will protect as much value as possible. He, himself, believes the company he is touting is "overpriced garbage," but he is nonetheless touting it to innocent investors. Ken is also an insider who has tipped Amos, so Amos (as the tippee) may not trade on the inside information. Amos is also shorting illegally in Canada in collusion with Ken.

Jacob's concealment of his involvement is interesting. He is having the stock he received donated to the church by his cousin, potentially entitling the cousin (if he were an American) to a tax deduction for the appreciated value of the stock, and relieving him of the capital gains tax. But the church is now going to sell the stock. As a church, it can ordinarily withdraw cash to distribute alms to the poor, but here the church and synagogue are being used by their clergy to illegally launder money. That will also jeopardize their status under Section 501(c)3 of the tax code, which gives religious organizations tax-exempt status.

Similar Charges

In a recent case that received much publicity, including an article by Adam Wills on *JewishJournal.com* entitled "Spinka Grand Rabbi, Four Others Plead Guilty," Grand Rabbi Naftali Tzi Weisz (the Spinka Rabbi) and his assistant, Rabbi Moshe Zigelman, pleaded guilty in Los Angeles to similar charges for acts similar to those of the pastor in the previous example, and each was sentenced to 24 months of imprisonment; they are now in Otisville with David Schick (see Chapter 16).[1]

If Ken's scam were to come out into the open, there could be many charges against Ken, Jacob, Eli, and the others. These include (at a minimum): (1) securities fraud, (2) tax fraud, (3) money laundering, and (4) conspiracy. Amos, though he lives in Canada, could also face charges both for illegally shorting and for trading on inside information. Finally, the cousin who got the cheap stock was clearly also a part of the conspiracy. The fact that Eli made the deal with Ken on his behalf is evidence of them acting in concert, so Boris's shares would be aggregated with Eli's and would lose their free-trading status (if they were ever truly free in the first place). Thus everyone in the chain would have a problem either with selling unregistered securities or with a statutory underwriting, or both.

Jacob's plan to trade the stock in a circle—A to B, B to C, and C to A—is also fraudulent parking and market manipulation. In short, what may have started out as a way to build a market so the company might be financed ended up as an illegal scheme that violated a host of laws.

(While the foregoing tale is based on an actual story, it has been augmented a bit with details from other stories that also all really happened. Eli has not yet been nailed, but Ken has. Stay tuned.)

Building awareness to create interest in a company can begin with good intentions. But as we have seen, in the execution a host of securities laws are often broken, and many unsavory characters are involved. If you see evidence of hyping a stock, don't walk. Run. In the opposite direction.

Chapter 15

Parachute into Prison

U.S. v. SCHRENKER

Federal enforcement of securities laws often proceeds slowly. Even when there are criminal charges, defendants can often remain free on bail for extended periods. Since, as we have seen, the penalties, when ultimately meted out, can be draconian, the temptation to flee can be great. Indeed, a number of folks who were caught committing financial fraud have sought to flee to avoid the consequences of their actions. Most are caught. Some have fascinating escapades along the way. Here are a few examples, starting with a parachute jump.

Disappearing Pilot Charged with Financial Scheme Fakes Own Death

An Indiana financial adviser, Marcus J. Schrenker, who was wanted on financial fraud charges, has been accused of trying to fake his own death in a plane crash. He has pleaded not guilty and was to undergo a psychiatric examination to determine whether he was able to stand trial.

The 38-year-old took off alone in his Piper aircraft on January 11, 2009, from Anderson, Indiana, heading for Destin, Florida. But over

Alabama he issued a Mayday call to air traffic controllers telling them his windshield had shattered and he was bleeding profusely. Police believe he then bailed out of the aircraft with his parachute.

Two F-15 jets were scrambled to intercept the aircraft, and the jet pilots reported that the plane was empty and apparently flying on autopilot. The fighters followed it until it crashed in East Milton, Florida, not far from a populated area.

Reconstructing What Happened

Here is a time line of events in the Schrenker plane mystery, as reported by the major news organizations.[1]

Schrenker first came to the attention of the authorities in January 2008. The Indiana Department of Insurance filed a complaint against him on behalf of seven investors who claimed he had cost them more than $250,000 because he never disclosed that they would face high fees to switch annuities.

A search warrant was obtained, and on December 31, 2008, officers executed the warrant and searched Schrenker's home for computers, notes, photos, and other documents related to his wealth management companies, looking for possible securities violations.

On January 9, 2009, a federal judge in Maryland issued a $533,500 judgment against Schrenker's Heritage Wealth Management Inc. and in favor of OM Financial Life Insurance Company.

That marked a turning point.

The very next day, Schrenker stored a red Yamaha motorcycle in a storage facility in Harpersville, Alabama, telling the facility's owner he'd be back on Monday to pick it up.

Two days later, on January 11, 2009, Schrenker, a pilot, took off in his single-engine Piper Malibu from Anderson, Indiana, with a flight plan supposed to take him to Destin, Florida.

While flying near Huntsville, Alabama, he issued what turned out to be a fake distress call, reporting severe turbulence, and told flight controllers that one of his windshields had imploded and that he was bleeding profusely.

Unbeknownst to anyone, he let his plane continue to fly on auto-pilot and parachuted out safely. It flew by itself for more than 200 miles before crashing and landing in a swamp near a residential area in the Florida Panhandle. Once flight controllers saw it going off-course, and after they were unsuccessful in their efforts to contact the pilot, two military jets were scrambled. They tried to intercept the small plane. The military pilots could see that the cockpit door was ajar and the cockpit was dark.

After the plane crashed, the wreckage was found scattered near Milton, Florida. It showed no signs that there had been any bleeding, and no blown-out windshield.

The mystery deepened, and all-points bulletins (APBs) were issued.

The next day, a man carrying Schrenker's license told police in Childersburg, Alabama—about 225 miles from the crash site—that he'd been in a canoe accident with friends. He was wet from the knees down, giving some credence to his story. Despite the APBs in Milton, the officers in Childersburg were unaware of the plane crash, so they took him to a hotel in nearby Harpersville, Alabama.

By the time the police figured out what had happened and came back, Schrenker was long gone.

Police discovered that had he had paid for his room in cash, and then had put on a black cap and run into the woods near the hotel.

That night, Schrenker, who apparently had his laptop with him when he jumped, wrote an e-mail to Tom Britt, a friend and neighbor. He characterized the situation as "a misunderstanding," apologized to his family for the trouble he'd caused, and wrote Britt that by the time Britt would be reading the e-mail, he would be gone.

Britt did the right thing, and turned the e-mail over to the authorities.

By January 13, 2009, Schrenker was very much a wanted man. The U.S. Marshals Service, an arm of the Department of Justice responsible for apprehending "fails to appear" (as those on the lam are technically called), intensified their efforts to hunt Schrenker down.

They got a lucky break. The manager of the storage place where Schrenker had stashed his motorbike came forward to say that the motorcycle was gone. A judge in Indiana issued an order for Schrenker's arrest, and charges of financial fraud were filed against him.

He was arrested later that night at a Florida campground, holed up in a tent with a slit wrist and bleeding profusely (for real, this time).

Schrenker pleaded guilty to intentionally crashing an airplane near a Florida Panhandle neighborhood in a botched attempt to fake his own death.

In a statement to *ABC News* Schrenker said,

> I am sincerely sorry for the pain, suffering, and dishonor my actions have caused my friends and family to endure. This has certainly been a regretful chapter in my life. My decision to unconditionally accept 100 percent responsibility is the first of many necessary steps to start the healing process. My greatest concern is that of my family whom [*sic*] has been undeservingly humiliated and ostracized because of my catatonic [*sic*] behavior.[2]

At sentencing, the U.S. attorney showed a videotaped deposition in a 2008 lawsuit in which Schrenker told attorneys he was seriously ill with multiple sclerosis, something that was never revealed in any of his flight or prison records. He lied separately to his stepmother and father in recent jail phone calls. He also told a girlfriend he was entering a witness protection program and wouldn't be returning to Indiana. He later sent her a cryptic text message asking her to meet him at a place where they had vacationed in the Florida Keys. He was sentenced on August 19, 2009, to four years and three months in federal prison, and he was also ordered to repay nearly $900,000 to the company that financed the plane that authorities say he intentionally crashed. The judge rejected Schrenker's tearful request for a shorter sentence, saying he agreed with a prison psychiatrist who diagnosed him as a narcissist who lacked empathy and desired attention from women.

The case is *U.S. v. Schrenker*, 09-CR-00011, U.S. District Court, Northern District of Florida (Pensacola). He still faces investigation by Indiana authorities and state criminal charges that he acted as an investment adviser without being registered. Meantime, he is federal inmate 12295-017.

Schrenker Is Not Alone

Others who fled to avoid trial and/or prison that we discuss in this book are Eddie Antar, Samuel Israel III, Monroa Harkness, Julian

Tzolov, Kobi Alexander, Sholam Weiss, Lou Pearlman, Arthur Nadel, and Norman Hsu.

It sounds trite and obvious, but those seeking to escape the wrath of securities laws by fleeing bring all of the prodigious resources of worldwide law enforcement to bear on their capture. Most times, they are caught and punished even more severely because of their escapes.

Chapter 16

Affinity Group Fraud

SCAMMING YOUR OWN COMMUNITY

Some scams target specific groups.

According to the SEC,

> Affinity fraud refers to investment scams that prey upon members
> of identifiable groups, such as religious or ethnic communities,
> the elderly, or professional groups. The fraudsters who promote
> affinity scams frequently are—or pretend to be—members of
> the group. They often enlist respected community or religious
> leaders from within the group to spread the word about the
> scheme, by convincing those people that a fraudulent invest-
> ment is legitimate and worthwhile. Many times, those leaders
> become unwitting victims of the fraudster's ruse.[1]

In affinity fraud, the perpetrators are taking advantage of the fact
that it's human nature that people tend to trust someone who is a
member of their own group. Many of the Ponzi schemes that we will
discuss owe their success to this fact. In particular, a number of the
Ponzi schemes targeted the Orthodox Jewish community. Perhaps
the most baffling case of affinity fraud, dating from the mid–1990s,
relates to David Schick.

David Schick—King of Otisville

The Otisville Federal Prison Camp (FPC) is located in Otisville, New York, a hamlet in the bucolic foothills of the Catskill mountain range in Orange County, just south of Sullivan County, and close to the old so-called Jewish Alps, also known as the borscht belt, that is still littered with the detritus of The Concord, Grossinger's, and other shuttered Jewish hotels from a bygone era.

Whenever new inmates arrive at the Otisville FPC, managed by the Bureau of Prisons (BOP), they will undoubtedly be pointed to David Schick, inmate 38713-054, who will immediately come over and inquire, "What do you need?"[2]

David Schick is larger than life and a legend in his own time. Incarcerated since 2005, he has to serve until the end of 2011. At 49, he is married, the devoted father of 10 children, and a grandfather several times over. Extremely well known in the *haredi* Orthodox Jewish community in Brooklyn, Schick is a very complex man.

Born into a well-known modern Orthodox and Zionist family, he had become an admirer of Rabbi Meir Kahane, and had migrated even more to the right as he grew older, adopting many Hassidic customs and closely aligning himself with the right-wing *haredi* Orthodox world of his forebears. Descended from a long line of famous and distinguished rabbis, he was the first nonrabbi in his family in 500 years.

During his 20s and 30s, he was a successful real estate attorney, and then, in the boom years for real estate, a phenomenally successful real estate tycoon, amassing holdings valued in the hundreds of millions of dollars in a short time. Schick used his position of wealth not only to donate generously himself, but also to raise prodigious sums for many worthwhile causes (especially centers of Orthodox Jewish learning and benevolent funds that aid *haredi* Jews) from business associates seeking to curry favor with him.

Prior to his incarceration, Schick led an utterly frenetic life, carrying a variety of cell phones, multiple pagers, and a BlackBerry, and using all of them at once while conducting meetings. However, he still found time to perform many acts of personal *hesed* (kindness). His circle of friends, partners, and acquaintances was legion and constituted a veritable who's who.

He was personally close to a U.S. president, numerous senators and representatives, as well as leading Israeli politicians. He also was close to, and often represented, the titular heads of the major leading Hassidic dynasties (Rebbis) as well as the heads of major non-Hassidic (Litvish) Yeshivot. His charity and good deeds were known far and wide, and Orthodox businessmen clamored to be allowed to participate in his deals.

His Dark Side

Schick also had a darker side. He was said by the United States Attorney to have caused losses of $200 million (mostly to Orthodox Jewish investors), and reportedly was a hairbreadth away from destroying a substantial law firm where he had been a partner, by laundering large sums of money through the firm's trust account; he pleaded guilty to diverting over $2 million in trust funds for his own use.[3]

The *New York Times* quotes him as saying, "I'm sorry. I'm a wicked person," when admitting to someone that he "took" the man's $1.7 million.[4] His own involuntary personal bankruptcy and his business losses set off a chain of bankruptcies of innocent people. After getting into trouble once and surrendering his law license, he rebuilt himself, only to get into trouble again a few years later.

Despite these facts, he presented one of the most impressive sets of detailed supporting letters and pleas for leniency from friends and prominent people that the judge had ever seen. None of that deterred her, however, from imposing the harshest possible sentence, a combined 97 months of imprisonment for both infractions. Numerous subsequent appeals all failed to overturn or modify the sentence.

Nonetheless, Schick's many friends and extended family remained overwhelmingly supportive, and visited him often in prison. His visitors included family members, of course, but also former business partners, friends, and many of the rabbinical and lay leaders of the *haredi* Jewish community.

Besides holding court in the visitor's room, Schick also held court regularly in his bunk or in the prison chapel. Any inmate of any religion who received a "shot" (an incident report related to a disciplinary infraction), who was served with legal papers, or who otherwise required legal assistance made a beeline for Schick, who never refused anyone. While he did delegate some of the actual legal drafting to one of several other (disbarred) lawyers serving time with him, he personally crafted the legal strategy in each case, and oversaw each case himself. He never charged for his services, and he was successful often enough that he earned the respect of all of the inmates at Otisville, as well as the grudging respect of the staff.

More important to Schick than all this activity was his vigorous program of serious daily prayer and study that included Torah, Bible, Mishnah, Talmud, and Kabala, and even (at the urging of his friends) a little bit of exercise. He also functioned as the gourmet *chef de cuisine* of the Sabbath meals, preparing tasty food under difficult, primitive conditions from limited and poor-quality ingredients while being forced to use microwave ovens because of kashruth concerns.

Schick was convinced that the BOP staff were, with a few exceptions, far from pro-Semitic, and often overtly anti-Semitic. He viewed most rules that could, no matter what their ostensible rationale, adversely affect the Jewish community as either disguised or overt anti-Semitic acts that needed to be combated forcefully, even at great personal risk.

He became expert in all the BOP's cumbersome and time-consuming procedures for redress of grievances, and when these were exhausted, he did not hesitate to exercise his right to file suit in federal court. He won often enough that the Otisville staff were clearly intimidated. Unfortunately for Schick, in the end they held most of the cards.

So when each of his three eldest children married, he was denied a furlough—even an accompanied furlough—to attend their weddings, notwithstanding the intervention of senators, well-known rabbis, and other VIPs on his behalf. Of course, he saw this as obvious retaliation and payback for his legal victories against the staff, but since the granting of furloughs is always discretionary, there was little that he could do about it but participate vicariously from afar in his family's *smachot* (joyous occasions). Other inmates tried to make him feel as comfortable as possible, and in each case, a large family delegation traveled up to see him at the first permitted opportunity.

It is hard to reconcile this David Schick with the David Schick who investigators and lawyers for investors say was engaged in a smorgasbord of schemes, from promises of risk-free investments yielding 15 to 20 percent profits to selling multiple mortgages on property he did not even own to simply stealing money entrusted to him and massive money laundering, and who, they say, orchestrated a $200 million Ponzi scheme, targeting his own co-religionists in a business atmosphere not unlike the diamond business, where deals are struck on trust and a handshake.

Haitian-American Affinity Ponzi Scheme

In numerous other schemes, affinity has also been a major element in the schemers' ability to develop the trust of their victims; in a number of cases, substantially the same ethnic group as was targeted. Here are a few of the more interesting ones.

On December 30, 2008, the SEC announced[5] that it had halted a $28 million Ponzi scheme that allegedly preyed on thousands of investors in the Haitian-American community nationwide through a network of purported investment clubs. The SEC alleges that Creative Capital Consortium LLC and A Creative Capital Concept$, LLC (collectively, Creative Capital) and its principal, George L. Theodule, began conducting the scheme as early as November 2007 by urging investors to form investment clubs to funnel funds to Theodule and Creative Capital.

Theodule solicited investors by guaranteeing a 100 percent return on their investments within 90 days based on his claimed successful trading of stocks and options. According to the SEC's complaint, investors also were promised that Creative Capital's trading profits were being used to fund new business ventures, including some to benefit the Haitian community in the United States, Haiti, and Sierra Leone.

The SEC alleges that Theodule has lost at least $18 million trading stocks and options just over the past year, and Creative Capital merely repaid earlier investors with monies collected from new investors in typical Ponzi scheme fashion. The SEC also alleges that Theodule has commingled investor funds with his personal funds and misappropriated at least $3.8 million for himself and his family.

"This alleged Ponzi scheme preyed upon unsuspecting members of a close-knit community, attempting to take advantage of the trust

they had in each other," said Linda Chatman Thomsen, director of the
SEC's Division of Enforcement. "As always, investors need to be wary
of investment opportunities that guarantee results and tout extraordinary
returns."

David Nelson, director of the SEC's Miami Regional Office,
added, "This case demonstrates that individuals will often rely on a
shared affinity to gain investors' trust. In this case, Theodule allegedly
abused that trust to con thousands of investors in the Haitian-American
community."[6]

Targeting the Deaf

On February 18, 2009, the SEC obtained a court order halting an
alleged $4 million Ponzi scheme perpetrated by Hawaii-based Billion
Coupons, Inc. (BCI) and its CEO, Marvin R. Cooper. The complaint
alleges that BCI and Cooper raised $4.4 million from 125 investors
since at least September 2007 and specifically targeted members of the
deaf community in the United States and Japan.[7]

The complaint, filed in federal court in Honolulu, Hawaii, alleges
that BCI and Cooper represented to the investors that their funds
would be invested in the foreign exchange (forex) markets, that investors would receive returns of up to 25 percent compounded monthly
from such trading, and that their investments were safe. According to
the complaint, BCI and Cooper actually used only a net $800,000 (cash
deposits minus cash withdrawals) of investor funds for forex trading,
and they lost more than $750,000 from their forex trading.[8]

The complaint further alleges that BCI and Cooper failed to generate sufficient funds from their forex trading to pay the promised
returns and operated as a Ponzi scheme by paying returns to existing
investors from funds contributed by new investors. The complaint also
alleges that Cooper misappropriated at least $1.4 million in investor
funds to pay for a new home and other personal expenses.

Affinity fraud succeeds because people let their guards down when
the scammer is a member of the same affinity group. As a result, courts
tend to view perpetrators of such scams harshly, usually meting out the
maximum punishment they can impose.

Chapter 17

Twentieth-Century Ponzi Schemes

LARGER AND LONGER-LASTING SCAMS

I n Chapter 4 we discussed some historical Ponzi schemes. In the next few chapters, we'll look at some twentieth-century Ponzi frauds, which can in many ways be considered a preamble to "the mother of all Ponzi schemes" that we discuss in Chapters 20 to 23.

Ponzi Schemes Cause Large Losses

Tamar Frankel, professor of law at Boston University School of Law, is an expert on Ponzi schemes. In testimony before Congress, she stated that in 2002 there were schemes aggregating $9.6 billion, and that in each of 1995 and 1997 investors suffered losses of more than $1.6 billion, while in 1976, 1990, and 1996 losses exceeded $1 billion per year.[1] So Ponzi schemes are big business.

As we discussed earlier, a Ponzi scheme inevitably fails whenever redemptions (including the fictitious gains) exceed new investments. Professor Frankel points out, however, that many Ponzi schemes last longer than the raw numbers might suggest, because many investors roll over their investments.[2] For example, she notes that in the case of the Baptist Foundation of Arizona, a fraud where 11,000 victims collectively lost $585 million, 94 percent of the investments in short-term loans were reinvested, and remained invested until the scheme collapsed in 1999.[3]

Unlike many older Ponzi schemes, which primarily preyed on small investors, many of the larger, more recent frauds targeted banks, hedge funds, and the superwealthy.

$680 Million Fake Commodities Ponzi Scheme Targets 20 Banks Worldwide

Twenty banks, including JPMorgan Chase, Fleet National Bank, PNC Bank N.A., KBC Bank N.V., Hypo Vereins Bank N.A., Dresdner Bank Lateinamerika AG, China Trust Bank, and General Bank, were victims of $680 million in losses in a Ponzi scheme orchestrated by Anil Anand, a former chief financial officer for Allied Deals, Inc.

Allied Deals, Inc., Hampton Lane, Inc., and SAI Commodity in the United States and RBG Resources in the United Kingdom (collectively, the Allied Deals companies) purported to be in the business of brokering trades in nonferrous metals. The Allied Deals companies were controlled by brothers Narendra Rastogi in the United States and Virendra Rastogi in the United Kingdom.

As part of their business, the Allied Deals companies purportedly would arrange for sales between buyers and sellers of metal in legitimate, arm's-length transactions (transactions negotiated by unrelated parties, each acting in his or her own best interest). To finance those metal sales, the defendants then arranged for loans with banks, usually to be repaid after 180 days. As collateral for the loans, the banks relied on Allied Deals' accounts receivable (the money due to Allied Deals from the customers for the metal transactions), expecting that the loans would get repaid when the customers repaid Allied Deals for the metal that had been purchased.

In fact, hundreds, if not thousands, of metal transactions on which the loans were based simply did not exist. Anand, the Rastogi brothers, and their co-conspirators had set up and controlled an elaborate network of hundreds of sham, nominee companies around the world (which they called "group companies") to serve as fake purchasers of metal from Allied Deals so that the defendants could get loans from the victim banks.

The Rastogis and their co-conspirators used loan proceeds from one victim bank to make the loan payments required by another victim bank, while concealing that the newly issued loans were not being used to fund actual, arm's-length metal transactions and that the money used to pay off the loans had not been provided by the buyers of metal in bank-financed sales.

How the Fraud Worked

According to prosecutors,[4] "the co-conspirators went to extraordinary lengths to mislead and convince banks into believing that the sham, 'controlled' customers were in fact real, independent companies with actual employees and offices and with no ownership or control relationships with the defendants," according to Michael J. Garcia, U.S. Attorney for the Southern District of New York.[5] Among other things, a number of co-conspirators posed as Allied Deals customers, established offices and phone lines for the sham companies in the United States and abroad, arranged for fake letterhead and bank accounts, and were prepared to field inquiries from bankers or auditors, according to federal officials.[6]

Anand allegedly was involved in helping the brothers establish a number of the sham controlled customers that were central to the scheme, by recruiting a number of his friends to set up fake metal companies in New Jersey, New York, and California. He and others then allegedly used these fake customers to generate millions of dollars in sham accounts receivable, which they used as collateral to obtain millions of dollars in loans from the victim banks.

To further the appearance that Allied Deals' customers were real, independent metal companies, Anand helped to establish fake credit histories for the sham customers. He also supplied sham customers with false financial data that was then provided to credit agencies to further the façade that the customers were real, bona fide metal companies engaged in real, bona fide metal trades.

As part of the fraud, the co-conspirators established a fake credit reporting agency, which generated false credit reports attesting to the creditworthiness of the sham companies. These credit reports were kept in a series of so-called credit files that Allied Deals maintained for each of its sham customers, which files could be shown to banks and/or auditors to further the deception that they were real customers.

Allied Deals employees forged many of the documents that the banks required in order to obtain loans. For example, the documentation department created fake purchase contracts at Allied Deals' office in New Jersey, cut and pasted signatures for the purported customers, and faxed the documents between fax machines at Allied Deals, in order to make it appear that the documents had come from overseas. Allied Deals employees also routinely forged such key shipping documents as steamship line bills of lading and chamber of commerce certificates of origin.

Anand also participated in key meetings with bank officials, during which he and his co-conspirators made representations regarding the nature of Allied Deals' metal transactions in order to obtain millions of dollars in loans.

Guilty Plea and Cooperation Agreement

Anand pleaded guilty to one count of conspiracy, one count of bank fraud, one count of conspiracy to commit money laundering, one count of tax evasion, and one count of making false statements to federal agents. Anand had pleaded guilty in 2002 and agreed to cooperate with the government's investigation into the fraud.

As part of his cooperation, he testified in 2004 in New York against six of his co-defendants, five of whom were convicted after trial. He also testified in London in the fall of 2007 at the U.K. trial of Virendra Rastogi and three others. That trial recently ended in the conviction of three of the defendants, including Virendra Rastogi, who was sentenced to nine and a half years in prison.

In all, 15 defendants were arrested in the United States in connection with this case. Nine—including Anand—pleaded guilty; five were found guilty at trial; and one was acquitted. Two defendants in the U.S. case remain at large.

Anand served only seven months in prison, rather than 30 years, because of his cooperation with investigators. In 2008, United States District Judge Richard M. Berman, who imposed the sentence in Manhattan federal court, also ordered Anand to pay forfeiture of $600 million and restitution of $683,632,800.[7]

Unlike smaller frauds that targeted individuals, Allied Deals targeted major financial institutions, inflicting enormous losses that presaged to losses in some of the even larger frauds to come to light in later years.

Chapter 18

Hit Charade

LOU PEARLMAN

U sually, Ponzi schemers have been unknowns before their ill-gotten gains catapulted them to fame. Not Louis Jay Pearlman, so his scheme makes for especially interesting reading.

Music Manager

He was known in the 1990s entertainment business for being the manager of the famous American boy bands the Backstreet Boys and 'NSync and later for being the owner of controversial talent scouting companies Wilhelmina Scouting Network, also known as Trans Continental Talent, and Fashion Rock/Talent Rock.

Pearlman is a first cousin of Art Garfunkel, the American singer, poet, and actor best known as half of the Grammy Award–winning folk duo Simon and Garfunkel. Garfunkel's fame and wealth helped to spark Pearlman's own interest in the music business. As a teenager he managed a band, but when success in music proved elusive, he turned his attention to aviation.

By the late 1970s, Pearlman had forged a partnership with German blimp tycoon Theodor Wüllenkemper. In the early 1980s, he started a helicopter commuter service. Next came a blimp advertising company, which suffered several controversies, including the crash of a Jordache blimp and claims of insurance fraud.

Lou Pearlman was also the CEO and money man behind NYPD Pizza, an Orlando-based pizza franchise that started selling franchise stores in 2005. Paul Russo, his longtime friend and the manager of several of the boy bands, assumed control of the NYPD Pizza company just before Lou's arrest. Paul Russo is now facing lawsuits from most of the franchisees of the doomed pizza company.

Boy Bands Mogul

"I got involved with Chippendales before Backstreet and it's Chippendales and New Kids on the Block that gave me the idea to pursue Backstreet," said Pearlman.[1]

After receiving an air charter request from New Kids on the Block, Pearlman became fascinated with the fact that the band had made hundreds of millions of dollars in record, tour, and merchandise sales. Thus he started Trans Continental Records. After a massive search (costing $3 million), Pearlman found the Backstreet Boys, who were signed to his label as its first act.

Management duties were assigned to a former New Kids on the Block manager Johnny Wright and his wife Donna. The Wrights are credited by everyone except Pearlman for actually making his first two boy bands famous, by their grooming the bands and making decisive contributions to the marketing strategy. "Pearlman provided the cash, and Wright did the rest."[2]

The Backstreet Boys went on to sell 100 million records worldwide, hitting gold and platinum in 45 different countries. Pearlman and the Wrights repeated this success with the band 'NSync, which sold over 56 million records globally.

With two major successes under his belt, Pearlman became a boy band mogul. Other boy bands managed by Pearlman were O-Town (created during the ABC–MTV reality TV series *Making the Band*), LFO, Take 5, and Natural. Other artists on the Trans Continental label included Aaron Carter, Jordan Knight, Smilez & Southstar, and C-Note.

Large and Long-Running Ponzi Scheme

Pearlman had another side. In 2006, it was discovered that Pearlman had perpetrated a major, long-running, and intricate Ponzi scheme, leaving more than $300 million in debts. For more than 20 years Pearlman enticed individuals and banks to invest in Trans Continental Airlines Travel Services Inc. and Trans Continental Airlines Inc., which existed only on paper. Pearlman used falsified Federal Deposit Insurance Corporation (FDIC), American International Group (AIG), and Lloyd's of London documents to win investors' confidence in his "Employee Investment Savings Account" (EISA) program, and he used fake financial statements created by a fictitious accounting firm, Cohen and Siegel, to secure bank loans.

Pearlman claimed to operate a travel agency called Trans Continental Travel Services, an aircraft leasing business, and a charter airline, Trans Continental Airlines, though in reality both existed in name only. To some, Pearlman was the best salesman ever known. "He told us he had 412 airplanes, the company had a value of $1.8-billion and the IPO was coming out at $17.50 a share. It was totally convincing."[3]

Trans Continental Savings Program

On December 17, 2006, the *St. Petersburg Times* wrote that the savings program was offering "high yield at no risk," a hallmark of a Ponzi scheme, and was presented as a way to participate in a special deal for Trans Continental Airlines employees. Unfortunately, it was too good to be true. Investors were notified by Trans Continental Airlines that it had stopped processing withdrawals from its "Employee Investment Savings Account," and the company wrote in a form letter to investors to "anticipate a resolution soon after the first of the year."[4] The letter neglected to say which year.

In February 2007, Florida regulators announced that Pearlman's Trans Continental savings program was a massive fraud, and the state took possession of the company. Most of the at least $95 million that had been collected from investors was gone. Orange County Circuit Judge Renee Roche ordered Pearlman and two of his associates, Robert Fischetti and Michael Crudelle, to bring back to the

United States "any assets taken abroad which were derived from illegal transactions." The court-ordered receivership froze company assets as the state investigation continued.

Claims against Pearlman Grow, Suicide of an Associate, and Litigation

Soon after, claims grew to more than $130 million, not including the $33 million judges had ordered Pearlman to pay in previous lawsuits. But according to Pearlman's letter to the *Orlando Sentinel* the claims of Florida state, the banks, and the investors were nothing but lies. "I know a lot of people come at me, as a deep-pockets theory," he said then.[5] "The more successful you get the more lawsuits you get, unfortunately." By February 6, 2007, there existed more than $317 million in claims, a figure that later grew to $500 million.

Tragically, on November 14, 2006, *WFTV.com* reported that Frank Vazquez, vice president of operations for the Trans Continental Companies, had taken his own life.

Several banks and groups of private investors filed suits against Lou Pearlman for failing to make payments on loans and investments. In its suit filed on December 28, 2006, Integra Bank called Pearlman a "deadbeat Ponzi operator."[6] The suit alleged, "While Pearlman's public persona is that of a man whose life seems lifted from a Horatio Alger story—a life filled with glamour, glitz and financial success beyond most people's dreams—Integra's recent dealings with Pearlman and his first company, TCA, would indicate that this outward mask conceals the fundamental economic instability more common to a Ponzi scheme."[7] There is a plethora of litigation against all of Pearlman's investments and enterprises.

Pearlman disappeared and was reported to be in Germany or Israel. After a worldwide manhunt, he was arrested in Indonesia on June 14, 2007, after being spotted by a German tourist couple.

He was then indicted by a federal grand jury on June 27, 2007, and charged with three counts of bank fraud, one count of mail fraud, and one count of wire fraud. A superseding "Information" was filed on March 3, 2008, and on March 6, 2008, Pearlman pleaded guilty to the charges in the Information.

Where Is the Money?

On May 21, 2008, Pearlman was sentenced to 25 years in federal prison after pleading guilty to charges of conspiracy, money laundering, and making false statements during a bankruptcy proceeding. In an unusual sentence, U.S. District Judge G. Kendall Sharp gave Pearlman the chance to cut his prison time by offering to reduce the sentence by one month for every million dollars he helps a bankruptcy trustee recover. According to the Bureau of Prisons, Pearlman is scheduled to be released in March 2029, so as of now, not much has been recovered. The judge also ordered individual investors to be paid before institutions in distributing eventual assets.[8]

Lou Pearlman is a complicated individual who scammed investors out of $500 million. It's hard to understand why he did it, given his opportunities to make serious money legally. Even allowing for a lavish lifestyle, it's unclear where all the money went. He seems to be a psychopath.

Chapter 19

Hedge Fund Ponzi Fraud

HEDGE FUNDS ARE FOR BIG BOYS

H edge funds are private investment funds. Alfred W. Jones is credited with the creation of the first hedge fund in 1949.

Unlike mutual funds, most hedge funds are structured to comply with one of the two major exemptions set forth in Sections 3(c)1 and 3(c)7 of the Investment Company Act of 1940. Those exemptions are for funds with 100 or fewer investors (a so-called 3(c)1 fund) and funds where the investors are qualified purchasers (a 3(c)7 fund).

A qualified purchaser is an individual with over $5 million in investment assets. (Some institutional investors also qualify as accredited investors or qualified purchasers.) A 3(c)1 fund cannot have more than 100 investors, while a 3(c)7 fund can have an unlimited number of investors. However, a 3(c)7 fund with more than 499 investors must register its securities with the Securities and Exchange Commission (SEC). Often, the minimum investment is $500,000 or more.

By limiting themselves in this way, hedge funds enjoy much lighter regulation and much less transparency. Within the four corners of whatever they write in their prospectuses, they can do pretty much as they please. Secrecy is their watchword.

The potential for fraud is thus much greater. Not surprisingly, the number of frauds has been growing. By 2008 the SEC had brought over 52 actions against hedge funds, alleging fraud of various sorts. Together, the wrongdoing is alleged to have totaled about $1 billion. None of the other frauds was anywhere close to the size and prominence of the Bayou Hedge Fund Group's fraud.

Bayou Hedge Fund Group

The Bayou Hedge Fund Group was a group of companies and hedge funds founded by Samuel Israel III in 1996. Initially, investors gave the funds $300 million. In all, the group raised approximately $450 million.

Investors were promised that the fund would grow to about $7.1 billion in 10 years. As it turned out, in 1998 and 1999 trading losses accumulated quickly. The company started a dummy corporation and hired it to audit the group and to provide misleading audited results that masked its true condition.

Bayou attracted prominent investors. Among investors with potential exposure are Stern Investment Holdings, an investment firm operated by Edward Stern, an heir to the family that founded Hartz Mountain Corporation, the pet-care supply company, said a person familiar with the matter. Stern Investment had an unknown amount of money indirectly invested in Bayou's hedge funds through a New York firm that pools clients' money in multiple hedge funds.

Hennessee Group, another so-called fund of funds manager that invests in numerous hedge funds, also had a big chunk of clients' money in Bayou. Another widely respected investment firm with several billion dollars under management, Silver Creek Capital Management of Seattle, was invested in Bayou. A well-known charity was also fleeced out of $4 million.

Fraudulent from Inception

According to federal prosecutors, Bayou had lied about its operations since the beginning; it had "overstated gains, understated losses, and reported gains where there were losses."[1] Court documents show that Bayou never made any money. In mid-2004, Bayou sent a letter to investors claiming that its assets were valued in excess of $450 million. Authorities began investigating after investors received a letter from Israel announcing that Bayou would return their money and shut its doors. The money did not arrive, and investors said they could not reach anyone at the fund.

In 2004, Samuel Israel III and Daniel Marino, the CEO and CFO, respectively, stopped trading and spent all resources on covering losses. Over the course of six days in July 2004, Bayou withdrew about $161 million from five bank accounts. Apparently feeling that the fraud might soon be detected, they planned to take the money and run. Israel and Marino were eventually caught trying to wire $100 million overseas. The Bayou hedge funds filed for Chapter 11 bankruptcy-court protection in White Plains, New York, in 2006. The $100 million that they had attempted to wire overseas was recovered and seized.

Criminal and Civil Charges; Hide and Seek

Israel and Marino went into hiding in the summer of 2005, and weren't found. However, in September they suddenly emerged from hiding. Israel pleaded guilty in federal court to conspiracy, invest-ment adviser fraud, and mail fraud. His chief financial officer, Marino, pleaded guilty to those charges and to wire fraud.

Israel was sentenced to 20 years in prison and ordered to forfeit $300 million. At his sentencing Israel said, "I lied to you and I cheated you and I cannot put into words how sorry I am."[2] In the same April 9 letter to Judge McMahon, he said he had become increasingly desper-ate as Bayou's losses mounted. But "when what I perceived as divine intervention occurred in the form of the fictitious investment programs, I leapt at the opportunity," he wrote.[3]

Israel makes other puzzling personal revelations in the letter. Although the Israel family is prominent in the Jewish community in New Orleans—Israel's father was recently honored by a local hospital for his philanthropic work, and their rabbi also submitted a letter of sup-port to the judge—Israel wrote that he has "always been a person of Christian faith, but through my saturating guilt and profound shame, I have reassessed what it means to be a Christian."[4] According to the *New York Times*, "Hearing of Mr. Israel's spiritual turn," David S. Goldstein, emeritus rabbi of the famed Touro Synagogue in New Orleans, said, "You could knock me over with a feather."[5] Rabbi Goldstein described Israel's parents, Ann and Larry, "as greatly anguished over these events. The Israel name is one of distinction in this community, and that's part of the embarrassment and the hurt."[6]

Marino also drew a 20-year sentence.

Jumping on the bandwagon, on September 29, 2005, the Commodity Futures Trading Commission (CFTC) also filed a civil complaint in the United States District Court for the Southern District of New York, alleging misappropriation and fraud involving the hedge fund manager Bayou Management, LLC; its principals, Samuel Israel III and Daniel E. Marino; and Richmond Fairfield Associates, Certified Public Accountants PLLC.

How Investors Were Fooled

Several investors say they were attracted to Bayou for the firm's remarkably steady returns, but also were comforted by the firm's unusually frequent reports to investors. Israel sent weekly updates telling investors what he was doing in the markets and reporting performance figures. He also held conference calls with investors once or twice a year.

As we will see, the Bayou fraud was in many ways similar to the much better known Madoff fraud that we will discuss presently. It had aspects of a Ponzi scheme, where later investments were used to pay off earlier investments that were withdrawn. It also named an obscure auditor (that in this case turned out to be nonexistent).

Gretchen Morgenson reported in her *New York Times* article "A Fib Here, a Scandal There" that there were significant differences between Israel's curriculum vitae in the Bayou Group's sales materials and the one, known as a CRD, that is on file with securities regulators in the Central Registration Depository (CRD) database.[7]

According to both, Sammy Israel began his Wall Street career in 1982 at Frederic J. Graber & Company, a small but respected institutional firm. He was at Graber for six years in all, the longest he stayed in one place during his 23 years in the investment arena.[8] This does not count his eight years running Bayou, which was based in Stamford, Connecticut.

Apparently, he did not make much progress at Graber. According to two salesmen at larger brokerage firms who dealt with him there, he never rose above the level of order taker. For the next five years, according to his CRD, he bounced around Wall Street, working at start-ups or small firms.[9] Only one of the five jobs that he held in this period shows up in Bayou's sales materials. In January 1993, he got his big break: a job at Omega Advisors, a huge hedge fund run by Leon Cooperman.

Prospective Bayou investors were told that Israel stayed at Omega for four years and rose to the position of head trader at the firm. "Mr. Israel was responsible for all equity and financial futures executions," the sales materials stated, "as well as sharing responsibility for hedging the portfolio through the use of futures and options."[10]

But an Omega official said that Israel's position at Omega was an administrative one, not a high-level trading job.[11] And his CRD has him at Omega for only 18 months, not four years. In June 1995, he left Omega to start Bayou, according to his CRD.[12] Investors were told, however, that his fund didn't open until 1997.[13] The reason for this discrepancy is not clear. Israel opened Bayou for business in 1996. While the fund's performance started out well, it soon went sour. Perhaps the sales literature wanted to obscure this.

Curious Aftermath

On June 10, 2008, the day that Israel was supposed to report to prison to begin serving his sentence, the press reported that he might have committed suicide after a car registered in his name was found abandoned on a bridge that spans one of the deepest stretches of the Hudson River in New York.[14] His vehicle was found abandoned on the Bear Mountain Bridge over the Hudson River with the words "Suicide is painless" written in the dust on the hood.

However, Israel had faked his suicide and had jumped bail. With the authorities in hot pursuit, he turned himself in to police in Southwick, Massachusetts, on July 2, 2008. In October 2008, U.S. District Judge Kenneth Karas in White Plains, New York, ordered a psychiatric examination of Israel at the Devens Federal Medical Center outside Boston—the very same prison camp to which he was supposed to report on the June morning that he disappeared. On March 17, 2009, Israel pleaded guilty to a single count of bail jumping. Debra Ryan, his girlfriend, also pleaded guilty to "aiding and abetting Samuel Israel III's failure to surrender to serve his sentence on June 8, 2008," according to the U.S. Attorney's Office for the Southern District of New York. She received a sentence of three years' probation. Israel had an additional two years tacked onto his 20-year sentence as punishment for the bail jumping and faked suicide.

Fraudulent Conveyance

There is another interesting footnote to the Bayou story that may be a precursor to what is still unfolding in the Madoff scam. As with any Ponzi scheme, the money of later investors is (at least partially) used to pay off illusory profits of early investors. In a landmark case, *In re: Bayou Group, LLC*, 372 B.R. 661 (Bankr. S.D.N.Y., August 9, 2007), seeking the return of cash from the Bayou Hedge Fund Group, federal bankruptcy Judge Adlai S. Hardin Jr. said that investors who withdrew money they had made from Bayou before it collapsed beyond what they had invested must return the cash so that it could be shared among those who had lost money, as these were actually fake profits.[15]

The only way this could be avoided was if investors could prove that they withdrew the money in good faith. The legal doctrine that was applied is called fraudulent conveyance, because the supposed profits paid out to the earlier investors were really the principal funds of later investors, and thus were paid out fraudulently and are returnable to their rightful owners. As we will see, the Madoff trustee is also seeking the return of the substantial illusory profits paid out to some investors.

The Wextrust Ponzi Scheme

In a another fraud that presaged "the mother of all Ponzi schemes," which came to light a few months later, Steven Byers and Joseph Shereshevsky were arrested in August 2008 and charged with operating an affinity fraud Ponzi scheme that primarily preyed on members of the Orthodox Jewish community, fleecing about 1,200 investors.

Byers and Shereshevsky and their companies, Wextrust Capital, LLC; Wextrust Equity Partners, LLC; Wextrust Development Group, LLC; Wextrust Securities, LLC; and Axela Hospitality, LLC, were charged in a $255 million Ponzi scheme and a $100 million fraud.

The government alleges that they conducted at least 60 securities offerings through private placements and created approximately 150 entities in the form of limited liability companies or similar vehicles to act as issuers or facilitators of the offerings, purportedly to fund the acquisition of specified assets, the majority of which were commercial real estate ventures. Contrary to representations in the offering memoranda that proceeds would be used for specific projects, the defendants allegedly diverted funds to pay returns to investors in prior offerings, or to fund expenses of the defendants. Shereshevsky, the SEC said, is a convicted felon who pleaded guilty to bank fraud in 2003. He took the lead in soliciting investors through his wide contacts in the Orthodox Jewish community, the SEC said.

In one offering, conducted in 2005, the SEC complaint alleges that defendants falsely represented to investors that the more than $9 million raised would be used to purchase seven specifically identified real estate properties that were leased by federal government agencies, such as the General Services Administration (GSA).[16] In fact, according to the complaint, the defendants never purchased the seven properties. Moreover, at the time the offering occurred, they knew or were reckless in not knowing that the seven properties would not be acquired. Significantly, while the offering was ongoing, the Wextrust entities borrowed more than $6 million from the funds raised in the GSA offering and used these funds for purposes unrelated to the GSA offering.[17]

Overall, the complaint alleges, defendants diverted at least $100 million dollars to unauthorized purposes.[18] The complaint alleges that the defendants are conducting at least four ongoing offering frauds intended to raise money to pay back investors from prior offerings. Shereshevsky allegedly sent an e-mail to a business partner that showed they both were aware that their activities were fraudulent:

> Please remember one thing. That although I always take care
> of you and myself, my goal in this thing as I have always told
> you from day one, is to get [W]exTrust out of all the s— before

the end of 09 or 10 at the latest. That is my primary concern. We have faced it until we made it for long enough and now we must clean it up.[19]

Jacob H. Zamansky, an authority on securities arbitration, noted in his blog how similar the Wextrust scam was to the case of Peter Dawson, a now-jailed investment adviser who ripped off dozens of retirees (Zamansky represented some of the investors in the Dawson case).[20]

Both situations are examples of affinity schemes: Wextrust Capital targeted members of the Jewish Orthodox community, specifically those who attended the B'nai Israel Congregation. Shereshevsky was close with the rabbi, who vouched for him regularly, according to the *Wall Street Journal*.[21] By the same token, Peter Dawson targeted members of the East Meadow Methodist Church and had close ties with its pastor.

One Dawson investor borrowed against his home. According to the *Wall Street Journal*, at least one investor, and potentially others, borrowed against the equity in their homes in order to invest in Wextrust Capital.[22] Managers of Wextrust Capital and its affiliates enjoyed lavish lifestyles, as did Peter Dawson, by allegedly fraudulent means. Dawson as well as Shereshevsky and Wextrust Capital commingled funds, which is a fancy way of robbing Peter to pay Paul.

Speaking about this case, Andrew M. Calamari, the SEC's associate director of enforcement, said, "Affinity frauds are especially pernicious because the victims tend to let their guards down in circumstances where they might otherwise proceed with much more caution."[23] Indeed they are. We tend to let our guard down when dealing with our in-group, and that can be a prescription for trouble. Affinity fraud is a serious menace. Nowhere was that more evident than in our next case, "the mother of all Ponzi schemes."

There is one other parallel to the Madoff case. Both were assigned to Judge Denny Chin. There has been a superseding indictment in the Wextrust case, everyone has lawyered up, and it has not yet come to trial. However, on April 13, 2010, Steven Byers, the former CEO, pleaded guilty to conspiracy and securities fraud. Byers admitted to a portion of the scheme that prosecutors said caused a loss to investors of about $9.2 million and agreed to forfeit that amount. "I knew what I was doing," Byers said. Byers faces 151 to 188 months in prison under a stipulated sentencing guidelines range as part of a plea agreement with prosecutors. Sentencing is set for September 13, 2010.

Shereshevsky is facing charges of conspiracy, securities fraud, wire fraud, and mail fraud. He has denied wrongdoing. The government is seeking $255 million in forfeiture in Shereshevsky's criminal case.[24]

The receiver, Timothy J. Coleman, recovered $5 million that was ordered distributed to investors on a pro rata basis. The receiver set up a web site, www.wextrustreceiver.com, which indicates that Wextrust did make some legitimate investments, which, once liquidated, may provide an additional payout for Wextrust investors.

Bayou and Wextrust were two substantial Ponzi schemes targeting hedge funds and sophisticated investors. Bayou was something of an affinity fraud, but scammed on an equal opportunity basis. Wextrust was primarily an affinity fraud. They eerily presaged the Bernie Madoff case.

Chapter 20

Madoff and the World's Largest Ponzi Scheme

THE MOTHER OF ALL PONZI SCHEMES

onzi schemes have been around long before Charles Ponzi himself, as we noted in Chapter 4. Charles Ponzi's scheme fleeced investors out of about $15 million, equivalent to about $300 million today. Investors in Bayou lost $300 million. Dozens of frauds have been perpetrated over the years, some as large as $3 billion. A search of the Securities and Exchange Commission (SEC)'s Litigation Releases shows nearly 1,000 documents related to Ponzi schemes.

NERA Consulting[1] studied SEC settlements in Ponzi schemes since July 31, 2002. In only 12 cases did the settlement exceed $50 million. It's likely that the sum total of all previous Ponzi schemes taken together probably does not equal the losses in a single well-known fraud that came to light just after the market crash of 2008.

The World's Largest Ponzi Scheme

Everyone not in a Rip Van Winkle–like extended sleep knows that Bernard L. Madoff, president and 75 percent owner of Bernard L. Madoff

Investment Securities, confessed, first to his sons and then to the FBI (he then also consented to SEC charges alleging these same facts), and finally in open court that he had organized what was arguably the longest-running and most extensive Ponzi scheme in history run by an individual, involving cash flowing through the accounts of $170 billion. Madoff consented to forfeiture in that amount.

As the story is so well known, but so important to the history of greed, I have tried in the next several chapters to place Madoff into the larger context of financial frauds while omitting nonessential detail.

Madoff told his investors they had $64.8 billion in their accounts. He told his sons that the fraud amounted to $50 billion. Investigators believe $36 billion was the real money that went into the whole scheme; $18 billion moved out before the collapse and $18 billion is missing, according to David Sheehan, chief counsel for trustee Irving Picard. The trustee has filed lawsuits, so far, to recover $15 billion for the benefit of thousands of defrauded former customers of the Madoff firm. Picard has told the court that he has identified about 2,336 account holders who collectively lost more than $13 billion. About half of Madoff's clients suffered a loss, in that they contributed more to their accounts than they withdrew, prosecutors said.

Early on in the case, the government got a judge to order forfeiture of all of Madoff's money and property traceable to the alleged fraud. However, the full extent of the fraud is still being unraveled by investigators.

In March 2009 Madoff was charged with 11 felonies:

1. Securities fraud.
2. Investment adviser fraud.
3. Mail fraud.
4. Wire fraud.
5. International money laundering to promote specified unlawful activity.
6. International money laundering to conceal and disguise the proceeds of specified unlawful activity.
7. Money laundering.
8. False statements.
9. Perjury.

10. Making a false filing with the SEC.

11. Theft from an employee benefit plan.[2]

The total maximum sentence of incarceration on all counts in the Information, the document to which Madoff pleaded guilty, is 150 years' imprisonment, and that was what U.S. District Judge Denny Chin meted out. The sentencing guideline is life imprisonment; the defense asked for 12 to 15 years, and the Department of Probation (which advises judges on sentencing) recommended 50 years. Madoff pleaded guilty to all the charges on March 12, 2009. In pleading guilty, he told Judge Chin, "I am actually grateful for this opportunity to publicly comment about my crimes, for which I am deeply sorry and ashamed."[3]

Madoff said that he started the fraud but that he believed it would be short and he could extricate himself. "As the years went by, I realized my risk, and this day would inevitably come," he said in a steady voice.[4] "I cannot adequately express how sorry I am for my crimes," he concluded. After the judge accepted his guilty plea, Madoff was scheduled to be sentenced on June 29, 2009, but was remanded to jail immediately, pending sentencing. On June 29, in the ceremonial courtroom of the federal court for the Southern District of New York, Judge Denny Chin heard from the victims, from counsel, from Madoff, and from the government, and then proceeded to mete out the maximum sentence he could, 150 years of imprisonment, thereby ensuring Madoff would be ineligible for imprisonment in a minimum- or low-security prison.

Judge Chin recommended commitment to a facility in the Northeast; the defense requested the Federal Correctional Institution (FCI) in Otisville, a medium-security facility housing male offenders in upstate New York, but the determination was up to the Bureau of Prisons, which sent him to Butner, North Carolina, where he found himself in the company of Adelphia Communications founder John Rigas and his son Timothy, both found guilty in 2004 of securities fraud. John Rigas, 84, is scheduled to be released in 2018, and Timothy Rigas, 53, in 2022. Former Rite Aid Corporation Vice Chairman Franklin C. Brown is also serving his 10-year sentence in a medium-security facility at Butner. Madoff may meet up with

Al Parish, a former economist at Charleston Southern University who pleaded guilty in 2007 to running what prosecutors alleged was a Ponzi scheme that defrauded investors of $66 million. Jonathan Pollard also is there. Pollard, a former Navy officer, entered a plea deal in 1987 after admitting to spying for Israel. He was eventually transferred to Butner's medium-security facility and is eligible for release in 2015.

At his sentencing, and in his allocution, reading from a prepared statement, Madoff said,

> I cannot offer you an excuse for my behavior. How do you excuse betraying thousands of investors who entrusted me with their life savings? How do you excuse deceiving 200 employees who spent most of their working life with me? How do you excuse lying to a brother and two sons who spent their entire lives helping to build a successful business? How do you excuse lying to a wife who stood by you for 50 years?[5]

The *Wall Street Journal* reported that Madoff said he made "a terrible mistake" and an "error of judgment" and that he lives in a "tormented state" now.[6] He also denied that he and his wife have been silent and not sympathetic to victims of the fraud.

"Nothing could be further from the truth," Madoff said.[7] "She cries herself to sleep every night."

In a statement issued after the sentencing, Ruth Madoff, his wife, said her silence on the case shouldn't be interpreted as indifference to the suffering of victims. "All those touched by this fraud feel betrayed; disbelieving the nightmare they woke to. I am embarrassed and ashamed," she said.[8] "Like everyone else, I feel betrayed and confused. The man who committed this horrible fraud is not the man whom I have known for all these years."

Judge Chin said in court, "Here the message must be sent that Mr. Madoff's crimes were extraordinarily evil." He went on to say, "I have a sense Mr. Madoff has not done all that he could do or told all that he knows." Judge Chin called the fraud "unprecedented" and "staggering."[9]

The judge said symbolism was important in this case to deter others from committing similar frauds, and Madoff "knew he was going to be caught soon" by the time he was arrested by Federal Bureau of Investigation agents in December.

While the exceedingly long sentence may have brought a measure of closure to victims in this famous case, it is far from over. The forfeiture order against Madoff left the onetime chairman of the NASDAQ Stock Market penniless, and Mrs. Madoff with $2.5 million; however, Irving Picard, the trustee liquidating Bernard Madoff's investment firm, is seeking to recover $44.8 million from Ruth Madoff, the swindler's wife of 45 years, in addition to the $80 million she had previously agreed to transfer to the government for the benefit of fraud victims.

In this unusual case, over 113 victims wrote heart-wrenching letters and e-mails to the judge, and a representative sample spoke at the sentencing. Judge Chin was clearly influenced by the letters; he read part of one in open court.[10]

Partial Settlement with SEC

Meanwhile, Madoff entered into a partial settlement with the SEC that prevents him from working in the financial industry again, which seems pretty improbable anyway but ensures that all the i's are properly dotted and the t's crossed. As part of the settlement, the SEC stated that "the facts of the complaint are established and cannot be contested by Madoff" when determining a monetary penalty still to be determined (which, if assessed, will be symbolic anyway, since Madoff forfeited all his assets and is locked up for life; he has little chance of earning any new money).[11]

The SEC's complaint, filed on December 11, 2008, in federal court in Manhattan, alleges that Madoff and defendant Bernard L. Madoff Investment Securities LLC have committed a $50 billion fraud and violated Section 17(a) of the Securities Act of 1933, Section 10(b) of the Securities Exchange Act of 1934 and Rule 10b-5 thereunder, and Sections 206(1) and 206(2) of the Advisers Act of 1940, and is similar to the criminal complaint.

The government's Information (list of charges) says that Madoff's fraud began in the 1980s.[12] At his plea hearing, Madoff said that he believes the scheme began in the early 1990s, even though the trustee believes that it began much earlier. A classic Ponzi scheme, Madoff's fraud depended on new money to pay for redemptions and apparently proceeded for years without detection. However, the market crash of 2008 prompted requests for $7 billion in withdrawals from his fund (mostly from hedge funds struggling to meet their own redemption requests), at a time when not much new money was coming in; this led to a liquidity crisis and the unraveling of the scheme.

Remarkably, Madoff, who was 70 at the time of his confession, was a legend on Wall Street. His firm was founded in 1960. He was one of those who started the NASDAQ stock exchange, and for a time he served as its president. He revolutionized trading, greatly reducing the costs, and his firm was a large market maker, accounting for a substantial percentage of the overall trading volume.

As it turns out, beginning no later than 1990, Madoff also ran money in a secretive fund operated by an investment arm on a separate floor, and that was allegedly kept separate from the brokerage business that employed his brother, his two sons, and assorted other relatives.[13] The FBI's criminal complaint states that when two federal agents arrived at the Madoffs' apartment (after his sons turned him in), they asked him if there was an innocent explanation. He told them, the complaint says, "There is no innocent explanation." The agents say that he also told them "he paid investors with money that wasn't there," that he was "broke," and that he expected to go to jail.[14]

Madoff then told the agents that he was "finished," that he had "absolutely nothing," and that "it's all just one big lie."[15] He said the investment arm of his firm was "basically a giant Ponzi scheme," and that it had been insolvent for years.[16]

While Ponzi schemes often promise unrealistic returns, Madoff promised (and for many years appeared to deliver) returns of 10 percent to 13 percent—large, but not totally unbelievable. The fund claimed annual returns of 10.5 percent on average since its inception in 1990. Nevertheless, there was skepticism for years on Wall Street over how Madoff managed to pay investors such consistently high returns in good years and bad.

Madoff Never Traded a Share

Irving Picard, the trustee liquidating Bernard Madoff's investment firm, said in a meeting of Madoff's creditors that his investigation has found no evidence that any securities were purchased on behalf of customers in at least 13 years.[17]

Speaking at a meeting of Madoff's customers, trustee Picard said the firm's customers will be able to recover up to the $500,000 they're entitled to from the Securities Investor Protection Corporation (SIPC). If they purportedly had cash in their accounts, they can recover up to $100,000 of that. Customers who have lost more than that amount can also share in assets recovered by the trustee. They may also be entitled to recapture taxes paid on the fictitious income for the five preceding years.

Not Like Enron or WorldCom

The Madoff fraud was very different from other large frauds, like Enron or WorldCom. While Enron was a real company, did own many substantial assets, and employed 22,000 people, many of Enron's recorded assets and profits were inflated, or even wholly fraudulent and non-existent. Debts and losses were put into entities formed offshore that were not included in the firm's financial statements, and other sophisticated and arcane financial transactions between Enron and related companies were used to take unprofitable entities off the company's books. Essentially, Enron was an accounting fraud, as discussed in Chapter 33. Ultimately, Enron's independent auditor, the worldwide firm of Arthur Andersen & Company, was forced out of business.

WorldCom, too, was primarily an accounting fraud, as discussed in Chapter 33. Assuming that the Madoff fraud clocks in at $65 billion, it would be more than six times larger than the accounting fraud that drove WorldCom into bankruptcy proceedings in 2002. This one was a classic Ponzi scheme.

Madoff's fraud was simply a Ponzi scheme, very carefully orchestrated. The firm provided detailed monthly statements purportedly showing many transactions. No one doubted them, but no one checked. Unlike the norm in most funds, there was no independent custodian for securities held for customers of Madoff's fund; the securities were supposedly kept at Madoff's own brokerage firm, but no one ever checked. Some of the CUSIP numbers (identification numbers used to identify securities) recorded in purported trades did not even exist.

There were simply no independent checks and balances. Moreover, there were many pass-through vehicles (i.e., funds that served as feeder funds and gave all or most of their clients' investments to Madoff, but purported to actively manage those investments themselves).

The pass-through vehicles were generally audited by leading big-name auditors, who merely accepted confirmations from Madoff without looking any further. PricewaterhouseCoopers, for example, audited Sentry funds, investment funds run by Fairfield Greenwich Group; they lost $7.5 billion of investors' money, half their capital.

Who Was Fleeced?

Madoff's investor list reads like a veritable who's who, especially of the Jewish world, where Madoff was once known as "the Jewish T-bill." However, over time, many others were victimized. Madoff's customer list includes more than 8,000 victims and is known to include (either directly or through a feeder fund):

- Ira Sorkin, Madoff's own lawyer.
- Zsa Zsa Gabor, 91, legendary actress.
- Sandy Koufax, the Hall of Fame baseball player.
- Fred Wilpon, owner of the New York Mets.
- Morton Zuckerman's Charitable Trust (funded by the builder and publisher).
- Ira Rennert, #57 on the Forbes 400 list before his losses.
- Norman Braman, former owner of the Philadelphia Eagles.
- Robert I. Lappin Charitable Foundation, a Massachusetts-based Jewish charity (Lappin and his family donated $5 million to restore the retirement savings of about 60 employees of various family enterprises, including the Robert I. Lappin Charitable Foundation, that were victims of Madoff).
- JEHT Foundation, founded by Jeanne Levy-Church (formerly Jeanne Levy-Hinte) to support left-wing causes.

- Yeshiva University, a New York–based private Jewish-sponsored university.
- The Technion—Israel Institute of Technology.
- Elie Wiesel, the Nobel laureate, and the Elie Wiesel Foundation for Humanity, his charitable foundation.
- Leonard Feinstein, the co-founder of retailer Bed Bath & Beyond.
- Senator Frank Lautenberg and the charitable foundation of the New Jersey senator's family.
- Steven Spielberg and the Spielberg charity, the Wunderkinder Foundation.
- Jeffrey Katzenberg, chief executive officer of DreamWorks Animation SKG Inc.
- Gerald Breslauer, the Hollywood financial adviser to Steven Spielberg and Jeffrey Katzenberg.
- Julian J. Levitt Foundation, a Texas-based charity.
- The Loeb family.
- Lawrence Velvel, dean of the University of Massachusetts School of Law.
- The J. Gurwin Foundation, a charity.
- The Ramaz School, a Jewish day school in New York.
- Congregation Kehilath Jeshurun, a synagogue in New York.
- The Maimonides School, a Jewish day school in Brookline, Massachusetts.
- Yad Sarah, an Israeli nonprofit Israel-wide network of volunteers aiding disabled, elderly, and housebound people aimed at making home care possible.
- Kevin Bacon and his wife, Kyra Sedgwick, Hollywood actors.
- Eric Roth, Hollywood screenwriter.
- Henry Kaufman, former Salomon Brothers chief economist.
- Marc Rich, the financier pardoned by President Clinton.
- Hadassah, the national Jewish women's organization.
- Alexandra Penney, writer.
- Rachminstrivka Chassidus in Jerusalem.
- North Shore–Long Island Jewish Health System (reported losing $5 million but said a donor will make it up to them).
- The family of the late Rabbi Alexander Schindler.

Leading banks and large hedge funds were also fleeced. So far, it is known that financial institutions reported losing $34 billion, although much of this was fictitious gains.

Much of the amount scammed was lost by wealthy individuals and families. However, many smaller investors lost their life savings. In all, by the July 2, 2009, deadline, 15,400 claims had been filed in bankruptcy court. Of these, 12,698 have been determined, 10,613 denied, and 2,085 allowed as of May 21, 2010, totaling $5,450,143,039.20. Of this, $689,134,117.01 is covered by SIPC protection, and allowed claims exceed statutory limits of SIPC protection by $4,761,008,922.19. Irving Picard, the trustee liquidating Bernard Madoff's defunct investment-advisory business, told a bankruptcy judge he has made "significant headway" in recovering assets, including $1.08 billion found as of June 30. Many hotly dispute the trustee's determination of their claims, and many lawsuits are pending.

Carl and Ruth Shapiro, and their charitable trusts, major donors to Brandeis University and Boston's Beth Israel Deaconess Medical Center, were listed as those who lost the most from Madoff. However, trustee Picard filed eight lawsuits against Madoff's biggest feeder funds and other investors, including Shapiro, that seek a total of $13.7 billion in damages to be used to repay victims. He also said he had received secured and general unsecured claims of about $282 million and 16 general unsecured broker-dealer claims totaling about $3.05 million.

As we will see, some of the largest investors are being investigated for complicity.

Osama Bin Laden Lost $1 Billion

According to the *Borowitz Report*, "al-Qaeda kingpin Osama bin Laden revealed that he lost over $1 billion in the fraud."[18]

> Mr. bin Laden made the rueful announcement in the form of a video, broadcast on the Arabic-language al-Jazeera network and around the world. Speaking from what appeared to be a cave, he said that he had invested with Mr. Madoff because the investment wizard had promised an annual return of 10 percent, adding, "Now I don't know who to trust."

The al-Qaeda leader remained vague about how he had first made contact with Mr. Madoff, saying only that they had a mutual friend at a Palm Beach country club. He added that the losses due to the Madoff fraud would have an immediate impact on al-Qaeda's financial health, forcing the terror network to shutter several regional offices and to cut back on the production values of Mr. bin Laden's videos.

While some expressed shock that a terrorist like Mr. bin Laden could become ensnared in a financial fraud like Mr. Madoff's, "It's not surprising at all," said North Korean president Kim Jong-Il from his office in Pyongyang. "I'm offered shady investment schemes every day of the week. This is why I keep all my money in treasuries."[19]

Although the *Borowitz Report* was poking fun, and the bin Ladin loss claim is satirical, many have alleged that billions of investments in Madoff came from highly dubious sources (the Russian Mafia is often mentioned). This may account for the fact that some of the heads of Madoff feeder funds have dropped out of public sight, and also may explain why Madoff wore a bulletproof vest to his court appearances.

Many Other Losers

Some overseas investors, who apparently invested unreported income, preferred to keep silent rather than alert the tax authorities. According to the *Huffington Post*, Colombian drug lords invested a purported $300 million with Madoff.[20] Russian oligarchs also were reported to have invested heavily and suffered large losses.

Some of the biggest losers were members of the Palm Beach Country Club, where many of Madoff's wealthy clients were recruited. Also, members of the Oak Ridge Country Club, a predominately Jewish club in Hopkins, Minnesota, reportedly lost $600 million collectively.

Irving Picard, who is overseeing the liquidation of Madoff, submitted a list of direct Madoff customers. It was filed in U.S. Bankruptcy Court and it is a 162-page list, compiled by the restructuring firm AlixPartners, of those considered customers of Madoff during the year prior to his December 11, 2008, arrest on fraud charges. Labor unions and their pensions, mostly in central New York State, figure prominently on the list.

A number of prominent nonprofits are listed as well, including the American Jewish Congress, the Brooklyn College Foundation, Columbia University, and the Long Island Museum of American Art, History, and Carriages. Also victimized was World Trade Center developer Larry Silverstein.

The *New York Times* looked at foundations that "probably" were hurt by Madoff, through either direct investment or one of the feeder funds.[21] The *Wall Street Journal* has reported that some of the prominent investors in the feeder funds that lost money included former Merrill Lynch chief executives Daniel Tully and David Komansky, along with former Merrill investment-banking chief Barry Friedberg, all of whom personally invested in hedge funds with Madoff exposure run by former Merrill brokerage chief John "Launny" Steffens, according to people familiar with the matter.[22] Steffens and J. Ezra Merkin were partners in the Spring Mountain fund, which invested substantially in Ascot Partners LP, Gabriel Capital Corporation, and Ariel Fund Ltd., funds run by Merkin.

JPMorgan Chase & Company, which reported essentially nil exposure to Madoff, reportedly yanked $250 million of its own funds from Fairfield Greenwich Advisors, another Madoff feeder fund, after a midyear review of its hedge fund risks.[23] However, it appears not to have told any of its clients that it had steered into the fund of its own decision, setting the stage for a possible lawsuit. Safra Bank also reported indirect exposure to Madoff. In all, Irving Picard, the trustee of Bernard Madoff's defunct firm, estimated that nearly 9,000 people were victims of the Madoff fraud.

Apparent Suicides

In addition to the apparent suicide of Thierry Magon de La Villehuchet, who was found dead in his Manhattan office on December 24, 2008, after personally losing about $50 million in the alleged Ponzi scheme, there is at least one other suicide that is being blamed on Madoff.

According to the *London Times*, "Mr. Madoff was accused of having 'blood on his hands' after a former soldier killed himself over the loss of his family's life savings.[24] The son of William Foxton, 65, said his father was so distraught after losing his family's entire savings in the alleged Ponzi scheme that he shot himself in a park in Southampton on Tuesday with a handgun. Willard Foxton from London, UK, said that his father, a grandfather of two and a former French Foreign legionnaire, was 'brought low by the greed of Bernie Madoff.'"[25]

"I spoke with my father recently and he confided in me that he was in 'an absolute s— fight' with his banks, as his life savings had been invested in two hedge funds; the Herald USA Fund and Herald Luxembourg Fund," Willard Foxton said.[26] "He had found out that the offices of these funds had closed and that the money had in fact been invested in the Madoff hedge funds. I feel a little helpless at the moment. Essentially I want Madoff and others involved in Herald funds to know that they have my father's blood on their hands."[27]

William Foxton served with the French Foreign Legion before joining the British Army in 1969 and working his way up to the rank of major. The father of two had his arm replaced with a metal artificial limb, and after leaving the forces in 1986 was made an MBE for services to the disabled. He later worked in the Balkans for the United Nations, where he was head of the European Commission Monitoring Mission during the Yugoslavian wars. He was awarded an Order of the British Empire (OBE) in 1999. His last overseas trip was running humanitarian projects in Afghanistan before his retirement last year.

Elie Wiesel Speaks Out

At a panel convened by *Condé Nast Portfolio*, Elie Wiesel, Nobel Prize winner, author, Holocaust survivor, and family friend of the author for over 40 years, spoke out. About 160 people, including Dan Rather, Georgette Mosbacher, and the *Daily Beast*'s Tina Brown, packed the 21 Club for the breakfast meeting moderated by Joanne Lipman, *Condé Nast Portfolio* editor-in-chief. Wiesel, whose charitable foundation was wiped out by Madoff, had mostly kept quiet about the alleged $50 billion Ponzi scheme. But at the meeting, the Holocaust survivor and Nobel Peace Prize recipient spoke out passionately about his betrayal by Madoff. He referred to him "variously as 'a crook, a thief, a scoundrel,' as well as a 'swindler' and 'evil.'"[28]

Wiesel said that in addition to having lost his foundation's assets, he lost his personal wealth to Madoff. "All of a sudden, everything we have done in 40 years—literally, my books, my lectures, my university salary, everything—was gone," he said.[29] His foundation, the Elie Wiesel Foundation for Humanity, lost substantially all of its $15.2 million in assets to Madoff. Including his personal investments, total losses may be as high as $37 million. "We gave him everything, we thought he was God; we trusted everything in his hands," Wiesel said.[30]

Wiesel met Madoff only twice, introduced through a friend who had known Madoff for 50 years and also invested with him. Knowingly or not, the intermediary played up Madoff's aura of exclusivity by telling Wiesel, "It's true, you are not rich enough."[31] But he agreed to make an introduction. Wiesel ultimately shared two dinners with Madoff and was impressed. Madoff "presented himself as a philanthropist," Wiesel said.[32] The men spoke, ironically, mostly about ethics and education.

Asked if he could forgive Madoff, Wiesel paused for a very long moment. "Could I ever forgive him?" he asked, almost to himself.[33] Finally, he said firmly, "No," to a burst of applause.[34] Wiesel did, however, come up with an imaginative punishment: "I would like him to be in a solitary cell with a screen, and on that screen . . . every day and every night there should be pictures of his victims, one after the other after the other, always saying, 'Look, look what you have done.' . . . He should not be able to avoid those faces, for years to come."[35]

He added, "This is only a minimum punishment."[36]

During the panel discussion, Wiesel rejected the idea that Madoff preyed on Jews, and that the scheme was some sort of affinity fraud. "It's not the Jewishness in him, it's the inhumanity in this man. . . . The man . . . was not only a liar, a swindler, but he was—not a crook—he was somehow always more than that. More. Once you enter evil, it's not static, it's dynamic."[37]

Wiesel believes charities that were scammed by Madoff should be bailed out by the government. "Just as we bail out banks and car agencies, bail out charitable institutions. . . . I think it would be a great gesture that the Obama administration should show that we really think of those who are helpless."[38]

Wiesel sees parallels between Madoff and his Holocaust experience. Although he emphasized that "Madoff is not the greatest story of our lifetime," he added that in recent years, "Madoff is one of the greatest scoundrels, thieves, liars, criminals. How did it happen? I have seen in my lifetime the problem is when the imagination of the criminal precedes that of the innocent. And Madoff had imagination. . . . We have no idea that a person is capable of that, but then I should have learned, of course, that a human being is capable of anything."[39]

Donations to the Wiesel foundation have come in unsolicited: "Literally hundreds of people that we have never known sent us money though the Internet. . . . Just as in 9/11, you remember 9/11 of course was the greatest tragedy, but it also brought out the best in the American people."[40]

An edited transcript of the meeting is available online at the *Condé Nast Portfolio* web site.[41]

Chapter 21

How Madoff Got Away with It

Madoff's fraud succeeded for so long for at least seven reasons:

1. Bernard Madoff was a legend on Wall Street for nearly 50 years, with an enviable reputation.
2. The returns were at the outer end but within the realm of believable, so while they appealed to an investor's greed, the usual warning that "if it's too good to be true, it probably is" could be ignored by avaricious investors. Or so they thought.
3. Madoff played hard to get. He was low-key and he mixed in all the right circles.
4. He turned down some investors; other prospective investors schemed for years before being granted entrance into his exclusive club. If Madoff took your money, that was proof that you had arrived. It was simply impolite to ask too many questions. As Jason Zweig, who writes "The Intelligent Investor" column for the *Wall*

161

    Street Journal, said, "When you are in an exclusive private club, you do not go rummaging around in the kitchen to make sure that the health code is being followed."[1]

5. Redemption requests were handled promptly for years, allaying any fears.

6. Oversight was incredibly lax. The Securities and Exchange Commission (SEC) said it poked around on eight occasions without finding anything significant.

7. Auditors (especially of feeder funds) were incredibly lax.

How Did Madoff Get Away with It for So Long?

Dara Horn wrote, "In the encounter between Tevye and Menachem-Mendl [which we discussed in Chapter 1], Sholem Aleichem demonstrates how much of financial disaster originates from the simple fact of trust—and trust within a family, at that."[2] (What Horn wrote at the time was based on what was known when she wrote it; we now know that over time, Madoff needed larger and larger sums to keep the fraud going. He shifted his focus to institutional investors. When they suffered massive withdrawals as the markets froze up, they sent in redemption notices for the liquid assets invested in Madoff, and the Ponzi scheme collapsed.)

    Still, many in the Jewish community were hurt, some very badly. Despite the blind Jewish fear of discussing money among a non-Jewish public, American Jews' discussions and investments with those they regard as family reveal an equally blind optimism. Horn said that the Jewish trust in those who are considered relatives is itself a by-product of what she called a "well-warranted" distrust of strangers.[3] She went on to conclude that the thoroughness with which Jewish communal organizations were devastated by the Madoff scam reflects less a problem of greed than a problem of trust.[4]

    Red flags had been raised. The first tip-off for some was the steady returns generated by the firm in every kind of market, which is virtually impossible to achieve year in and year out. As a result, there were those who questioned Madoff's tactics. On May 7, 2001, *Barron's* published a story by Erin E. Arvedlund presciently entitled "Don't Ask,

Don't Tell" that questioned Madoff's remarkably consistent investment performance. She talked with experts who were highly skeptical about Madoff's claimed results. One financial adviser that she quoted had pulled his clients' funds out of Madoff's shop.

She wasn't alone. So-called prophets of doom were ignored. Harry Markopolos, a former Boston investment professional, was quoted in the *Wall Street Journal* saying that he repeatedly tried to get the SEC to investigate Madoff, first contacting the agency's Boston office more than a decade before the fraud was exposed. "Madoff Securities is the world's largest Ponzi scheme," Markopolos wrote in a letter to the U.S. Securities and Exchange Commission in 1999.[5]

He wasn't clear only to the SEC. He wasn't shy about sharing his views with money managers as well. His warnings resonated with some money managers (the fortunate ones), who advised their clients to steer clear of investing with Madoff. For instance, Jim Vos, who runs Aksia LLC, a firm that advises investors, investigated Madoff and came away worried after examining the Madoff operation. He kept his clients away from Madoff.

Neither Markopolos nor Vos was alone. I was told privately by a senior vice president of Merrill Lynch that after a due diligence review, Merrill refused to put its clients into Madoff as Merrill was concerned about the lack of transparency, absence of an independent custodian, and use of a little-known auditor.

The *Wall Street Journal* also noted another potential red flag: "Mr. Madoff operated as a broker-dealer with an asset management division. Why not simply act as a hedge fund and pocket big gains, rather than profit from trading commissions as the firm seemed to be doing?" some asked.[6] Of course, the reason was that a hedge fund needs to use an independent custodian who makes sure the assets are all there.

Such conflicts of interest were also noted by others. "There was no independent custodian involved who could prove the existence of assets," said Chris Addy, founder of Montreal-based Castle Hall Alternatives, which vets hedge funds for clients seeking to invest money.[7] "There's a clear and blatant conflict of interest with a manager using a related-party broker-dealer. Madoff is enormously unusual in that this is not a structure I've seen," he added.

Joe Aaron, a longtime hedge fund professional, found that Madoff's structure was suspicious and in 2003 warned a colleague to steer clear of the fund. "Why would a good businessman work his magic for pennies on the dollar?" he queried.[8]

A Swiss bank, Union Bancaire Privée (UBP), kept hundreds of millions of dollars of its wealthy clients' money in Bernard Madoff's alleged Ponzi scheme despite warnings from its own research team, according to people familiar with the matter. While others in the investment community had questioned Madoff's strategy and chosen to stay away, the instance offers a sign that red flags were raised within one of the large institutions that actually invested with Madoff. By early 2007, UBP's research department had raised various concerns about Madoff's business, and later it recommended that he be stricken from a list of fund managers approved for UBP's clients' investments, according to people familiar with the matter and internal e-mails reviewed by the *Wall Street Journal*.[9]

Allegedly, some of the bank's most senior executives were aware of the concerns and discussed them. It is unclear how the matter was resolved, but UBP ultimately left hundreds of millions of dollars of its clients' money with Madoff. An adviser to J. Ezra Merkin's funds, Victor Teicher (who ironically had a conviction for securities fraud), allegedly warned Merkin that Madoff's returns "were not possible."[10] Merkin and Teicher talked about Madoff on and off for years. Teicher scoffed. "The thing seemed ridiculous," Teicher told Merkin.[11] But then, *New York* magazine speculates, "Ezra must have thought, Teicher generally didn't like anyone's ideas but his own."[12]

Lax Oversight

According to those familiar with the case, Madoff was never inspected by U.S. regulators after he subjected his company to oversight two years earlier by registering it with the SEC.

The Financial Industry Regulatory Authority (FINRA), a self-regulatory body for the securities industry, serves as the first line of defense for the Securities and Exchange Commission by inspecting about 5,000 registered U.S. broker-dealers. The securities industry regulator investigated 19 complaints about trading by Bernard Madoff's broker-dealer operation since 1999, but could not ask questions about the investment advisory business at the center of his now admitted fraud because it was not legally authorized to do so.

FINRA did not know that the SEC had received allegations that Madoff was running a Ponzi scheme, according to Herb Perone, a spokesperson for FINRA. The agency does not examine investment advisers, but it has been drawn into the debate over regulatory failures because the broker-dealer was the only business subject to examinations before Madoff registered his investment-advisory arm in 2006. FINRA released a lengthy public report that noted lapses in its examination process. The report found that FINRA's lack of ability to oversee investment advisers did contribute to its failure to detect the Madoff fraud. Even so, the report said, "Finra examiners did come across several facts worthy of inquiry with the Madoff scheme that, with the benefit of hindsight, should have been pursued."[13]

A 2007 examination, the report said, uncovered "commissions from a London affiliate that now appear to have served as a money laundering operation for Madoff's investment advisory business."[14]

Richard Ketchum, FINRA's chief executive officer, said that the group is planning to launch a new Office of Fraud Detection and Market Intelligence in response to the report's findings. "Finra must institute a number of internal reforms to better safeguard investors and the broader financial system," he said.[15] "The report calls attention to the many regulatory challenges related to jurisdictional issues and product definitions."

The SEC hadn't examined Madoff's books since he registered with the agency in September 2006, according to Bloomberg, which quoted two people who declined to be identified because the reviews aren't public. The SEC tries to inspect advisers at least every five years and to scrutinize newly registered firms in their first year, former agency officials and securities lawyers said.

The *Wall Street Journal* reported that Bernard L. Madoff Investment Securities LLC was "examined" at least eight times in 16 years by the Securities and Exchange Commission and other regulators, who often came armed with suspicions but found only very minor problems.[16]

SEC officials followed up on e-mails from a New York hedge fund that described Bernard Madoff's business practices as "highly unusual."[17] FINRA reported in 2007 that parts of the firm appeared to have no customers.[18] Madoff was interviewed at least twice by the SEC, and regulators seem to have conducted eight separate investigations.[19] But regulators never came close to uncovering the Ponzi scheme that investigators now believe began in the 1970s.

While the SEC requires the broker-dealer industry to regulate itself, there is no comparable arrangement for 11,274 registered investment advisers. Only 10 percent of registered advisers are examined on a cycle of every three years, though others may be subject to sweeps or random examinations, the SEC said. The SEC no longer routinely examines newly registered advisers in their first year. Madoff's investment advisory business was not examined after registering in 2006. An SEC spokesman said that it shares information with FINRA based on "individual facts and circumstances."[20]

Perhaps the most interesting and devastating testimony was provided by Harry Markopolos. He submitted 375 pages of testimony and documents. Markopolos charged that the SEC simply could not understand the entities and transactions it was supposed to be regulating.

After listening to his testimony, one of the members of the subcommittee, Representative Gary Ackerman, blasted the SEC, saying, "I am frustrated beyond belief. We are talking to ourselves and you are pretending to be here. You've told us nothing. What the heck went on? What went wrong? One guy with a few friends and helpers found this fraud over a decade. You guys couldn't find your backside with two hands when the lights are on."[21]

On September 29, 2009, H. David Kotz, the SEC's independent inspector general, issued two reports on the SEC's failures. Kotz urged overhauling how investigators scrutinize tips, plan probes, tap expertise, verify information, and train employees. Kotz's eight-month investigation found that the SEC since 1992 had missed at least six opportunities to uncover the world's largest Ponzi scheme after assigning inexperienced lawyers to inquiries, conducting inspections that were too narrow, and failing to press Madoff when catching him in lies. The reports suggest 37 changes to the examinations office and 21

was "kind of like a vacation" in which Madoff's firm paid his hotel tab and paid for expensive dinners with colleagues.[33]

Non-family members also had shares in the London firm, including Maurice J. Cohn, known as Sonny. Madoff and Cohn were shareholders in Cohmad Securities, a Madoff feeder. Filings show that in 1987 Cohn had shares of Madoff Holdings Ltd., a predecessor to the current firm. In 1998, he held 35,624 nonvoting shares, some of which he transferred to "BL Madoff" in 1998; the rest he "disposed of" in 2004. A lawyer for Sonny Cohn has said he had no knowledge of fraud.

Interestingly, "[a]nother shareholder was Paul Konigsberg, a New York City accountant and a longtime friend of the Madoffs who audited the Madoff Family Foundation tax returns." The *Wall Street Journal* goes on to quote Charles Stillman, an attorney for Konigsberg, who said his client "received the nonvoting shares when he did work for the London operation roughly 25 years ago when it was first opening, [and that he] didn't have any 'meaningful business role' in the London operation, and didn't receive dividends or compensation."[34]

In addition to Mark and Andrew Madoff, there were seven other directors, including their father and Peter Madoff. Records suggest the directors were well compensated. In 1999, the directors received "emoluments" (fees) totaling £688,570 ($946,577). The operation reported profits of £1.03 million. In 2007, directors received £1.09 million. The highest-paid director, not named, got £301,437 in 2007. The primary business was trading stocks using the firm's own capital. The amounts managed by each trader were relatively modest, typically in the tens of millions of dollars, according to a former employee there. There was only minimal contact with the U.S. trading operation, traders said.[35]

Money Laundering

"What is particularly useful about money-laundering charges in this context is that you can be convicted of money laundering in the U.K. if the original crime has taken place outside the U.K.," Martin Saunders, a London-based partner at law firm Clifford Chance who focuses on white-collar crime, told the *Wall Street Journal*.[36] "If the alleged fraud took place in the U.S. . . . unless there was some act to help perpetrate the fraud in the U.K., you cannot be convicted of fraud in the U.K.," he said.[37]

Proving money laundering can also be easier. Prosecutors would only need to show that the person in the United Kingdom receiving the funds at least suspected they might have been fraudulently obtained, as opposed to proving the person knew. "It's a lower bar," Martin Saunders said.[38] U.K. authorities' considering the possibility of money-laundering charges was earlier reported on *Portfolio.com*. The SFO says it does appear Madoff's London office had legitimate trading operations but in the end, it declined to bring any charges.

Did Madoff Act Alone?

Many have said that in a fraud of this magnitude, numerous people must have been involved. Bernie Madoff's brother Peter, sons Mark and Andrew, and niece Shana all worked for the trading business, and allegedly not in the investment-advisory business. In his court allocution, Madoff was careful to claim that he acted alone. He said his brother, Peter, and two sons, Andrew and Mark, worked for his brokerage and trading business, which was separate from the fraudulent investment-advisory business and was "legitimate, profitable and successful."[39]

However, Irving Picard, a court-appointed trustee for his bankrupt firm, has said, "We have found nothing to suggest there was any difference, any separateness. It was all one."[40] Investigators are trying to determine whether the other family members knew anything about the alleged scheme. Representatives for Mark, Andrew, and Shana have said they had no knowledge of the alleged scheme. Frank DiPascali Jr., a key lieutenant to Madoff for more than 30 years, said he headed stock options trading and was the point man for investment-advisory clients who were told he executed their trades.[41]

DiPascali "is a potential point man in the investigation." DiPascali, 52 years old, has pleaded guilty and is cooperating with authorities. Federal investigators are interested in information he can provide about "the inner workings of Mr. Madoff's operation, who—if anyone else—knew about the alleged fraud, and where the money went, according to people familiar with the matter." DiPascali, according to the *Wall Street Journal*, who "was one of the firm's most senior employees at the time of Mr. Madoff's arrest, often wore jeans and a sweatshirt to his office in a Third Avenue tower known as the Lipstick Building in midtown Manhattan. He also handled requests for redemptions, and could be a valuable source of information for investigators trying to determine which investors profited from the scheme by making redemptions in recent years that could be taken back by the firm's court-appointed trustee."[42]

Boyer Palmer, the father-in-law of Tim Murray, a Minneapolis investor who did business with Madoff, said he often spoke with Frank DiPascali about his family's account and investments. DiPascali "was in charge," said Palmer. Murray said he had called DiPascali to change details on some of his family's trust accounts with Madoff about a decade before, and DiPascali had become annoyed with the paperwork. He said DiPascali told him that if more work was required on the account, he would close it. Said Murray, "Frank was kind of a tightly wound guy." Murray said he eventually got all the paperwork he needed.[43]

On August 11, 2009, DiPascali pleaded guilty to helping his boss carry out a $65 billion Ponzi scheme and was immediately sent to jail by a judge who said he might flee. He pleaded guilty in federal court in Manhattan to 10 counts, including conspiracy, fraud, and money laundering. DiPascali has been cooperating with prosecutors, explaining how he and others helped Madoff defraud investors by using money from new clients to pay earlier ones at Bernard L. Madoff Investment Securities LLC.[44]

In his allocution, DiPascali told U.S. District Judge Richard Sullivan: "I knew I was participating in a fraudulent scheme. I knew everything I did was wrong, and it was criminal, and I did it knowingly and willfully. I accept complete responsibility for what I did. I apologize to every victim and to my family and the government. I am very, very, very sorry."[45]

DiPascali admitted that he fabricated account statements, lied to investors, perjured himself before the SEC, and created phony books and records at the company. He said he was a supervisor on the 17th floor of Madoff's midtown Manhattan offices, where the fraud took place. He said he "never meant to hurt anyone," and that he thought Madoff had enough assets to cover redemptions by clients. In pleading guilty, DiPascali admitted that he evaded taxes for 2002, 2005, 2006, and 2007 and owes an additional $2 million in taxes.[46]

"I know my apology means almost nothing," DiPascali said. "But I hope my actions going forward with the government will mean something."[47]

Judge Sullivan was unmoved and denied a $2.5 million bail request by prosecutors and DiPascali's lawyer, who argued that sending him to jail would hamper his cooperation. U.S. marshals handcuffed DiPascali after the two-hour hearing and took him into custody. The judge said he might reconsider DiPascali's bail request. He did. DiPascali was released to house arrest on November 11, 2009.[48]

JoAnn "Jodi" Crupi, longtime employee of Madoff, received a subpoena on January 16, 2008, for documents about her compensation and her dealings with certain firm clients, including charities, according to a person familiar with the matter. The agency also asked for access to her personal computer, this person said. "We have been served with a subpoena and we will comply with it as the law requires," Crupi's lawyer, Eric R. Breslin, told the *Wall Street Journal*.[49]

As we go to press, other than two programmers, none of those who sat on the 17th floor with DiPascali, including Robert Cardile, a 24-year Madoff veteran who is married to DiPascali's sister; Eric Lipkin, a second-generation Madoff employee; JoAnn "Jodi" Crupi; and Erin Reardon have been charged with wrongdoing.

Reuters reported that court documents filed in the wealthy Massachusetts island of Nantucket suggest Frank Avellino, an accountant who had delivered investors to Madoff since the 1960s, continued to channel money to Madoff and may have known crucial information about the losses a week before the revelation of Madoff's Ponzi scheme shocked world financial markets.[50]

Nevena Ivanova, a Bulgarian who cleaned Avellino's summer home on Nantucket, said in court papers filed in Nantucket District Court on December 29, 2009, that she invested her family's $200,000 savings with Avellino and was told the money was gone on December 1 (10 days before Madoff's arrest). "It's an indicator that he may have known what the Madoff scheme was all about," said Jay Gould, a former investment management attorney at the Securities and Exchange Commission who heads the hedge fund practice at Pillsbury Winthrop Shaw and Pittman

LLP. "Did Madoff tell him 'look, your money is gone. You're not going to get it back.' Is that why he knew? Or is it that he didn't know and he wasn't a participant, but he took money from these other people and didn't intend to give it back. It's hard to say."[51]

Two other investors have filed a lawsuit against Avellino in the Nantucket court seeking to recover more than $1 million lost to Madoff. But legal experts say Ivanova's case is unique in suggesting a Madoff middleman may have known of the losses before Madoff's arrest. Ivanova said she tried to withdraw the money in July, saying she needed it to send her daughter to college and to help buy a home, but she was told she could get her money back only at the end of the year, according to the court papers. According to court documents, she was told by Frank Avellino and his wife, Nancy, that the money was lost on December 1, 2008.[52]

Reuters quotes David Mark, a lawyer representing Victor Barnett of Palm Beach, Florida, who invested $10 million with Madoff, as saying, "If that is correct information, it would be very interesting." The Nantucket cases renew scrutiny on Avellino, who in 1992 with fellow accountant Michael Bienes was brought before the Securities and Exchange Commission for illegally raising $440 million for Madoff. In that case, Avellino and Bienes were accused of offering notes that promised returns of between 13.5 percent and 20 percent since about 1962.[53]

They operated a so-called feeder fund, handing the money over to Madoff to invest. It became so profitable they scrapped their accounting business in 1984 to focus purely on securities trading, court documents show. The SEC shut down the operation in 1992 for selling unregistered shares. The two neither admitted nor denied liability, but agreed to pay a fine and repay investors in a settlement that forced Madoff to return the money they raised for him. Interestingly, they were represented in that case by Ira Sorkin, Madoff's current attorney.

Madoff's Auditor Arrested and Charged by SEC

David G. Friehling, the sole practitioner at Friehling & Horowitz, CPAs, PC, was been arrested and charged in a criminal complaint with securities fraud, aiding and abetting investment adviser fraud, and four counts of filing false audit reports with the SEC. Friehling, 49 years old, faces up to 105 years in prison on all of the charges if he were ordered to serve the sentences consecutively. He too pleaded guilty, is cooperating with authorities, and awaits sentencing.

The accounting firm was formed in 1988 with David Friehling's father-in-law, who is now deceased, the SEC said.[54] Friehling is the firm's only CPA and its sole shareholder. Prosecutors alleged that from the early 1990s to December 2008 he created false and fraudulent certified financial statements for Madoff's firm, Bernard L. Madoff Investment Securities LLC. The government alleged, and he admitted, that he failed to conduct audits of Madoff's firm that complied with generally accepted auditing standards and conformed with generally accepted accounting principles, and falsely certified he had done so.

In a sworn affidavit, Keith D. Kelly, a Federal Bureau of Investigation agent, said Friehling's audit work papers for the Madoff firm were "inadequate to support the findings contained in the audited financial statements" and reflected "insufficient independent verification" of information provided to Friehling by employees of the Madoff firm. The papers didn't include documentation that he had conducted an independent verification of the Madoff firm's assets, had examined a bank account through which billions of dollars in Madoff client funds flowed, or verified the purchase and custody of securities by the firm, according to the FBI agent. "Friehling and F&H did not perform anything remotely resembling an audit of BMIS and, critically, did not perform procedures to confirm that the securities BMIS purportedly held on behalf of its customers even existed," the SEC said in its complaint.[55]

Friehling admitted to making false filings with the SEC in 2004, 2005, 2006, and 2007, prosecutors said. The financial statements portrayed the Madoff firm as "a financially sound broker-dealer," the SEC said. Madoff's firm paid Friehling between $12,000 and $14,500 a month for his services between 2004 and 2007, prosecutors said. Meanwhile, the SEC said Friehling and his firm received $186,000 a year in fees from the Madoff firm for providing the purported audit work, as well as bookkeeping services for Madoff and various Madoff family members. Friehling or his wife also maintained a client account at the firm from the early 1980s to the present, according to the FBI agent's affidavit.[56]

The SEC said Friehling and his accounting firm obtained "ill-gotten gains" through compensation paid by Madoff and his firm and by withdrawing "millions of dollars from accounts" held at Madoff's firm in the name of David Friehling and his family members. The SEC press release said accounts held by Friehling and his family at the Madoff firm had a balance of more than $14 million as of November 30, 2008, and withdrawals from the largest account totaled more than $5.5 million since 2000.[57]

"Although Mr. Friehling is not charged with knowledge of the Madoff Ponzi scheme, he is charged and pleaded guilty to charges of deceiving investors by falsely certifying that he audited the financial statements of Mr. Madoff's business," said acting U.S. Attorney Lev Dassin in a statement. "Mr. Friehling's deception helped foster the illusion that Mr. Madoff legitimately invested his clients' money." Friehling's arrest came days after his 80-year-old father-in-law and former partner, Jeremy Horowitz, who had been suffering from cancer, died in Florida on the same morning that Bernie Madoff pleaded guilty.[58]

Someone who identified himself as Horowitz's son Irwin posted a poem about his father on the day of his death on a web site called Newwest.net. The poem called Horowitz "a decent, honorable man." It provided some insight into his final weeks and months and described how Madoff's fraud affected his family.

"The irony that Bernard Madoff pled guilty to 11 counts of fraud, perjury and money laundering on this day is beyond measure," Irwin Horowitz told the *New York Times*. "My father's passing has become part of this great American tragedy. He served as Mr. Madoff's auditor for over three decades. . . . He never suspected the crime that was happening . . . my father, who had spent his entire life building up both a reputation for honesty and integrity as well as an investment nest egg that would provide for my parents' retirement . . . has suffered mightily simply from the association with Mr. Madoff."[59]

Both David Friehling and his late father-in-law, according to people who know the two men, had invested with Madoff and lost substantial sums. Lev Dassin, then acting U.S. attorney for the Southern District of New York (SDNY), which includes Manhattan, said that the investigation is continuing.[60]

On July 17, 2009, a criminal Information was filed, and on November 3, 2009, a superseding Information was filed. Friehling pleaded guilty the same day and is cooperating with the government.[61]

Friehling admitted in his allocution to Judge Alvin Hellerstein that he failed to conduct independent audits of Bernard L. Madoff Investment Securities LLC's financial statements, saying he took the information given to him by Bernie Madoff or Madoff's employees at "face value." However, he denied any knowledge of Madoff's Ponzi scheme and said he entrusted his own retirement investments and his family's investments to Madoff, and in what he said was "the biggest mistake of my life, I placed my trust in Bernard Madoff," saying he had about $500,000 with the Madoff firm.

Friehling is cooperating with prosecutors. Although he theoretically faces a statutory maximum of 114 years in prison on the charges, he is likely to get a far lighter sentence, both because of his cooperation and because most of the time sentences in the multiple counts run concurrently rather than consecutively. The maximum possible sentence on each count does not exceed 20 years.[62]

Who Else Can Be Made to Pay?

In an interesting lawsuit filed in the Southern District of New York, two investors have sued the SEC for gross negligence. The lawsuit was filed by Phyllis Molchatsky, a disabled retiree and single mother who lost $1.7 million, and Steven Schneider, a doctor who lost almost $753,000. The SEC earlier denied the investors' administrative claims, clearing the way for them to file suit under the Federal Tort Claims Act. The suit is styled *Phyllis Molchatsky and Steven Schneider v. United States of America*, U.S. District Court, Southern District of New York Case # 1:09-cv-08697-LTS. It makes for interesting reading. While there is scholarly debate about the merits of the suit (sovereign immunity is a difficult hurdle to overcome), the suit does a great job of summarizing the case and the SEC's failures.

The secretary of state of Massachusetts had a successful enforcement action against Cohmad Securities, which was co-owned by Madoff. The Massachusetts office is investigating, and has revoked Cohmad's license.[63]

From January 3, 2007, to December 2, 2008, Cohmad received approximately $7,046,678.96 from Madoff Investments, amounting to 84 percent of its revenues. Ruth Madoff, the wife of Bernard Madoff, allegedly withdrew $5.5 million from Cohmad Securities on November 25 and an additional $10 million on December 10, according to two wire transfer receipts attached to a complaint filed by William Galvin, the Massachusetts secretary of state, in the weeks before Madoff's arrest. Also, according to Secretary Galvin, Cohmad is alleged to have been sent for payment of "professional services" in excess of $52 million from Madoff Investments. Cohmad is also alleged to have paid $526,000 to Sonja Kohn on behalf of Madoff.[64]

In a statement, however, a lawyer for Kohn said she had not received any of the funds suggested in the complaint, nor is she aware of any of the activities referred in the complaint by and between Cohmad and Madoff. The lawyer added that Kohn "has not seen or otherwise been involved with Cohmad or with Maurice Cohen, Cohmad's largest shareholder, for many years." Kohn is the chairwoman of Bank Medici AG in Vienna, which invested $3.5 billion in client funds with Madoff. She has said she is a victim who had no knowledge of the fraud.[65]

According to a report in the *Wall Street Journal*, "The secretary's office said the complaint and supporting documents 'speak for itself.' Internal Cohmad documents filed with the complaint show that the Madoff firm made payments to Cohmad for Kohn—sometimes referred to in the documents as 'SK' or 'Sonya Kohn'—of $87,792 a year for six years," the complaint said. U.S., U.K., and Austrian prosecutors are investigating and believe that Kohn was paid more than $40 million in kickbacks to funnel billions of dollars of investments to Bernard Madoff, according to sources quoted in the *Wall Street Journal*.[66]

Prosecutors from all three investigations believe Madoff paid kickbacks to Sonja Kohn while she was chairwoman of Austria's Bank Medici AG via separate companies she controlled, according to affidavits detailing the investigations and hundreds of documents collected by Austrian prosecutors that were reviewed by the *Wall Street Journal*. "I am actually the greatest Madoff victim. It is a tragedy for my family, my company and for me personally," Kohn was quoted as having told the *Journal*. However, she declined to discuss details of the allegations against her.[67]

According to the *Wall Street Journal* in an article entitled "Madoff Kickbacks Alleged in Austria," an affidavit from the U.S. Justice Department filed with Vienna prosecutors in April 2009 stated that Kohn is under investigation in the United States for potential criminal charges of conspiracy, fraud, and wire fraud in connection with the alleged kickbacks. U.S. prosecutors allege that Kohn acted on her own behalf in receiving kickbacks. They also allege that Kohn and Bank Medici failed to disclose to investors that their funds were being invested wholly with Madoff. The affidavits don't suggest Bank Medici knew of the alleged kickbacks to Kohn. Two streams of alleged payments are under investigation. Early in 2009, U.S. investigators noticed a flow of payments totaling about $32 million over 10 years from Madoff's investment-advisory firm, Bernard L. Madoff Investment Securities LLC, to Infovaleur Inc., a New York company that was "owned by Sonja Kohn personally," according to a U.S. affidavit filed on April 6. The U.S. affidavit said U.S. prosecutors were unable to locate a registration for Infovaleur Inc.[68]

"It does not appear that Kohn, or Bank Medici, ever disclosed to investors in the feeder fund that Kohn was personally receiving payments from Madoff at the same time as she was investing the feeder funds with [Madoff's fund]," the affidavit says. Madoff was "actually in full control" of Bank Medici's investments, according to the affidavit.[69]

Prospectuses for the Bank Medici funds that Kohn oversaw claimed they were investing in a basket of 35 to 50 Standard & Poor's 100-stock index shares, as well as in U.S. Treasuries, the affidavit says. The prospectuses didn't mention Bernard Madoff or his company, when in fact all of the funds' money was being forwarded to Madoff, the affidavits say.[70]

"It is suspected that the research papers were completely worthless and that the reports were never in fact used by [Madoff Securities International] for business decisions," the affidavit said. Kohn is being investigated in the U.K. in connection with potential criminal charges of money laundering and falsifying documents to receive kickbacks, according to the affidavit.[71]

The U.S. and British affidavits asked Austrian prosecutors to seize or share documents, witness statements, and bank records related to companies and accounts controlled by Kohn. The Justice Department also asked to observe an interview with Kohn.

Kohn was questioned by Austrian prosecutors at a court in Vienna, with a team of six U.S. officials present from the Justice Department, the Securities and Exchange Commission, and the Federal Bureau of Investigation. In the interview, she said she had no recollection of Erko, a company that deposited a check written by Madoff International into a Vienna bank." She said she had produced research for Madoff International, but was never paid for it, according to the court summary.[72] Authorities believe that the account was controlled by Kohn.

Kohn answered routine questions, according to the Vienna State Court's nine-page summary of the questioning, such as: age: 60; education: high school diploma; income: none. She also listened to questions based on the U.K. affidavit, but declined to respond, saying the questions were a surprise and she would need to prepare a response, the summary shows.[73]

Trustee Sues Feeder Funds

Trustee Picard has already filed lawsuits in bankruptcy court in Manhattan to try to force hedge funds and other large investors to return nearly $14 billion in fictitious profits paid by Madoff's firm, alleging they should have known about the fraud. According to Reuters ("Madoff Trustee Sues Medici Fund for $578 million," by Martha Graybow, July 14, 2009), Picard sued Medici, as well as the fund's custodian, a unit of HSBC Holdings Plc, for $578 million. The case was filed in the U.S. Bankruptcy Court for the Southern District of New York.[74]

"I have a duty to investigate and to go to court to recover from persons and entities who received more than their share," said Picard. "In actual fact, persons who are subject to these recovery efforts actually received money stolen from others."[75]

The trustee of Bernard Madoff's defunct firm also sued investment funds run by Fairfield Greenwich Group for $3.5 billion. The lawsuit, filed in federal bankruptcy court in Manhattan, alleges that the funds, which placed client money with Madoff, "should have known" he was engaged in fraud. The suit doesn't provide evidence that Fairfield or its officers had knowledge of the Madoff fraud but says the firm didn't perform adequate due diligence that it promised its clients. The suit alleges that Fairfield missed numerous warning signs, including trades listed in its accounts that could never have occurred, and seeks the return of money it withdrew on behalf of its clients since 1995.[76]

Trustee Picard has filed similar suits seeking $10 billion from other funds that fed client money to Madoff. Will he be able to recover money? "Lawyers familiar with the cases say Mr. Picard, an attorney at Baker & Hostetler LLP, who is charged with recovering assets for investors burned in the fraud scheme, will have difficulty collecting from the defendants even if the suits succeed. That's because the money may already be in the hands of Fairfield's own clients, who are likely off limits to Picard, since they weren't direct investors with Mr. Madoff," reports the *Wall Street Journal*.[77]

Who Else Knew?

Amir Efrati, who has been covering the Madoff case for the *Wall Street Journal* since it first broke, has reported that "the criminal investigation into who knew about Bernard L. Madoff's massive fraud has expanded to include some of his highest-profile investors, according to people familiar with the matter."[78]

He suggests that although prosecutors are continuing to probe Madoff family members and employees, the investigation now includes investors who have claimed to be among the hardest-hit victims of the fraud, both directly and through their foundations. Jeffry Picower and Stanley Chais, two philanthropists who invested heavily with Madoff, and Carl Shapiro, one of the money manager's oldest friends, are among at least eight Madoff investors and associates being scrutinized by the U.S. attorney's office in Manhattan, these people said. Indeed, Picard has already sued both Picower and Chais to retrieve all of the monies paid to these individuals, their families, and trusts related to them. Picower was sued in May 2009 and accused of taking fake profits of $6.7 billion for himself and his affiliates over a 20-year period. Picard's demand increased to $7.2 billion on September 30, 2009. Chais was sued for over $1 billion.[79]

Amir Efrati goes on to claim, "Federal investigators have gathered evidence they think will show that Messrs. Picower and Chais told

Madoff how much in returns they wanted. Their accounts soon would reflect those amounts, people familiar with the investigation said. Aiding investigators is their discovery that Madoff was a 'meticulous' record keeper who kept correspondence between some clients and the firm, said people familiar with the probe," according to the report.[80]

In the civil suit against Picower (*Complaint against Jeffry M. Picower et al.*, May 12, 2009), Picard alleged that Picower sought—and then received—better returns than thousands of other Madoff investors. He made a similar allegation against Chais (*Complaint against Stanley Chais et al.*). Trustee Picard claimed that "the high returns reported on defendants' accounts were a form of compensation by Madoff to Picower for perpetuating the Ponzi scheme by investing and maintaining millions of dollars" with Madoff.[81]

The Picowers, who had two dozen accounts with Madoff, received annual returns of more than 100 percent in 14 instances, Picard said. "In some cases, their returns reached 300% or 950% a year," the trustee has alleged. "Messrs. Picower and Chais have denied the claims, either directly or through their lawyers."[82]

The *Wall Street Journal* claims that prosecutors are "now weighing whether the actions and evidence cited in the civil lawsuits rise to the level of criminality, according to people familiar with the matter."[83]

Among the other Madoff investors and associates whose account records and other information kept by the Madoff firm are being scrutinized by the government for signs of complicity, according to people familiar with the matter: Frank Avellino, the Florida and Nantucket accountant who ran an investment fund that channeled client money to Madoff; Noel Levine, a real estate investor who works out of a two-room office located next door to where Madoff ran his fraudulent investment operation on the 17th floor of the Lipstick Building in Manhattan; and Palm Beach investor Robert Jaffe, a son-in-law of Carl Shapiro, who referred potential investors to Madoff. None of these individuals have been accused of criminal wrongdoing by the government.[84]

According to the *Wall Street Journal*, "It's unclear why Mr. Madoff would allegedly have given some investors such high returns and why some investors allegedly made requests for specific gains. Mr. Picard's lawsuit against Messrs. Picower and Chais doesn't speak to possible motive, only alleging that the defendants knew or should have known they were 'reaping the benefits' of 'manipulated purported returns, false documents and fictitious reports.'"[85]

Accounts of Chais and his family averaged annual returns of 40 percent with Madoff, and returned as much as 300 percent, Picard alleged. Chais also requested fictitious losses from Madoff's firm, apparently to offset gains he made through other investments in order to avoid taxes, Picard alleged. Chais's foundation, wiped out in the scandal, had $178 million in assets as of 2007. In a letter to clients about the trustee's suit, Chais said it was filled with "inaccuracies." Eugene Licker, a lawyer for Chais, said Chais is extremely ill, suffering from a blood disorder.[86]

Correspondence between Picower or one of his employees and the Madoff firm suggests complicity, Picard alleged in the complaint. In May 2007, for example, a foundation employee named April Freilich requested gains on Picower's behalf, according to the suit. The Madoff firm then recorded purported trades in his account as having occurred in January and February 2006, according to the lawsuit. That and similar moves in May 2007 netted Picower $55 million in fictitious gains, the suit alleged. Altogether, the Picowers are accused of profiting more than $7 billion from Madoff. Barbara Picower found her husband Jeffry's body at the bottom of the pool at his oceanside mansion on October 25, 2009, police said. He was 67, and apparently died of a heart attack, coroners ruled after an autopsy. Trustee Picard said that his lawsuit will proceed nonetheless.[87]

"Federal investigators," according to Amir Efrati, "are reviewing evidence that they think suggests Shapiro also knew his returns were fraudulent, according to people familiar with the matter. Unlike Messrs. Picower and Chais, Shapiro, a women's clothing entrepreneur, was never in the finance business. He is one of Madoff's oldest friends and biggest financial backers and helped Madoff start his investment firm in 1960. In 1971, Shapiro sold a clothing brand for about $20 million. Over the years, that sum, the vast bulk of which was 'invested' with Madoff, grew to hundreds of millions of dollars and some say more than $1 billion, according to people close to Shapiro. Shapiro personally 'lost' an estimated $400 million from the fraud, including $250 million invested with Madoff 10 days before the fraud collapsed, said people familiar with the matter. His foundation lost more than $100 million."[88]

Bloomberg reported that Picard is also seeking to recover $150 million transferred from the firm to Banque Jacob Safra (Gibraltar) Ltd. for the benefit of British Virgin Islands–based Vizcaya Partners Ltd. He also sued Kingate Global Fund Ltd. and Kingate Euro Fund Ltd, which were set up by the Italian Carlo Grosso as feeder funds that channeled $1.7 billion worth of his client's money to Madoff beginning in the mid-1990s, according to another lawsuit, also filed in bankruptcy court in Manhattan.[89]

The lawsuit did not name Carlo Grosso and did not allege his funds had any involvement in the Madoff fraud. Grosso's funds allegedly withdrew $255 million from Madoff's firm in October and November 2008. Hareley International, a hedge fund run by Cayman Islands–based Euro-Dutch Management Ltd., allegedly withdrew $425 million from Madoff "which it knew or should have known was nonexistent principal and other investors' money," according to the filing in bankruptcy court.[90]

Most Assets Forfeited

Federal prosecutors have also identified more than $100 million in real estate, cash, bonds, art, automobiles, boats, and other assets owned by Madoff and his wife Ruth, which they have seized, including the couple's Palm Beach, Florida, residence; a yacht called *Bull* and a smaller boat; and properties in France, on Long Island, and on Park Avenue in Manhattan.

Bernie Madoff's brother, Peter Madoff, agreed to an asset freeze. Under the agreement, he can spend up to $10,000 per month for living expenses, including mortgage loans and insurance premiums. The agreement prohibits Peter Madoff from transferring assets or property. The liquidators of Bernard Madoff's business in the United Kingdom also sued Peter Madoff to recover a vintage Aston Martin car bought with funds from the U.K. business. The court-appointed liquidators said in the lawsuit that Madoff's business, Madoff Securities International Ltd., wired a total of £135,000 ($201,353) to Aston

Martin in March and May 2008 to buy the car for Peter Madoff and his wife. A lawyer for Peter Madoff disclosed that his client also had agreed to an asset freeze with federal prosecutors as early as December 2008.[91]

A state-court judge in Connecticut temporarily froze the assets of three investment funds that helped bring client money to Madoff's fraudulent investment operation, as part of a lawsuit brought by the town of Fairfield, Connecticut.

In 2007, Bernard Madoff used a firm account to lend $9 million to his brother, the firm's chief compliance officer, the filing said. The firm also gave money to two entities owned by Madoff family members, including $1.7 million in capital contributions to Madoff Energy Holdings LLC, owned by Andrew, Mark, and Shana Madoff, who also worked at the firm, the filing said. The Madoff firm also paid out $4.5 million to support Ruth Madoff's real estate–related investments, it said. More than $11.5 million was used to buy two yachts for the Madoff family, the filing said, and other funds appear to have been used by Andrew Madoff to purchase an apartment. Mr. Picard is seeking the return of all of these monies.[92]

The Sorkin Connection

Prosecutors preparing the case against Madoff identified potential conflicts of interest involving his defense attorney, Ira Lee Sorkin. The possible conflicts involved Sorkin's 1992 representation of a Florida accounting firm that had invested with Madoff, as well as the fact that Sorkin's deceased father had a retirement account with Madoff. "This is about a potential conflict over my 1992 case with Avellino and Bienes and my father had an account," Sorkin told Reuters.[93]

In 1992, Sorkin represented the Florida accounting firm Avellino & Bienes (A&B) after it was sued by the SEC. A&B agreed to pay a civil penalty of $250,000, and Frank Avellino and Michael Bienes each agreed to pay civil penalties of $50,000 in their settlement with the SEC. According to recent congressional testimonies by SEC officials, Messrs. Avellino and Bienes allegedly raised $441 million from 3,200 investors through unregistered securities offerings, which were then invested in discretionary brokerage accounts with Madoff's firm. Madoff in turn invested the money in the securities market.

Sorkin's name also appeared on a 162-page mailing and customer list released by the trustee liquidating Madoff's business. Sorkin said at the time: "I have never had at any time an account either as a customer, investor, [or] client or had any beneficial interest in any account at Bernard L. Madoff Investment Securities."[94] His father had a retirement account that invested with Madoff, which was passed to his mother when he died in 2001, according to Reuters, which added that Sorkin said he received her mail for several years before her death in 2007. At a hearing, Madoff waived the potential conflicts with Sorkin, and the judge accepted the waivers.

Chapter 22

Madoff Plea and Its Aftermath

GOVERMENTS GO AFTER MERKIN, KOHN, AND
MAYBE OTHERS IN THE MOTHER OF
ALL PONZI SCHEMES

So the Madoff investigation continues.

No Plea Bargain

One theory that was floating around (and reported by The Big Picture) was that Madoff would cut some kind of a deal that will implicate the major banks (HSBC, Royal Bank of Scotland, Santander, BNP Paribas, Nomura); funds of funds; and referrers (feeder funds) in his massive fraud. Should he implicate these others, it would open the door to massive civil and criminal litigation.[1]

This theory was greatly strengthened as Madoff waived his right to a formal grand jury review of the complaint, which is usually the first step toward a plea agreement to charges contained an Information, which is the list of charges a defendant pleads to. It didn't happen.

Lev Dassin, then acting U.S. Attorney for the Southern District of New York, emphasized in court that there was no plea deal with Madoff. He said later that prosecutors would "bring additional charges against anyone, including Mr. Madoff, as warranted" in their ongoing investigation.[2]

Madoff's plea, as the U.S. Attorney was quick to point out, "does not end the matter." In this connection, Peter J. Henning, a professor at Wayne State Law School, quoted Winston Churchill, who said (after the victory at the Battle of El Alamein), "It is the end of the beginning." The government's investigation will continue, according to Professor Henning, "and the fallout from the fraud will reverberate for years," he opined.[3]

Why No Agreement to Cooperate

As Professor Henning points out, "entering a plain guilty plea to the criminal complaint without any agreement to cooperate also means Mr. Madoff could be a witness for anyone else charged in connection with the Ponzi scheme, including any family members who might be charged. If prosecutors indict others for assisting him, the defense lawyers could call him to testify that he was the only one responsible for the fraud and that he deceived those who worked for him as much as the investors."[4]

Would a jury actually believe Madoff? All a defendant has to do is raise a reasonable doubt about his or her own guilt, and having the primary perpetrator take all the blame could be an effective defense to charges of complicity in the scheme. "Odd as it may sound," Professor Henning says, "Mr. Madoff could be a valuable defense witness if the government seeks to convict others for assisting in the execution of the Ponzi scheme."[5]

However, the *New York Post* quotes former federal prosecutor Bradley Simon, who said he believes that "the lack of a plea agreement is simply for public consumption." Simon said a Madoff lawyer, Ira Sorkin, is likely cut a secret deal for the mega-swindler to "provide a road map" to the money he stole after he goes to prison. "No lawyer is going to walk a client in for 150 years and say: 'Sorry, that's it,'" Simon said. "I believe the government has said to Madoff and his lawyer, 'If you cooperate with us after sentencing, we'll ask the court to reduce the sentence.'"[6]

Faced with 150 years in prison, Madoff has all the reasons in the world to cooperate in exchange for a reduction of his sentence.

Did Madoff Buy Lax Oversight?

Barry Barbash, a former head of the SEC's investment management division, said the agency has tried to focus its inspections on money managers who pose the biggest risks. The regulator uses criteria such as which securities a firm is buying and who its clients are, said Barbash, a partner at Willkie Farr & Gallagher LLP in Washington.[7] Any suspicions about Madoff may have been dampened because of his association with industry groups, watchdogs, and politicians. He sat on a committee of academics, regulators, and executives formed in 2000 by former SEC Chairman Arthur Levitt to advise the agency on new stock market rules in response to the growth of electronic trading. Madoff has led the trading committee at the Securities Industry Association, Wall Street's biggest trade group, and served as chairman of the NASDAQ Stock Market.

Since 2000, he has given at least $100,000 to the Democratic Senatorial Campaign Committee and more than $23,000 to the party's candidates, including Senator Charles Schumer of New York and Senator Frank Lautenberg of New Jersey, who leads a charitable foundation that invested with Madoff. "You can see where people would pull the shades down over their eyes in terms of recognizing what could be one of the great frauds of our time," Levitt said in a Bloomberg Television interview, according to Bloomberg.com. "I've known him for nearly 35 years, and I'm absolutely astonished."[8] Levitt is a senior adviser to the Carlyle Group and a board member of Bloomberg LP.

Still, none of these answers is satisfactory. As Louis Pasteur said, "Where observation is concerned, chance favors only the prepared mind."[9] It's fair to say that none of the government's investigators had a "prepared mind," and at the end of the day, that's probably the bottom-line reason that the fraud was missed.

Is the Money Hidden or All Gone?

Most reputable media have concluded that nearly all the money held with Madoff is likely gone, much of it to pay off earlier investors (as in most Ponzi schemes), and that Madoff acted more or less alone.

Madoff indeed may have acted more or less alone, as he says, concludes Professor Peter J. Henning after reviewing the evidence.[10]

In contrast to the mainstream view, on the *Randi Rhodes Show*, the left-leaning comic Randi Rhodes made an extraordinary, if unsubstantiated, claim that Madoff had accomplices abroad, and that $40 billion is hidden in Israeli banks with the knowledge of the U.S. government. The story was subsequently taken down from the web site.

In a story datelined December 31, 2008, the web site *TBRNews.org* quoted William Storch, who says of himself: "We have been accused of being neo-Nazis, Communists, anti-Semites, Christian haters, certainly not Bush friendly and guilty of treason, aggravated mopery, theft of mattress tags from cheap motels, chronic jaywalking and disturbers of the political peace."[11] Storch makes the following claims:

> The real story of the Bernie Madoff rip-off is being kept under official U.S. lock and key since it has become very evident that most of the stolen funds were sequestered in Israeli banks and with the active connivance of top Israeli government officials. . . . The problem with some of this information is that not one word of it will ever be seen in the American media and the swindled will stay that way. . . . Bernie had accomplices, both in New York, Washington and Tel Aviv.[12]

Professor Lawrence R. Velvel, dean of the Massachusetts School of Law, wrote to the judge on behalf of the Steering Committee of Madoff Survivors, a Google group of 300 victims of Madoff (he among them), claiming, among other things, that "billions of dollars" of investor money were stashed away in offshore accounts and in bank accounts in Israel, but he does not offer any proof. He allocates much of the blame for losses on the Securities and Exchange Commission (SEC), which gave Madoff a clean bill of health. He believes that the government should bear responsibility for some of the losses.

Lucinda Franks, a Pulitzer Prize–winning journalist and author and the wife of longtime New York District Attorney Robert Morgenthau, agrees. She quotes an anonymous federal investigator as saying, "He lied so blatantly about his financial assets, in addition to the fiction that he carried out this ruse alone, I thought that he was going to come into court and enter an insanity plea."[13] She also claims that a money-laundering investigation that is being conducted jointly by British and U.S. authorities has found that investors' capital was moved from international bank to international bank so that it couldn't be traced.[14]

So far, she says at least six banks are involved in the scheme, in Luxembourg, Gibraltar, Switzerland, Ireland, England, and Chile, and probably Austria and Italy.[15] She also claimed in a report published on August 17, 2009, that "two people close to the Bernie Madoff investigation tell Lucinda Franks prosecutors will issue more indictments after Labor Day [2009], and new evidence is pointing toward family members."[16] So far, that has not happened.

In the meantime, Madoff is sitting in a federal jail, so hopefully the Bureau of Prisons will prevent him from either killing himself or being killed by others. Also, it seems unlikely in the extreme that Israel's banking laws would shield this type of theft (they never have in the past), or that anyone in the Israeli or U.S. governments would have an interest in protecting Madoff or in preventing restitution. If money is hidden, it is likely that it will be recovered by government investigators or the army of lawyers who stand to profit from the money's return to its rightful owners.

Funds Set Aside for Madoff Claims

The Securities Investor Protection Corporation (SIPC) and the trustee in the Madoff case, Irving Picard, said that as of May 21, 2010, a total of $689 million in funds have been set aside for claims from victims of the Ponzi scheme, with another $2.74 billion authorized for potential recoveries in the future.[17]

A total of $5.45 billion in claims have been allowed, including $4.76 billion that exceed the statutory limit of protection. Customers with allowed claims will share on a prorated basis in customer property recovered by the trustee. The SIPC noted that its protection is intended to cover only up to $500,000 per customer.

The SIPC and Picard also stressed that trustee expenses aren't paid out of customer property, contrary to rumors. The SIPC covers those costs.

Ezra Merkin—Victim or Colluder?

Over the course of a few weeks, beginning when the Madoff story broke, J. Ezra Merkin lost more than $2 billion with Bernard Madoff, board positions with at least three nonprofit institutions, and his flagship fund, which is liquidating. He also was forced to step down as chairman of GMAC LLC. The attorney general of New York State has opened a formal investigation and has issued subpoenas. Merkin also lost his anonymity. Until Merkin, 55, got caught up in the Madoff scandal, some residents of 740 Park Avenue in Manhattan didn't know that their bearded neighbor was a money manager. Some guessed he was a rabbi because he wore a skullcap, according to Michael Gross, author of *740 Park: The Story of the World's Richest Apartment Building.*[18]

"Ezra Merkin was a figure of some mystery, even to people in and around the building where he lived," Gross said in an interview with Bloomberg.com. His no-nonsense demeanor impressed the co-op board, though, and members were so intimidated they asked few questions before he moved in, Gross said. According to Bloomberg, Merkin was equally brusque with executives of a New York charity he asked to invest with one of his funds, said Laura Goldman, who runs money management firm LSG Capital in Tel Aviv. After arriving more than an hour late to a meeting in 2000, he became impatient when asked for details, Goldman recalled. The charity, which she served as an informal adviser and wouldn't name, decided against giving him funds.[19]

"This Merkin had sway over people like crazy. They were grown men and they barely got out of the meeting without signing over their lives," Goldman commented. "He's very arrogant, and when you ask questions he makes it like, 'Why are you asking me a question?'"[20]

Born in April 1953, Ezra is the eldest son of Hermann and Ursula Merkin. They had six children, among them Daphne Merkin, a writer who has contributed to the *New York Times* and wrote a novel about growing up with a distant father who sheltered his daughters from the family finances. An investor who died in 1999, Hermann Merkin endowed a Manhattan concert hall that bears the family name and was a Yeshiva University trustee for three decades. Ezra Merkin graduated magna cum laude from Columbia College in New York in 1976 and from Harvard Law School in Cambridge, Massachusetts, with honors, according to his official biography. After practicing law at the New York firm Milbank, Tweed, Hadley & McCloy from 1979 to 1982, he worked at Halcyon Investments from 1982 to 1985.

After losing money for Manhattan clients, including New York University and the Ramaz School, a private Jewish school, Merkin may no longer be able to avoid answering. He is the defendant in at least four lawsuits that say he deceived investors by not telling them he placed their money with Madoff. He has been sued by New York University, Yeshiva University, New York Law School, and Mortimer Zuckerman's charitable trust, as well as by Andrew Cuomo, New York attorney general.

"Mr. Merkin shares the sorrow of all investors who have been cheated by Madoff," Andrew Levander, Merkin's famous lawyer, said in an e-mailed statement to Bloomberg.com. Merkin, whose own losses are in the "many tens of millions of dollars," declined to comment, Levander said. In the Madoff affair, "everybody's a victim," said Joseph Sprung, a member of the Fifth Avenue Synagogue, co-founded by Merkin's father Hermann. "They have to deal with the betrayal. How would you feel if your fiancée was cheating on you and that betrayal was publicized all over?"[21]

Merkin followed his father as president of the synagogue, whose congregants include financiers Ira Rennert and Ron Perelman, and Nobel laureate Elie Wiesel. On Tuesday nights, Merkin often attends a Talmud class, according to Rabbi Yaakov Kermaier. A passionate New York Yankees fan (he can't be all bad, then), Merkin "is a Renaissance man, at ease discussing literary classics, Talmudic texts, modern art, or baseball strategy," Kermaier told Bloomberg.com. Bruce Greenwald, who served as a governor with Merkin of Bard College's

Levy Economics Institute, agrees. Merkin is "considerate, articulate, intellectual, and he seems thoughtful," he said. "I'm shocked that he got sucked into this."[22]

The Levy Economics Institute at Bard, in Annandale-on-Hudson, New York, removed Merkin after discovering it had lost $3 million in one of his funds. The financier also resigned as chairman of the investment committee and as a trustee of New York's Yeshiva University, which said it lost $14.5 million in investments, fictitiously valued at $110 million, mostly through his funds invested with Madoff. Merkin served on the boards of several New York–based nonprofits, which were subpoenaed by New York Attorney General Cuomo. Merkin also resigned as chairman of the investment committee of UJA-Federation of New York, a major Jewish charity, and resigned as chairman of GMAC LLC, the finance arm of General Motors Corporation, now partly owned by Cerberus Capital Management LLC, which is controlled by Stephen Feinberg, an occasional investing partner of Merkin. Merkin also stepped down as president of the Fifth Avenue Synagogue when his term ended, rather than becoming its chairman, which is the usual custom, after his staying on became front-page news in the *New York Post*.

Merkin's ties to Madoff have substantially diminished many already bruised university endowments.

In addition to New York University, Merkin also managed money for Tufts University in Medford, Massachusetts, which lost $20 million as a result of Merkin's reliance on Madoff. New York's Yeshiva University, where Merkin served as a trustee and chairman of its investment committee, lost $110 million (it seems that much of that was illusory gains from a $14.5 million investment). Mort Zuckerman, the developer, has also filed suit against him, saying he invested $25 million with Merkin's Ascot Fund Ltd. in 2006 through his charitable remainder trust, CRT Investments Limited. Zuckerman said he also personally invested $15 million with Merkin's Gabriel Capital. On December 12, 2008, the day after Madoff's arrest, Merkin sent Zuckerman two facsimiles informing him the money was invested with Madoff and was "likely gone," according to court papers. The case is *CRT Investments Ltd. v. J. Ezra Merkin*, 601052/2009, filed in New York State Supreme Court in Manhattan.[23]

The New York attorney general's office has requested documents and testimony from J. Ezra Merkin as part of an inquiry into whether nonprofit organizations were defrauded by three of his investment funds that were partially or completely invested with money manager Bernard Madoff. The probe by Andrew Cuomo's office is focused on nonprofits on which Merkin was a board member, according to a person familiar with the matter. Cuomo's office is examining, among other things, what disclosures Merkin made to the nonprofit investors about his funds, how much he earned in fees, and what percentages of the groups' investments were placed with Madoff's firm. Merkin agreed to New York Attorney General Andrew Cuomo's demands to step down as manager of his hedge funds and place them into receivership.[24]

Cuomo sued Merkin, saying in the complaint that he "held himself out to investors as an investing guru. . . . In reality, Merkin was but a master marketer." The attorney general doesn't allege that Merkin was aware that Madoff was running a multibillion-dollar Ponzi scheme. In a response to the attorney general's suit, Merkin filed documents with that court that he says show some clients of his funds and financial advisers had knowledge of the Madoff connection. Among them were Yeshiva University, where both Messrs. Merkin and Madoff were board members; Solaris Group, which was a financial adviser to at least one Merkin investor; and Union Bancaire Privée (UBP), the biggest investor in Merkin's Ascot Fund.[25]

However, a spokesman for Solaris, which was a financial adviser to New York Law School, said Merkin told the firm he himself was actively managing the school's money.[26]

Trustee's Suit

Irving Picard, the trustee for Bernie Madoff's defunct investment-advisory business, has also sued Ezra Merkin, asking for the return of about $558 million that his investment funds withdrew from Madoff's firm. Trustee Picard alleges that telltale signs should have tipped off Merkin that Madoff's returns were fictitious. The returns for Merkin's funds averaged 11 percent to 16 percent annually. And, unlike Stanley

Chais, Merkin didn't have personal accounts with Madoff's firm. Instead, Merkin collected a management fee.[27]

In his lawsuit against Merkin, Picard, the Madoff receiver, stated that, as a sophisticated fund manager, Merkin should have noticed the myriad warning signs that could have indicated Madoff was engaged in fraud. Among the clues: Purported trades made by Madoff that were listed in account statements sent to Merkin could never have taken place, a fact that Merkin could easily have detected, the suit alleges. Also, two of Merkin's funds had losses in only four out of 144 months for which Picard has records.

New York State Sues Merkin

The attorney general of New York, Andrew Cuomo, sued Merkin for violating New York's Martin Act by perpetrating a fraud in connection with the sale of securities, as well as the state's executive law for persistent fraud in conducting business and New York's not-for-profit corporation law for breaching his fiduciary duty in connection with serving on the boards of nonprofit organizations (*New York v. Merkin*, 450879/2009, New York State Supreme Court, Manhattan). Cuomo alleges that Merkin steered the assets to Madoff in exchange for $470 million in fees.

The nonprofits that invested with Merkin may have lost more than $100 million, said a person familiar with the matter. He took a 1.5 percent fee for managing the fund. According to disclosure documents, Merkin managed about 10 percent of the endowment of Yeshiva University. The 2003 disclosure to the board, a copy of which was obtained by *New York* magazine, reported that Ezra Merkin was managing about 10 percent of Yeshiva's endowment through four different funds. For his efforts, he collected over $2 million in fees, almost $1 million for the Ascot Fund alone. Essentially, his management consisted of turning the money over to Madoff.[28]

The Madoff trustee, Irving Picard, also filed suit against Merkin, seeking to recover over $500 million. The lawsuit in U.S. Bankruptcy Court in New York said that Merkin and his Gabriel Capital Corporation received tens of millions of dollars in fees from dealings with

Madoff. The case is *Irving H. Picard v. J. Ezra Merkin, Gabriel Capital, L.P., Ariel Fund Ltd., Ascot Partners, L.P., Gabriel Capital Corporation*, 09-01182 in U.S. Bankruptcy Court for the Southern District of New York (Manhattan).[29]

Vultures Circle around Him

Merkin's setbacks have inspired him to sell his $150 million collection of Mark Rothko paintings, The abstract works, some as large as 9 feet by 15 feet (2.7 by 4.6 meters), appear to dissolve into the walls of the family duplex at 740 Park Avenue, said London-based critic David Anfam, who has visited the home. "If you go up to that apartment, you would drop your socks," Ben Heller, who helped the couple arrange subdued rugs, furnishings, and dim lighting to complement the Rothkos, told Bloomberg.com. Merkin, at the urging of the Rothko family and Attorney General Cuomo, sold his art collection to an unnamed buyer. The monies, less expenses and amounts still owing on the art, will be held in escrow, pending resolution of the various lawsuits. In all, it is expected that another $200 million could become available for victim restitution from this sale.[30]

The Merkins' corner apartment, purchased for $11 million in 1995, had 18 rooms and eight bathrooms when built. It occupies two floors, according to documents obtained by *740 Park* author Gross. Blackstone Group chairman Stephen Schwarzman and cosmetics billionaire Ronald Lauder are neighbors in the 75-year-old building, property records show. Merkin also owns a home in Atlantic Beach, New York, on the south shore of Long Island, valued at $1.7 million, and a property in Eagle County, Colorado, worth $506,000, according to public records.[31]

The evening before Madoff's arrest, Merkin and his wife hosted patrons of Jerusalem's Israel Museum at their Park Avenue duplex. The Friday night after the arrest, Merkin appeared at the synagogue for a 100-person dinner honoring a member, said Rabbi Kermaier. "Nobody could have possibly expected Ezra to show up," Rabbi Kermaier said. "He felt that as president of the synagogue and someone who loves this community, he should be there."

A class action suit against Merkin on behalf of investors in his funds (which lost 75 percent of their value) has also been filed.

The authorities, including the U.S. attorney's office in Manhattan, are focusing on whether other individuals helped Madoff carry out the alleged fraudulent scheme and on recovering assets for burned investors. The attorney general's office is seeking information from Ezra Merkin and his Gabriel Capital Corporation, Ariel Fund Ltd., and Ascot Partners LP. Merkin invested "substantially all" of Ascot's $1.8 billion with Madoff, and roughly a quarter of the assets in his Ariel Fund Ltd. and Gabriel Capital LP also were invested with Madoff.

Merkin Warned about Madoff

The university said in its lawsuit (*New York University v. Ariel Fund Ltd.*, 8603803/2008, New York State Supreme Court, Manhattan) that none of the Ariel fund prospectuses disclosed that "Victor Teicher, a convicted felon, and his staff were the persons actively managing the majority of the Ariel assets, and that hundreds of millions of dollars of Ariel's funds had also been delivered for management to Madoff— even though Teicher had warned Merkin than Madoff's returns were not possible." Victor Teicher began advising Merkin's Ariel Fund in 1993 *after* he had been convicted of several counts of securities fraud, including using insider information in trading puts and calls. According to the filing, Teicher advised Merkin until 2001.[32]

Merkin Reportedly Brought in Fairfield Greenwich Advisors

Reportedly, Ezra Merkin was the one who brought in Fairfield Greenwich Group, which lost $7.5 billion (48 percent of its capital) with Madoff. He is said to have received a 4 percent finder's fee from Madoff, worth $300 million, and Fairfield was the single largest investor in Madoff. Walter Noel, who heads Fairfield, and his family were all very unflatteringly portrayed by Vicky Ward in *Vanity Fair*. She implies that Fairfield co-principal Jeffrey Tucker's wife Melanie, "a dedicated tennis player" from Scarsdale, was the one who had the connection. Her family, Ward says, "knew Bernie Madoff."[33]

Fairfield charged management fees of 1 percent to its clients as well as 20 percent of the returns—twice the normal rate for a typical fund of funds. Reportedly, Merkin received over $600 million in fees from Madoff in all, and, as noted, trustee Picard has sued to recover the funds for the benefit of defrauded investors.[34]

Daphne Merkin Comes to Her Brother's Defense

In an op-ed piece in the *New York Times*, the writer Daphne Merkin, Ezra Merkin's sister—her books include *The Discovery of Sex*—subtly comes to her brother's defense, blaming everything on Madoff, the con man. She writes, "I did not know Mr. Madoff nor did I invest with his firm, but have a sibling who did business with him."[35] However, she does not identify Ezra Merkin by name, and does not tell her readers of any of the accusations against her brother. Essentially saying that Madoff fooled everyone, she writes, "When I think of Mr. Madoff himself, I am reminded of Geoffrey Wolff's wonderful memoir of his con-artist father, *The Duke of Deception*. A small-scale operator by comparison to Mr. Madoff, Mr. Wolff's father had 'bluster in his voice' and lied about everything, from his religion to his college, for what appears to be no reason at all."[36]

Duke Wolff was a kind of visionary—charming, charismatic, endlessly inventive—driven less by greed than by the desire to support himself and his family in the grand style to which he insisted on remaining accustomed. He was a forger, a passer of bad checks, a car thief, a deadbeat extraordinaire, a compulsive spender, a dandy, and a heavy "drinker." Madoff, by most accounts, including Merkin's, was "[b]y all accounts," "the quintessential nice guy . . . offering a cover of benign paternalism." Nonetheless, Merkin writes, "[p]erhaps that is as good a definition of what it is to deal with a sociopath as any, but to call Mr. Madoff a sociopath isn't really to explain him so much as to explain our failure to pick up on his scam. Enter the sorcerer, the *ganef*, the man without qualities but with steady returns—and, I might add, a family man to the end. Mr. Madoff has not implicated his family; after all, even sociopaths have their loyalties. Enter us, the believers, the ones who signed on for the ride until it went off the rails, leaving wreckage as far as the eye could see."[37]

Sheryl Weinstein, former chief financial officer at Hadassah, claims in a book, *Madoff's Other Secret: Love, Money, Bernie, and Me*, that she had a longtime extramarital relationship with Madoff, and (nevertheless) lost all her money, as well as a chunk of Hadassah's, to Madoff, suggesting that Merkin's assertion that Madoff was a loyal family man was off-base.[38] It also seems doubtful that prosecutors share the same view as Merkin that her brother was a casualty rather than an enabler; litigators for investors who lost everything with him certainly don't share her view.

Sonja Kohn—Madoff Victim or Collaborator?

Sonja Kohn, chairwoman of Bank Medici AG in Vienna (where she is 75 percent owner and Milan-based UniCredit holds 25 percent), is another colorful person who was a feeder to Madoff. As noted in Chapter 21, the Commonwealth of Massachusetts has been investigating Kohn's connection to Cohmad, and payments said to have been filtered through Cohmad by Madoff.[39] She agreed to answer questions from the *Wall Street Journal* about how her bank ended up in Madoff's Ponzi scheme and lost $3.5 billion of its clients' money.

"It is a shattering experience to be thoroughly taken," Kohn, who had been working in her office with a government-appointed official over the prior 10 days, said in statements e-mailed to the *Wall Street Journal*.[40] "Mr. Madoff has duped a literal 'Who's Who' of international business and finance." Kohn was profiled by Haig Simonian and Eric Frey in the *Financial Times*, and quoted without attribution in ZionistGoldReport blog, which was a Christian site that said of itself, "We know political Zionism, or talmudic Zionism to be racism, and the antithesis of how Jesus told us we should love one another."[41] According to the authors, much of the reason for Kohn's success lay in her striving character. "She was a good but not exceptional student," recalled a school-time acquaintance who asked not to be named. "But she was always ambitious."[42]

Kohn, née Türk, spent her early years among Vienna's small postwar Jewish community. After marrying Erwin Kohn, a scion of an entrepreneurial, but also modest, Jewish family, the couple turned their attention abroad. By the 1970s, they had established an import-export business, trading in watches, among other things, and moved to Milan. Political instability in Italy soon prompted another move, this time to Switzerland, helping to establish the international network that later proved to be so useful. By the mid-1980s, the couple was living in Monsey, New York. A former Wall Street penny-stock broker, Kohn turned a 19-person firm called Bank Medici into a major hub of interrelated funds for Madoff's investments.

Now, $3.5 billion of Bank Medici client funds have been lost in Madoff's alleged $50 billion Ponzi scheme, and the bank's management is being overseen by an official appointed by the Austrian government. Kohn was named, together with Madoff and others, in a lawsuit by an investor who lost at least $700,000. The lawsuit, filed in New York federal court by a British Virgin Islands corporation called Repex Ventures SA, says that Kohn didn't disclose that the client's money was being funneled to Madoff and that the Bank Medici chairwoman didn't do enough due diligence on behalf of her clients.[43]

Kohn, in her e-mail statement, said: "When I first heard word [Madoff] had been arrested . . . I thought it was some sort of bizarre practical joke. When it became obvious that it was true, I felt as if a huge tsunami had hit me. . . . It is still beyond belief and I still am in a state of shock."[44] She also said that Bernie Madoff, whom she met when she worked on Wall Street in the 1980s and 1990s, was not a personal friend.[45] She wrote that her work schedule "did not allow for socializing or private friendships—neither with Mr. Madoff nor others."[46]

According to the *New York Times*, in recent years Kohn had become very Orthodox.[47] She wears a bouffant red wig, in accordance with the Orthodox Jewish tradition that requires that married women cover their hair. Her home in Monsey is in an enclave of Orthodox and ultra-Orthodox Jews. Apparently, she sold it when she started spending most of her time in Europe. Many but certainly not all of her investors were also members of the Jewish community around the world.

After the Madoff scandal broke, Kohn dropped out of sight, leaving her firm, Bank Medici, in the hands of Austrian regulators, who took it over. Embarrassment from investing heavily with Madoff could explain wanting to disappear from public view. But another theory widely repeated by those who know her is that she may be afraid of some particularly displeased investors: Russian oligarchs whose money made up a chunk of the $2.1 billion that Bank Medici invested with Madoff.

"With Russian oligarchs as clients," said a Viennese banker who knew Kohn and her husband socially, "she might have reason to be afraid." A spokeswoman for Bank Medici, Nicole Back-Knäpp of the public relations firm Ecker & Partner in Vienna, said Kohn did not want to speak to the press. "She is a victim and the Bank Medici as well," Back-Knäpp said. She declined to comment on whether Kohn was in hiding. In any case, she did not respond to the *New York Times'* inquiries, nor to those of the *Financial Times* relating to monies that she received from Cohmad Securities.[48]

Although its headquarters are in Vienna, Bank Medici focused on marketing and distributing the Madoff-linked investment vehicles through other banks and asset managers in Europe and beyond. Nearly all of Bank Medici's $2.1 billion exposure to Madoff comes from clients outside Austria. In recent years, according to the *Financial Times*, Sonja Kohn traveled constantly to Milan, Zurich, London, Israel, and New York, returning from time to time to an apartment in an upscale neighborhood of Vienna near the Parliament building. She also maintains a villa outside Zurich.[49]

The Hebrew-language edition of *Haaretz*, a leading Israeli newspaper, recently reported that Kohn and her husband regularly visited Israel and have an apartment in an upscale section of Jerusalem, and that she had invested in a number of Israeli companies, including that of recently deceased industrial titan Benny Gaon. At this time, no one can say that Kohn's version of the facts—that she was a victim—is not accurate. However, as noted earlier, the Commonwealth of Massachusetts alleges that she was paid at least $526,000 by Cohmad on behalf of Madoff.[50]

In March 2009, the Vienna state prosecutor launched a criminal investigation against Sonja Kohn on suspicion of fraud and breach of

trust relating to more than $2.1 billion in funds her bank funneled to
Madoff. A prosecutor's office said the investigation was directed against
Kohn, Bank Medici, and several current and former bank managers.[51]
The complaint argues that Bank Medici presented the funds as low-
risk vehicles and hid the fact that the customers never acquired actual
ownership rights over the shares they received.[52]

Reuters reported that the Austrian magazine *Format* said the sum
funneled to Madoff by the bank could be as much as $8 billion, cit-
ing evidence from the Federal Bureau of Investigation recorded by
Vienna police investigators in a report dated March 9, 2009. "The
present investigation by U.S. authorities has shown that between
$5–8 billion flowed from Bank Medici or [Medici chairwoman]
Sonja Kohn to Bernard Madoff," the report said, according to the
magazine. The investigators said Kohn received $900,000 per quar-
ter from Madoff for research activities, probably ever since her bank
was formed in 2003, according to *Format*. Earlier this year Kohn
denied receiving direct payments from Madoff. "Bank Medici did
not supply any money to Madoff or Madoff companies," the bank
said in a statement. It said Herald Fund SPC and Herald Lux, funds
for which it was investment manager or distributor, were victims of
the fraud.[53]

On May 28, 2009, the Austrian Financial Market Authority
(FMA) said it withdrew the banking license of Bank Medici AG
because its capital stock was too low. Since the Madoff swindle came
to light, Bank Medici has fought to reorganize its business model and
survive the blow, but the FMA said in a statement that its capital
stock has fallen below the €5 million ($6.9 million) required to run
banking operations in Austria. The bank has also renamed itself 20.20
Medici AG. The British, as well, have opened a criminal investigation of Bank Medici and Kohn. According to the *Financial Times*,
U.K. investigators are probing the head of an Austrian bank that
funneled billions of dollars into Madoff's Ponzi investment scheme.
Sonja Kohn, president and majority shareholder of Bank Medici,
is suspected of charging the London outpost of the Madoff empire
millions of pounds for worthless research, said people familiar with
the matter.[54]

The allegation—denied by a lawyer for Kohn—is part of a request for legal assistance sent to Austrian prosecutors in March by the United Kingdom's Serious Fraud Office "in connection with fraudulent activities of Bernard Madoff," the people said.[55] Among the claims is that London-based Madoff Securities International paid Kohn £7 million ($11.6 million) from 2002 to 2007 for reports that Madoff Securities International workers say were useless.

Chapter 23

Mopping up after Madoff

LAWYERS FEAST ON MADOFF FEEDERS IN THE
MOTHER OF ALL PONZI SCHEMES

Madoff feeder funds generally took 1.5 percent per year as a management fee and some took a share of the profits, up to 20 percent. In addition to J. Ezra Merkin's funds and Bank Medici's, the Lambeth Fund, operated entirely by Beverly Hills investor and arbitrage maven Stanley Chais (also sued by Madoff trustee Irving Picard), served as a feeder, as did Thierry Magon de La Villehuchet's Access International. Many of the banks that reported losses received fees as well.

Other Feeders

Philanthropist Robert Jaffe was another feeder. Jaffe started out as a stockbroker. From 1969 until 1980 he worked for E.F. Hutton and from 1980 to 1989 as a manager at Cowen & Company. In 1989 he became the manager of the Boston office for Cohmad Securities, a firm co-owned by Bernard Madoff that helped attract investors to his fund. The Massachusetts secretary of state has subpoenaed Cohmad seeking details of its relationship with Madoff's firm. Cohmad was owned by Maurice "Sonny" Cohn and Bernie Madoff, and the two apparently had very close ties. Regulators are now trying to force Jaffe to testify; but so far he has refused. He is married to the former Ellen Shapiro, the daughter of Carl Shapiro, an apparel tycoon who launched Kay Windsor Inc., which he sold to Vanity Fair Corporation in 1971. Shapiro has said he lost more than $400 million personally, according to people familiar with his situation.[1]

The Jaffes recently built an 11,000-square-foot mansion just two doors down from Madoff's home overlooking the Intracoastal Waterway, near the Palm Beach Country Club. Members of the club said Madoff would often have lunch with Jaffe or Shapiro when he was on the grounds. The *New York Post's* Page Six wrote: "The wife of Bob Jaffe—the Palm Beach bon vivant in the doghouse for getting the tony island's millionaires to invest with Bernard Madoff—is fighting for her beleaguered husband's honor."[2]

Author Laurence Leamer says Ellen Shapiro Jaffe is waging a fierce campaign to get Leamer's own upcoming lecture at the Kravis Center axed because of unflattering cracks he made about her hubby in *Boston magazine*. "She is especially pissed and she's pressuring them," Leamer told *Page Six*. "You would think she'd be in social hibernation and have better things to do." In the article, Leamer called Jaffe "a 60-something peacock in a black dinner jacket . . . [with] an aging gigolo's looks, with sleek black hair and a face that if not lifted by plastic surgery . . . looked not youthful so much as the caricature of youth."[3]

Page Six went on to write, "Jaffe, originally a Boston shoe sales-man, 'was looking for a rich wife and Ellen was the best he could do,' said one source, who describes him as a Madoff 'middleman . . . steer-ing eager clients his way and collecting easy fees in return.'" Page Six also wrote, "Jaffe's rep, Elliot Sloan, said that Ellen, a Kravis Center board member, made only two calls to officials there about Leamer's book because 'all it does is open up hurtful wounds in the community.' Sloan also slammed the article as 'full of inaccuracies,' insisting Jaffe has not had plastic surgery, noting he's been married to Ellen for 40 years and they 'are very much in love.' Jaffe's name has been mud since the Madoff scandal broke. In December, he was called a 'dirty bastard' and nearly pummeled at Mar-a-Lago by Nine West founder Jerome Fisher, who lost $150 million."[4]

Jaffe too was named by the Securities and Exchange Commission (SEC) in its suit, which charged the defendants with actively marketing investment opportunities with Madoff while knowingly or recklessly disregarding facts indicating that Madoff was operating a fraud. The SEC's Litigation Release says, "The SEC's complaint against the Cohmad defendants alleges that while bringing investors to Madoff, they ignored and even participated in many suspicious practices that clearly indicated Madoff was engaged in fraud. For example, the SEC's complaint alleges that the Cohns and Cohmad filed false Forms BD and FOCUS reports that concealed Cohmad's primary business of bringing in investors for BMIS [Bernard L. Madoff Investment Securities]. This referral business comprised as much as 90 percent of Cohmad's revenue in some years, brought in more than 800 accounts, and billions of dollars into BMIS' advisory business, for which BMIS paid them more than $100 million."[5]

Perhaps more tellingly, the SEC's complaint also alleges that "the compensation arrangement between BMIS and Cohmad indicated fraudulent conduct at BMIS. Cohmad was paid an annual percentage of the funds its representatives (except Jaffe) brought into BMIS offset by any withdrawals from those investor accounts. This compensation arrangement indicated to Cohmad and the Cohns that BMIS was not providing any real returns to investors. For example, where the client's principal investment had been $10,000, Cohmad stopped receiving fees if a client withdrew $15,000 from an account, even if under BMIS' management the account had purportedly grown to $100,000. In Cohmad's internal records, such an account was designated with a negative $5,000 number."[6] The SEC alleges that Jaffe also participated in Madoff's fraud by soliciting investors and bringing more than $1 billion into BMIS. The complaint alleges, among other things, that Madoff compensated Jaffe with outsized returns in Jaffe's personal accounts that he knew, or was reckless in not knowing, were manufactured by BMIS employees entering fictitious, backdated trades onto trade confirmations and account statements for his personal accounts at BMIS."[7]

Jaffe, through his attorneys, has denied the charges and moved in court to have them dismissed. "While salaciously branding Jaffe a henchman of Bernie Madoff," Jaffe's attorneys wrote in a motion filed in U.S. District Court in New York, "the complaint here is a textbook example of failure to state a claim." "The fundamental defect that runs through the SEC's case against Jaffe—and that is not remedied by the SEC's attempt to re-write the Complaint in their opposition brief—is the SEC's utter failure to allege facts identifying particular 'deceptive' acts that 'actually misled a single person,'" Jaffe's attorneys stated (SDNY, Case 1:09-cv-05680-LLS Document 26 Filed 11/06/2009).[8] In a decision filed on February 2, 2010, most of the SEC's claims were dismissed for failure to show that Cohmad or Jaffe were aware of Madoff's frauds (https://ecf.nysd.uscourts.gov/doc1/12717363471). In a subsequent order, the SEC was given until June 18, 2010 to file an amended compliant (https://ecf.nysd.uscourts.gov/doc1/12717722657).

Jaffe's lawyers also take a swipe at the SEC's motives, suggesting that "times of great passion can lead regulators to overreach."[9]

Jaffe also filed a dismissal motion for similar charges brought against him and Cohmad by Irving Picard, the U.S. Bankruptcy Court trustee charged with recouping assets for Madoff victims.[10]

Jaffe's lawyers, Stanley S. Arkin and Peter B. Pope, said in a statement that the complaints were deficient and unfairly hurt Jaffe's reputation. "Both the SEC and the trustee have tried to tar Bob Jaffe. But as our motions show, they just do not have the facts to back up their name calling. Bob Jaffe is not the guy they say he is. He is a good guy caught in a bad storm."[11] In a scathing rebuke to the SEC, its suit was thrown out by Judge Louis Stanton without letting the case go to trial. Fraud claims against Cohmad chairman Maurice "Sonny" Cohn, chief operating officer Marcia Cohn, former vice president Robert Jaffe, and the firm were all dismissed. Other claims remain pending in the lawsuit. "There is nothing inherently fraudulent about referring customers to an investment adviser for fees," Judge Stanton wrote. "Nowhere does the complaint allege any fact that would have put defendants on notice of Madoff's fraud."[12]

Another of Madoff's biggest feeders was Richard Spring, of Boca Raton, Florida. Spring said that for years he received payments from Cohmad, though he declined to give amounts. He said the fees were in exchange for bringing investors and investment ideas to Madoff. Spring hasn't received any requests for information from any regulators or law-enforcement bodies, according to his attorney, Kenneth Lipman.[13]

Andres Piedrahita was another feeder. He was known for throw-
ing lavish parties at his home in the expensive Madrid neighborhood
of Puerta de Hierro. There he gathered Spanish and Latin American
high society, including the heirs to Spain's biggest banking and industrial fortunes, according to people who know the couple. These con-
nections helped make Piedrahita one of the key figures in the spread
of Madoff's reach from Palm Beach to far-flung world capitals. After
marrying one of the daughters of Fairfield Greenwich co-founder
Walter Noel, the Colombian-born Piedrahita joined Fairfield and
eventually became the fund's point man in Europe and Latin America.
He and his wife, Corina, moved to London, then Madrid, becoming
ambassadors for the fund among Europe's wealthiest families.[14]

Santander Extends an Olive Branch— Did It Have a Choice?

Clients of Banco Santander's Geneva-based hedge fund unit, Optimal
Investment Services SA, had €2.33 billion invested in Madoff's firm, the
bank has said.[15] The exposure was the largest by a commercial bank. At
an extraordinary meeting of Santander's shareholders, there were heated
exchanges between shareholders—many of whom are also clients—and
executives over Santander's treatment of its customers in connection with
Madoff. However, the meeting achieved its unrelated purpose of approving
a capital increase for the purchase of Sovereign Bancorp in the United States.

"Bastards! Look at them applauding him," one executive said to his colleagues on the podium in a comment picked up by a microphone after the
bank had been criticized by a speaker from the floor.[16] Later, Emilio Botín,
chairman, ordered a vociferous critic silenced and removed from the hall.

Banco Santander SA has said that it plans to compensate private
banking clients who lost money by buying its Optimal products linked
to Madoff, and Emilio Botín said that the bank was itself looking at
legal action to try to recover its clients' funds. The bank also said that it
is offering thousands of its private-banking clients €1.38 billion ($1.82
billion) in compensation for losses arising from investments in Madoff's
alleged Ponzi scheme, the first financial company to do so. The offer by
the Spanish bank, which doesn't apply to institutional investors, came

as Banco Santander customers filed the first lawsuit seeking class-action status against the bank, accusing it and other defendants of gross negligence and breach of fiduciary duty.

According to the *Wall Street Journal*, Santander's clients in Latin America have been quietly approached by Santander representatives with an offer to return their original investments in the form of preferred stock in Santander.[17] Under the terms of the offer document, a copy of which was reportedly reviewed by the *Wall Street Journal*, the preferred shares will be issued by Santander and pay a 2 percent rate of annual interest. In return, Santander's clients must promise not to sue and must keep all of their current business and deposits at the bank. The offer shows the extent to which Santander is worried about its reputation for having invested with Madoff and is trying to keep clients from taking their money elsewhere.

"We are offering commercial compensation with the clear objective of preserving the value of our private-banking franchise," José Antonio Alvarez, Santander's chief financial officer, said in an interview with the *Wall Street Journal*.[18] But the move wasn't enough. Some of those who had privately received the offer were unhappy with its terms and vowed to hold out for a better deal. Clients would get preferred shares equal to the value of their original investment and wouldn't get credit for any gains they believed they had earned. The shares would be quoted on an exchange and clients could sell them, but likely at a steep discount. Santander can call them after 10 years.

The shares would have a face value of €1.38 billion, and the bank said it would set aside about €500 million to cover the cost, to be taken entirely in its 2008 results. In an effort to close the door on the affair, the bank's representatives have been offering a series of incentives to their best clients to get them to sign up to the deal. Some wealthy clients are being given the possibility to use the preferred shares as collateral for a loan charging 3 percent annual interest. The loan, which can amount to 85 percent of the clients' original investment in Madoff funds, can be either taken by clients in cash or reinvested in bonds paying 6 percent interest, say investors who have received the revised offer.

Santander has also offered another sweetener. It sent a letter to clients affected by Madoff saying they no longer would have to maintain their bank accounts in Santander in order to be eligible for the preferred stock swap, offered as part of the January 2010 package.

Around three-quarters of clients have already signed up to the offer, and the bank is hoping to get the overwhelming majority to do so. Santander's Alvarez said the deal was by no means an admission of wrong doing by the bank. "This is a trade-off, which does not imply any recognition that things were done badly, because they weren't—they were done right," he said.[19]

Some say Santander had no choice. According to Bloomberg.com, Banco Santander SA's hedge fund unit used risk software that according to its developer may have "waved red flags" about Bernard Madoff investments. "You definitely would have seen it," Riskdata SA chief executive officer Ingmar Adlerberg told Bloomberg in a phone interview from Paris. Many of the company's 80 customers have thanked it for flagging risks linked to Madoff, he said. He refused to name them or comment specifically on Santander. Geneva-based Optimal said Riskdata's FOFiX product was key to "quantitative risk analysis" for hedge fund investments in a 30-page due-diligence questionnaire dated in April 2008.[20]

"'Risk profiles are calculated for each hedge fund in order to estimate the systematic factors influencing the returns of the fund,' Optimal said in the document, which was reviewed by Bloomberg News. 'Deviation from expected risk profiles need to be explained.' 'Potential breaches of the risk parameters would be immediately notified to the chief operating officer and if appropriate the chief executive officer,' Optimal said in the document. Riskdata's FOFiX is a tool for fund of hedge fund investors that compares the performance of products with the same strategy to find aberrations in the pattern of results. It also analyzes returns to help explain how a fund made or lost money. The system costs 50,000 euros to 200,000 euros a year."[21]

According to the Bloomberg report, when the software sifted through 2,281 comparable funds, it highlighted 20 with "suspicious" performance, including those linked to Madoff and one run by Bayou Group LLC headed by Samuel Israel. Israel, aged 49, whom we discuss in Chapter 20, pleaded guilty to faking his own suicide the day he was due to start serving a 20-year sentence for a $400 million fraud. "Red flags the system would have throw up include 'returns smoothing,' as well as performance inconsistent with Madoff's stated strategy, which he described as 'split-strike conversion,' [Riskdata CEO] Adlerberg said."[22]

In the end, Santander also settled with the Madoff trustee, agreeing to repay $235 million for distribution to others who lost money with Madoff.[23]

Other Banks Compensating Victims

The following are ways that banks tried to repay for lost debt.

- Celfin Capital, a midsize investment bank in Chile, announced a restitution plan for its own clients on December 20, 2008, about a week after the alleged swindle was revealed. It is returning about $11 million—the total original sum—to 100 investors.
- The National Bank of Kuwait has also returned $50 million to affected investors.
- Union Bancaire Privée (UBP), the second-biggest investor in hedge funds, offered partial compensation to clients hit by $700 million of losses from the Bernard Madoff fraud—as long as they waive the right to sue.
- UBP, based in Switzerland, said it was willing to pay half of client losses but compensation would be based on the value of initial investments, excluding the fraudulent gains that evaporated when Madoff was arrested. The UBP offer will involve paying out 10 percent of clients' original investments each year for five years, plus 2 percent interest.

Was Banco Safra a Feeder, Too?

The *Financial Times* believes that Banco Safra of São Paulo for several years marketed a fund called Zeus Partners Limited, one of many feeder funds that channeled money to Madoff from investors around the world.[24] According to the *Financial Times*,

> Safra Group denies any involvement with Bernard Madoff Securities. A Safra spokesperson in New York said Banco Safra in Brazil had no involvement with Mr. Madoff's funds and that none of the Safra banks promoted any Madoff funds, although

some Safra-family banks outside Brazil did invest in some Madoff funds if customers requested them to do so. He added: "The Zeus fund is not a Safra fund."[25]

But documents obtained by the *Financial Times* from investors in Brazil include a single-sheet description of the fund headed "Safra Group" and "Zeus Partners Limited" and bearing the Safra Group logo. The *Financial Times* also obtained an "executive summary" of the fund that lists Banque Jacob Safra (Gibraltar) Limited, part of the Safra Group, as the fund's custodian. The description of the fund bears several of the hallmarks of Madoff funds, including the now notorious "nontraditional . . . split-strike conversion" strategy supposedly employed by Madoff, and almost unbroken monthly gains over five years from early 2002.[26]

One investor in São Paulo (who asked not to be identified) said he was usually reluctant to buy funds but received "a very hard sell" from his Safra representative. "They said this was a very good fund with an excellent track record and that [Joseph] Safra himself [the head of Safra Group] had put a lot of his own money into it." Banco Safra in Brazil did not respond to requests for comment on the Zeus fund and its involvement with Madoff. People familiar with the matter said the fund invested at least $300 million on behalf of Safra's customers.[27]

Be that as it may, and following a similar move by Spain's Banco Santander in January 2009, the *Wall Street Journal* reported that the Safra Banking Group nevertheless in March 2009 began offering to partially cover losses by some private-banking clients who lost money with Madoff, according to people familiar with the matter.[28]

The offers came as Brazilian officials said they had opened a probe into marketing of Madoff-related investments in Brazil. Brazilian officials confirmed that they are taking a closer look at how banks may have marketed Madoff-linked funds in the country. The Comissao de Valores Mobiliarios, Brazil's version of the Securities and Exchange Commission, has an ongoing investigation into the marketing of Madoff-related funds in Brazil, a spokeswoman said. The family-owned Safra banking empire, which has Brazilian and Lebanese roots, operates in several countries. Investors are being offered "perpetual" bonds of an amount equal to their original investment, paying 2 percent a year, according to a report in Brazilian newspaper *Estado de São Paulo*, the details of which were confirmed by a person familiar with the matter.[29]

Lawyers' Feast

As one might expect, the mother of all Ponzi schemes may turn out to be the mother of all legal squabbles. In addition to the suits discussed earlier, the *Financial Times* reported that UBS has begun to reimburse certain investors in the Luxalpha fund, one of the main European funds affected by Madoff.[30]

Sofra, SA, the French investor that won a freeze of Luxalpha assets held in a UBS managed account, is expecting to receive its €1million ($1.32 million) investment back, said Karine Vilret-Huon, a lawyer representing Sofra and other investors. Other clients who had either subscribed to Luxalpha or sold shares during November—before news of Bernard Madoff's arrest broke on December 12, 2008—had also received notice that they would be reimbursed, she said.[31]

The moves follow a Luxembourg court ruling that UBS should release €30 million to French investment group Oddo Cie, whose investment had been sold on November 17. UBS has appealed the verdict. A UBS spokesman confirmed the bank had repaid Oddo but said he was unaware of other reimbursements. UBS was accused of "serious failure" by the Commission de Surveillance du Secteur Financier (CSSF), Luxembourg's financial regulator, over its custodianship of the $1.4 billion fund that funneled money to Madoff.

The regulator said the "poor execution of [the bank's] due diligence obligations constitute a serious failure of its surveillance role as a depositary bank." CSSF gave the Swiss bank's Luxembourg arm three months to improve its procedures and structures. The CSSF also said the bank should pay compensation, although only a court can order it to do so.[32]

The CSSF has moved to shut down the Luxalpha fund, but the public "denouncement" of UBS on February 25, 2009, was highly unusual, legal experts told the *Financial Times*. Its action comes as Luxembourg fights charges, particularly from France, that investors in the grand duchy are less protected than those in other European Union countries. Many of Luxalpha's investors were French. UBS said it was "unfair" to blame the bank. "The investors in Luxalpha were sophisticated and explicitly agreed that the safekeeping of the securities was Madoff's responsibility and not UBS's," it said. But UBS remained "keen to continue to co-operate with the authorities."[33]

Meanwhile, the legal repercussions of the scandal widened as angry investors filed lawsuits against three French intermediary banks to demand information on how their money had been used. BNP Paribas confirmed it had received a summons to disclose documents on behalf of one or two clients. "This case concerns a few sophisticated individuals who acted on the recommendation of someone else. BNP Paribas did not advise clients to invest in Madoff funds."[34]

The strategy has been led by Véronique Lartigue, of Lartigue-Tournois law firm, who represents a group of wealthy private individuals with investments totaling about €25 million in Luxalpha. Many of these clients have been unable to pursue their claims against Luxalpha or UBS, which acted as the custodian bank for the fund, as they are not recognized as the shareholders. Their shares were purchased through intermediaries, and both UBS and Luxalpha have failed to respond to their requests, lawyers said.[35]

Until now UBS and HSBC, as custodians for the Madoff feeder funds in Europe, have been the foci of investor lawsuits. The affair has sparked a political spat between Luxembourg and France, where some of the country's wealthiest individuals are believed to have been caught out by the Ponzi scheme.

Christine Lagarde, French finance minister, has called into question Luxembourg's interpretation of EU rules on investment funds and said that differing interpretations risked weakening investor confidence.[36] Luxembourg has insisted that its regulations are as strict as those of its neighbors. Lawyers say that to be made whole, investors will have to look to the vast array of intermediaries who failed to spot red flags before Madoff's unprecedented pyramid scheme unraveled in December 2008, prompting his arrest by federal authorities.[37]

"These third parties were paid fees, significant fees, to manage these accounts and they did not do due diligence," Sandra Stein, an attorney who helped win a record $7.2 billion award for investors bilked by failed energy trading company Enron from banks that underwrote the company's fraudulent activities, told the *Jerusalem Post*.[38]

As noted in the previous chapter, suits have been filed against Sonja Kohn and Bank Medici, and Bank Austria and its parent, UniCredit of Italy, as well as HSBC Holdings, the fund's custodian; Ernst & Young, its auditor; and Bank Medici's former chief executive, Peter Scheithauer. In presentations for potential investors in the feeder funds, as well as internal marketing documents from Bank Medici that have now come to light, there is no mention of Madoff Securities. The lawsuit claims Madoff specifically forbade the managers who gathered assets for him from mentioning his name in their marketing literature and other reports.

Bank Medici may face a second lawsuit. Robert Schachter, a lawyer for New York law firm Zwerling, Schachter & Zwerling, told the *New York Times* that he was preparing a claim on behalf of a dozen individuals and institutions in Austria and Germany with total investments of "tens of millions of dollars."[39]

Hagens Berman Sobol Shapiro LLP filed a class-action lawsuit in the United States District Court for the Central District of California on behalf of individuals and groups that invested capital in Bernard L. Madoff Investment Securities (BMIS) through Stanley Chais or through the Brighton Company, one of the many alleged feeder funds run by Chais.

Lawsuits filed against J. Ezra Merkin and his funds were discussed earlier.

Fairfield Greenwich has also been sued by investors, in addition to having been sued by trustee Picard for $3.2 billion, all the money Fairfield Greenwich took off the table on behalf of clients from 2002 on (including $1.2 billion in the final three months). The funds' account records showed prices for 280 stock trades that did not match the actual price range for those stocks when the trades supposedly occurred. Some trades were shown as occurring on days that were actually holidays or weekends, according to the complaint. "These trades were clearly fictional," the complaint said.[40]

According to Bloomberg.com, Fairfield Greenwich Group's Greenwich Sentry fund invested $220 million and its Fairfield Sentry fund invested $7.3 billion solely in Madoff. According to the investor lawsuit, which was filed in New York State Supreme Court in Manhattan,

Fairfield Greenwich jeopardized investors' interests while collecting "millions of dollars in fees." The suit is seeking class-action status.[41]

The lawsuit accuses Fairfield Greenwich Group founding partners Walter Noel, Andres Piedrahita, and Jeffrey Tucker with breach of fiduciary duty, negligence, and unjust enrichment.[42] The complaint makes the same charges against Brian Francouer and Amit Vijayvergiya of FG Bermuda, an affiliate, Bloomberg.com said.

In a settlement, Fairfield Greenwich Group agreed to pay $8 million to settle civil fraud charges filed by Massachusetts Secretary of State William Galvin.[43]

A related lawsuit styled *Tremont Group Holdings; Tremont Partners Inc.; Rye Investment Management; Oppenheimer Acquisition Corporation; Oppenheimer Funds Inc.; Massachusetts Mutual Life Insurance Company/Richard Peskin on behalf of investors in Spectrum Select L.P.* has also been filed and makes similar charges. Maxam Capital Management and others also have been sued in a case styled *Family Management Corporation; Seymour Zises; Andrea Tessler; Andover Associates LLC; Beacon Associates LLC; Beacon Associates LLC; Beacon Associates Management Corp.; Beacon/Andover Group; Maxam Absolute Return Fund L.P.; Maxam Capital Management LLC; Fulvio & Associates, LLP/David Newman and others on behalf of investors in FM Low Volatility Fund L.P.*

Ten actions were already filed by mid-January 2009. An up-to-date summary is maintained by Kevin LaCroix of D&O Diary and a partner in OakBridge Insurance Services, Beachwood, Ohio. At this writing, the list runs to nearly 30 pages. It includes 19 separate actions and can be downloaded at http://www.oakbridgeins.com/clients/blog/madofflawsuitlist .doc. As discovery proceeds, additional suits will undoubtedly be filed and other auditors, custodians, and assorted "deep pockets" who had some role will also find themselves becoming defendants.

Global Litigation

The *Financial Times* reported that a Spanish law firm working with hundreds of investors who lost money to Bernard Madoff's alleged $50 billion Ponzi scheme is trying to put together a multinational group of lawyers to seek compensation from banks that sold Madoff-related funds in at least 17 countries. "We believe this is the first global fraud affecting confidence between clients and financial institutions, the banks," Javier Cremades of Cremades & Calvo-Sotelo told the *Financial Times*. "We are selecting law firms in every jurisdiction so that we can provide a global answer to this global fraud."[44]

American Lawyer reported that Cremades said his firm was representing about 600 clients—400 individuals and 200 institutions such as hedge funds and university foundations—from Spain, Switzerland, Israel, and Latin America. Most were clients of Santander or its affiliate, Banesto, but other banks involved included Fortis, UBS, Caja Madrid, and Banco Espirito Santo.[45]

The litigation being prepared by Cremades and his colleagues, including a proposed class-action lawsuit in Florida, will argue that banks misrepresented the products as low-risk investments and failed to perform sufficient due diligence. The *Financial Times* quoted Cremades as saying, "They want their money back. They don't want litigation. . . . [But] if we don't reach a settlement, we will litigate in every jurisdiction, including in the U.S."[46]

A lawsuit, filed in Florida, is directed against Santander's Optimal hedge fund unit and three of its executives, including its former chief executive, Manuel Echeverría. It also names Optimal's auditors, PricewaterhouseCoopers, and an HSBC Holdings PLC unit, which acted as custodian for the assets. The plaintiffs in the suit are Inversiones Mar Octava Limitada, a Chilean company, and Marcelo Guillermo Testa, a resident of Buenos Aires, according to court documents provided by their lawyers. Octava lost "all or substantially all" of a $300,000 investment in Optimal Strategic U.S. Equity, a feeder fund operated by Madoff's firm, the court documents said. Testa lost everything he invested, the lawsuit claims.[47]

David Rosemberg, a litigator at Broad and Cassel in Miami who represents investors who lost money with Madoff, said Safra had approached some of his clients. They "were not impressed by the offer," Rosemberg said, because "it's not a refund of the investment." A spokesman for the Safra banking group, however, said that the "Safra banking group's proposal is being well received by clients."[48]

A lawyer representing clients in Brazil said some clients were being asked to sign confidentiality agreements before receiving terms of any deal. A spokesman for the Safra banking group declined to comment. It isn't clear how much Safra's private banking clients invested with Madoff, but a person familiar with the matter said a published estimate that the bank could spend $40 million restituting clients was accurate.[49]

The foregoing is but a sampling of litigation to date. Every major and many smaller law firms with securities law practices will have an opportunity to eat from this enormous litigation pie, as they represent litigants in this "mother of all Ponzi schemes."

Auditors and Accountants Being Asked to Pay up, Too

Numerous accounting firms missed the fraud at Bernard L. Madoff Investment Securities LLC as they inspected the investment company's books or those of so-called feeder funds that helped steer money to it. As a result, those accountants could now be legally vulnerable to claims that they should have uncovered red flags, according to legal and accounting experts.[50]

For example, notes the *Wall Street Journal*, Madoff's firm was audited by Friehling & Horowitz, a suburban New York firm with one active accountant who pleaded guilty to a six-count criminal complaint of securities fraud and aiding and abetting investment adviser fraud and of making false filings to the Securities and Exchange Commission. Lynn E. Turner, former chief accountant for the SEC, said he finds it hard to believe that auditors of so-called feeder funds checked out Madoff's auditor as a way of bullet-proofing their confidence. "If they didn't," he said, "then investors will have to hold the auditor accountable."[51]

Following the collapse of Enron Corporation, the Public Company Accounting Oversight Board (PCAOB) was set up under the Sarbanes-Oxley Act of 2002 to help detect fraud. Auditors of brokerage firms were supposed to be registered. However, the SEC suspended the rule for private financial partnerships such as hedge funds, which by the end of 2008 were collectively handling about $1 trillion.

Friehling & Horowitz wasn't registered with the PCAOB. Nor was it peer reviewed, a system in which auditors check out one another for quality control. David Friehling, the firm's only active accountant (who was arrested on securities fraud charges) was enrolled in a peer-review program at the American Institute of Certified Public Accountants (AICPA), but wasn't required to participate because he told the trade group that he didn't handle audits, according to the AICPA.[52]

In a typical lawsuit, Madoff feeder fund Maxam Absolute Return Fund LP claims in a lawsuit filed in Connecticut Superior Court against its own auditor, McGladrey & Pullen LLP, that the firm was "in the best position to understand that an operation of Madoff's size required a much larger audit team."[53]

KPMG LLP also allegedly overlooked a "highly suspicious claim" as it audited the books of a big Madoff feeder fund managed by Tremont Group Holdings, according to a lawsuit filed by an investor. According to Madoff's statements, Tremont's assets went entirely into Treasury bills every December 31. But that was inconsistent with Bernard Madoff's claims that he was investing in a complex "split strike" strategy, "which required the purchase and sale of a panoply of financial instruments such as stocks and derivatives," according to the suit against Tremont and KPMG by the Tomchin Family Charitable Trust filed in New York State Supreme Court. KPMG spokeswoman Kathleen Fitzgerald said, "Our audit conformed to all professional standards." Pointing out that lawsuits have been filed against many top auditing firms, she stated, "This is not a KPMG issue."[54]

PricewaterhouseCoopers Ireland is being sued in Miami by investors in a fund marketed by Banco Santander SA, Europe's second-largest bank by market value, which lost an estimated $3 billion. The bank also is a defendant in the suit. PricewaterhouseCoopers's Canadian affiliate has dismissed claims that it was negligent in its audit of Madoff feeder fund Fairfield Greenwich Group. Both overseas units say the claims are baseless. "PwC was not the auditor for Bernard Madoff Investments where the alleged fraud occurred," the Canadian affiliate said in a statement. Fairfield also is a defendant in the suit.[55]

In addition to firms with a formal auditing role, some individual investors are taking a closer look at Sosnik Bell & Company, the accounting firm Madoff encouraged them to use for routine record keeping. Hundreds of individuals who invested with Madoff hired the small New Jersey firm to handle their monthly statements. Sosnik

Bell compiled profits, losses, and gains and prepared tax-summary statements and schedules to be used by a client's regular accountant for income tax returns. Some used Sosnik Bell at the suggestion of Cohmad Securities.[56]

In a 2001 letter, a Cohmad representative instructed a new investor to mail a check to Bernard L. Madoff Investment Securities. "For accounting purposes I suggest you call Scott Sosnik and Larry Bell," the letter said, according to a copy released by Massachusetts regulators. "They do accounting for many Madoff clients and can provide a summary at a very reasonable price."[57]

Sosnik Bell charged about $800 annually for "simple work," according to Robert Anello, the firm's lawyer. The firm generated perhaps one page each month, as well as quarterly statements. "Sosnik Bell was not asked to perform analysis or due diligence with respect to the monthly statements or the tax summary statements and did not serve as an investment adviser for such clients," Anello says. He also commented that Sosnik Bell, with client permission, often received data directly from Madoff. "There was nothing fishy that would raise any concern on the face of the documents," he says. The partners of Sosnik Bell personally lost "millions of dollars" in Madoff investments, Arnello added.[58]

Asking the Taxpayer for Help

In addition to trying to get money from accountants and advisers, investors will get relief from the government. Some may be entitled to relief from the Securities Investor Protection Corporation (SIPC), an organization designed to help investors at failed brokerage firms. However, losses in brokerage accounts from theft are usually limited to $500,000 in securities and $100,000 in cash. It is unclear if money held in the names of feeder firms will be covered as one account or as individual accounts. In addition, Madoff-related losses may be claimed as ordinary theft losses, which can be used to offset ordinary income. Some advisers are also telling investors to file amended returns for up to five prior years (some had paid taxes on phantom income for literally dozens of years, but as of now only more recent taxes can be recovered).

While tax experts weren't initially sure how the IRS would rule on these and other issues creating uncertainty, the IRS was pressured to issue guidelines that promise relief for taxpayers. "Beyond the toll of human suffering, the Madoff case raises numerous issues for the victims of losses from Ponzi-type investment schemes," Douglas Shulman, IRS commissioner, told a congressional hearing. Shulman said losses from such schemes would be treated as "investment theft losses" and taxpayers may deduct all of the purported earnings on which the investor paid taxes as well as the cash invested in the Ponzi scheme.[59]

The taxpayer's assessment of how much of a deduction to claim, however, would hinge largely on prospects of recovering money, whether through claims made with the Securities Investor Protection Corporation—the nongovernment agency that helps customers of failed brokerages—or through civil lawsuits.

Under the plan, the IRS would allow investors to claim a theft-loss deduction amounting to 95 percent of their investments, minus any recoveries, including SIPC claims. Investors who are suing third parties can claim a 75 percent theft-loss deduction. Investors would be able to claim the loss as having occurred in 2008, and can carry back the theft-loss deduction in many cases as much as five years, according to the guidelines.[60] Investors who placed money with so-called feeder funds—which subsequently channeled money to Madoff—would also get relief. The funds would be allowed to claim theft-loss deductions and would distribute them proportionally to individual investors. The guidelines apply to the Madoff fraud as well as other similar Ponzi schemes deemed to be criminally fraudulent.

"This is a mess," Leslie B. Samuels, a former assistant Treasury secretary for tax policy and now a lawyer at the Cleary Gottlieb Steen & Hamilton law firm in New York, is quoted as saying by the *Wall Street Journal*.[61] "Nobody knows yet what all the facts are," and all the confusion over tax issues "just adds insult to injury" for the alleged victims.

Senator Charles E. Schumer of New York has proposed (on December 10, 2009) a Madoff Investors' Tax Bill of Rights that would dramatically expand federal tax benefits aimed at helping devastated smaller investors recoup some of their losses.[62]

Shutting the Barn Door

In all, more than 150 Ponzi schemes collapsed in 2009, compared to about 40 in 2008, according to the Associated Press's examination of criminal cases at all U.S. attorneys' offices and the FBI, as well as criminal and civil actions taken by state prosecutors and regulators at both the federal and state levels.[63]

Clearly, the Madoff scandal will be analyzed and dissected for many years, and at this writing many questions still remain unanswered. You can confidently expect that the SEC will step up its investigation efforts now that this horse has run through the open barn door. Securities and Exchange Commission Chairman Christopher Cox said as much in a statement issued on December 16, 2008. Pathetically, the statement says (in part):

> The Commission has learned that credible and specific allegations regarding Mr. Madoff's financial wrongdoing, going back to at least 1999, were repeatedly brought to the attention of SEC staff, but were never recommended to the Commission for action. I am gravely concerned by the apparent multiple failures over at least a decade to thoroughly investigate these allegations or at any point to seek formal authority to pursue them. Moreover, a consequence of the failure to seek a formal order of investigation from the Commission is that subpoena power was not used to obtain information, but rather the staff relied upon information voluntarily produced by Mr. Madoff and his firm.[64]

Predictably, investors who lost money are calling for a government bailout, and to the extent it happens, we will all be paying for Madoff's many sins.

Many Questions Remain

Professor Lawrence Velvel, dean of Massachusetts Law School and himself a victim, says that many questions remain unanswered. In a post on his blog he writes, "It also is not yet known precisely who knew of the fraud and, of those, who knew that the nature of the fraud was that it was a Ponzi scheme. Unless and until the prosecutors affirmatively give clean bills of health to Ruth Madoff, Peter Madoff, Shana Madoff, and Madoff's two sons, Mark and Andrew, an awful lot of people are going to think they had to know something was wrong." He also says, "Shana Madoff must have known that Cohmad and BLMIS were paraded as being separate but really weren't; as was said in a complaint, she was the compliance officer for both Cohmad and BLMIS."[65]

Dr. Velvel continues, "If you ask me, it is more likely that there was someone else involved in the deal who got a lot of the money—some think the American mafia, some think the Russian mafia, some think the Mossad and/or the CIA, some think others. Some think a lot of the money is still in banks overseas and one wonders about all the excess billions withdrawn by Picower—where, or to whom, did that money go?"

He goes on to write, "Then there are the questions about the IRS. Why did it approve Madoff as a so-called nonbank custodian for IRAs in June of 2004 when he was in serious violation of crucial regulations the IRS itself had established to insure that persons with IRAs will not lose their money because of misconduct by or unfortunate events occurring to nonbank custodians? How did Madoff get the IRS to approve his company as a nonbank custodian despite his serious violations of the IRS' own regulations, and despite the fact that inspection of Madoff by the IRS to insure that its regulations were met would have disclosed the fraud? Was there criminal conduct on the part of the members of the IRS—acceptance of bribes, for example? Was there 'only' simple gross negligence, incompetence and gross dereliction of duty (as, perhaps, by failing to inspect Madoff to be sure he complied with the regulations)?"

No matter what you think of Professor Velvel's questions or his thinly veiled conspiracy theories, it seems certain that an army of lawyers will be pursuing the case for many years, and that Madoff will have a preeminent place in the annals of financial fraud.

Giving Madoff the Last Word

Speaking from prison, in an in-person interview facilitated by Madoff's attorney and his wife, Madoff candidly discussed his Ponzi scheme and how he got away with it. Joseph Cotchett, a lawyer who is representing about a dozen of Madoff's victims, says the disgraced financier repeatedly apologized to his victims during the nearly five-hour interview. Madoff also described how securities regulators were unable to catch him during the decades-long fraud.

"We're talking about billions of dollars that this guy was able to take out of our society, [which] created a lot of victims, without the Securities and Exchange Commission paying a lot of attention to what he was doing," said Cotchett. "The general impression that I came out with was this was a guy that had an extraordinary reputation on Wall Street and for many reasons, people left him alone." Cotchett says he plans to use the information to add defendants to a lawsuit being filed in Manhattan.

While much has come to light about the Madoff fraud, many details, including who helped whom and who knew what, are still not fully known at this writing. Nevertheless, the Madoff fraud is clearly a watershed event. It will not be soon forgotten and will likely be studied for generations. It will significantly impact securities regulation, auditing standards, and the due diligence process. It was a game changer.

Chapter 24

Other Recent
Ponzi Schemes

MADOFF WAS A CROOK BUT HE HAD NO
MONOPOLY ON RECENT PONZI SCHEMES

Madoff's Ponzi scheme so dominated the news that one could be forgiven for thinking that it was an outlier and an isolated event. Not so. In this chapter, we recount some of the other interesting and more recent schemes that have come to light. Far from being an isolated event, the ineluctable conclusion is that there are Ponzi schemes everywhere, and extreme vigilance is required.

Norman Hsu—The *Other* Ponzi Scheme

In October 2008, Norman Hsu, the disgraced Democratic Party fund-raiser and pal of President Clinton, and the largest fund-raiser for Hillary Clinton, was charged by the U.S. Attorney for the Southern District of New York and the Securities and Exchange Commission (SEC) with operating a $60 million Ponzi scheme between 2003 and 2007, in which he allegedly used investor funds to pay politicians and support his "luxurious lifestyle." The complaint charges that Hsu operated and was also the managing director of two companies, Components Ltd. and Next Components Ltd. These companies purported to provide investment programs that were supposed to extend short-term financing to businesses. He recruited victims by guaranteeing that they would receive 14 to 24 percent returns every 70 to 130 days for using the money to make short-term loans to businesses on short-term investments. For a while, after he got their money, Hsu actually did repay both the victims' interest and their principal, just like he said he would do.

This convinced the victims that both he and the companies were legitimate and that they had the chance to make themselves a good profit. So, many of them agreed to let their investments roll over into new investments, put in even more money, or convinced friends to invest. However, the companies were not legitimate, but just fronts for Hsu's Ponzi scheme. He ended up defrauding at least 250 victims of $60 million. He is also accused of violations of election laws. Previously he was a fugitive from justice after having skipped out from a 1992 court hearing where he was to enter prison for three years in a fraud scheme involving the sale of latex gloves. In separate cases, Hsu pleaded guilty to running a Ponzi scheme and was convicted by a jury of campaign violations. On September 29, 2009, U.S. District Judge Victor Marrero in New York sentenced Hsu to a term of 24 years and four months in prison for campaign finance violations and for defrauding investors of more than $20 million.

In an unrelated case, Hassan Nemazee, a top fund-raiser for President Barack Obama and Hillary Clinton, was arrested and indicted by a grand jury in September 2009 for defrauding Citigroup Inc., HSBC Holdings Plc, and Bank of America Corporation of $292 million.

Everywhere a Ponzi Scheme

Highly embarrassed by its failure to uncover the Madoff scheme, the SEC is now busy looking under rocks to find other Ponzi schemes. It exposed five schemes within a couple of weeks of each other, all shortly after the Madoff scheme came to light (through no fault of the SEC) on December 11, 2008. The SEC, which doesn't keep an official count, averaged 35 enforcement actions against alleged Ponzi schemes during each of the two years 2007 and 2008. Between January and July of 2009, the SEC has initiated 40 Ponzi scheme enforcement actions. That tally doesn't include actions on the state level, where many allegations of securities fraud are routinely pursued. "In recent months, Ponzi schemes have become an even higher priority," Robert Khuzami, the SEC's director of enforcement, recently said. "This is both because of the (Bernard) Madoff fraud and because the financial crisis has exposed so many Ponzi schemes." "Because of the economy, people are seeking redemptions more than they ever have and that's making a lot of these scams go belly up," Bart Chilton, commissioner of the Washington-based Commodity Futures Trading Commission (CFTC), said. Chilton called the problem "rampant Ponzimonium" and "Ponzipalooza" (a play on Lollapalooza, an American music festival featuring a long list of acts). The CFTC shares oversight with the SEC.[1]

Joseph Forte's $50 Million Ponzi Scheme

In early January 2009, the SEC announced that it had charged Joseph S. Forte with conducting a multimillion-dollar Ponzi scheme that it claims bilked 80 investors out of $50 million. The complaint alleges that, through the sale of securities in the form of limited partnership interests in his firm, Joseph Forte, L.P., that Forte told investors that he would invest the funds in an account that would trade in securities futures contracts, including Standard & Poor's (S&P) 500 stock index futures. According to the complaint, despite the impressive and consistent returns he reported to investors, Forte consistently lost money in the limited trading that he did, withdrew millions of dollars in so-called fees for his personal use based on the falsely inflated value of Forte LP, and used investor funds to repay other investors.[2]

"Forte engaged in lies, deception and rapacious behavior at the expense of innocent investors, many of whom considered themselves his friends and close acquaintances," said Daniel M. Hawke, director of the SEC's Philadelphia Regional Office. "Using other people's money, Forte promised and reported outrageous returns over more than a 10-year period, and because of his relationships with investors was able to lull them into trusting him with their funds."[3]

The SEC's complaint goes on to allege that Forte had been conducting a Ponzi scheme since at least 1995, and that Forte, who has never been registered with the SEC in any capacity, has admitted that he misrepresented and falsified Forte LP's trading performance from the very first quarter. From 1995 through September 30, 2008, Forte and Forte LP reported to investors annual returns ranging from 18.52 percent to as high as 37.96 percent. However, from January 1998 through October 2008, the Forte LP trading account had net trading losses of approximately $3.3 million. According to the SEC, Forte claimed that "he used approximately $15 to $20 million of investor funds to repay other investors—the hallmark of a Ponzi scheme."[4] His portfolio reported a value of more than $150 million at a time when his trading account contained less than $147,000, according to the SEC complaint. Forte pleaded guilty to parallel criminal charges related to the SEC's charges and faced a maximum possible sentence of 80 years in prison, a $1.75 million fine, five years supervised release, a $400 special assessment, full restitution to the victims of his crimes, and forfeiture of all property that constitutes or is derived from his criminal proceeds. He was sentenced on November 24, 2009, to 15 years of imprisonment.[5] The case is 2:09-cr-00304-JD, *USA v. Forte*, in the Eastern District of Pennsylvania.

CRE Capital, a Fraudulent Currency-Trading Ponzi Scheme

On January 15, 2009, the Securities and Exchange Commission charged Atlanta-area firm CRE Capital Corporation and its president, James G. Ossie, with operating a Ponzi scheme. The SEC has obtained an emergency court order freezing their assets and appointing a receiver for CRE.

According to the SEC's complaint, CRE and Ossie fraudulently obtained at least $25 million from investors during 2008 by representing that CRE would use their money to engage in a currency trading program.[6] Most investors were advised that they would receive guaranteed returns of 10 percent every 30 days, although a few investors were promised as much as 20 percent. In fact, CRE's currency trading was not profitable and returns were paid to investors out of principal and money invested by later investors. CRE also falsely claimed that the firm and its program were audited by an outside accounting firm, which had concluded that CRE was not a Ponzi scheme. The SEC's complaint also charged CRE and Ossie with fraud relating to their offer to sell $100 million in CRE stock that was slated to begin in early 2009. Ossie pleaded guilty to parallel criminal charges and was sentenced to nearly seven years in prison.

Arthur Nadel's Undetected $350 Million Ponzi Scheme

Investors in a Sarasota, Florida–based hedge fund could be out $350 million, and the man behind it vanished (at least for a while). Managers of the fund are telling clients that their money is gone, and they do not know if any will be recovered. The SEC was not involved until one of the fund's partners reported that all the money was gone.

Fund principal Arthur G. Nadel, a prominent player in Sarasota social and philanthropic circles, disappeared. His wife, Peg, filed a missing person report with law enforcement after finding a suicide note.

Investors in the funds (branded Viking, Valhalla, and Scoop)—from individuals to the Sarasota YMCA Foundation—were stunned to learn they may be victims in what could become the largest investment swindle in southwest Florida history. Despite the carnage on Wall Street during the year, investors were told that their investments had earned more than 8 percent as of November 2008. "I feel abused. I feel beaten. I don't know who to believe," said Dr. Brad Lerner, who expects to lose nearly $730,000 in an individual retirement account (IRA) fund with Nadel and Neil Moody.[7]

In a statement issued to investors, Moody confirmed that the funds appear to be depleted. "Unfortunately, just yesterday afternoon we became aware of an extremely serious situation suggesting that the funds may have virtually no remaining value," Moody wrote. Moody told several investors that the funds' value totaled $350 million. The Nadels were known for their civic activities, serving on boards and donating money. Habitat for Humanity, Jewish Family & Children's Services, and Girls Inc. all received cash gifts and pledges from the couple in recent years. None had any money invested in the hedge funds. "We're very fortunate in that way," said Rose Chapman, president of Jewish Family & Children's Services. Moody was co-chairman of the organization's capital campaign. "We've received gifts from them over the years, but they were all cash," said Stephanie Faltz, Girls Inc.'s executive director. "We had no funds with them. The Nadels have been very generous. This makes me very, very sad." At Habitat for Humanity, the Nadels were the home-building charity's largest donors. One recent year, at the group's "Hammers & Hope" fund-raiser, Peg Nadel pledged an equal amount if Habitat raised $250,000.[8]

Investors said they realized something was wrong when they failed to receive their December statements, or when they did not receive requested distributions. Scoop could not meet a year-end demand for $50 million in withdrawals from investors, Dr. Lerner said. He said he invested $500,000 in the Viking IRA fund three years before, and through November it had grown to $729,844. The fund managers claimed the fund had earned 8.56 percent in 2008, down only in October, during a year when Wall Street suffered catastrophic losses. "I had no reason to believe it wasn't real," Dr. Lerner said. Moody contacted him to say that his money was gone and that Nadel had disappeared.[9]

Lerner, a physician specializing in internal medicine, was one of several investors who filed reports with the Sarasota Police Department. Another Sarasota investor, who requested anonymity, said she had asked for a year-end distribution but was stalled for a few days. Then she was told that "Art Nadel was missing with all the money." She had invested with the firm for 10 years.[10]

Foundations also appear to have been hurt. The YMCA Foundation of Sarasota believed that $1.1 million, or 13 percent of its total assets, was generating returns of at least 10 percent per year in the Valhalla Management LLC fund. Moody, a director of the YMCA and first vice chair, informed YMCA president Karin Gustafson that the money was gone. He resigned from the board at the same time, she said.[11]

Moody, also well known in social and civic circles, made an initial donation in January 2005 and bumped the total up by $1 million starting in 2007 and into 2008. "Neil made a significant gift but asked that it be invested at Valhalla," Gustafson commented. "With Neil's fund, because it was outside our investment guidelines, he did a personal guarantee of 10 percent," she added. In other words, if the fund did not generate at least 10 percent per year, Moody promised to make up the difference.

The YMCA received regular reports from Scoop Management Inc., with the last showing a November balance of $1,188,000. Gustafson could not describe how the money was invested.[12]

Tellingly (and eerily similar to Madoff), the Sarasota-based *Wall Street Digest* lauded Nadel's and Moody's experience, especially Nadel's "black box" computer trading program, in a 2003 report. On January 21, 2009, the SEC charged Nadel with defrauding investors at six hedge funds and overstating the value of investments by about $300 million. According to the SEC, Nadel provided false and misleading information to investors. The SEC said the funds appeared to have total assets of less than $1 million, contradicting materials from three of the funds that they had $342 million in assets as of November 30, 2008.[13]

The SEC's complaint alleges that the defendants provided false and misleading information to the relief defendants for dissemination to investors through account statements and through offering memoranda. For example:

- Offering materials for three of the funds represented that they had approximately $342 million in assets as of November 30, 2008. In contrast, those funds had a total of less than $1 million in assets at that time.
- Offering materials for several of the funds represented monthly returns of around 11 to 12 percent between January and November 2008. In contrast, at least three of the funds had negative returns during that time and another fund had lower than reported returns.
- One investor in one fund received an account statement for November 2008 indicating that her investment was valued at almost $420,000. In contrast, the entire fund had less than $100,000 at that time.

The SEC obtained an emergency court order to freeze Nadel's assets and included a temporary restraining order. The SEC is seeking injunctions, disgorgement with prejudgment interest, and civil money penalties.

Nadel had recently transferred at least $1.25 million from two of the funds to secret bank accounts, according to the complaint, and the SEC alleged that two groups associated with Nadel provided investment advice and also engaged in fraud as a result of his actions.[14]

Scoop Capital LLC and Scoop Management Inc. said they would consent to the preliminary injunctions and asset freezes issued by the SEC, but wouldn't admit or deny the allegations of the complaint.

Nadel was arrested by Federal Bureau of Investigation agents in Florida several days later on a criminal complaint out of New York. According to court documents, he has been charged with securities fraud and wire fraud for allegedly making misrepresentations to investors about their investments. The scheme allegedly ran from 2004 to January 2009.[15]

Nadel had been missing for about 10 days. According to a criminal complaint, he left a note for family members reflecting that "he was no longer going to be around" and, according to the criminal complaint, he overstated the value of total assets by more than $300 million. He pleaded not guilty to a 15-count indictment, and is being held pending his trial, as he was unable to make bail. Nadel initially pleaded not guilty in federal court to 15 fraud counts tied to the meltdown of his $360 million hedge fund operation. The *Sarasota Tribune* suggested that Nadel's strategy may be to show that he did not act alone, and to implicate as many people as possible, including his former partner. On February 24, 2010, before Judge Jonn G. Koeltl in New York, he pleaded guilty to causing losses to victims of $162 million.[16] Neil and Chris Moody, general partners in three of Scoop's hedge funds, have been accused in civil suits.[17] In a May 5, 2010 settlement in which they neither admit nor deny the SEC allegations, the Moodys agreed to a five-year ban from associating with any investment advisers. A federal judge issued permanent injunctions against future securities fraud violations (http://www.sec.gov/litigation/admin/2010/ia-3020.pdf).

Castaldi's $77 Million Ponzi Scheme Lasted Over 20 Years, U.S. Attorney Says

A suburban Chicago businessman who promised hundreds of investors between 10 and 15 percent annual interest rates on promissory notes he sold them was charged with operating a Ponzi scheme for more than 20 years, resulting in losses estimated in tens of millions of dollars. The defendant, Frank A. Castaldi, was charged with mail fraud in a federal criminal complaint filed on January 23, 2009, in U.S. District Court, announced Patrick J. Fitzgerald, United States Attorney for the Northern

District of Illinois, and Robert D. Grant, special agent-in-charge of the Chicago office of the Federal Bureau of Investigation.

According to the complaint, during approximately the early to mid-1980s, Castaldi, his father, and a business partner started two businesses—CZ Travel and CZ Realty. They later purchased ownership interests in First State Travel Service, Inc.; Parkway Towers Insurance Agency, Inc.; and Cumberland Realty, Inc., which later became known as Remax Cumberland Realty; Frank Castaldi was identified as the president of each business. Beginning in approximately 1986, Castaldi allegedly started offering and selling six-month promissory notes to investors, the majority of whom were people referred to him by other investors, including friends, family members, and customers of his businesses. While the vast majority of notes stated that the annual interest rate was 0 percent, Castaldi allegedly verbally guaranteed that he would pay investors annual returns between 10 and 15 percent.

Castaldi allegedly made false representations to most investors about investing their principal in his various businesses, as well as the source of the funds that he used to make their interest payments. At least five years ago, Castaldi allegedly began falsely telling investors that he was placing their money with financial institutions with which he had a special relationship and would guarantee their principal and high returns. Instead, Castaldi obtained loans and used certain investors' principal payments to make interest payments to other investors, without disclosing the true source of the interest payments, the charges allege.

The complaint affidavit stated that there were approximately 200 to 300 investors whose principal had not yet been returned and estimated that the outstanding principal owed to these investors was in the tens of millions of dollars.[18] In 2008 alone, Castaldi allegedly renewed or issued promissory notes bearing a total face value of approximately $68 million to $69 million, in many instances representing the face value of investors' initial notes plus the investors' accumulated interest, which had been rolled back into the notes.

In addition to using new investors' principal to make interest payments and return principal to earlier investors, Castaldi also lost investors' money by funding his failed banquet hall and other failing businesses, and to purchase some stocks, the charges alleged. It was believed that neither Castaldi nor his businesses had the money to pay back the investors, the complaint stated. There was no indication that the SEC was involved in the investigation leading up to Castaldi's arrest. He pleaded guilty on August 26, 2009, and awaits sentencing.

Ron Stringer's Hedge Fund Was a Ponzi Scheme, SEC Says

On January 20, 2009, U.S. District Judge Sam R. Cummings, for the Northern District of Texas, Lubbock Division, appointed a receiver and froze the assets of a former bail bondsman who was purportedly managing a hedge fund worth at least $45 million on behalf of 31 individual investors. Defendant Rod Cameron Stringer, of Lamesa, Texas, claimed that his stock trading strategy had generated annual returns as high as 61 percent, and total returns in excess of 600 percent. The SEC's complaint alleged that, in truth, Stringer had been operating a fraudulent scheme since at least 2001, during which time he misappropriated millions of dollars of investor funds to support an extremely lavish lifestyle and to make Ponzi payments to earlier investors with new investor funds. Many of Stringer's investors were elderly.

Specifically, the complaint alleged that defendant Stringer used less than 20 percent of the investors' funds to engage in securities transactions, and those transactions resulted in substantial losses, not gains, as reported to investors.[19] While Stringer's alleged fraudulent scheme began as early as 2001, an expedited investigation by the Federal Bureau of Investigation and the SEC focused on Stringer's activities since January 2007. Since that time, the complaint alleged that Stringer raised at least $8.5 million from approximately 12 to 15 investors. Contrary to Stringer's representations, only approximately $1.5 million of this amount made its way into three securities brokerage accounts, each of which was maintained in Stringer's personal name.

The exact disposition of the remaining funds is unknown at present, but it is clear that Stringer used substantial amounts of investor funds to, among other things, finance a horse-racing partnership, purchase a luxury boat, build a swimming pool at his office, purchase several pieces of expensive jewelry, pay off mortgages on at least two houses, and purchase several expensive cars and trucks. Further, since January 2007, the complaint alleges that Stringer used at least $2.4 million of the $8.5 million invested by his hedge fund clients to pay distributions and purported profits to other investors. Stringer pleaded guilty on June 29, 2009, and was sentenced on October 2, 2009, to 10 years of imprisonment and ordered to pay $7,458,238 in restitution. The civil case (*Securities and Exchange Commission v. Rod Cameron Stringer, d/b/a RCS Hedge Fund*, 5:09CV0009-C) is still pending in U.S. District Court of the Northern District of Texas.[20]

Cosmo Causes $413 Million in Losses

Right on the heels of the earlier arrests, Nicholas Cosmo, a Long Island investment firm owner, surrendered to federal authorities and was charged in an alleged $370 million Ponzi scheme, prosecutors said on January 27, 2009.[21] They later increased the amount to $413 million.

In a statement, the U.S. Attorney's office in Brooklyn, New York, said that Cosmo, 37, the owner and president of Agape World Inc. and Agape Merchant Advance LLC (AMA), has been charged with mail fraud. He faces up to 20 years in prison on the mail fraud charge. He previously pleaded guilty to mail fraud in a separate case and was sentenced to 21 months in prison in 1999. He was released in August 2000, according to the U.S. Bureau of Prisons web site.

"This defendant, who operated a classic Ponzi scheme to enrich himself and his colleagues at the expense of investors, is now in custody and the government's investigation is continuing," said U.S. Attorney Benton J. Campbell in a statement.[22]

In a letter to the court, prosecutors argued that Cosmo should be permanently detained prior to trial, saying he was a flight risk, citing his prior fraud conviction, and asserting he was an "economic danger" to community. "For the reasons set forth . . . , in particular the size and scope of the current fraud, the fact that the scheme was executed only a few years after Cosmo's prior federal fraud conviction, and the fact that he continued to perpetrate the fraud even after he was aware of the possibility of a criminal investigation, indicate that this defendant clearly poses an economic danger to the community," Assistant U.S. Attorney Grace M. Cucchissi wrote in her written statement to the court.[23]

Prosecutors said Cosmo was seen entering his offices on Long Island on January 26, 2009, by Federal Bureau of Investigation agents, but was gone by the time agents attempted to serve an arrest warrant about 1:30 P.M. EST. His vehicle was abandoned in the company's parking lot. After being contacted by the authorities, he surrendered at the U.S. Postal Inspection Service's office in Hicksville, New York. In a statement shortly after his surrender, his lawyers, Steven Feldman and Arthur Jakoby, said he intended to work with prosecutors "to allay investors' concerns."[24] Prosecutors alleged that Cosmo and others, at his direction, represented to investors that the money they invested with the Agape companies would be used to provide short-term loans to businesses and the investors would received substantial returns, ranging from 48 percent to as high as 80 percent a year.

By paying investors partial returns—represented to be profits from interest-generating loans—Cosmo persuaded current investors to invest additional funds in Agape and AMA, and also encouraged new victims to invest in the two companies. To conceal the fact that the returns paid to investors were really funds provided by new investors, Cosmo falsely inflated profits from some of the commercial loans that were actually made. For example, he distributed approximately $5.2 million to more than 100 investors, claiming that the money represented the principal and profits related to a single commercial loan. In fact, that particular loan generated less than $45,000 in interest for Agape, and the balance of the $5.2 million return was drawn from funds provided by new victim-investors.

On its web site, Agape World (now defunct) described itself as a "private bridge lender" that arranged equity participations, joint ventures, bridge loans, and other services.[25] Its sister company, Agape Merchant Advance, described itself on its web site as a provider of cash advances to merchants against their future credit card sales. A small number of loans were made to commercial borrowers, but the majority of the money was used to pay prior investors, to pay more than $55 million to brokers who recruited the investors, and to fund seven commodity futures trading accounts controlled by Cosmo, the government said. Between October 2003 and October 2008, Cosmo lost more than $80 million in those commodities accounts, prosecutors said. They also said that only a small fraction of investors' $370 million was used to make loans.

There was only about $746,000 remaining in the Agape companies' bank accounts, the government said. As is typical of Ponzi schemes, "many victims have thus far reported that they were solicited to invest with the defendant by means of family ties or friendship," said Cucchissi.[26] "Recent efforts by many victims to obtain some form of explanation from the defendant about the whereabouts of their funds have been met either by silence from representatives of the defendant, or recent additional misrepresentations about the fund being unavailable because of defaulting loans."

More than 1,500 individual investors entrusted Cosmo with their money, and more than $370 million was deposited in the Agape companies' accounts between January 2006 and November 2008, the government said. Prosecutors have moved to freeze bank accounts related to the Agape companies, Cosmo, and others, and has seized $1.5 million so far. Cosmo pleaded not guilty to 10 counts of wire fraud and 22 counts of mail fraud. According to court filings, his defense claims that the government has vastly overestimated the amount of missing money.[27] After some wrangling, he was released to monitored home confinement to await trial, but on October 9, 2009, U.S. District Judge Denis Hurley ordered him jailed immediately after a two-day hearing demonstrated that he had violated strict bail conditions barring him from access to any computer or the Internet. His trial before Judge Hurley is scheduled to begin on January 10, 2011. In a related development, federal prosecutors filed an arrest warrant for one of Cosmo's closest associates, Richard Barry, charging him with conspiracy to commit mail fraud. Settlement discussions are apparently ongoing.

Alleged $553 Million Fraud—Ponzi Scheme or Plain-Vanilla Fraud?

Two money managers have been accused of misappropriating at least $553 million and using it to fund a lifestyle of lavish homes, horses, and even an $80,000 collectible teddy bear in a fraud alleged to have begun in 1996. Paul Greenwood, 61 years old, of North Salem, New York, and Stephen Walsh, 64, of Sands Point, New York, were arrested by Federal Bureau of Investigation agents and face criminal charges of conspiracy, securities fraud, and wire fraud by the U.S. Attorney for the Southern District of New York. They were released on $7 million bail each.

Federal prosecutors allege that since 1996, Greenwood and Walsh ran a fraudulent investment-advisory scheme involving several companies, in which they promised to invest funds in an "enhanced stock indexing" program. It was represented as a conservative trading strategy that had outperformed the Standard & Poor's 500 index for more than 10 years. Prosecutors allege the men raised more than $668 million from institutional clients, and misappropriated most of the money. Court documents list several companies as being controlled by the two, including WG Trading Co. and WG Trading Investors LP in Greenwich, Connecticut, and Westridge Capital Management Inc., based in Santa Barbara, California. They owned Westridge with another individual, prosecutors say.

Greenwood and Walsh also face civil charges from the SEC and the Commodity Futures Trading Commission, which became involved in the case because it regulates futures markets. The alleged fraud involved trading in financial futures pegged to stock indexes. In its civil complaint, the SEC alleges that Walsh and Greenwood used client funds from WG Trading Investors as "their personal piggy-bank to furnish lavish and luxurious lifestyles, which include the purchase of multimillion-dollar homes, a horse farm, cars, horses, and rare collectibles such as Steiff teddy bears."[28]

Greenwood's horse farm boasts show ponies that can fetch more than $100,000, according to his web site. The CFTC said more than $160 million was used for their personal expenses, including rare books and a $3 million home for Walsh's ex-wife.

The SEC said that alleged victims include Carnegie Mellon University, which had invested more than $49 million, and the University of Pittsburgh, which put in more than $65 million, court records show. The Iowa Public Employees Retirement System said it had invested about $339 million, or 2 percent of its portfolio. The Sacramento County Employees' Retirement System in California said on its web site that it had invested $89.9 million, or 1.6 percent of its total fund.

The two universities, Carnegie Mellon and the University of Pittsburgh, filed a civil lawsuit against Greenwood and Walsh and several of the companies allegedly affiliated with them, seeking an asset freeze. According to the lawsuit, filed in U.S. District Court in Pittsburgh, the schools grew concerned after learning that the National Futures Association (NFA), an industry self-regulatory association, on February 12 had suspended the two men from NFA membership and had prohibited them from soliciting new investments.

The two "failed to cooperate with NFA and produce books and records" during an audit by the NFA, according to documents filed in the case. According to the lawsuit, on February 15, 2009, two senior Carnegie Mellon executives called James Carder, president of Westridge Capital. Carder told the two men that he "was 'devastated' by the apparent actions of Greenwood and Walsh, and their refusal to cooperate with the NFA," the lawsuit alleges. Carder "went on to say that his 'career is over,'" these documents say. The NFA's audit of Messrs. Greenwood and Walsh's firm "started the dominoes falling," an association spokesman said.[29]

If proved, this latest case "will be the biggest direct hedge-fund fraud we've seen," Chris Addy of Montreal-based Castle Hall Alternatives, which provides risk-assessment services for investors in hedge funds, was quoted as telling the *Wall Street Journal*. Donna M. Mueller, chief executive of the Iowa pension fund, said: "This is an indication that regulators moved quickly to address suspicions and are acting on our behalf."[30]

An article about Greenwood on the North Salem Bridle Trails Association web site describes him as a former economics professor who wrote a dissertation on stock-portfolio theory. The article said he had bought Old Salem Farm from the actor Paul Newman, and later sold his interest in it. A *New York Times* article in 1989 described the farm, then owned by Greenwood, as "the grandest stable for show horses" in Westchester County.[31]

The SEC described the alleged fraud as "ongoing." As recently as February 6, 2009, the defendants obtained a $21 million investment from a large state educational institution that was a client, the SEC's complaint said. Greenwood was elected supervisor (the rough equivalent of mayor) of North Salem, New York, a bucolic town north of New York City, in 2007.[32]

Westridge is structured like a hedge fund in that it raised money from big institutional clients, pooled the funds, and charged fees based on asset size and profits. Westridge Capital managed $1.8 billion in assets, the firm told the SEC in an adviser registration filing in January 2009. It oversaw a total of 20 accounts primarily for institutions including pension funds, charitable foundations, and hedge funds, according to the filing. It lists Walsh and Greenwood as principals since 1999.[33]

WG Trading Company reported consistently positive returns, according to HedgeFund.net, a provider of fund data to investors.

From January 1995 to September 2008, WG Trading never reported a negative month. Typically it gained from 0.1 percent to 1 percent a month during that time, as part of a low-risk strategy designed to out-perform major market indexes. The firm charged a management fee of 0.25 percent of assets it managed plus 30 percent of any trading profits, a higher percentage than the 20 percent typical of most hedge funds.[34]

While Greenwood and Walsh pleaded not guilty and await trial, Deborah Duffy, chief compliance officer, has pleaded guilty to money laundering, securities fraud, and conspiracy. In her allocution to the court, she said, "I assisted in the unlawful transfer to my bosses of more than ($100 million) to my bosses' benefit as loans." She is cooperating with prosecutors. At first, she said, she believed the transfers were loans that would be repaid. "After a period of time, I realized that the money was not being returned," Duffy told U.S. District Judge Naomi Buchwald.[35]

Mark Bloom Arrested on the Same Day

A third man, Mark Bloom of New York City, was charged separately by the U.S. Attorney's office in U.S. District Court in New York with securities fraud and wire fraud for allegedly defrauding investors in the North Hills Fund, an investment partnership he started, and operated separately, while working for WG Trading (which was run by Paul Greenwood and Stephen Walsh). Bloom was released on $3 million bail. On July 31, 2009, he pleaded guilty to U.S. charges that he stole at least $20 million from clients and lied to them, and that he helped sell illegal tax shelters while working earlier at BDO Seidman LLP.

Bloom pleaded guilty to five charges, including securities fraud. He admitted he stole millions from investors in the North Hills Fund, an investment partnership with more than $30 million in assets that he managed. He agreed to forfeit as much as $20 million and to cooperate with prosecutors in their continuing investigation.

"I committed securities fraud," Bloom, 57, told U.S. District Judge John Koeltl in New York. "I committed mail fraud."[36]

Bloom, a certified public accountant, said he helped sell illegal shelters to wealthy clients when he rejoined BDO Seidman, an accounting firm, in 2001. Three other BDO Seidman executives have pleaded guilty in the expanding shelter case, including its former vice chairman, Charles Bee. The case is *U.S. v. Bloom*, 09-cr-367, U.S. District Court, Southern District of New York (Manhattan).

Hedge Fund Claimed to Win in 98 of 99 Months

The U.S. government charged hedge fund manager James Nicholson with securities and bank fraud in U.S. District Court in Manhattan. Some $900 million was invested with his firm. On December 11, 2009, the former fund manager admitted to running a four-year Ponzi scheme that prosecutors say cost investors about $133 million.

The SEC, which also filed a civil complaint, alleged that Nicholson and his firm solicited investors with false claims of an almost unbroken eight-year string of investment successes. At least one Westgate fund claimed positive returns in 98 of 99 consecutive months, the SEC complaint said. Nicholson created a fictitious accounting firm and provided some investors with bogus audited financial statements, the SEC alleged. The regulator added that he created the firm under the name of an actual accountant while using his own telephone number and driver's license to set up a "virtual office."[37]

William McGrogan, an FBI special agent, wrote in the criminal complaint that the emergence of the alleged Madoff fraud in December 2008 prompted numerous investors in Westgate funds to redeem investments. Nearly two dozen received checks, collectively totaling about $5 million, but all of them were returned for insufficient funds.[38]

"I stand before you a man who is greatly ashamed," Nicholson told U.S. District Judge Richard J. Sullivan in Manhattan. "Words cannot explain how sorry I am. I take full responsibility."[39]

Nicholson, of Saddle River, New Jersey, faces up to 20 years in prison on securities fraud and mail fraud charges. He is scheduled to be sentenced June 30, 2010.

Prosecutors from the U.S. Attorney's office in Manhattan have alleged the scheme, which began in 2004, fell apart in December 2008 after a number of investors sought to redeem their investments following the arrest of convicted Ponzi scheme operator Bernard Madoff. The defense claims that Nicholson's fraud was "only" $42.3 million and asked for a sentence of 9 to 11 years; he could receive a sentence of up to 45 years.

Fake Day-Trading Ponzi Scheme

The suddenly reenergized SEC announced in February 2009 that it had filed securities fraud and other charges against former registered representative William L. Walters, formerly of Lone Tree, Colorado, for operating a Ponzi scheme promising annual returns ranging from 20 percent to 40 percent. According to the complaint, from 2003 through 2006, Walters raised approximately $16.8 million from more than 80 investors under the false pretense that he would invest their funds in day trading in the securities markets. As set forth in the complaint,[40] Walters lured investors with the promise of high returns that he falsely claimed he could achieve based on his personal expertise and prior success in day trading.

In reality, the SEC alleges, Walters deposited only a small fraction of investor funds into brokerage accounts, conducted very little trading in these accounts, and sustained heavy losses on the trading he did conduct. The SEC further alleges that Walters used approximately $11.4 million of investor funds to pay off prior investors in a classic Ponzi scheme pattern, using the rest largely to support his lavish lifestyle, with expensive cars and homes in Colorado and Hawaii. He has only been charged in a civil lawsuit.

Currency Scheme Causes Suicide and $40 Million in Losses

Many of the financial scams started small but grew fast to support lavish lifestyles. Take, for example, the suspected $40 million, five-year Ponzi scheme that came to light early in 2009 when a North Carolina man, Bruce Kramer, committed suicide, according to a Reuters report.

Claiming he was an expert mathematician, Kramer is accused of persuading 79 people to invest in what he said was a foreign currency trading operation, Barki LLC. He promised monthly returns of at least 3 percent to 4 percent, the CFTC said. Instead, he funneled money into a Maserati sports car, a $1 million horse farm, and artwork while holding "extravagant" parties, according to a CFTC complaint.[41] As the economy soured, Kramer struggled to find new clients to keep the scheme going.

In the days before his suicide, his investors demanded their money back and grew suspicious when they couldn't access their own funds, said Bart Chilton, CFTC commissioner.

The sad conclusion of this chapter is that Ponzi fraud is much more widespread than previously believed. Its victims are individuals, hedge funds, and leading institutions. The common denominator of all these frauds is that returns that appear too good to be true often are.

Chapter 25

Stanford Group

MASSIVE $7 BILLION, MULTINATIONAL FRAUD COMES TO LIGHT

H ad not Madoff pushed most other frauds out of the headlines, the Stanford case, one of the biggest alleged frauds in banking history, would likely have garnered much larger headlines.

Stanford

On top of all the smaller (and not so small) Ponzi schemes that have come to light at the end of 2008 throughout 2009, and which were recounted in the previous chapter, it appears that a $7 billion fraud may have also collapsed in February 2009. R. Allen Stanford (Sir Allen), the billionaire, fifth-generation Texan who was knighted in 2006 by Antigua, part of the British Commonwealth, is an international cricket sponsor, Washington political donor, and private banker to Latin America's wealthy. He has been accused of engaging in $9.2 billion fraudulent financial schemes that cheated 50,000 customers.

Stanford boasted about having customers in 140 countries. In addition to Stanford International Bank (SIB), his companies included the

Houston-based broker-dealer and investment adviser Stanford Group Company (SGC), and investment adviser Stanford Capital Management. They were all charged by the Securities and Exchange Commission (SEC) with massive fraud. The SEC also charged SIB chief financial officer James Davis as well as Laura Pendergest-Holt, chief investment officer of Stanford Financial Group (SFG), in the enforcement action. After graduating with a degree in finance, Stanford worked at the investment company founded by his grandfather. He made several hundred million dollars from buying cheap properties during a collapse in the Texas economy in the 1980s and selling them on at a big profit. In 1993, he took over the family business from his father and went on to expand the developing wealth-management company into Mexico and Latin America.

One of the biggest alleged frauds in banking history was stumbled upon accidentally late in 2008 by Alex Dalmady, a Venezuelan financial analyst, when he was doing a favor for a friend who planned to invest in SIB, according to the *Times* of London.[1] SIB, based in the former British colony of Antigua, seemed on the surface to be a safe bet. It boasted 30,000 clients in 131 countries, had $8.5 billion in assets, and was part of a group claiming to oversee $50 billion in assets.

Within hours, Dalmady, 48, had warned his friend that there appeared to be a gaping hole in the bank's account. "I was stunned. First, it looked so simple, so unsophisticated," he said.[2] No matter how hard he tried, he could see no way in which SIB's business model could produce the returns that it claimed to or fund the dividends that it was continuing to pay its investors. Once his findings were published in a Venezuelan magazine, the regulators took notice.

Warnings Ignored

Leyla Basagoitia, a former Stanford employee, had raised a series of red flags about the tycoon's empire in a 2003 employment dispute with her company at a tribunal run by FINRA, the finance industry's self-regulatory body. Basagoitia also alerted the SEC at about the same time, her lawyer said, echoing criticisms that the agency ignored early warnings about the alleged Ponzi scheme run by Bernard Madoff.[3]

In October 2003, Basagoitia told an arbitration panel at the National Association of Securities Dealers (NASD) that she suspected that Stanford Group Company, one of Sir Allen's key businesses, was "engaged in a Ponzi scheme to defraud its clients,"[4] according to case documents seen by the *Financial Times*. In 2007, the NASD became the Financial Industry Regulatory Authority (FINRA), which has come under scrutiny since the Stanford allegations emerged.

In a nine-point critique, Basagoitia indicated many concerns later cited by the SEC in its charges against Sir Allen's businesses, including allegations about the lack of a credible auditor, inappropriate sales of investment products, and the promise of consistently high returns that did not correspond to the reality of the markets. Basagoitia's allegations were denied by Stanford and subsequently dismissed by the dispute resolution panel. In addition, she was ordered to pay Stanford $107,782 in damages, in repayment of a loan advanced to her while an employee of the company.

Michael Falick, the lawyer who acted for Basagoitia, described the outcome of the case as "very, very sad."[5] He added that his client had contacted the SEC with details of the alleged fraud in tandem with her NASD complaint. The SEC declined to comment on Basagoitia's case, although it said that it had begun investigating the Stanford empire in the spring of 2005, well over a year earlier than officials had indicated previously.

Raids on Stanford's Offices

The federal government raided the Stanford financial empire in Houston, Memphis, and Tupelo, Mississippi. The SEC stated, "At the request of the SEC, Special Agents of the Federal Bureau of Investigation's Richmond Division today located and identified Stanford Financial Group chairman Allen Stanford in the Fredericksburg, Va., area. The agents served Mr. Stanford with court orders and documents related to the SEC's civil filing against him and three of his companies."[6]

No one knows where more than $8 billion of customer money went. FBI agents in Houston are running a parallel investigation, according to a U.S. official who spoke on condition of anonymity because the criminal probe is ongoing.

SEC Says It's a Ponzi Scheme

In an amended complaint filed a few days later, on February 27, 2009, the SEC claims that in carrying out this scheme, Stanford and Davis misappropriated billions of dollars of investors' money and falsified the Stanford International Bank's records to hide their fraud. "Stanford International Bank's financial statements, including its investment income, are fictional."[7] The SEC said it now also has evidence that Stanford and Davis misappropriated at least $1.6 billion of investor money through bogus personal loans made to Stanford personally by the bank. An undetermined amount of investors' money was also put into speculative and unprofitable private businesses. By the end of 2008, overvalued real estate, undocumented loans, and private equity made up the bulk of the bank's portfolio even though the company marketed it as a "well-diversified portfolio of highly marketable securities."[8]

To hide the fraud, the SEC said Stanford and Davis fabricated the performance of the bank's investment portfolio. Each month, the men decided on a predetermined investment return for Stanford International Bank's portfolio and had the bank's internal accountants reverse engineer its financial statements to report investment income the bank never earned.

Prosecutors Arrest Stanford and Co-Conspirators

On June 19, 2009, the Justice Department announced charges against Stanford and six others who allegedly helped the tycoon run a $7 billion swindle. At a court hearing in Richmond, Virginia, a federal judge agreed with prosecutors that Stanford posed a flight risk and ordered him to remain in custody until a future detention hearing in Houston.

Among those charged were executives of Stanford Financial Group and a former Antiguan bank regulator who prosecutors say should have caught the fraud but instead took bribes to let the scheme continue.

Robert Khuzami, the enforcement director for the Securities and Exchange Commission, said investigators have built "an impressive criminal case from the rubble of this massive fraud."[9]

If convicted of all charges in the 21-count indictment, Stanford could face as much as 250 years in prison, officials said.[10]

Dick DeGuerin, Stanford's lawyer, said in a written statement that Stanford was "confident that a fair jury will find him not guilty of any criminal wrongdoing."[11]

The indictment unsealed in Houston charged that Stanford and other executives at his firm falsely claimed to have grown $1.2 billion in assets in 2001 to roughly $8.5 billion by the end of 2008. The operation had roughly 30,000 investors, officials said.

Investigators said that even as Stanford claimed healthy returns for those investors, he was secretly diverting more than $1.6 billion in personal loans to himself.

Court papers charged that Stanford and top executives orchestrated the massive fraud by advising clients to buy certificates of deposit (CDs) from the Antigua-based Stanford International Bank. Stanford and the other executives were charged with wire fraud, mail fraud, and conspiracy to commit securities fraud. Stanford was also charged with conspiring to obstruct an SEC proceeding.

"This case is a typical Ponzi scheme, robbing Peter to pay Paul," said Gregory Campbell of the U.S. Postal Inspection Service.[12]

Prosecutor Steven Tyrrell said at the hearing that more than $1 billion from Stanford's alleged scheme remained unaccounted for, and if anyone had access to it, it was Stanford.[13]

The others indicted in the case were Stanford executives Laura Pendergest-Holt, Gilberto Lopez, and Mark Kuhrt. A separate indictment unsealed in Florida accused a fourth Stanford worker, Bruce Perraud, of destroying records important to the investigation.

Prosecutors charged Leroy King, the former chief executive officer of Antigua's Financial Services Regulatory Commission, with conspiracy to obstruct an SEC investigation. In February 2009, King told reporters the commission properly scrutinized Stanford's business. However, prosecutors allege King accepted more than $100,000 in bribes to help Stanford continue his fraud.

The SEC complaint was filed in a civil action as *Securities and Exchange Commission v. Stanford International Bank*, 09cv00298, U.S. District Court, Northern District of Texas (Dallas). The criminal indictment was unsealed and filed as *U.S. v. Stanford*, 09cr00342, in the U.S. District Court for the Southern District of Texas (Houston).

The SEC's complaint also alleged an additional scheme relating to $1.2 billion in sales by SGC advisers of a proprietary mutual fund wrap program, called Stanford Allocation Strategy (SAS), by using materially false historical performance data. According to the complaint, the false data helped SGC grow the SAS program from less than $10 million in 2004 to more than $1 billion, generating fees for SGC (and ultimately Stanford) of approximately $25 million in 2007 and 2008. The fraudulent SAS performance was used to recruit registered investment advisers with significant books of business, who were then heavily incentivized to reallocate their clients' assets to SIB's CD program.

Asset Freeze Hurts Depositors

"Once again regulators are playing catch-up," said James Cox, professor of law at Duke University.[14] Sir Allen's web of companies has drawn the attention of regulators for years. The charges filed in February 2009 against Sir Allen and two top executives involved with Stanford Financial Group and SIB stemmed from a probe that was opened in October 2006 following a routine examination.

"The SEC 'stood down' on its investigation at the request of another federal agency in the spring of 2008 but resumed it in December 2008," Stephen Korotash, an associate regional director of enforcement at the SEC's Fort Worth office, said.[15] He declined to name the other agency. Allegations of fraud and possible drug money laundering have been made against Stanford in the past 10 years, but the SEC took action only after two former employees filed a lawsuit in civil court.

The SEC shut down three of Stanford's companies, and obtained a freeze on assets. Two outfielders on the New York Yankees baseball team have been hurt by the asset freeze, according to media reports reported by Reuters. *Fox Sports* and the *New York Post* reported that Johnny Damon and Xavier Nady are among investors whose assets were frozen.[16] "My money has been frozen for four or five days," Damon told the *Post*. "Hopefully it won't be much longer. I can't pay my bills," he added.

Nady told *Fox Sports* he also has been affected. "I have the same [adviser] as Johnny," he said.[17] "He said I didn't have money with Stanford, but all my credit card accounts are frozen right now because of that situation. I'm trying to get an apartment in New York. I can't put a credit card down to hold it." Damon, 35, is earning $13 million for the 2009 season, while Nady, 30, is set to earn $6.55 million, according to Fox Sports.

Both players are clients of agent Scott Boras, who could not be reached for comment. However, Boras told *Fox Sports* his clients had no reason to worry. "Our personal-management auditors have looked into the financial elements of it," Boras said.[18] "None of our clients is in any financial jeopardy."

Other Governments Take Action

Latin American authorities moved against the local operations of the Stanford business empire, as thousands of individual depositors across the region waited anxiously for news of their savings. Venezuela seized the local operations of Antigua-based Stanford International Bank, which was charged with fraud by U.S. regulators, after hundreds of investors scrambled to recover their funds.

In Peru, the authorities moved to take control of Stanford's local business, while Mexico's banking regulator said it was investigating the local Stanford bank affiliate for possible violation of banking laws. Officials in Ecuador, Antigua, and Venezuela have also taken control of Stanford's outposts in those countries. Stanford was especially active in Venezuela, taking advantage of ongoing capital flight sparked by President Hugo Chávez's attempts to implement what he calls "twenty-first-century socialism."

"Stanford Bank Venezuela will be put on sale as soon as possible—we already know of groups interested in acquiring the bank," said Ali Rodriguez, Venezuela's finance minister.[19] Bank regulators in Antigua and Barbuda seized control of Stanford Financial Group's offshore banking operations, officials said.

Stanford's main business was headquartered on the Caribbean island of Antigua. In the past decade, Stanford and his companies spent more than $7 million on lobbyists and campaign contributions in efforts to loosen regulation of offshore banks. The authorities there fired Leroy King, and extradition proceedings are pending.

Lack of Coordination Hampers Investigation

A lack of coordination among federal agencies—and the difficulty of obtaining information from Stanford's bank in Antigua, where financial oversight is relatively light—kept regulators from gaining a full picture of the situation, current and former officials said.[20]

Two years earlier, in October 2006, the SEC's Fort Worth, Texas, office had opened a formal investigation into Stanford's sale of certificates of deposit, which eventually led to civil charges against Stanford and associates by the SEC. The 2006 probe followed a lawsuit filed earlier that year in Florida state court. In 2006, a former Stanford employee, Lawrence J. DeMaria, filed suit against Stanford in Florida state court. He alleged that the firm "was operating a 'Ponzi' or pyramid scheme, taking new money to its offshore bank, laundering the money and using the money to finance its growing brokerage business, which did not have any profits of its own."[21]

Stanford Lived High on the Hog

The lavish lifestyle enjoyed by Sir Allen was laid bare by court documents from 2007. A $10 million Florida mansion, bills of up to $75,000 for Christmas presents and children's holidays, and a $100 million fleet of private jets topped a list detailing Stanford's expensive lifestyle.

In the case, which was a paternity suit, Louise Sage Stanford said the family once lived together in a $10 million mansion known as the Wackenhut Castle after its builder, the former FBI agent and private security tycoon George Wackenhut. Her claims—admitted by Sir Allen—included his chartering of the yacht, the purchase of gifts and vacations costing from $30,000 to $75,000, and his ownership of a fleet of private jets.

Improbable and Unsubstantiated
Returns Lure Investors

Prospective investors were initially lured in by the high rates of return on certificates of deposit, far exceeding the prevailing rates. In November 2008, for example, investors were offered 5.375 percent on three-year CDs, compared with about 3.2 percent from other banks at that time. In early 2009, Stanford was offering 10 percent for a five-year lockup, the SEC said.[22]

The SEC alleged that the certificates promised "improbable and unsubstantiated high interest rates."[23] The rates were supposedly earned through SIB's unique investment strategy, which had purportedly allowed the bank to achieve double-digit returns on its investments for the past 15 years. The SEC says that Stanford misrepresented to CD purchasers that their deposits were safe, falsely claiming that the bank reinvested client funds primarily in "liquid" financial instruments (the portfolio), monitored the portfolio through a team of 20-plus analysts, and was subject to yearly audits by Antiguan regulators.

Ironically, SIB had attempted to calm its own investors by falsely claiming the bank had no "direct or indirect" exposure to the Madoff scheme. However, the SEC said Stanford and Davis were told on December 15 that the bank had lost roughly $400,000 based on indirect exposure to Madoff, contrary to its past assurances to investors.[24]

Lawyer Bails; Experts Say Lawyer Was Right

On February 14, three days before the civil charges were filed, the lawyer for Sir Allen, Thomas Sjoblom of Proskauer Rose LLP, resigned from representing him and his companies. He sent a note to the SEC in which he said, "I disaffirm all prior oral and written representations made by me and my associates to the SEC staff regarding Stanford Financial Group and its affiliates."[25]

Am Law Daily contacted a number of legal ethics experts to discuss Sjoblom's decision to come clean about a client's alleged frauds, especially given the possibility that in doing so he disclosed confidential client information to the government. Experts said Sjoblom did precisely the right thing—and, more importantly, that the federal Sarbanes-Oxley (SOX) Act likely made his decision much easier than it otherwise might have been.[26]

The SOX Act contains a provision that explicitly states that any attorney before the Securities and Exchange Commission "may" reveal confidential client information to investigators if that attorney believes that doing so will prevent a violation of the law or help rectify losses investors have already suffered, according to Bruce Green, a law professor and ethics expert at Fordham University. Nevertheless, Sjoblom withdrew from Proscauer Rose and was sued by Pendergest-Holt for representing both her and Stanford in an SEC hearing, which she believes is a conflict of interest and led to her being charged because of the poor advice that she received.

An August 27, 2009, class-action lawsuit, filed in federal court in Dallas, accuses law firm Proskauer Rose and partner Thomas Sjoblom of aiding and abetting the alleged fraud. Subsequently, Chadbourne & Parke, where Sjoblom had previously been a partner, was added as a defendant.

Multiple Red Flags Ignored

Multiple red flags were ignored by regulators. In November 2007, FINRA imposed a $10,000 fine against Stanford in relation to the company's promotion of certificates of deposit by a "bank affiliate." FINRA said the Stanford Group "failed to disclose a potential conflict of interest between it and the bank, and did not provide "fair and balanced" treatment of the risks and potential benefits of the CD investments.[27] In 2007, the SEC found that the Stanford Group did not have adequate capital to meet the requirements of being a broker-dealer.

The company paid $20,000 to settle those charges. A violation of so-called net capital requirements is fairly rare and is considered to be a serious red flag. In 2008, Stanford paid $30,000 to resolve a third set of accusations by FINRA that the company had failed in its research reports to adequately disclose a variety of research methods and the way it was valuing certain securities. Additionally, no one seems to have noticed that the bank reported identical portfolio returns of 15.71 percent for two straight years, 1995 and 1996, according to the federal complaint. For 2008, when the S&P 500 lost 39 percent, the bank said that its portfolio lost only 1.3 percent.

Duke law professor Cox said, "This case shows the inadequacies of how the SEC has carried out its inspections in the past. There needs to be a dramatic restaffing of the inspections team with people who have a lot of direct experience in the markets."[28] Alex Dalmady, the Venezuela-based financial analyst who had first claimed the company was a fraud, said that it took him just 20 minutes to create the spreadsheet that formed the basis of his analysis.

Federal authorities told *ABC News* that the FBI and others have been investigating whether Stanford was involved in laundering drug money for Mexico's notorious Gulf cartel. As part of the investigation, which has been ongoing since last year, Mexican authorities detained one of Stanford's private planes. According to officials, checks found inside the plane were believed to be connected to the Gulf cartel, reputed to be Mexico's most violent gang.[29] Stanford was charged with criminal money laundering and bribery of foreign officials as part of the 21-count indictment.

Authorities said the SEC action against Stanford may have also complicated the federal drug investigation. Perhaps the Drug Enforcement Agency was the agency that reportedly asked the SEC to "stand down."[30]

Stanford Was a Generous Contributor to the Clintons, Pelosi, and Other Politicians

A possible explanation for the limited oversight over the Stanford Group is that Sir Allen Stanford was a generous contributor to many politicians. According to the *New York Times*, "For years, Mr. Stanford and entities associated with him have been raining money on Congress, through campaign donations, trips and conferences in resort destinations. There is no evidence that this influenced the way regulators handled the company."[31]

However, since 2000 Sir Allen and his firm, along with its employees and its political action committee, had given $2.4 million in campaign contributions, according to the Center for Responsive Politics—about two-thirds to Democrats. Top recipients, the center said, included

Senator Bill Nelson, Democrat of Florida, $45,900, and Senator John McCain, Republican of Arizona, $28,150. Moreover, campaign finance records show that in 2008 Stanford gave at least $28,000 to committees controlled by Representative Charles B. Rangel, Democrat of New York. Rangel has been an outspoken champion of legislation benefiting the economic interests of Caribbean countries and residents.

Stanford and entities associated with him have also courted lawmakers with trips. For example, the Stanford Group took Senator John Cornyn, Republican of Texas, and his wife on a three-day trip to Antigua and Barbuda for a "financial services industry fact-finding mission" shortly after the 2004 election, according to data compiled by LegiStorm, which tracks Congressional ethics disclosures."[32]

The New York Times also noted,

> Mr. Stanford is also associated with the Inter-American Economic Council, a nonprofit that brings political and corporate leaders together to discuss Caribbean and Latin American business issues. Donors to the council are not public, but when it gave him a leadership award three years ago, it said he had "strongly supported" its work.
>
> The council spent more than $300,000 from 2003 to 2007 providing about 85 trips to lawmakers and their staff members—mostly to resort locations like Jamaica and the Virgin Islands, LegiStorm's data shows. Democrats took 58 trips and Republicans 27.[33]

A video posted on the Stanford firm's web site shows Allen Stanford being hugged by Speaker of the House Nancy Pelosi and praised by former President Bill Clinton for helping to finance a convention-related forum and party put on by the National Democratic Institute (NDI). "I would like to thank the Stanford Financial Group for helping to underwrite this," Clinton said to the crowd at the event.[34]

Stanford Financial was listed as the "lead benefactor" for the gathering, and Stanford was permitted to address the audience of several hundred. Stanford contributed $150,000 to underwrite the event, said NDI president Kenneth Wollack.[35] At the time the NDI had no idea of Stanford's trouble, and it has not had any contact with him since the December event, said Wollack. "We had no reason to believe that a very public company that was also engaged in philanthropic work might be suspect," said a spokesperson for the National Democratic Institute, Amy Dudley.[36]

Over the past decade, Stanford spent more than $7 million on lobbyists and campaign contributions to Washington politics in both parties, although the vast majority of the money went to Democrats. A total of $1.56 million was given to Democrats, according to OpenSecrets.org. Republicans received $840,000. Stanford also hired big-name lobby firms like DLA Piper and Parry, Romani and DeConcini.

Many of the members of Congress who received Stanford contributions vowed to turn the money over to charity. Senator Bill Nelson (D-FL) was the single biggest recipient of Stanford contributions, according to the Center for Responsive Politics. He received $45,900 from Stanford over the past 10 years. "I will give to charity any campaign contributions from him or his employees," Senator Nelson said in a statement through his spokesperson.[37]

Special Review Committee

On April 13, 2009, the Board of Governors of the Financial Industry Regulatory Authority established a special review committee to review FINRA's examination program, with particular emphasis on the examinations of FINRA member firms associated with R. Allen Stanford and Bernard L. Madoff. Between 2003 and 2005, the National Association of Securities Dealers—FINRA's predecessor entity—received credible information from at least five different sources claiming that the Stanford CDs were a potential fraud. The most striking was a July 2005 five-page referral letter from the SEC's Fort Worth office that explained in detail why the purported investment strategy of the offshore bank could not have produced the consistently high returns being paid by the CDs. The letter stated that the CD program was a "possible fraudulent scheme" and that the returns were "too good to be true."[38] According to this letter, "as of October 2004, [the Stanford firm's] customers held approximately $1.5 billion of CDs.[39]" Despite the existence of this red flag and others described in the body of this report, FINRA did not launch an investigation of whether the Stanford

CD program was a fraud until January 2008. The report acknowledged that "FINRA missed a number of opportunities to investigate the Stanford firm's role in the CD scheme."[40]

Missed Opportunities

A *Wall Street Journal* story[41] called attention to a report by the SEC's inspector general that "says SEC examiners concluded four times between 1997 and 2004 that Mr. Stanford's businesses were fraudulent, but each time decided not to go further. It singles out the former head of the SEC's enforcement office in Fort Worth, Texas, accusing him of repeatedly quashing Stanford probes and then trying to represent Mr. Stanford as a lawyer in private practice."

The *Journal* article says, "In 1997, just two years after Mr. Stanford's businesses registered with the agency, a Fort Worth examination official told her branch chief to 'keep your eye on these people'—a reference to Mr. Stanford—'because this looks like a Ponzi scheme to me and some day it's going to blow up.'"

That was among the first such findings, and it was followed by similar conclusions in 1998, 2002, and 2004, according to the inspector general."[42]

Despite the clarity of the allegation, the inspector general's office found that enforcement staff "minimally reviewed" the letter, but "decided not to investigate or open an inquiry into the matter." The enforcement chief who made the decision told investigators that the decision was made in part to "wait and see if something else would come up."

"SEC Inspector General David Kotz's report suggests the agency's mistakes in the Stanford case were in part the result of a culture that favored easily resolved cases over messier ones," the article concluded.

Pleas and Trial

James M. Davis, the former chief financial officer for Stanford Financial Group and Stanford International Bank Ltd., pleaded guilty in August

2009 to criminal charges in connection with the collapse of Stanford International Bank.

Davis pleaded guilty to one count of conspiracy to commit mail, wire, and securities fraud; one count of mail fraud; and one count of conspiracy to obstruct SEC proceedings. He faces up to five years in prison on the two conspiracy charges and up to 20 years in prison on the mail fraud charge. He agreed to cooperate with the government in its investigation. As part of the plea deal, he also agreed to a $1 billion forfeiture judgment. The government reserved the right to ask for a "downward departure" of Davis' sentence if it determines his cooperation rises to the level of "substantial assistance."[43]

Laura Pendergest-Holt, the chief investment officer for Stanford Financial Group, was also charged for obstructing and conspiring to obstruct the federal investigation into Stanford's sham money manager. She pleaded not guilty. On January 27, 2010, a federal judge ordered Lloyd's of London to pay her legal bills, as well as those of Stanford, expected to be in excess of $20 million.

The trial of Stanford and Holt, along with former Antiguan banking regulator Leroy King, who allegedly helped hide the scam from authorities, is now scheduled to begin in January 2011, as per the order of U.S. District Judge David Hittner.

Once again, we have seen how a politically well-connected, high-living executive could continue an allegedly massive Ponzi scheme for a very long time, despite obvious signs and many specific warnings.

Chapter 26

Ultimate *Chutzpah*

THE STRANGE TALE OF MARC DREIER, ESQ.

"**M**arc S. Dreier knew the 45th-floor conference room of Solow Realty well. He had been in it many times as a trusted lawyer for the company's founder," reported the *New York Times*.[1] So, nothing seemed amiss when he showed up one afternoon in October 2008 and told a receptionist he had a meeting with her boss, people associated with Solow say. Dreier was elegantly dressed, as always. He had three people with him. The receptionist ushered the group past her desk. They were sitting there, visible inside the glass-walled room, a few minutes later when the boss, Steven M. Cherniak, happened to walk by.

Cherniak would reportedly later tell people at the company how surprised he had been to see Dreier. He had not scheduled any meeting with him, and he had no idea what Dreier was up to. So the tale begins.

Arrested Twice

Marc Dreier, a prominent New York plaintiffs' lawyer and founder of Dreier LLP, a 250-person law firm, was arrested and charged by U.S. federal prosecutors with securities and wire fraud in a case alleging a multimillion-dollar real estate fraud involving hedge funds. A week before, on December 3, 2008, he had been arrested in Canada on charges alleging he tried to obtain tens of millions of dollars fraudulently.

According to the initial complaint, people in Solow's office gave little thought to Dreier's odd visit until November, when the company's founder, Sheldon H. Solow, received a disturbing call.[2] The caller wanted to let Solow know that Dreier had offered him the chance to buy promissory notes that had been issued by the company, people associated with the firm said.[3]

They were fake notes, and shortly thereafter, the real lawyers for Solow Realty got in touch with federal authorities to report their suspicions that Dreier might be engaged in financial fraud. In October 2008 a hedge fund that was considering buying some promissory notes was puzzled by the documents' fine print. Seeking more detail, the fund, Whippoorwill Associates Inc., got in touch with the auditor whose name was on the documents and soon learned they had been forged, say people familiar with the matter.

The auditor, Berdon LLP, and Solow Realty & Development Co. both informed federal authorities, who began examining the marketing of the notes. Meanwhile, Dreier's law firm, one with a national reputation and celebrity clientele, was set to collapse.

In Canada, Marc Dreier was arrested for impersonating someone else in connection with an attempt to sell notes, purportedly issued by a former client of Dreier's to a third party, at a substantial discount. Since the opening tip provided by Solow, federal authorities had been tracking what they describe as a brazen swindle of some of New York's savviest investors by one of New York's more accomplished lawyers. In all, he was accused of misappropriating over $700 million (originally thought to be $400 million).

Prosecutors also attempted to tie a former broker, Kosta Kovachev, to the fraud. Kovachev was charged with one count of conspiracy to commit wire fraud. The complaint alleges, among other things, that Kovachev pretended to be the controller of a realty company in order to effect a meeting with a hedge fund. Dreier was indicted and was charged with conspiracy, securities fraud, and five counts of wire fraud.

Dreier LLP filed for Chapter 11 protection in bankruptcy court in Manhattan. In its petition, Dreier LLP claimed to have liabilities totaling between $10 million and $50 million. Subsequently, it ceased operations, and 250 lawyers and a support staff about twice that size were all looking for new employment.

While what Dreier took is a tidy sum, it pales in comparison to the $65 billion fraud alleged to have been perpetrated by Bernard Madoff, and the Madoff story, which broke a few days later, pushed Dreier out of the headlines. Still, in many ways, it tops Madoff in sheer brazenness.

Chutzpah Par Excellence

The Talmud (B. Talmud, Tractate Sotah 49b) tells us that on the eve of the arrival of the Messiah, *hutzpa* (impudence) reaches its apogee, and the face of the generation will be as the face of the dog (i.e., everyone out for himself). To that extent, Marc Dreier must be the annunciator heralding the coming of the Messiah. It is hard to envision a scam with more *chutzpah*.

(For more information on Marc Dreier's story, see Ann Woolner's account for Bloomberg at http://tinyurl.com/9g8ld5.)

Dreier repeatedly pulled off tricks worthy of a Hollywood B movie.

As the U.S. Attorney's office in Manhattan tells it, he would lie his way into an accounting firm's or real estate developer's offices as if he had business there. He then would use their conference rooms for meetings with hedge fund officials to make it seem that the accountants or developers were in on the deal, according to the feds.

He forged the accounting firm's letterhead, fabricated financial statements, and forged audit letters. He would arrange conference calls between hedge fund representatives and someone pretending to be the chief executive of Solow Realty, the developer and former Dreier client whose fake notes the feds say Dreier was trying to sell.

That someone was former broker Kosta Kovachev, who posed as Solow's controller or chief executive and was Dreier's dirty tricks guy, prosecutors in New York alleged. If the ruse needed a new telephone number or e-mail address, no problem.

"Mr. Dreier is the Houdini of impersonation and false documents," Assistant U.S. Attorney Jonathan Streeter told a magistrate judge in Manhattan. "He has been fooling some of the most sophisticated institutional investors in the world."[4] A judge nevertheless ordered him released to tight conditions of house arrest.

If it weren't for the shadow cast by Madoff's gigantic con, which came to light a few days later and grabbed all the headlines, the story of Marc Dreier's chutzpah would be provoking the sort of dumbstruck amazement that Madoff's tale now elicits.

Dreier, described as an abrasive fellow, relied on outrageous deceptions rather than on his reputation for honesty and integrity.

Maximum Chutzpah

Perhaps Dreier's nerviest caper was the final one. Fortress Investment Group, a New York–based asset management firm he was courting to sell them notes, wanted to meet with the Ontario Teachers' Pension Plan, the alleged note holder, according to the *Toronto Globe and Mail*.

Fortress wanted assurances the fund would guarantee its assets, so Dreier arranged a face-to-face meeting in the fund's offices, supposedly between Fortress and a pension executive, the newspaper reported.

The only problem was that the pension fund had no idea Dreier had cooked up this deal in which it played no role. So Dreier arranged to meet in Toronto with Michael Padfield, a senior lawyer to the pension plan, regarding an unrelated deal. This gave Dreier entry into the fund's offices, where Padfield exchanged business cards with Dreier.

The meeting lasted only about 15 minutes, as Padfield wasn't interested in the deal Dreier was proposing. So when Dreier asked if he could wait in the fund's office for his plane to be ready for the trip back, Padfield agreed. About an hour after that, Fortress executive Howard Steinberg showed up at the fund's offices, where Dreier intercepted him, brought him into a conference room, and pretended to be Padfield, according to authorities and news accounts. They say he gave Steinberg the business card Padfield had given him and signed papers in Padfield's name. He was offering to sell performing Solow Realty notes with a $44.7 million face value for $33 million, a whopping discount.

Who Was That Man?

Dreier might have pulled it off if Steinberg hadn't found the lawyer's behavior odd. After Dreier, posing as Padfield, left the meeting, Steinberg asked the pension fund's receptionist whether the man he'd been with was Padfield. The answer was no, the Toronto newspaper reported. Dreier was arrested by local police on a charge of impersonation, spent three days in jail, posted a $100,000 bail, and flew to New York on December 7, where he was arrested at LaGuardia Airport.

This time it was U.S. authorities who nailed him, as they had been watching him since they were tipped off by Solow and the accountant whose name Dreier admitted (in his plea) to forging. In fact, the episode in Toronto unfolded not long after that accountant confronted Dreier in a telephone conversation. Dreier didn't deny his deception, but said he was "ashamed" of his "very serious" misdeeds.[5]

Unbeknownst to Dreier, the accountant was recording the conversation for the U.S. Attorney's office in Manhattan, which would prove to be Dreier's undoing.

Outlandish as his schemes may seem, he managed to fool at least 13 hedge funds. One fund wired $100 million to buy the fake notes. Another sent $13.5 million. It wasn't just outsiders Dreier targeted, according to authorities.[6] He was also draining clients' escrow funds, according to statements lawyers within his firm gave to the SEC. Any lawyer knows that client escrow funds are sacrosanct, not to be touched, and not to be used by the law firm or its lawyers except for the client's purposes. Dipping into that money is grounds for disbarment, lawsuits, and criminal charges.

At the Dreier firm, only Marc Dreier could move funds into and out of client escrow accounts. In fact, any disbursement from just about any of the firm's bank accounts had to be approved by Dreier, according to the firm's controller, John Provenzano, and one of its partners, Joel Chernov.

Missing Funds

The firm discovered that some $27 million was missing from client accounts. The employee who oversaw the escrow accounts told Chernov she had moved $37.5 million out of a single client's fund from a $38 million deposit. So when Dreier called after his arrest in Toronto and asked Provenzano to wire him $8 million, Provenzano refused. Dreier called the next day and asked for $10 million to be wired to one of his personal accounts. Provenzano again said no. "He asked me to connect him to someone at the firm's bank, and I did so, and I heard him instruct the bank employee to make the transfer," Provenzano said in a statement to prosecutors.[7]

There are still many unanswered questions. Foremost, of course, is "Where did the money go?"[8] Some of it surely seems to have gone for expensive artwork and a lavish lifestyle. Dreier's assets include a waterfront home in the Hamptons, a Manhattan triplex, and a place on Ocean Avenue in Santa Monica, California. In addition, he kept a Mercedes 500 in New York, an Aston Martin in California, and a 121-foot blue-and-white Heesen motor yacht with a Jacuzzi and a crew of 10 docked in Manhattan or St. Maarten. Still, it seems that his lifestyle doesn't fully account for the $700 million.

New York Magazine suggested that Dreier LLP overexpanded too quickly, and that Marc Dreier agreed to pay excessively lavish salaries to recruit name talent.[9] In a superseding indictment, Drier was charged with a new count of money laundering. From 2004 to 2008, prosecutors allege, the attorney deposited funds from his note sales into accounts held by his former law firm, Dreier LLP. The attorney now faces a total of eight criminal counts, including conspiracy, securities fraud, and five counts of wire fraud.

Prosecutors demanded, and the judge ordered, that Dreier forfeit about $700 million, including all of his interest in a yacht, luxury cars, and more than 200 works of art by such masters as Henri Matisse and modern artists Andy Warhol, Jasper Johns, and Roy Lichtenstein.

Dreier pleaded guilty to conspiracy to commit securities and wire fraud, securities fraud, wire fraud, and money laundering. The charges carry a potential prison term of 30 years to life in prison. Authorities say Dreier received $670 million between 2004 and 2008 from the sale of fictitious securities. Investors may have lost as much as $400 million. "I understand that everything I was doing was illegal," Dreier told U.S. District Judge Jed Rakoff on the day before his 59th birthday, Bloomberg.com reported.[10] Prior to sentencing, he was confined to his home and monitored. The prosecution asked for a sentence of 145 years; the defense requested 10 to 12 years. Judge Rakoff ultimately gave him a 20-year sentence, ordered the forfeitures, and also ordered him to pay $387.7 million in restitution. The judge scolded prosecutors for wanting to jail Dreier for as long as Ponzi swindler Bernard Madoff. "Is the government serious about asking for 145 years?" he asked. "To me, for the government to ask for 145 years is to demean the sentence Judge [Denny] Chin imposed on Mr. Madoff.[11] It says the government is not sensitive to the need to be fact-specific. . . . He [Dreier] is not going to get any sympathy from this court, [but] he is no Mr. Madoff under any analysis."

Kosta Kovachev pleaded guilty to one count of conspiracy to commit securities fraud and to one count of wire fraud. "I helped him," Kovachev said.[12] He faced 51 months to 63 months in prison as part of a stipulated sentencing guidelines range under a plea agreement with prosecutors. On March 31, 2010, he was sentenced to a term of three years and ten months of imprisonment.

Vanity Fair ran a long story based on presentencing interviews with Dreier entitled "Marc Dreier's Crime of Destiny," by Bryan Burrough, a former *Wall Street Journal* reporter.[13] What emerges is a sad story of a brilliant, compulsive, and narcissistic lawyer whose reach exceeded his grasp, so he succumbed to illegal means to get what he felt he needed, and who sincerely regrets his actions.

The case is *U.S. v. Dreier*, 09–cr–85, U.S. District Court, Southern District of New York (Manhattan).

It is likely that eventually more of the story will tumble out. It will probably make for a good movie, in which case any monies Dreier earns will go toward victim restitution.

Marc Dreier's bold frauds were allowed to continue for so long because he appealed to greed by promising outsized returns, he was an attorney with a patina of respectability, and due diligence was lax.

Chapter 27

Detecting Fraudulent
Financial Schemes

HOW MUCH TO REGULATE?
HOW MUCH TO VERIFY?

I t's obvious, from all of the frauds that we have recounted, that the status quo for detection of financial fraud is woefully inadequate. In this chapter, we look at some of the remedies that have been proposed.

More Regulation Is *Not* the Answer

The magnitude of losses inflicted by the many Ponzi schemes and other financial frauds suggests that something must be done. Congress held hearings on the Madoff scheme to try to understand what happened, and what to do to prevent a recurrence.

In her testimony before Congress, and to her credit, Professor Tamar Frankel of Boston University Law School made a compelling case that more regulation is *not* the answer. The rules, she says, are already in place. They just aren't always followed, and by the time the rule breaking is discovered, a lot of damage has already been done.

To help detect Ponzi schemes early, Professor Frankel suggests that the government must conduct thorough and frequent examinations of broker-dealers, advisers, and money managers, whether they are registered or exempt from registration, so long as they control significant amounts of investor money.

Trust, but Verify

In making this suggestion, Professor Frankel (perhaps unwittingly) is embracing a concept called *trust, but verify*, which was a signature phrase of President Ronald Reagan. He usually used it while discussing relations with the Soviet Union and he almost always presented it as a translation of the Russian proverb *doveryai, no proveryai*. For example, at the signing of the Intermediate-Range Nuclear Forces Treaty (INF Treaty) in 1987 he used it, and his counterpart Mikhail Gorbachev responded: "You repeat the phrase every time we meet," to which Reagan answered "I like it."[1] (The phrase has been attributed to Damon Runyan, 1884–1947.)

Some managers have already adopted this strategy. The *Financial Times* reported that DE Shaw, one of the largest U.S. hedge funds, plans to appoint independent administrators to provide third-party checks that its investments exist, in an effort to reassure investors panicked in the wake of the alleged various large Ponzi schemes.[2] The move by DE Shaw comes amid a growing clamor from hedge fund investors for more use of independent administrators, already standard in Europe but rare among U.S. funds.

"Up until recently, valuation was the issue investors in alternatives were most focused on," said Darcy Bradbury, a spokesman for DE Shaw, which appointed HSBC last year to provide independent checks of asset prices. "Now we're going beyond that and looking at third-party administration arrangements where an administrator would also substantiate positions and cash balances."

Shortly after Bernard Madoff was arrested, Union Bancaire Privée (UBP), the second-biggest investor in hedge funds and a major loser from the alleged fraud, began warning some of the biggest U.S. hedge funds to introduce independent administrators or see it pull out. The funds without independent administrators from which it threatened to pull out included DE Shaw and Millennium, as well as ESL Investments, run by Eddie Lampert, chairman of department store group Sears Holdings; Renaissance Technologies, run by billionaire mathematician Jim Simons; Chicago's Citadel, run by Ken Griffin; SAC Capital, run by billionaire art collector Steven Cohen; Cerberus, one of the oldest hedge funds; Dallas-based HBK Capital; and Caxton Associates, run by billionaire Bruce Kovner.

Madoff's confessed fraud was possible because he operated a brokerage, giving him custody of assets, something highly unusual in the hedge fund industry. However, he also had no independent administrator to check valuations or assets, unlike the practice at many funds.

Administrators and European hedge fund lobby groups argue that having the additional check of an independent administrator is one of the main reasons there is little or no hedge fund fraud in the region, although managers in Europe are also regulated.

"Innocence Is Gone"

Erin Arvedlund, who questioned Madoff's purported returns in *Barron's* back in 2001, wrote a piece for http://www.portfolio.com in December 2008. She observed, "Today, the innocence is gone. That Madoff mythology has evaporated, and in its wake even the most smug hedge fund investors are worried."

"There will be a lot more Madoffs discovered," says Edward Seidle, founder of Benchmark Financial Services, which specializes in investigations of pension fraud and money management abuses.[3] "It will no longer be impolite to ask for the documents, sit down, and figure out whether the manager is for real."

Regulators: Fix Yesterday's Problems with More Regulation

"Whenever frauds like Sadleir's or Madoff's are exposed, people clamor for government regulation," George Robb, a professor at William Patterson University in Wayne, New Jersey, and author of *White-Collar Crime in Modern England: Financial Fraud and Business Morality 1845–1929*, told Bloomberg. "The problem with regulation is it's always reactive; they solve the last scandal. In 10 years people forget and crooks figure out a way to circumvent it," he concluded.

Taking the opposite view of Professor Frankel, Adair Turner, chairman of the British Financial Services Authority, called for "profound" regulatory change to prevent future financial crises. Parliament went through a similar exercise after Sadleir's fraud in 1856, including Treasury select committee hearings. Among the results was the introduction of limited liability banks in which each investor was liable only for the amount of money he or she put into the company, a change designed to protect shareholders from the misdeeds of others.

SEC Weighs In

During the congressional hearings, SEC officials admitted that the agency should address weaknesses in the rules that permitted Madoff to operate without much skepticism. They singled out a rule that allows an investment adviser to keep money and securities at an affiliated brokerage firm or entity, instead of a wholly independent body that would safeguard the assets. The SEC said more than 1,000 investment advisers entrust the custody of their accounts to an affiliate. "It gives the possibility for fraud. That is one of the changes I hope the commission will strongly consider in the days ahead," said Lori Richards, head of the SEC's inspections group.[4]

In hearings at the Senate Banking Committee, Linda Thomsen, chief of the Securities and Exchange Commission's enforcement division, suggested that federal prosecutors may pursue charges against Madoff over what they believe were his lies to SEC officials during past examinations. However, she declined multiple times to comment specifically on the SEC investigation or its past examinations of Madoff's firm, citing the current inquiry. "We want to be sure to preserve the integrity of any criminal investigation," she told the committee. She also said that "some of the conduct in the prior investigation may itself have amounted to crimes," such as "violations of perjury" laws.[5] "During the current crisis, the SEC has become particularly concerned about possible hedge-fund offering frauds, where fraudsters use the non-transparent and largely unregulated status of hedge funds to conceal large Ponzi schemes," SEC Commissioner Elisse Walter told the House Financial Services Committee.[6]

New Regulation

A bill to improve enforcement of securities fraud and financial institution fraud involving asset-backed securities and fraud related to federal assistance and relief programs has been reported out of the Senate Judiciary Committee. CCH Financial Crisis News Center reported that the bill was introduced by Senator Patrick Leahy, chair of the Judiciary Committee, and Senator Charles Grassley. Fraud contributed to an unprecedented collapse in the mortgage-backed securities market, he noted, and as Congress passes legislation to make sure this kind of collapse cannot happen again, a component of reform must be the reinvigoration of federal anti-fraud measures.

The Fraud Enforcement and Recovery Act of 2009 (Public Law 111-21), signed into law on May 20, 2009, makes a number of important improvements to fraud and money laundering statutes to strengthen prosecutors' ability to combat this growing wave of fraud. Specifically, the legislation amends the federal securities fraud statute to cover fraudulent schemes involving commodity futures and options, including derivatives involving the mortgage-backed securities that caused such damage to the banking system.

The legislation includes important improvements to federal fraud and money laundering statutes to strengthen prosecutors' ability to confront fraud in mortgage lending practices, to protect Troubled Asset Relief Program (TARP) funds, and to cover fraudulent schemes involving commodity futures, options, and derivatives, as well as making sure the government can recover ill-gotten proceeds from crime.

The bill also amends the definition of the term *financial institution* to extend federal fraud laws to mortgage lending businesses that are not directly regulated or insured by the federal government. These companies were responsible for nearly half the residential mortgage market before the economic collapse, yet they remain largely unregulated and outside the scope of traditional federal fraud statutes. This change will apply the federal fraud laws to private mortgage businesses, just as they apply to federally insured and regulated banks.

Expanding the term *financial institution* to include mortgage lending businesses will also strengthen penalties for mortgage frauds and the civil forfeiture in mortgage fraud cases. It would also extend the statute of limitations in investigations of mortgage fraud cases to be consistent with bank fraud investigations. The new definition would also provide for enhanced penalties for mail and wire fraud affecting a financial institution, including a mortgage lending business.

The bill amends the major fraud statute to protect funds expended under the Troubled Asset Relief Program and the economic stimulus package, including any government purchases of preferred stock in financial institutions. This change will give federal prosecutors and investigators the explicit authority they need to protect taxpayer funds. In addition, this amendment will make sure that federal prosecutors have jurisdiction to use one of their most potent fraud statutes to protect the government assistance provided during this most recent economic crisis, including money from the TARP and circumstances where the government purchased preferred stock in companies to provide economic relief.

This bill will also strengthen one of the core offenses in so many fraud cases, money laundering, which was significantly weakened by a recent Supreme Court case. The bill would amend the federal criminal money laundering statute to make clear that the proceeds of specified unlawful activity include the gross receipts of the illegal activity, not just the profits of the activity. The money laundering statutes make it an offense to conduct financial transactions involving the proceeds of a crime, called specified unlawful activity in the statutes. These statutes, however, do not define the term *proceeds*, and the term has been left to be defined by the courts. For 22 years, since the money laundering statutes' enactment in 1986, courts have construed *proceeds* to mean gross receipts and not net profits of illegal activity consistent with the original intent of Congress.

However, in *United States v. Santos*, 128 S.Ct. 2020, the Supreme Court suggested that the term *proceeds* was ambiguous and gave the term a narrower meaning. In this decision, according to the chair, the Court mistakenly limited the term *proceeds* to the profits of a crime, not its receipts, and as a result, the decision limited the money laundering statute to only profitable crimes, and permits criminal defendants to reduce their culpability for money laundering by deducting the costs of their criminal conduct.

For example, under the decision, an executive who committed securities fraud could not be charged with money laundering if the fraud were unsuccessful in making a profit, even though there was a fully completed financial transaction. This decision is contrary to the intent of Congress in passing the money laundering statutes, said the chair, and weakens one of the primary federal tools used to recover the proceeds of illegal activity, including mortgage and securities frauds.

In April 2010, U.S. Senator Charles Schumer and SEC Chairman Mary Schapiro began advocating for self-budgeting authority for the SEC amid concerns Congress may strip the measure from its regulatory overhaul.[7]

How to Spot a Fraudster

Dr. Henry Jarecki, longtime managing director of Gresham Investment Management, a $4 billion fund, shared some unique insights with the *Financial Times* about how to spot a fraudster. He is uniquely qualified to do so, being not only a money manager but also a psychiatrist, formerly on the faculty of Yale Medical School. He pointed out these personal characteristics of the con artist. "I've been encountering them through my work for over 30 years, and there are some interesting common characteristics I've noticed," he said.[8] "Many of them are, or appear to be, religious, or at least assume a pose of religiosity."

He went on to say that one unnamed Middle Easterner he knew told him, based on a few centuries of his family's experience in the banking business, "Never do business with a religious fanatic." He also noted that most scam artists don't drink to excess as they may fear a sudden burst of candor.[9]

"On the other hand," he said, "they throw big parties in the Jay Gatsby manner. The parties are useful for another characteristic, which is a penchant for collecting celebrities and politicians."[10]

Dr. Jarecki also observed that, like Madoff, they are usually very clean, almost obsessively so. Their offices are often spotless, with little of the normal clutter of someone engaged in a real business. It's as if they want to rid themselves of the invisible dirt.

He also believes that the scam artist often either won't look you in the eye or looks you in the eye too directly for too long. "They deal well with crisis," he said, "since they have always known it was coming to an end someday."[11]

"There are few women at this level of crime. It seems to be more of a boy's adventure thing. While they're surrounded by acolytes and acquaintances before discovery, in the end it turns out that nobody really knew them well, and they didn't have any real friends," he concluded.[12]

How One Bank Avoided Problems

C. Hoare & Company, a family-owned bank that has operated on London's Fleet Street since 1672, credits its status as the sole U.K. bank to reject limited liability for its success in navigating the credit crisis unscathed. "Unlimited liability, the joy of it is it keeps you jolly nervous," CEO Alexander Hoare said in an interview with *Bloomberg .com*. "Everything apart from the shirt on our back is at risk."[13]

Harvey Pitt's Suggestions

Harvey Pitt, the former SEC chairman, advises that to prevent future frauds a new audit system overseen by the SEC be implemented. "What is needed is a system in which everyone who takes money from the public should be inspected every year, or for smaller firms perhaps every other year, by a completely independent, wholly outside expert entity." The audit would determine whether there were "actual assets" behind financial statements. Pitt also believes "people who invest money should be required to deal through a non-affiliated entity" to prevent self-dealing.[14]

Jim Chanos, the fund manager and well-known short seller, stated in the same "Round Table" discussion that he believes that "if Bernie Madoff had been public, he probably would have never gotten as far" because of scrutiny by journalists, short sellers, or internal whistle-blowers.[15]

Both Pitt and Chanos said they believed there is criminality among some of the major financial institutions hit by the financial crisis. "There was criminality going on in the executive suites of these firms . . . because they were materially misrepresenting the financial shape of these firms as they were raising tens of billions of dollars from new investors," Chanos said. "The level of accounting chicanery that is going on in these major institutions is stunning." Pitt agreed there was criminality, though he added, "I can't say whether it was the executive suite or not."[16]

Pitt said the SEC isn't properly staffed to ferret out fraud. "You can't take young people, two, three, four years out of college, pay them $50,000, $60,000, $70,000, and expect them to have the sophistication to assess a $20 billion hedge fund," he said. Later, he said there is "a lack of real sophistication" at the SEC. "I can say this as a lapsed lawyer . . . the SEC is overlawyered in the sense that it's heavily dependent on lawyers. There aren't enough economists, there aren't enough MBAs, there aren't enough market specialists in the agency providing the kind of additional sophistication" that the SEC needs.[17]

Rating Agencies Need More Oversight

Separately, Mary L. Schapiro, SEC chair, indicated to Congress that the agency may need to seek broader authority from Congress to oversee credit rating firms. The agency was granted some authority over them for the first time in 2006, allowing the agency to pass some rules relating to disclosure and curbing conflicts of interest. Since then, credit rating firms have been criticized by some for exacerbating the financial crisis after they gave good ratings to mortgage-backed products.

The SEC is still considering some proposed rules related to credit rating firms as part of its mandate from the 2006 legislation, but Schapiro indicated she may wish to go beyond the scope of that bill. "I'm not sure if it's enough, to be perfectly honest," she told lawmakers before the House Appropriations Financial Services Subcommittee.[18]

Whistle-Blower Tells All and Makes Suggestions

Perhaps the most interesting and devastating testimony was provided by Harry Markopolos, an investment manager turned financial fraud investigator, at hearings conducted by the House of Representatives.[19]

Markopolos charged that the SEC simply could not understand the entities and transactions it was supposed to be regulating.

One of the members of the subcommittee, Rep. Gary Ackerman, after listening to Markopolos's testimony, blasted the SEC, saying to its head of enforcement, "I am frustrated beyond belief. We are talking to ourselves and you are pretending to be here. You've told us nothing. What the heck went on? What went wrong? One guy with a few friends and helpers found this fraud over a decade. You guys couldn't find your backside with two hands when the lights are on. You have totally failed in your mission."[20]

Markopolos told the committee, "As early as May 2000, I provided evidence to the SEC's Boston Regional Office that should have caused an investigation of Madoff. I re-submitted this evidence with additional support several times between 2000 and 2008, a period of nine years. Yet nothing was done. Because nothing was done, I became fearful for the safety of my family until the SEC finally acknowledged, after Madoff had been arrested, that it had received credible evidence of Madoff's Ponzi Scheme several years earlier. . . . I gift wrapped and delivered the largest Ponzi scheme in history to the SEC, and somehow, they couldn't be bothered to conduct a thorough and proper investigation because they were too busy on matters of higher priority. If a $50 billion Ponzi scheme doesn't make the SEC's priority list, then I want to know who sets their priorities."[21]

More significantly, he claimed that the SEC was improperly staffed. He advocated upgrading SEC employee qualifications and education, adopting industry compensation guidelines to better compete for talent, and revamping the examination process. Markopolos characterized the current state of the SEC as a group of "3,500 chickens tasked to chase down foxes, which are faster, stronger and smarter than they are."[22] He said that the SEC staff would have trouble finding first base at Fenway Park if seated in the Red Sox dugout and given an afternoon to find it.

Markopolos Makes Recommendations to Catch Fraudsters

Markopolos outlined his recommendations for upgrading SEC employee qualifications and educational budgets to improve the quality of the staff.

He pointed out that there is no entrance exam or test of an employees' knowledge of the capital markets for SEC employees. "By failing to hire industry savvy people, the SEC immediately sets their employees up for failure and so it should not be surprising that the SEC has become a failed regulator," he said.[23]

To remedy this, Markopolos suggested that a suitable test of financial industry knowledge such as the Chartered Financial Analyst Level I exam should be given to prospective SEC employees. He also advised that a skills inventory of current SEC staffers should be undertaken to measure skills shortfalls and gauge where the SEC stands.

Markopolos said the new SEC chair, Mary Schapiro (who had just been confirmed before his testimony), "will find that she has too many attorneys and too few professionals with any sort of relevant financial background."[24]

The SEC should also seek diverse skill sets and backgrounds for its employees, according to Markopolos, who said that "right now the SEC is overlawyered." Another suggestion he made to improve employee quality would be an expanded tuition reimbursement program that would pay 100 percent of relevant postgrad classes if the employee commits to one year of additional government service for each year of education. In addition, Markopolos stressed that SEC staffers should be allowed and encouraged to attend industry conferences, particularly those that feature new securities, as well as subscribe to industry publications to stay on top of marketplace trends and potential fraud.

"Sending SEC staff to conferences with a written information collection plan, under the supervision of a senior person, with the goal of obtaining information and marketing literature about new products and querying attendees about frauds within the industry is a cost-effective solution for keeping the SEC on level ground with the industry it regulates," said Markopolos.[25]

In order to properly regulate, Markopolos said that the SEC must hire staffers that know how to "take apart complex financial instruments and put them back together again." Beyond upgrading staff at the junior and middle level, he also advocated recruiting what he termed "foxes" for senior, high-paying positions. These foxes would ideally "have gray hair," and a position at the SEC would be a capstone on an already illustrious career. The SEC would need to offer lucrative pay for these foxes, with incentive pay for catching fraudsters and bringing them to justice, he added.[26]

Compensation in particular needs to be updated for a new, effective regulatory body, said Markopolos. He said that compensation should be increased and expanded to include incentives or bonuses tied to enforcement revenues or fines brought in by each office. "Each SEC regional office should get back some pre-set percentage of the fines it brings in, and I recommend a 5 percent level initially towards that office's bonus pool," explained Markopolos.[27] He also recommended that fines be triple the amount of actual damages so taxpayers would not have to pony up any money for the bonus pools. In addition, those fined would also pay the actual costs of the investigation.

In terms of staff salaries, Markopolos said they should be increased to $200,000 in financial centers such as New York, Boston, Chicago, Los Angeles, and San Francisco and $100,000 to $150,000 in regions with a lower cost of living, plus annual year-end bonuses when merited. "All compensation over and above the base compensation would come from each Regional Office's bonus pool and be tied directly to the fines that each office generates," he stated.[28]

Markopolos also advised using metrics to quantify the regulators' effectiveness. These could include fines, dollar damages to investors recovered, dollar damages to investors prevented, fine revenues per employee per regional office, and the number of complaints from Congress to the regulators complaining about the severity of the fines or the thoroughness of the investigations. Markopolos also made the point that the SEC should not stop just because some action is not illegal and should not ignore unethical behavior in the marketplace. "Policy standards and requirements including good ethics, fair dealings, full transparency and full disclosure need to be adopted and enforced," he said.[29]

Finally, Markopolos was adamant that the examination process at the SEC should be revamped. He explained his personal experience with the SEC's examinations. He said that as a portfolio manager and a chief investment officer at a multibillion-dollar equity derivatives asset-management firm, "an area considered high-risk by the SEC," his firm was inspected every three years.

Some of the flaws he pointed out were:

- The SEC never once sent an examiner with any derivatives knowledge.
- SEC audit teams were very young and rarely had any industry experience.

Audit teams come into the firm with a list of documents and records they need to examine. They go directly to the compliance officer for these records and then hole up in a conference room to pore over the documents. "The team only interacts with the inspected firm's compliance team, not the traders, not the portfolio managers, not the client service officers and not management. . . . They're sitting like ducks in the inspected firm's conference room and getting fed controlled bits of paper by the firm's compliance staff."

Using Social Networking and Technology Tools

Bradley W. Block makes an interesting suggestion in his Huffington Post article, "Madoff, Merkin and the Epidemiology of Fraud." He says:

> Analyzing the social networks of Madoff and his clients will give us a better understanding of how trust, exclusivity, and connections accelerated the spread of the Madoff virus. This information will not only show how social networks fuel decisions with far-reaching consequences, but could also shed further light on the differences between the networks of enterprises that are legitimate and those that are not.[30]

Block seems to have struck a chord. Mary Schapiro, the new SEC chair, said: "I have also spent much of my first week and a half on the job in meetings with my fellow Commissioners and the agency's senior staff to discuss other ways in which we can reinvigorate the SEC's enforcement program, including improving the handling of tips and whistleblower complaints and focusing on areas where investors are most at risk. And I anticipate that we'll be making further improvements in the coming weeks and months to ensure swift and vigorous enforcement."[31]

Stephen Labaton reported in his *New York Times* article entitled "S.E.C. Chief Pursues Tougher Enforcement: "Ms. Schapiro and her aides have begun consulting officials at intelligence and law enforcement agencies about the technology they use to sort through mounds of information. Her hope is to borrow techniques that could help the commission sift through hundreds of thousands of tips it receives annually from informants. Last year, the agency received more than 700,000 such tips."[32]

In addition, Schapiro is streamlining the process of pursuing investigations and settlements. In one of her first decisions, she reversed a policy of her predecessor, Christopher Cox, which had required enforcement lawyers to obtain the consent of commissioners before moving to resolve major cases. With the commission dominated by opponents of government regulation, this had the effect of discouraging cases and reducing penalties. "This agency did not pursue some critical issues and problems," she said in a brief interview last week. "We need to be transparent about what we missed. We need to learn from these tragedies."[33]

Schapiro also stated that the SEC will make changes that will deal with issues including custody of customer assets and auditing of investment advisers—both problem areas exposed by the Madoff affair. Madoff had said he operated as a broker-dealer and an investment adviser. He held custody of the advisory accounts at his brokerage arm, in line with SEC rules that permit self-custody under certain circumstances. The Madoff firm was audited by a three-person auditing firm in the New York City suburbs that wasn't registered with the Public Company Accounting Oversight Board, which conducts inspections of auditors. For years the SEC allowed brokers that weren't publicly traded to use unregistered auditors.

All of these steps, taken together, can help to catch frauds earlier, but are unlikely to eliminate them totally.

The inspector general of the SEC, H. David Kotz, released two separate reports—one for the agency's inspections and examinations office and one for its enforcement branch—detailing a number of process fixes, many of which stemmed from errors made in apprehending Bernard Madoff. The two reports contain a total of 58 recommendations, all of which were accepted by the SEC.

In addition to having at least two experienced persons review each tip and complaint, the report also seeks to have the SEC set up a more sophisticated system for handling incoming information. The system would require documentation of why a complaint "was or was not acted upon."[34]

Kotz also recommends that the agency establish and annually review guidelines that require all complaints that appear to be credible to be followed up with "in-depth" interviews to assess the validity of the claims.

Responding to concerns that SEC investigators of the Madoff scam did not have sufficient experience, Kotz said the agency should put in place procedures to ensure that investigations are assigned to teams, where one individual has "specific" knowledge of the subject matter, such as Ponzi schemes.

This recommendation responds in part to one point discussed in the September 2 report, which revealed that the majority of a 2005 investigation into Madoff was performed by a staff attorney who had recently graduated from law school and had joined the SEC only 19 months before she was assigned the investigation. The attorney had never been the lead staff attorney on any investigation before, the report said.[35]

Kotz also noted that the agency's Office of Compliance, Inspections and Examinations (OCIE), the agency unit responsible for evaluating complaints and for periodically examining the books of institutions registered with the agency, didn't "properly evaluate" a complaint from "highly credible sources" about problems with Madoff's fund.[36]

Other recommendations were that the SEC set up a collection system for gathering tips and complaints, and that all tips considered by the inspections office be vetted within 30 days of being received, with any examinations of funds that take place because of the tips commencing within 60 days after the complaint is received.

Another recommendation suggested establishing guidelines for searching and screening news articles and other information from industry sources that may indicate securities-law violations by investors and broker-dealers.

"The protocol should include flexible searching capability to help identify specific areas of risk or concern and should include access to all relevant industry publications. The protocol should also include adequate screening criteria to eliminate unnecessary results and/or to more narrowly define a search in order to generate sufficient results," according to the report. "The screening criteria and any changes should be documented and the protocol should be reassessed regularly to determine if any modifications are appropriate."[37]

SEC chief Mary L. Schapiro accepted all of the recommendations.

Improved Transparency

On March 13, 2009, the SEC took action to help increase the transparency of credit default swaps by approving conditional exemptions that will allow the Chicago Mercantile Exchange Inc. (CME) to operate as a central counterparty for clearing them. These conditional exemptions, based on a request by the CME and Citadel Investment Group LLC, provide the SEC with regulatory oversight of the central counterparty, and should enhance the quality of the credit default swap market and the SEC's ability to protect investors. On December 24, 2008, the SEC approved temporary exemptions allowing LCH.Clearnet Ltd. to operate as a central counterparty for credit default swaps. On March 6, 2009, the SEC approved similar temporary exemptions for ICE US Trust LLC.

The SEC has worked in close consultation with the Board of Governors of the Federal Reserve System and the Commodity Futures Trading Commission, executing a memorandum of understanding in November 2008 to lay out a framework related to central counterparties for credit default swaps. Improved transparency may help avert a situation such as occurred with American International Group (AIG).

Obama Proposes Sweeping Changes— And Then Backs Off a Bit

In June 2009, the Obama administration proposed the most sweeping changes in regulation of the financial sector since the 1930s. The administration will urge Congress to grant new powers to the Federal

Reserve to oversee the economy. Officials want the rules to be tough enough to correct some of the damage caused by the financial crisis of 2008 but not so restrictive that they stifle innovation. The administration claims it has stopped short of calling for all changes that could be seen as "desirable" and has pushed only for those they see as "essential" to reform.

"We must act now to restore confidence in the integrity of our financial system," the proposal says. "The lasting economic damage to ordinary families and businesses is a constant reminder of the urgent need to act to reform our financial regulatory system and put our economy on track to a sustainable recovery."[38] The administration's proposal would give the government the power to take over and wind down a large financial company, a power that government officials lacked in 2008 when the financial crisis was intensifying. It would also give the central bank more powers over the payments and settlements systems in U.S. financial markets to prevent a breakdown that officials fear could destabilize the economy.

The plan would abolish the Office of Thrift Supervision and create a new national regulator for financial institutions, aimed at making it harder for companies to shop between supervisors. Hedge funds and other private pools of capital would have to register with the Securities and Exchange Commission. Thousands of financial institutions would be required to hold more capital in reserve to protect against unexpected losses, and companies would also have to retain a portion of the credit risk for loans they have packaged into securities.

The Federal Reserve emerges from the plan with the power to oversee from top to bottom almost any financial company in the country, including the firms' foreign affiliates. It would also hand the central bank another victory by allowing it to oversee any commercial company that owns a banking charter known as an industrial loan company.

To soothe lawmakers unhappy with the Fed's growing power, the proposal also recommends capping it in some ways. The administration proposes the creation of a consumer-protection agency that would have the ability to write rules related to mortgages, credit cards, and other consumer products, taking away powers previously held by the central bank.

In addition, the plan would require the Fed to receive approval from the Treasury Department before it took dramatic action to stabilize the economy, which it did several times in 2008 after it cited "unusual and exigent" circumstances.

Reaction to the plan, as might be expected, was mixed. Here are two samples from a larger number culled in a blog managed by the *Wall Street Journal.*

> The proposals are generally quite sensible. The unfortunate aspect is that political constraints have caused the administration to stop short of a full solution in certain areas, most notably in the consolidation of regulatory functions into fewer hands. Nonetheless, the country should be better off if these proposals are passed than if we were to remain as we are now.
>
> —Douglas Elliott, Brookings Institution[39]

> The Obama administration deserves a C−, which is not a passing grade in graduate school. This thing will now invite the worst kind of mud wrestling in DC. We could have done so much better if Obama had been willing to be real about what went wrong and what needs fixing. There were some good points, particularly about too big to fail and over-the-counter derivatives trading. But most of the good ideas are presented vaguely, and are surrounded by bad ideas and huge omissions. Important problems and remedies, such as U.S. housing policies that subsidized leverage and regulatory rules that mis-measure risk, are ignored completely or mentioned in passing. Too much weight is attached to populist objectives. And the huge reallocation of power toward the Fed is inadvisable.
>
> −Charles Calomiris, Columbia University
> Business School[40]

Although the administration is pushing for early passage of its plan, changes of this magnitude will undoubtedly get quite a lot of public scrutiny, and while the president may have the votes to force through his plans, he will likely try to build a consensus, even if it means compromising somewhat.

The regulatory apparatus failed in many of the cases we have discussed. Obvious warnings were ignored. Everyone agrees that something must be done. The general consensus seems to be that securities law enforcement staff is underpaid, undertrained, unco-ordinated, low-tech, and otherwise ill-equipped to deal with the more sophisticated frauds that we have seen go undetected for long periods. While some (as always) believe that more regulation is the answer, we can expect to see an overall upgrading of watchdog systems, better coordination, upgraded staffing, and, inevitably, more bureaucracy as well.

Chapter 28

Fraudulent Offerings

A SHORT LOOK

An essential requirement when taking money from the public is adequate and truthful disclosure so that prospective investors (and their advisers) can make informed decisions. Generally, the securities laws require that the disclosure be in writing, disclose all reasonably foreseeable risks, and not be misleading or fail to include relevant information. In a fraudulent offering, this is not what happens.

Transnational Engaged

Here is one typical example.

The Securities and Exchange Commission (SEC) announced that on January 23, 2009, a final judgment by consent was entered against defendants Michael P. Luckett, 37, a former resident of Boston, Massachusetts, and Transnational Fund, Inc. in an enforcement action.[1] Luckett and Transnational Fund were enjoined from violating the antifraud and registration provisions of the federal securities laws and held liable for disgorgement of $312,400 plus prejudgment interest of $17,250. Luckett previously pleaded guilty to related criminal charges and was sentenced to 36 months imprisonment in a prosecution brought by the U.S. Attorney for the District of Massachusetts.

The SEC's complaint alleged that from July to September 2007 Transnational and Luckett conducted a fraudulent offering of unregistered securities known as "Transnational Certificates" using Transnational's web sites, which the court ordered Luckett and Transnational to cease operating. According to the SEC's complaint, the defendants promised to pay investors at a rate of 6.35 percent annual percentage yield in nine months. The complaint alleged that at least 15 investors in six different states (Arizona, Kansas, Michigan, Missouri, Pennsylvania, and Texas) purchased these certificates, investing a total of at least $432,400.

Furthermore, the complaint alleged that, in soliciting investors, Transnational and Luckett made material misrepresentations and omissions in that they:

- Failed to disclose to investors and potential investors that Luckett would use investor funds for personal purposes.
- Misrepresented that Transnational was just like a bank.
- Misrepresented the fact Transnational had been in business for years.

The complaint alleged that Luckett took thousands of dollars from at least one Transnational bank account into which he had deposited investor funds and used the money to pay, among other things, rent on a luxury condominium in Boston and the lease on a Toyota automobile. According to the complaint, he also used bank cards issued on bank accounts holding investor funds for various personal living expenses.

The federal government does not try to decide whether a particular investment has merit (some states do have merit reviews). However, it rightly insists that the information about the investment be complete, accurate, and not misleading. When company executives try to use an offering to fund a lavish lifestyle or as a personal piggy bank, they can be subject to civil and criminal penalties.

Chapter 29

Auction-Rate Securities

A $330 BILLION FRAUD?

U p until May 2008, auction-rate securities (ARSs) were classified as "cash alternatives/municipal securities" on the customer statements issued by UBS Financial Services, and well into March 2008 Merrill Lynch customers who checked their accounts online found their auction-rate securities investments listed under "other cash." The investments proved to be illiquid, however, with investors unable to access their supposedly liquid funds.

A still unfolding (and underreported) drama is the tale of how investors everywhere were pushed to invest in supposedly liquid auction-rate securities. Many suffered large losses. The major brokerage houses that were touting them also ended up suffering large losses, as they were pushed by the government to repurchase the illiquid securities from their clients, contributing heavily to their own capital crises, and in some cases, subsequent forced mergers and government bailouts. But in the end, much of the loss will be borne by the taxpayers.

What Are Auction-Rate Securities?
What Is a Dutch Auction?

We all know that time is money. But time is also directly related to risk. Therefore, the longer you lock up your money, the larger the return you expect. Even the safest investments—U.S. government Treasury notes—pay higher yields for longer loans. An auction-rate security is a debt instrument (corporate or municipal bonds) with a nominal long-term maturity that was designed to neutralize the risk of long-term debt by regularly resetting the interest rate (as often as weekly) through a Dutch auction.

A Dutch auction, named for the methodology used in the flower auctions in Aalsmeer and other locations in Holland, is a type of auction where the auctioneer begins with a high asking price that is lowered until some participant is willing to accept the auctioneer's price, or a predetermined reserve price (the seller's minimum acceptable price) is reached. The winning participant pays the last announced price. This is also known as a clock auction or an open-outcry descending-price auction.

The total number of shares available to auction at any given period is determined by the number of existing bondholders who wish to sell or hold bonds only at a minimum yield. Existing holders and potential investors enter a competitive bidding process through broker-dealer(s). Buyers specify the number of shares, typically in denominations of $25,000, they wish to purchase with the lowest interest rate they are willing to accept.

Each bid and order size is ranked from lowest to highest minimum bid rate. The lowest bid rate at which all the shares can be sold at par establishes the interest rate, otherwise known as the clearing rate. This rate is paid on the entire issue for the upcoming period. Investors who bid a minimum rate above the clearing rate receive no bonds, while those whose minimum bid rates were at or below the clearing rate receive the clearing rate for the next period.

Why Were Auction-Rate Securities Invented?

The idea behind the auction-rate security (ARS) is that it would enable borrowing long-term while paying lower short-term rates, based on the fact that the interest rate is constantly being reset based on market conditions. The auction-rate security was invented by Ronald Gallatin at Lehman Brothers in 1984; the first auction of ARS securities for the tax-exempt market was introduced by Goldman Sachs in 1988.

If the investor was not able to sell the security at auction, the municipality was required to pay a real interest rate penalty (penalty rate) sometimes as high as 10 percent or more to compensate the investor for now having in effect an illiquid long-term security (hence additional time risk). At the same time, this clause provided incentive for the issuer to make the investor whole as soon as possible and call the issue back, cashing out the investor.

By early 2008, the ARS market had grown to over $200 billion, with roughly half of it being owned by corporate investors. By the end of 2008, the market had grown to $330 billion. Most holders of auction rate securities are institutional investors and high net worth individuals, and they generally have minimum denominations of $25,000.

The ARS Markets Collapse

An essential element for the viability of auction-rate securities, of course, is the existence of a robust market so that the bids at each auction will approximate market conditions and investors will perceive the securities as safe, liquid, and readily marketable. During the week of February 11, 2008, the $330 billion market for ARS virtually collapsed overnight. The liquidity of many of these investments disappeared and their safety was reportedly in jeopardy.

Beginning on Thursday, February 7, 2008, auctions for these securities began to fail when investors declined to bid on them. The four largest investment banks that had been making markets in these securities (Citigroup, UBS AG, Morgan Stanley, and Merrill Lynch) declined to act as bidders of last resort as they had in the past. This was a result of the scope and size of the market failure, combined with the firms' needs to protect their capital during the 2008 financial crisis. No one could sell their supposedly safe and liquid ARS securities except at a huge loss of principle (of 20 percent or more).

What had been described as safe AAA credits, comparable to money market funds, instead became a nightmare for investors. The *Saint Louis Post-Dispatch* reported on January 11, 2009, about the plight of an elderly couple, Glenn Linke, 80, and his wife Norma, 73, who couldn't climb stairs the way they used to. So, about a year earlier, they decided to add a first-story bedroom to their house in Creve Coeur, Missouri.

When the construction bills began rolling in, they called their broker at Stifel Nicolaus and asked him to sell some of their "weekly CDs." That's when they got the bad news: Their money was frozen. Some of it remained frozen in early 2009, because even though in Missouri the secretary of state's office negotiated such buy-back agreements with Wachovia Securities in St. Louis and Commerce Bank, the Linkes' broker, Stifel Nicolaus, wasn't a part of the settlement. The firm refused to buy back the securities, arguing that it had done nothing wrong. Other regional brokerages, such as Raymond James Financial, also were resisting.

A similar story was reported in nearby Sunset Hills. Donald and Barbara Correll couldn't get their hands on $425,000 in their Stifel account. Donald Correll, 82, said he decided to get out of the stock market in 2006, and he moved the proceeds into a money market fund. "I was happy with that," the retired manufacturer's representative said.[1]

In 2007, his broker called and said, "I have a situation and I think I can do better than a money market," Donald Correll recalled. "I said, 'Is this as safe as a money market?' and he said, 'Yes.'" It was not the case.[2]

"Thirty-three formal complaints have been filed by Stifel's auction rate customers with the Missouri secretary of state's office," said spokeswoman Laura Egerdal.[3] Dozens more Stifel customers have called but haven't filed written complaints, she added. The complaints all allege that the investors were told that the investments were safe and liquid. Tragic situations like this have occurred all over the country. Shepherd, Smith & Edwards, LLP, a Texas law firm, maintains a blog called Stockbroker Fraud Blog (www.stockbrokerfraudblog.com). They state that investors were defrauded by ARSs.

Is ARS the Biggest Fraud Ever?

An anonymous but "exclusive" article linked to the law firm of Shepherd, Smith & Edwards asks whether "what started out as a creative and market-based structured product got corrupted by greed, disregard of market principles, deceit, nondisclosure, self-dealing and material omission of fact which ended in the one of largest massive alleged frauds ever committed by Wall Street houses on their clients?"[4]

As a result of the failure of the brokers to make a market, the ARS securities, listed at par on investors' statements, are not and maybe never were ever truly worth par. Without the brokerage liquidity they were worthless, and in the case of the auction-rate preferred securities (ARPSs—investments in closed-end mutual funds that bought ARSs) they were worth about 60 cents on the dollar. Almost all ARPSs have AAA status and were marketed as completely safe. However, AAA-rated or not, unless there is a secondary market, investors have to sell these securities at a discount so that interested investors will earn what they demand for investing in a 50-year illiquid security.

The anonymous blogger linked to the Shepherd web site argues that it is not the ARPS market that has dried up. It is just that the manipulated market that artificially propped up 60 cents to be worth one dollar has abandoned them. In a sense investors were sold a 50-year security that was paying them a fraction of what similar-term securities pay out. The same principle, but to somewhat of a lesser degree, applies to ARSs.

Government-Prodded Settlements

Beginning in March 2008, class-action lawsuits were filed against several of the large banks. The lawsuits were filed in federal court in Manhattan alleging that these investment banks deceptively marketed auction-rate securities as cash alternatives. The government prodded costly settlements. To appreciate the magnitude of the problem, we look briefly at some of the largest banks that were prodded to make costly settlements.

Citigroup: On August 1, 2008, the New York State attorney general notified Citigroup of his intent to file charges over the sale of troubled auction-rate securities and claimed Citigroup destroyed documents. On August 7, 2008, in a proposed settlement of state and federal regulators' charges, Citigroup agreed in principle to buy back about $7.3 billion of auction-rate securities it had sold to charities, individual investors, and small businesses. The agreement also called for Citigroup to use its "best efforts" to make liquid all of the US$12 billion auction-rate securities it had sold to institutional investors, including retirement plans, by the end of 2009. The settlement allowed Citigroup to avoid admitting or denying claims that it had sold auction-rate securities as safe, liquid investments, which would protect its banking license and also reduce the potential for the settlement to be used against Citi in private lawsuits.

Merrill Lynch: Also on August 7, just hours after Citigroup's settlement announcement, Merrill Lynch announced that effective January 15, 2009, and through January 15, 2010, it would offer to buy at par $10 billion in auction-rate securities it had sold to its retail clients. Merrill Lynch's action created liquidity for more than 30,000 clients who held municipal, closed-end funds, and student loan auction-rate securities. Under the plan, retail clients of Merrill Lynch would have a year in which to sell their auction-rate securities to Merrill Lynch if they so wished.

Morgan Stanley: On August 11, 2008, Morgan Stanley announced that it would repurchase at par those securities bought by its clients prior to February 13, 2008. This program was scheduled to commence no later than September 30, 2008, and to include all investors with accounts valued at $10 million or less. The total size of the buy-back program was anticipated to be in the area of $4.5 billion.

UBS AG: On August 9, 2008, UBS AG also agreed to repurchase from its clients nearly $19 billion in auction-rate securities as part of a settlement reached with federal and state regulators. UBS AG scheduled its buy-back program to commence in October 2008. Separately, on February 18, 2009, UBS agreed to pay $780 million to avoid criminal prosecution for money laundering.

Wells Fargo and Wachovia Securities: Reuters reported on November 18, 2009 (http://goo.gl/mkTz) that Wells Fargo Investments LLC would repay about $1.3 billion to investors, charities, and small businesses whose funds were frozen in the auction-rate securities market in the latest of a series of settlements with state securities regulators, an industry association said in a statement.

The company, a unit of San Francisco–based Wells Fargo & Company, agreed to offer to buy back auction-rate securities by mid-February 2010, according to the North American Securities Administrators Association. Wells Fargo will also reimburse clients who sold securities at a discount after the market froze and pay $1.9 million in penalties to states.

On August 18, 2008, Wachovia Securities agreed to buy back $9 billion in auction-rate securities from clients. In addition, Wachovia has agreed to pay $50 million in fines.

Commerce Bancshares Inc. and Bank of America Corporation: On August 18, 2008, Commerce Bancshares offered to buy back $545 million in auction-rate securities from its clients. Bank of America Corporation has agreed to buy back as much as $4.7 billion in auction-rate securities.

More Litigation

On July 17, 2008, Carey & Danis filed a class-action lawsuit in the U.S. District Court for the Southern District of Illinois on behalf of persons who purchased auction-rate securities from Bank of America Corporation, Bank of America Investment Services, Inc., and Bank of America Securities, LLC between June 11, 2003, and February 13, 2008, and who continued to hold the securities as of February 13, 2008. The same firm has also filed a class-action lawsuit on behalf of persons who purchased auction-rate securities from H&R Block, Inc. and H&R Block Financial Advisors, Inc., and from Stifel Financial Corporation (NYSE: SF) and Stifel, Nicolaus & Company, Inc.

Many of these now illiquid securities were then sold to the government under TARP or were accepted by the Federal Reserve Bank as collateral. In August 2008, the Securities and Exchange Commission's Division of Enforcement engaged in preliminary settlements with several of the larger broker-dealers, including Citigroup, JPMorgan Chase, Merrill Lynch, Morgan Stanley, RBC Group, and UBS. The proposed settlement called for these broker-dealers to repurchase outstanding ARSs from their individual (but not institutional) investors and to pay substantial fines.

The attorney general for New York State, Andrew Cuomo, sued UBS for insider trading, alleging that several senior executives traded $21 million worth of auction-rate securities knowing the market was about to collapse.

David Aufhauser, formerly the general counsel of UBS's investment bank, has agreed to pay $6.5 million in order to settle a claim of insider trading involving auction-rate securities. Aufhauser is notable because not only was he a top executive at UBS, but he was also the highest-ranking in-house lawyer at the Treasury Department and served on the Justice Department's corporate fraud task force. He agreed to give up a $6 million bonus he was to receive from UBS and will pay a $500,000 penalty. In addition, he is barred from working in the securities industry for two years and may not work as an attorney for two years.

Of the $320 billion in ARS securities that were frozen in February 2008, about $195 billion had been unfrozen by the end of 2008, leaving $135 billion still frozen. According to Shepherd's anonymous blogger,

> It is inconceivable to think that any client would be interested in these products if it had been properly disclosed, in a very direct and frank manner, that absent true liquidity these securities were worth as little as 60 cents on the dollar.
>
> Almost all investors in these products thought they were investing in a safe, secure and liquid investment akin to a money market. This is especially true since the rate of interest offered by these securities [was] just slightly higher than money market and indicative of what very safe short term securities paid. Risky securities offered more than double the return. In essence investors took on double the risk for half of the return. There was no apparent risk/reward ratio.[5]

PIMCO Relents

According to the *Wall Street Journal*, money manager Pacific Investment Management Company (PIMCO) was being forced to buy back some of the auction-rate preferred securities issued by its closed-end funds. This was a reversal for the firm, co-founded by bond maven Bill Gross, which had refused to redeem these securities for months after the auction-rate market froze up. But in an ironic twist, deteriorating markets and legal requirements were forcing PIMCO to redeem them after all. Under similar circumstances late in 2008, PIMCO relented and made a partial redemption. Bloomberg.com reported that as of

May 31, 2009, "Pimco is the only one of the five largest managers of publicly traded closed-end funds that hasn't initiated a buyback to let investors cash out."[6]

PIMCO's closed-end funds, like dozens of others, had for years issued auction-rate preferreds to borrow money and add leverage to the funds. Early in 2008, PIMCO and affiliate Nicholas-Applegate Capital Management (both are owned by Allianz SE) had about $5.3 billion in auction-rate securities outstanding. PIMCO wouldn't comment for the record.

The *Wall Street Journal* said, "Under federal law, closed-end funds can't announce or distribute dividends if their auction-rate leverage is more than 50% of total assets." The five PIMCO funds said they would redeem some of their auction-rate securities to be able to pay or declare dividends. Analysts expect the Nicholas-Applegate funds to follow suit.[7]

An indefinite and delayed suspension of the dividend hurts the reputation of the funds and the firm. "The only reason that investors buy these income funds is for income," said Cecilia Gondor, an analyst at Thomas J. Herzfeld Advisors Inc. "If investors can't rely on the income, they may go elsewhere," she added.[8]

Late in 2008, all seven of these funds failed to meet their leverage ratios. After delaying dividend payments for nearly two months in some cases, the funds eventually redeemed about $1.7 billion, or a third of the total outstanding.

"It's happened to Pimco twice; it's happened to other funds only once," Sangeeta Marfatia, closed-end fund analyst at UBS Wealth Management Research, told the *Wall Street Journal*. She said that while other funds were also forced to delay their dividend payments and deleverage, lately they've avoided a reoccurrence by proactively reducing leverage. Unlike PIMCO, they haven't waited until right before the dividend payment is due to announce the problem.[9]

$61 Billion Returned—Why So Little Attention to ARS?

As of year-end 2009, $61 billion was returned to investors, the largest return of funds in history, according to the North American Securities

Administrators Association. Still, according to the *Wall Street Journal*, some 400 companies that had sunk their free cash into the investments—from retailer Abercrombie & Fitch Company to tiny Nanophase Technologies Corporation—still held more than $20 billion of auction-rate securities at the end of 2009 that couldn't be sold or were sharply reduced in value. That was forcing the holders to restrain their spending, thus creating yet another drag on the economy as it struggled to recover.

If, as is alleged, ARS and its cousin ARPS add up to a $330 billion scam, why has it gotten relatively little notice, especially as compared with the Madoff scandal? On BloggingStocks.com, a blog aggregator that follows the markets, Peter Cohan said that he believes the reason the Madoff scheme has gotten more media attention than the ARS collapse is because Madoff's victims include high-profile celebrities, such as Steven Spielberg and Kevin Bacon. In my opinion, the lack of attention is related to the complexity of the instruments, which most members of the media and the investing public don't understand.

An ARS Fraud That Wasn't?

On September 3, 2008, federal authorities in Brooklyn indicted two former Credit Suisse brokers.[10] The government alleges that they tricked large corporations into buying more than $1 billion of so-called auction-rate securities tied to mortgage debt in recent years when investors didn't want a mortgage-backed security; so they just didn't call it a mortgage security. They were charged with conspiracy, securities fraud, and wire fraud. In essence, the government is charging that the brokers pitched ARSs, but were actually selling unwanted mortgage-backed securities.

The client companies had hired Credit Suisse to invest their short-term cash reserves in auction-rate debt backed by ARSs that were federally insured student loans, according to the indictment. Instead, the brokers often placed clients in auction-rate issues backed by subprime home loans and other mortgage-related debt known as collateralized debt obligations (CDOs)—because those issues paid them "significantly higher" commissions, the government says. The brokers, Julian

T. Tzolov, 36, and Eric S. Butler, according to the SEC, disguised their actions by falsifying e-mail confirmation statements sent to clients, the government said.

The two replaced any mention of the words "mortgage" and "CDO" with "student loan" or "education," according to the indictment and an accompanying Securities and Exchange Commission civil suit. For example, the SEC charges, one of the brokers placed a client in a $20 million security issued by Greenpoint Credit that was backed by mobile-home loans. But the broker told the client in an e-mail that the security was issued by "Greenpoint Student Assistance," which had not been the issuer.

FBI Assistant Director-in-Charge Mark J. Mershon stated, "Investors who were told they were purchasing relatively low-risk securities backed by student loans were unwittingly purchasing high-risk mortgage-backed securities. For a nearly three-year period, what Tzolov and Butler sold their clients was a bill of goods. The FBI remains committed to policing the securities industry to protect investors from all forms of unscrupulous and illegal conduct."[12]

Julian Tzolov, the former Credit Suisse broker, who some believed fled to his native Bulgaria, returned to New York from Germany, where both an indictment and an FBI arrest awaited him. Initially, he pleaded not guilty to charges that he and Butler misled investors about purchases of auction-rate securities.

"Julian Tzolov is innocent of these charges," said Tzolov's attorney, Paul Hastings' Kenneth Breen. "We're going to show that these were sophisticated investors who were Mr. Tzolov's clients and that they knew exactly what their investments were. Julian Tzolov should not be blamed for an unforeseen market failure."[13]

Paul Weinstein, a lawyer for Butler, said his client believed in the triple-A securities he had sold to customers. "He believed he was doing the best for his clients, and they agreed, until the entire auction-rate securities market failed, which had nothing to do with him," he said.[14]

Tzolov disappeared on May 9, 2009, from a Manhattan home where he had been under house arrest, being first arrested in 2008 and then released to house arrest after surrendering his passport and posting a $3 million bond. An electronic monitor on his ankle had been removed. Defense attorney Ben Brafman had said he lost contact with his client weeks ago. "We have no idea where he is or what may have happened to him," the lawyer said. Brooklyn Federal Judge Jack Weinstein angrily ordered prosecutors to seize $3 million in assets that were posted as bail for Tzolov. They moved to seize $3 million worth of property belonging to two men who had signed Tzolov's bond, Dimitre Ivanov and Kamen Kiriakov.

The government seized Tzolov's ninth-floor apartment at 225 Fifth Avenue in Manhattan, Ivanov's 18th-floor apartment at 325 Fifth Avenue in Manhattan, and Kiriakov's residence in North Miami Beach, Florida. Both of the latter men identified themselves on court papers as Tzolov's friends.

After a worldwide manhunt, Tzolov was captured on July 15 just outside Marbella, Spain, accompanied by a bodyguard and carrying false documents, according to Spanish authorities. He waived extradition and was returned to New York. This time, he pleaded guilty to federal securities fraud charges.

Asked by the judge why he absconded, Julian Tzolov replied: "I got scared."[15]

The former broker for Credit Suisse's private banking division also pleaded guilty to bail jumping and visa fraud, among other charges.

Butler was sentenced to five years in prison. The guidelines called for a much longer sentence, but Judge Weinstein did not agree with the government's $1.1 billion loss calculation. He also took into account family circumstances. The judge also fined Butler $5 million, and ordered him to forfeit $500,000. The judge said Butler's trial "laid bare the pernicious and pervasive culture of corruption in the financial-services industry" which he said is "beset by avarice."

"The blame for this condition is shared not only by individual defendants like Butler, but also the institutions that employ them," he said.

Weinstein cited several factors that he said may have contributed to Butler's crimes, including a failure by government regulators and legislators to monitor and supervise the markets, the investors who didn't "exert reasonable control and supervision" over transactions, and "a failure by Credit Suisse, Butler's employer, and other financial institutions to adequately supervise."[16]

Tzolov, who is being held without bail, still awaits sentencing scheduled for September 27, 2010; he will likely receive an additional sentence for absconding, and will be deported after he serves his sentence.

Civil complaints that were filed in connection with the Credit Suisse case by STMicroelectronics, a semiconductor company, paint a classic picture of greed and glory on Wall Street. In one instance, the two brokers, they allege, misled a client, claiming there was an administrative error in filing a trade ticket, when in fact the auction for the client's securities had failed. They then persuaded the customer to invest $25 million more in securities backed by student loans. Instead, they invested that money in riskier securities. David Walker, a spokesman for Credit Suisse, said, "Credit Suisse immediately informed our regulators, and we have continued to assist the authorities." But STMicroelectronics, one of the bank's clients, disputes Credit Suisse's version of events. The company claims that Credit Suisse Securities engaged in a "bold and sophisticated scheme to defraud ST."[17] The company suggests that Credit Suisse was aware that its brokers were moving clients' money into risky auction-rate securities as part of a scheme to get those securities off the bank's own books and earn higher fees for its services.

Walker, the Credit Suisse spokesman, said: "We do not comment on meritless lawsuits."[18] However, in a securities filing and a related press release, STMicroelectronics said that an arbitration panel of the Financial Industry Regulatory Authority (FINRA)—in a full and final resolution of the issues submitted for determination—awarded STMicroelectronics, in connection with the sales by Credit Suisse Securities (USA) LLC of unauthorized auction-rate securities to the company, an amount of approximately $406 million comprising compensatory damages, as well as interest, attorney's fees, and consequential damages, which were assessed against Credit Suisse. In addition, ST was entitled to retain the about $25 million interest award, which had already been paid.[19]

Tzolov and Butler were also accused on July 14, 2009, in a separate 14-count indictment in the Southern District of New York in Manhattan of operating a wire fraud scheme to sell auction-rate securities. Manhattan and Brooklyn are separate judicial districts.

The case is *U.S. v. Tzolov*, 08–CR–370, U.S. District Court, Eastern District of New York (Brooklyn).

ARS securities significantly contributed to and were affected by the market collapse of 2008. They involved many of the largest financial institutions and not just rogue brokers. The civil and criminal cases ironically arose from a fraud pitched as an ARS when it really wasn't, even though the ARS securities market itself blew up.

Chapter 30

$132 Million Tax-Free Exchange Fraud

SECTION 1031

I n many cases we have seen, the client is complicit in the fraud, or is willfully blind to the impossibility of continued outsized returns. Not always. Sometimes, the client is just an innocent victim. In this chapter, we look at a mysterious and little-known corner of the financial world, whose sole raison d'être is [legal] tax deferral. The niche was created by Section 1031 of the tax code, and like other arcane niches is little understood, underregulated, and ripe for fraud.

The Tax Code

The sale of real property is subject to capital gains tax based on the sales price less adjusted basis (cost less depreciation deducted). For appreciated properties held for many years, this can be a substantial sum. Under Section 1031 (1031 cases) of the United States Internal Revenue Code (26 U.S.C. § 1031), the exchange of certain types of property may defer the recognition of capital gains or losses due upon sale, and hence defer any capital gains taxes otherwise due.

Originally, 1031 cases needed to be simultaneous transfers of ownership. But since *Starker vs. U.S.* (602 F.2d 1341), a contract to exchange properties in the future is practically the same as a simultaneous transfer. It is under this case, decided in 1979, that the rules for election of a delayed 1031 originated. To elect the 1031 recognition, a taxpayer must identify the property for exchange before closing, identify the replacement property within 45 days of closing, and acquire the replacement property within 180 days of closing.

Qualified Intermediary

A qualified intermediary (QI) must also be used to facilitate a 1031 exchange. The qualified intermediary (also known as an accommodator) should be a corporation that is in the full-time business of facilitating 1031 exchanges. The role of a QI is similar to, but not identical to, the role of an escrow company.

The QI enters into a written agreement with the taxpayer wherein the QI transfers the relinquished property to the buyer, and transfers the replacement property to the taxpayer pursuant to the exchange agreement. The QI holds the proceeds from the sale of the relinquished property beyond the actual or constructive control of the exchangor. The QI also prepares the necessary documents to accomplish a tax-deferred exchange.

Since the QI is holding a lot of money, there is always the potential for fraud.

Government Charges Ed Okun

In March 2007, Edward H. Okun, who ran a 1031 exchange business, was indicted in a $132 million scheme to defraud clients of funds allegedly held in trust. He was charged with mail fraud, bulk cash smuggling, and making false statements, Assistant Attorney General Alice S. Fisher and U.S. Attorney for the Eastern District of Virginia Chuck Rosenberg announced. The indictment stems from Okun's alleged scheme to defraud and obtain millions of dollars in client funds held by

The 1031 Tax Group, LLP (1031TG), a qualified intermediary company owned by Okun.

According to the indictment, from August 2005 through April 2007, Okun used 1031TG and its subsidiaries to obtain funds by promising clients that their money would be used solely to effect 1031 exchanges as outlined in the exchange agreements. After making such promises, Okun misappropriated approximately $132 million in client funds to support his lavish lifestyle, pay operating expenses for his various companies, invest in commercial real estate, and purchase additional qualified intermediary companies to obtain access to additional client funds.

The indictment also alleges that Okun instructed employees to withdraw $15,000 in cash from the bank account of Investment Properties of America (IPofA), a company owned by Okun, and smuggle the cash to his personal yacht on Paradise Island in the Bahamas to avoid federal currency reporting requirements, and that he made material false statements under oath before the U.S. District Court for the Eastern District of Virginia relating to conversations he had with the chief legal officer of IPofA. Authorities said there were 577 victims across the country.

Edward Okun of Miami, Florida, and Lara Coleman, the chief operating officer, were charged in a superseding indictment on July 11, 2008, with 27 counts of conspiracy, fraud, and money laundering charges. During the trial, prosecutors presented evidence that from 2005 to 2007 Okun and co-conspirator Lara Coleman spent million of dollars from his Virginia-based 1031 Tax Group and its subsidiaries to fund a lavish lifestyle which included a home on Miami Beach's Hibiscus Island, planes, cars, boats, jewelry, and a lavish wedding.

Okun's attorney, Barry Pollack, told the jury his client believed he was doing nothing wrong when he borrowed money that his companies collected from their clients who were seeking to defer capital gains taxes on property sales. He said Okun intended to repay all the money but couldn't.

Victims' Stories

Jurors in March 2009 found Okun, 58, guilty of conspiracy, wire fraud, money laundering, smuggling, and perjury following a three-week trial.[1]

Bonnie Schloss of Silver Spring, Maryland, said she lost $335,000 from the sale of a house she had purchased with an inheritance and choked back tears after hearing the verdict. "It doesn't bring back the money, but it does make you feel like somebody paid attention and cared about us," she told *ABC News*.[2]

Barry and Sandy Cogan said they lost about $500,000 from the sale of a small strip mall that had been in Sandy Cogan's family since the late 1920s. In response to the verdict, Barry Cogan, 67, stated, "I think it was just and it was fair, and I think he will never ever again be able to destroy people's lives. This page in our lives has been turned."

100-Year Sentence

U.S. District Judge Robert Payne in Richmond, Virginia, where Okun's company was based, sentenced him to 100 years in prison for running the $126 million fraud scheme. Prosecutors had sought a sentence of 400 years, or a similar term amounting to life in prison.

"The sentence must deter those who have access to funds of others," Judge Payne said. "If you ruin lives of others, your life stands to be ruined."[3]

Coleman, Others Plead Guilty

Lara Coleman, who pleaded guilty and could have been sentenced to up to 25 years in prison and $500,000 in fines, agreed to 10 years' imprisonment under a plea deal. Robert D. Field II, the chief financial officer for Okun Holdings, Inc., the parent company of Okun's businesses, agreed to a sentence of five years for conspiracy to commit mail fraud and money laundering; and Richard B. Simring, the Okun Holdings chief legal officer, also pleaded guilty. Coleman and Field were sentenced on August 13, 2009, under the terms of plea agreements reached with the government. Judge Payne said the five years called for under the plea agreement for Simring may be appropriate, but said he wanted more information about Simring's emotional condition.

The case is *U.S. v. Okun*, 3:08–cr–132, U.S. District Court, Eastern District of Virginia (Richmond).

Fraud by qualified intermediaries operating an exchange fund is a particularly pernicious crime, as its victims are beyond reproach. Lack of transparency and independent controls over exchange funds made it easy for Okun and others to inflict grave financial harm on their victims by misuse of funds essentially held in trust for clients who were acting legally. Unfortunately, some who hold significant monies for others believe they can get away with "temporarily" borrowing funds and convince themselves they can repay the funds with no one getting hurt. Inevitably, the appetite comes with the food; they keep stealing and eventually are caught, but not before they inflict grave harm on their innocent victims.

Chapter 31

Not Smart

THE SMART ONLINE TRADING SCAM

W hen market manipulation involves bribes to brokers, criminal charges often follow. Here is an interesting tale of *The
Little Engine That Could*, but didn't, because it got off track.

Six Arrested

On September 11, 2007, the U.S. Attorney's office for the Southern
District of New York announced the arrest of Dennis Michael Nouri
(then CEO of Smart Online), his brother, and four brokers, bringing
to a close an interesting fraud that nearly made it all the way. Many
penny-stock frauds have obvious red flags: they involve mergers with
shells, they often trade on the Pink Sheets, and there is a paucity of
disclosure. This scam was different. The signs were much more subtle.

The Nouris were not content to make a few million. Their goal
was to make a few hundred million, at least. For this, they were willing
to be patient and to invest time and (as it turned out) other people's
money. The company was fully reporting. And but for a few greedy
slipups, they might have made it. The story began in 1993, before the
dot-com era. Michael Nouri, an émigré from Iran, founded Smart

Online, a publisher of mundane, fill-in-the-blanks software for making wills, writing simple contracts, and other low-tech activities. The company sold their self-help software on diskettes and later on CD-ROMs through traditional retail outlets for boxed software. For many years, they operated as a private company, having raised and lost considerable money from private investors along the way.

Laying the Foundation

Nouri decided that if he used enough smoke and mirrors, tightly limited the stock supply, and rigged the market long enough, he could get the stock price above $10, trade it on the NASDAQ, and build a robust enough market to take gobs of money off the table. The first hurdle to overcome was to concoct a story, as his older story had played out and was by then very tired. Nouri decided to latch onto the software as a service (SaaS) modality that was beginning to emerge, which would give his company sex appeal. Then, he needed to raise cash. He had no money of his own and had scandals in Italy and in France in his past. But Nouri had access to hot European money, and a secret, silent European partner living in Holland who had strong ties to Israel.

First, he retroactively gave himself a large salary, and then issued himself restricted shares in lieu of receiving the salary, thus giving himself control. Then he made a partnership with a convicted felon. The partnership used the felon's hot money to invest in Smart Online at $0.50 per share, but Nouri had voting control of the partnership so he could vote its stock, giving him control of Smart Online. While not totally omitted from the prospectus, the felon's role was carefully hidden.

He proceeded to conduct a series of offshore deals selling stock to overseas funds at $1 per share, but with a commitment to register their shares in a resale prospectus. Nouri also offered his software to various large banks as a benefit to their customers, to be accessible free from the prestigious partners' web sites. This earned him some customization fees, but he also gave equity in return and was able to claim the customers as investors in his company. Thus, JPMorgan Chase and other banks, *Inc.* magazine, *BusinessWeek*, and Hewlett-Packard came to be strategic partners and shareholders. At least a third of the reported revenue was from an offshore entity owned by the same European investor.

By this time, Nouri's company had eaten through more than $28.6 million in accumulated losses, a large chunk of which had gone to him, to his brother, and to his wife. At the time of the first prospectus, a total of nearly 14 million shares were issued or issuable, and Nouri, his family, and his offshore partner controlled half of them. Nouri himself now had no basis in the company, as he had taken out all of his own money, but told everyone that he had invested many millions in it.

Going Public without an IPO

Smart Online filed a resale prospectus with the SEC to register shares of the investors and partners. Once it became effective, one of the brokers forced trading to commence by selling short a few hundred shares. A local shareholder who had bought in at $0.25 obligingly sold his stock at $5, which covered the short and got things going, establishing an initial price. Various small stock purchases were engineered by the conspirators and sold by obliging small investors happy to take their profits. Nouri registered the shares as was required, but he had intended that no one sell until he was ready, meaning that he had done enough public relations, investor relations, and so on so that a market would develop.

However, once the registration had been declared effective, some shareholders jumped the gun. They deposited their shares with their brokers and asked to have the shares sold, as they were now free-trading. Nouri's transfer agent called and asked counsel for a free-trading opinion. Since there was an imbalance of orders, Nouri tried to buy time by improperly holding up the opinion.

This was a huge mistake. It turned out that the brokers had already sold the shares on behalf of the sellers, so they were short. Since the price had appreciated, the sellers were bought in by the brokerage house at a higher price, and the investors lost money. Unbeknownst to Nouri, they wrote a letter of complaint to the Securities and Exchange Commission (SEC). In the meantime, all was apparently well. Using some money raised and the high share price, Nouri engineered two acquisitions to buy a little real revenue. He also needed more shareholders to qualify for the NASDAQ, so he went on a campaign, which we will discuss later, to add more round-lot shareholders (those holding at least 100 shares). Based on the stock's price, which got up as high as $11.25, and the number of shares outstanding, the market capitalization met the requirement for a NASDAQ listing. The stock was scheduled to move to the NASDAQ and then, just minutes before trading was to commence, on January 17, 2006, the SEC exercised its emergency powers and suspended trading for 10 days for "possible manipulative conduct in the market for the Company's stock."[1]

The NASDAQ, of course, immediately canceled the impending listing. SEC subpoenas were immediately served. After reviewing the documents to be handed over, the company's independent directors saw some fishy things. They hired counsel to conduct an independent investigation. Several unusual things turned up. It turned out that Nouri and others had been paid enormous fees as compensation for arranging for the various financings, and it just so happened that Nouri got large unsecured loans from those who received fees. In addition, he signed large contracts for two separate firms for IR services from two unknown offshore firms that just happened to share the same address in an offshore haven known for its secrecy. He got loans from them, too.

After the Fall

Well, the apparent upshot of all this was that trading resumed on the Pink Sheets at a much lower, but still unrealistic, price of $2.40. The company's audit committee hired counsel to conduct an independent investigation and said, "The Audit Committee did not conclude that any of our officers or directors have engaged in fraudulent or criminal activity. However, it did conclude that we lacked an adequate control environment," and said that the company "has taken action to address certain conduct of management that was revealed as a result of the investigation. The Audit Committee concluded that the control deficiencies primarily resulted from our transition from a private company to a publicly reporting company and insufficient preparation for, focus on and experience with compliance requirements for a publicly reporting company."[2] The company made some changes in its internal governance, and it managed to obtain still more financing. Sales were still small, and the company continued to burn through money. There matters apparently stood still until September 12, 2007, when the U.S. Attorney announced the arrests.

The criminal complaint alleged that Smart Online stock began trading publicly on the OTC Bulletin Board in April 2005. Defendant Michael Nouri, the CEO of Smart Online, sought to qualify the company for listing on the NASDAQ by increasing the number of shareholders and trading volume of Smart Online stock. In order to do so, he allegedly began paying bribes to stockbrokers, including defendants Anthony Martin, James Doolan, Ruben Serrano, and Alain Lustig, to solicit customers to purchase Smart Online stock.

Moreover, the complaint alleges that between May 2005 and January 2006, Michael Nouri paid over $170,000 to brokers, who sold more than 267,000 shares of Smart Online stock (or approximately 10 percent of the trading volume during the period) to investors. The complaint also alleges Eric Nouri, an employee of Smart Online, also negotiated bribe payments with a broker to solicit purchases of stock at various amounts and prices. Michael Nouri concealed the bribes as "consulting fees" paid pursuant to sham consulting agreements.

The complaint further alleges that the brokers did not disclose to their customers that they were receiving bribes to sell Smart Online stock, and that Michael Nouri understood that the brokers were concealing the bribes from their customers. A seven-count grand jury indictment was filed on November 8, 2007. On May 19, 2009, a superseding indictment was filed, apparently after the attorneys could not agree on a disposition.[3] New charges were added.

The main defendants went to trial. Dennis Michael Nouri, his brother Reza, and stockbroker Anthony Martin were found guilty on all counts after a three-week jury trial before United States District Judge Denny Chin, the same judge who handled the Madoff case.

According to a press release issued by the office of the U.S. Attorney for the Southern District of New York, "In recorded conversations that took place after the Securities and Exchange Commission ('SEC') suspended trading of Smart Online stock on the NASDAQ, . . . [Nouri] described how to lie to investigators to cover up the scheme and how to conceal the nature of the illegal kickbacks to brokers. In another meeting . . . [Nouri] took a cooperating broker's cell phone to delete a phone number the broker had been using to contact him, and gave the broker a number to call when speaking with him in the future."[4]

Each of the defendants was found guilty of one count of conspiracy to commit securities fraud, wire fraud, and commercial bribery, and one count of securities fraud. Dennis Michael Nouri and Reza Eric Nouri each were found guilty of three additional counts of wire fraud and one count of commercial bribery. The conspiracy and commercial bribery charges each carry a maximum sentence of five years in prison and a maximum fine of the greater of $250,000 or twice the gross gain or loss from the offenses. The securities fraud and wire fraud charges each carry a maximum sentence of 20 years in prison. The securities fraud charge carries a maximum fine of the greater of $5 million or twice the gross gain or loss from the offense. Each of the wire fraud charges carries a maximum fine of the greater of $250,000 or twice the gross gain or loss from the offense. Following the jury's return of a guilty verdict against all of the defendants on all nine charges in the indictment, Judge Chin remanded Michael Nouri, who had been out on bail pending trial, into custody immediately. Reza Eric Nouri and Martin were allowed to remain out on bail.

Earlier, co-defendants and stockbrokers Alain Lustig and Ruben Serrano pleaded guilty to conspiracy to commit securities fraud, wire fraud, and commercial bribery in addition to securities fraud.

Nouri had argued that even if he did bribe brokers, that is not a crime, an argument dismissed by the judge.

He also asked to suppress the government's recording because he had been represented by counsel at the time that the government intercepted his phones. The government, not surprisingly, forcefully rejected all of Nouri's arguments, and the judge agreed.

Separately, Nouri filed suit against Smart Online in Delaware to compel the company to continue to pay for his defense even after its directors and officers insurance policy payments were exhausted.

In an SEC filing, the company estimated the fees it would incur to be $826,798 in addition to legal fees and costs of over $1.3 million previously paid by the company's insurance carrier for the benefit of the Nouris in these matters. The company added in its filing that it "intends to vigorously contest the complaint."[5]

Sentencing, which had been scheduled for October 6, 2009 was put off to allow the government time to calculate the total loss in the case, which is an important element in determining both sentence and amount of restitution, and for the defendants to prepare their objections.

Earlier, on October 18, 2007, Robyn L. Gooden filed a class action lawsuit in the United States District Court for the Middle District of North Carolina naming Smart Online, and certain current and former officers and directors, Maxim Group, LLC, and Jesup & Lamont Securities Corp. as defendants. The lawsuit was filed on behalf of all persons other than the defendants who purchased our securities from May 2, 2005 through September 28, 2007 and were damaged.

The complaint asserts violations of federal securities laws, including violations of Section 10(b) of the Exchange Act and Rule 10b-5. It asserts that the defendants made material and misleading statements with the intent to mislead the investing public and conspired in a fraudulent scheme to manipulate trading in company stock, allegedly causing plaintiffs to purchase the stock at an inflated price. The complaint requests certification of the plaintiff as class representative and seeks, among other relief, unspecified compensatory damages, including interest, plus reasonable costs and expenses, including counsel fees and expert fees.

On June 24, 2008, the court entered an order appointing a lead plaintiff for the class action. On September 8, 2008, the plaintiff filed an amended complaint that added additional defendants who had served as directors or officers during the class period as well as independent auditor. The class action was settled as to the company and the outside directors. The settlement, once signed, would be subject to court approval. The tentative settlement contemplates a cash payment of $350,000 to be made by the company and the issuance to the class of 1,475,000 shares of company common stock, in consideration for which all claims against the settling defendants would be dismissed with prejudice, with no admission of fault or wrongdoing by the company or the other defendants. The company's additional charge to expenses for 2009 as a result of this tentative settlement is approximately $2,150,000. Nouri's[6] motion for a new trial was denied, so plaintiffs in the complaint will have a relatively easy time in prevailing against Nouri. However, it may prove to be a pyrrhic victory, as the company's directors and officers insurance was exhausted paying for legal fees, and Nouri will undoubtedly forfeit all of his assets to the government. Perhaps aware of the difficulties, there has been no substantive activity in the class action case since December 2008.[7] The government had requested terms of imprisonment of 20 to 25 years for Michael Nouri and 8 years for Eric Nouri. In May 20, 2010, Judge Chen sentenced them respectively, to terms of 8 years and 18 months.

(Disclosure: The author, a former director of Smart Online, resigned on June 23, 2006, long before the arrests were made. He was not charged or named in the criminal complaints. He was named, in his capacity as a former director, in the class-action suit, but he and the other former directors were subsequently dismissed from the case by the plaintiffs without having to make any payment whatsoever.)

Lessons to Be Learned

Had Smart Online focused on its business, and not obsessively on the market, it could have had been a successful enterprise, and it could have supported a much smaller but realistic market capitalization. Illegally attempting to control the price created an unrealistic market capitalization and attracted short sellers and regulatory attention. Eventually, a stock finds its level. Post the arrests, the stock price dropped to as low as $0.55 in the quarter ending September 30, 2007, and more recently it has been trading at around $1.00 to $1.50.

There were multiple tragedies in this story. Innocent investors lost money; hardworking employees lost their jobs as well as their savings. Smart Online is still hemorrhaging money (for the first six months of 2009, it reported a loss of $3,328,689 or $0.18 per share, based on 18,333,140 shares outstanding and only $1,542,654 in gross revenue; it reported a loss of $1.39 per share in the quarter ended September 30, 2008, and an operating profit margin of negative 78 percent), so its survival is still in question. Greed is the great destroyer.

Smart Online was an early entrant into cloud computing, a burgeoning field. Had its founder been content to build a business, he might well have succeeded. By greedily attempting to manipulate the market and to bribe brokers, he not only crossed a criminal line; he nearly destroyed the company.

Chapter 32

Boiler Rooms

"Boiler rooms" or "bucket shops" are the names given to high-pressure brokerage firms that cold-call clients to sucker them into buying smaller-cap stocks. At the end of the nineteenth century, there were places called bucket shops that looked like the stock exchange, with stock boards or ticker-tape machines, but they were really casinos. You could bet on the performance of a stock or an index—almost anything. While nothing of real value was traded, lots of money was lost nonetheless.

Wild speculation in these bucket shops contributed to a panic and the stock market crash of 1907, the one that resulted in the formation of the Federal Reserve Bank. States began campaigns to ban them, and they were finally made illegal in 1920. Public participation in the bucket shops preceded the popularity of the stock market during the Roaring Twenties.

Some of the antics of modern-day bucket shops were immortalized in the movie *Boiler Room*, directed and written by Ben Younger and starring Giovanni Ribisi, Vin Diesel, Nia Long, and Ben Affleck, which was released in 2000. It's about con men who pitch worthless stocks. A boiler room is a "churn-and-burn operation."[1] The stocks being touted, even if they go up for a while, inevitably crash.

In a typical investment-related boiler room, the brokers (registered reps) may sit crowded together in a room with long tables with up to seven phone stations per table. The firm likely holds mandatory sales meetings every morning, at which time sales techniques are demonstrated and scripts for the firm's house stock are distributed. Brokers are expected to follow the script and give customers only the information it contains. They are discouraged from doing any outside research, and are told to rely on the firm's research and representations. After the morning sales meeting, the reps are expected to spend the entire day on the phone. The firm expects a high volume of sales, and if brokers don't stay on the phone, they are fired. One registered rep told an examiner that he made 250 calls on a good day, 70 on a bad day. All of his calls had been previously qualified by an unregistered cold caller.

Though *Boiler Room* was fictional, some real-life bucket shops (long since closed by regulators) that come to mind and which operated similarly are A.R. Baron, D.H. Blair, Stratton Oakmont (and its illegitimate sister, Monroe Parker Securities), Whale Securities, and First Jersey Securities (whose founder, Robert E. Breenan, was sentenced to a prison term of nine years and two months after being found guilty of bankruptcy fraud). There are also any number of obscure little firms that did the same thing.

A review of the film *Boiler Room* in the *New York Observer* had a few memorable lines: "*Boiler Room* has some new dictums for their real-life counterparts: 'Don't pitch the bitch' (meaning, never sell stock to women); 'Act as if' (meaning, 'Act as if you've got a nine-inch cock'); and selling stock is 'the white-boy way of slinging crack rock' (meaning, it will make you rich fast).

"'A friend's firm that I visited was exactly like this one,' a PaineWebber broker said after the screening. 'It was on Long Island. The parking lot was full of Porsches, BMW's, Ferraris. There were a hundred guys in there. Every single one of them was under 25. Most of them were just high school graduates. They were all wearing Rolexes.'"[2]

How a Boiler Room Works Today

Blogger Warren Meyer describes how a boiler room operator tried to scam him at the end of 2008.[3] "I got another boiler room broker call today, so I guess the recent downturn has not flushed out all the cockroaches. A while back I discussed the frequent calls I get from boiler room stock promoters."

Here is what he recounts:

So the other day, I accidentally let one of them go further than I usually allow. He said he was from Olympia Asset Management. (There is an Olympia Asset Management web page, but I don't know if it is the same company and the web page has not been updated for several years.) I let him run for a bit because a friend of mine runs a very well-respected financial planning firm with a different name but also with Olympia in the title, and for a moment I thought it might have been one of his folks.

Anyway, he proceeds to try to convince me that we have talked before and discussed a certain security. "Remember me? We talked six months ago about ____." Of course, I had never heard of the guy. At this point I usually hang up, because I have heard this crap before—it is a common pitch. It's pretty clear to me now that this is what he is doing:

Trying to imply that we have some kind of relationship we actually don't have. Or worse . . .

Trying to convince me that he touted stock A six months ago, so now he can tell me stock A has gone up in price. Many reputable brokers built their reputation by cold calling people and saying: Watch these three stocks and see how they do and I will call you back in six months. That way, you can evaluate their stock picking without risk. The modern sleazy approach is to pick a stock that has gone up a lot in the last six months, and then call some harried businessperson and pretend you called them with that pick six months ago, hoping that they will give you the benefit of the doubt.

The guy today called me and asked me if I remembered him calling six months ago predicting the downturn in the mortgage market and the crash of the financial stocks. You are not crazy—no matter how certain the guy seems, you really did not talk to him six months ago.

By the way, I am not the only one getting this pitch. Ed Moed got the same pitch from the same script from the same company. Many of his commenters share similar experiences.[4]

Some things never change.

Renaissance Financial Securities and Stanley Cohen

One little bucket shop I want to tell you about is Renaissance Financial Securities Corporation of not-so-blessed memory. Like many of them, it was based in Long Island, in and around Garden City. Renaissance is interesting, not as a bucket shop, because in this it was no different from many other little bucket shops on Long Island, but because of a plot within the plot.

Renaissance did only a few tech underwritings before flaming out. It was ostensibly run by Todd Spehler, who previously had been with a different shuttered bucket shop, but still held the requisite licenses. However, Spehler was only the front man. The real power was a man named Stanley Cohen. His story is told at length in an appeals court decision.[5]

Renaissance chose its name carefully, in order to be confused with Renaissance Technologies, a highly successful hedge fund management company started by James Simons in 1982. Cohen had owned a broker-dealership in the early 1970s, and after getting into trouble there had been banned in 1973 from ever exercising a supervisory role at a brokerage firm.

Some 20 years later, after a varied career that included serving as part-time mayor of Great Neck Estates, Cohen wanted to reenter the brokerage business. Sponsored by a small firm, he applied to the National Association of Securities Dealers (NASD) to be hired by the firm in a nonsupervisory capacity. He remained at the small firm for two years, garnering modest commissions. Then, without the NASD's permission, he switched jobs and joined Renaissance. In direct violation of the NASD's ban, he assumed full trading control, and even signed checks.

Marking the Close

Cohen also engaged in various manipulative practices, one of which is called "marking the close" (an illegal practice of artificially pumping up the price at the end of the trading day) so the closing price reported in the newspapers and in all the Internet sites will be higher than the stock trading all day. This technique also had the effect of increasing the overnight value of Renaissance's inventory, which was important for meeting its net capital requirements.

Cohen also instituted an illegal policy of "crossing the stock," meaning that no sell order could be issued for a security that Renaissance was pushing unless the broker found a matching buy order. A broker who couldn't find a buyer had to buy the stock for his own account. Eventually, someone tipped off the NASD that Cohen was running the firm without even being registered there, much less having a license to operate as a principal.

Lying to the NASD

What ultimately did in Renaissance, as well as Spehler, Cohen, his son Adam, and his daughter, Jamie Scher, was lying under oath to the NASD. Everyone conspired to deny that Cohen was really running Renaissance, and denied under oath the illegal sales practices that were employed. Ultimately, their ruse was found out, and they were all charged with perjury in the first degree and found guilty at trial. Cohen was also convicted of two counts of fraudulent securities practices and sentenced to a term of imprisonment of one to five years, and five years of probation, while the others received lesser sentences. Once again, we see that the cover-up was worse than the crime.

Boiler rooms deservedly earned a reputation for sleaze. They operate on the edge of the law. Many use high-pressure tactics and subterfuge to illegally prop up the price of a stock until it ultimately collapses of its own weight (oversupply of sellers and paucity of buyers). But that's only half the story here. The other half is that, as in the case of Martha Stewart, the crime can get you into trouble, but the cover-up can make it much worse.

Chapter 33

Accounting Frauds

With Examples

Accounting fraud might not seem to be a form of alchemy, but it is. Very small, presales companies are priced based on hope. Larger companies with sales and earnings are usually priced in the market as a multiple of either sales or earnings. If they are reporting rapidly increasing sales and profits, the market will reward them with a larger multiple. Also, many analysts forecast estimates of the expected numbers, and beating the estimates will cause the stock price to go up, while missing them, even by as little as a penny a share, may cause it to plummet.

Many boards of directors tie executive compensation directly to meeting targets that may include sales, earnings, or even share price. Such incentives put tremendous pressure on management to come up with the right numbers, and in many accounting frauds, executives simply fudge the numbers in order to reach their benchmarks.

Recording Phantom Sales and Earnings

I could write an entire book recounting stories of accounting frauds, and in fact many such books have already been written. One that

I recommend is *Fraud 101*, Second Edition, by Howard Silverstone and Howard R. Davia(John Wiley & Sons, 2005). I had a difficult time deciding which of the many accounting frauds perpetrated over the years to discuss here. I finally settled on three in addition to the story of Crazy Eddie, which we discussed in Chapter 6 and which included massive accounting fraud among its many misdeeds. One was a fraud with no real factual basis (WorldCom), one had phantom sales and earnings (America Online [AOL]), and one had managed sales (Computer Associates). In all three cases, the perpetrators ended up with lengthy sentences.

WorldCom

WorldCom was once the second-largest telecommunications company. It grew largely by acquiring other telecommunications companies, most notably MCI Communications. It ended up failing in July 2002 with the dubious distinction of being the largest bankruptcy in history until it was eclipsed by the Lehman Brothers' bankruptcy in 2008.

Beginning in 1999 and continuing through May 2002, the company, under the direction of Bernie Ebbers (CEO), Scott Sullivan (CFO), David Myers (controller), and Buford "Buddy" Yates (director of general accounting), used fraudulent accounting methods to mask its declining earnings by painting a false picture of financial growth and profitability so as to prop up the price of WorldCom's stock. The fraud was accomplished primarily in two ways:

1. Underreporting line costs (interconnection expenses with other telecommunication companies) by capitalizing these costs on the balance sheet rather than properly expensing them.
2. Inflating revenues with bogus accounting entries from "corporate unallocated revenue accounts."

In 2002, a small team of honest (and skeptical) internal auditors at WorldCom worked together, often at night and in secret, to investigate and unearth $3.8 billion in fraud. Shortly thereafter, the company's audit committee and board of directors were notified of the fraud and acted swiftly: Sullivan was fired, Myers resigned, Arthur Andersen withdrew its audit opinion for 2001, and the Securities and Exchange Commission (SEC) launched an investigation.

By the end of 2003, it was estimated that the company's total assets had been inflated by around $11 billion and Bernie Ebbers, MCI's founder and longtime CEO, was tried and found guilty. He is currently serving a 25-year prison term at Oakdale Federal Correctional Complex in Louisiana.

AOL's Round-Trip Accounting

In 2005, AOL (now a subsidiary of Time Warner, which we discussed in Chapter 4), settled civil SEC charges by agreeing to pay a $300 million penalty. The SEC's investigation at that time focused largely on so-called round-trip transactions, in which AOL paid sites that bought advertising space on its network, essentially paying itself for that space.

Time Warner also had to restate more than two years' worth of results—from the fourth quarter of 2000 through 2002—reducing advertising revenue at AOL by $500 million over that stretch. However, the deal with the SEC did not call for it to admit any wrongdoing.

More recently, in May 2008, the SEC charged eight former AOL executives with a $1 billion accounting fraud. The SEC charged that the former AOL executives executed fraudulent round-trip transactions in which AOL–Time Warner effectively funded its own advertising revenue by giving purchasers the money to buy online advertising that they did not want or need.

Online advertising revenue was a key measure by which analysts and investors evaluated the company. The defendants made or substantially contributed to statements to investors that included the company's fraudulent financial results. John Kelly and Mark Wovsaniker, both certified public accountants, also were charged with misleading the company's external auditor about the fraudulent transactions.

According to the complaint, "In one example from November 2000, emails and instant messages obtained by the government show AOL employees rushing to turn a negotiated discount on telecom services from a supplier, Telefonica, into advertising revenue. Telefonica agreed to buy AOL ads with the money it would have returned as a rebate."

In a fascinating twist, even Scott Sullivan, the former chief financial officer of WorldCom, who is now serving a five-year prison sentence for his role in the biggest accounting fraud in history (see preceding discussion), saw AOL's accounting as a sham. "This has turned into a money-changing scheme, and it can't continue," reads a November 2001 e-mail from WorldCom cited in the SEC complaint.[1]

In the arrangement that prompted the rebuke from Sullivan, WorldCom twice agreed to waive penalties that AOL owed on an unrelated contract. "If you want $17 million in advertising, then pay $17 million instead of the credit and we will place ads, even though we don't need them," a clearly frustrated Sullivan wrote, according to the SEC.[2] "If you want $25 million in advertising, then pay $17 million instead of the credit, pay another $8 million and we will place the ads, even though we don't need them."

The complaint also alleges that in order to book revenue from Telefonica before the financial quarter that ended on December 31, 2001, AOL created "its own purported ads" for Telefonica that misspelled the company's name as Telephonica and linked to a dead web page. "No graphics, no links, no nuthin'! LOL," an unnamed AOL employee wrote in an instant message cited in the complaint.[3] Replied another colleague: "Welcome to the new world of e-commerce."[4]

Four of the executives charged agreed to settle the charges without admitting or denying liability, and also agreed to pay millions of dollars in penalties and disgorgements. Two received lengthy bars from serving as an officer or director of a public company. Interestingly, one of those charged, Joseph A. Ripp, formerly chief financial officer, had been hailed earlier as a whistle-blower, and through his attorney he vigorously denied the charges and has not settled them. As Tim Arango asked out loud in the *New York Times*, "how did Ripp, who successfully minded the finances of Time Inc. for 25 years and has been lauded by Justice lawyers as a pivotal figure in exposing criminal fraud at AOL, wind up in the crosshairs of the SEC?"[5]

The SEC claims in its complaint that Ripp "knowingly or recklessly engineered, oversaw and executed a scheme to artificially and materially inflate the company's reported online advertising revenue."[6] About 16 months after the case was first filed, in the first substantive ruling, Judge Colleen McMahon on September 30, 2009, denied

Defendants' Motion to Dismiss, meaning that the case can proceed to discovery and, if no settlement is reached, to trial. It seems that the case (1:08-cv-04612-CM-GWG) is likely to drag on for several years.

Computer Associates

Computer Associates (CA) is a software company that grew to be a multibillion-dollar business largely by making acquisitions. Although the company did not invent either sales or earnings, for many years it would manage its earnings. According to the plea agreement of the CFO, he met with two other senior CA executives on January 6, 2000, to discuss the company's sales for the previous quarter. The sales fell short of Wall Street analysts' forecasts, so the men decided to continue to book new sales as if they had taken place in the previous quarter, according to the plea. To hide the backdated sales from auditors, employees of CA deleted time stamps that showed when the contracts had actually been faxed to the company.

As Alex Berenson noted in the New York Times, "the actual accounting fraud to which the men pleaded guilty is relatively narrow. They admitted to deliberately booking sales and profits for CA on contracts that were signed shortly after the end of the quarter in which the sales were booked. Unlike the esoteric accounting gimmicks that current and former employees have said CA used to inflate its reported profits, the practice of backdating contracts is not unheard of at publicly traded companies."[7]

However, CA carried the practice to an extreme, according to the guilty pleas. In some quarters, more than 20 percent of the company's revenue came from backdated contracts. In any case, prosecutors have focused on the backdating of contracts in lieu of trying to win convictions on the more complicated techniques that they suspect CA used, the New York Times stated.[8] Overall, the government said the fraud amounted to $2.2 billion.

As in many other fraud cases, once the fraud has been detected, there is often an attempt to cover it up. The government usually terms this obstruction of justice. One witness said that CA's general counsel, who was also a target of the federal investigation, purportedly told him "to respond to questions from Wachtell, Lipton, Rosen & Katz" (the law firm that conducted the internal investigation) with "half-truths and vague answers."[9] The general counsel himself personally denied to me ever having made such a statement, but rather he said he told witnesses the answer the direct questions and not to volunteer information.

When all was said and done, Sanjay Kumar, CA's CEO, received a sentence of 12 years and was fined $8 million for helping inflate the company's sales figures in 1999 and 2000, as well as for lying to federal investigators and authorizing a bribe to a potential witness. He was ordered to pay $798.6 million in restitution. The CFO received a sentence of seven months in prison and seven months of home detention because prosecutors said he was instrumental in the prosecution of Kumar. The former head of sales was handed a seven-year sentence. The general counsel was sentenced to one year and one day, and four others also received relatively short sentences.

As is often the case, it was the actions after the fraud was uncovered (the attempted cover-up) that accounted for the bulk of the punishments.

Transparency of information goes to the heart of our market-based capitalist system. Investors in public companies rely on the information provided in company filings. Investors rely on independent public accountants to audit the numbers and confirm their accuracy. While auditors disclaim responsibility to detect fraud, in practice they can be called to account for audit failures and can be held liable. When, in response to whatever pressures, the filings are misleading or fraudulent, the market system is compromised, making accounting fraud the serious crime that it is.

Chapter 34

Stock Option Frauds

ALCHEMY THAT BENEFITS INSIDERS

S tock option fraud is a form of alchemy that illegally benefits insiders. It's another way of turning paper into money, at the expense of the public shareholders.

How Options Work

An option is a right to buy a stock in the future at a price that is set on the date of issuance. It's often used as a way of compensating employees, because it motivates them by making their interests parallel those of the shareholders. In Silicon Valley, options were the main form of compensation until the end of the dot-com era.

Obviously, options are valuable only if a stock's price goes up. Such options are said to be "in the money." So, for example, if Miracle Widgets' stock is trading at $5 and it issues an employee an option to buy 100,000 shares of its stock at $5 ("at the money"), exercisable for five years, and the stock then goes to $10, the employee is sitting on $500,000 of value. If the stock price declines to $4, the option has no value.

How Backdating Fraud Works

Say Miracle Widgets usually trades in a range of $40 to $50. If, at the time that it's trading at $50, options are issued at $40, then there is $10 of compensation in the option. It is in the money. Under the accounting rules, that has to be disclosed, and is booked as compensation expense (there are maximum limits for it to be deductible as compensation expense). There's nothing wrong with that.

However, let's say the company's chief financial officer goes back in time, locates a day when the stock closed at $40 (say three months earlier) and pretends to issue the stock on that date, by backdating the option. He has just pulled off a fraud. Ostensibly the options were issued at a fair market value, at the money—that is, at the market price— but in fact, they were really $10 in the money. So an employee could exercise them immediately, sell the shares, and make $10 a share, risk free. If the option allows for cashless exercise, as many do, then the employee doesn't even have to lay out any money. This is obviously illegal, but it seems that in some circles it was done regularly.

Comverse Is the Poster Child for Backdating

The first criminal conviction for backdating of options related to Comverse, the company that invented voice mail, among other advanced software technologies. It seems that Kobi Alexander, the former long-time CEO, and the former CFO, David Kreinberg, took the practice of backdating options to new extremes, as charged by the U.S. Attorney for the Eastern District of New York in 2006.

Not only did Comverse issue millions of in-the-money options, a large portion of which went to Alexander and Kreinberg, but it also issued options in false names, in order to warehouse them and make them available to new hires later by surreptitiously changing the names of the option holders. The scam went on for many years. Once it came out, Alexander allegedly offered large bribes to Kreinberg to take sole responsibility. Kreinberg and William Sorin, the company's general counsel, both pleaded guilty to the charges. Sorin was sentenced to serve a year and a day, and did. Kreinberg signed a cooperation agreement with the government, so his sentence was held up pending completion of his cooperation (against Alexander).

Meanwhile, Alexander fled the country, and ended up in Namibia, transferring at least some $64 million to Israel, much of which was then transferred to Namibia. He was then charged in a superseding indictment with money laundering on top of the 34 counts in the earlier indictment. In addition to prison, the government sought forfeiture from Alexander of $138 million in assets, which was the profit he is alleged to have made on exercising the options (but only $6.4 million of this was as a result of the backdating). In the meantime, the U.S. government is blocking $50 million of Alexander's that it found held in his U.S. accounts.

In Namibia, money laundering is not a crime, and neither is backdating of options. Alexander has been fighting extradition, so far (as of May 2010) successfully. His attorney in Namibia noted that Alexander did not attempt to conceal any of his money from law enforcement authorities when he transferred about US$57 million (about N$451 million) from a U.S. bank account in his own name to accounts in Israel, also in his own name, in July 2006.

He also pointed out that the $138 million the government seeks from Alexander is more than seven times the amount of money that Alexander is alleged to have earned through illegal stock options backdating before 1998. Louis Du Pisani also stated: "So there can be no suggestion that any of the funds brought into Namibia by our client constitute the proceeds of alleged unlawful activities."[1] "The only alleged activities from which the United States authorities can claim our client profited are activities in respect of which our client is not charged criminally [and therefore would not be extraditable]."[2]

Alexander is still in Namibia. He has been living in the southern African desert country with his wife Hana and their children since July 2006, and has bought a $543,000 house, launched an annual $20,000 scholarship for gifted students, and invested $2.9 million in an 84-unit low-income housing project. On May 27, 2009, Justice Collins Parker in Namibia granted him an order that he may lawfully reside and carry on business in Namibia. In the judgment, Judge Parker stated that Alexander has shown on a "preponderance of probabilities that he has a right that this court should protect in the interim."[3]

On June 18, 2009, the SEC settled its case against Comverse Technology, Inc. with Comverse agreeing not to violate securities laws in the future. The SEC also announced the filing of settled civil charges against Ulticom, Inc., a majority-owned subsidiary of Comverse whose stock is also publicly traded, for fraudulent options backdating and earnings management practices.[4]

On April 12, 2010, Alexander won an important victory in Namibia. The Namibian Supreme Court, in a judgment of Acting Judge of Appeal Johan Strydom, declared that section 21 of the Extradition Act of 1996 is unconstitutional. The provision held that an extraditable person must remain in prison until the appeals process is exhausted. The court has yet to rule on the extradition request, but meanwhile, Alexander may live and work in Namibia.[5]

Not Just Comverse

While Comverse was the poster child for stock option fraud, it was by no means alone. In all, at least 160 public companies have owned up to being investigated or charged with backdating of options, and they include such well-known companies as Apple.

Backdating of options, while a common practice, is still a fraud on the market even though some high-tech companies viewed it as either not a crime at all or a victimless crime. While most of the cases that have come to light have been discovered by the companies themselves and have been resolved civilly, the most egregious cases resulted in criminal charges and prison sentences.

Chapter 35

Odd and Unusual
Financial Frauds

NOT YOUR EVERYDAY FRAUD

T his chapter recounts some of the more odd and unusual financial
frauds that have been come to light.

$90 Million Tax Refund Fraud

In a coordinated investigation involving the IRS, the FBI, and the
Postal Inspection Service, three people (Lacy Bethea, Gladys Maria
Pena, and Jose Franklin Duarte) were arrested in February 2009 and
charged with massive fraud in a scheme to steal millions of dollars by
filing fraudulent federal tax returns, falsely claiming refunds, and then
diverting the refund checks that had been sent by the U.S. Treasury.

Since approximately June 2007, federal law enforcement agents
have been investigating a massive scheme involving the fraudulent
use of stolen Social Security numbers and other identity information to submit fraudulent state and federal tax returns. To date, the
investigation has uncovered the electronic filing of tens of thousands

of federal tax returns and tens of millions of dollars of fraudulently obtained tax refunds.

The scheme involved the electronic filing of thousands of tax returns using Social Security numbers assigned to residents of the Commonwealth of Puerto Rico. Residents of Puerto Rico are issued Social Security numbers, but typically do not file federal tax returns with the IRS because, in general, such filing is not required as long as all of the Puerto Rican resident's income is derived from Puerto Rican sources (they do pay income tax to the Commonwealth). In this scheme, the fraudulent tax returns falsely claim that the filer resides in one of the 50 states of the United States. The use of Puerto Rican Social Security numbers minimizes the risk that a legitimate federal tax return was already filed by the legitimate holder of the Social Security number.

The investigation determined that, during the one-month period between January 16 and February 18, 2009, approximately 8,000 federal tax returns were electronically filed via Internet web sites run by a particular company. Substantially all of those returns were filed from the Dominican Republic, and nearly every one sought a refund. The total amount of refunds sought by those approximately 8,000 federal tax returns exceeded $90 million. Moreover, 3,300 of those returns, seeking approximately $32 million in refunds, had been accepted by the IRS, which means that refund checks would have been sent out. Thus far, however, the IRS has determined that approximately 2,000 of those returns were fraudulent because the returns indicated that the taxpayer had earned wages from a particular employer in 2008 when, in fact, that was not true.

One of the ways the participants in the scheme arranged to actually receive the refund checks that were sent out was to request that they be mailed to various addresses in New York and elsewhere. The addresses were often clustered around a particular location. Participants in the scheme would then arrange with Postal Service letter carriers to steal the checks from the mail and provide them to the participants in the scheme, normally for a per-check fee. For example, thousands of the returns in question requested that refund checks be sent to addresses on the Bronx postal route assigned to Bethea, who is a letter carrier.

Once the scheme was uncovered, decoy letters and checks prepared to resemble federal tax refund checks were placed in the mail for delivery on Bethea's route. But instead of delivering the checks or returning them to the post office, she left the post office with them after work. Pena is alleged to have received unlawfully taken decoy mail on February 23, 2008, and Duarte is alleged to have attempted to receive decoy mail on that day as well. Each of the defendants was arrested and released on bond. Duarte pleaded guilty in September 2009 and was sentenced to 78 months in prison. The other cases were still pending as of April 2010.

Fake Billion-Dollar Client

On March 9, 2009, the SEC charged Leila Jenkins with inventing an investor. The SEC charged Jenkins, a money manager with offices in New York and Rhode Island, with falsely creating a billion-dollar client in order to gain credibility and attract legitimate investors. In its complaint, the SEC charged Leila Jenkins and her firm, Locke Capital Management Inc., with making up the supposedly massive client and then repeatedly lying about its existence to land real clients.[1] The SEC alleges that Jenkins lied to the SEC staff about the existence of the invented client and furnished the SEC staff with bogus documents in 2008, including fake account statements that she created.

"Today's enforcement action demonstrates that investment advisers who lure clients with false claims will be held accountable for their actions," said George Curtis, deputy director of the SEC's Division of Enforcement.[2] "In this case, the conduct was particularly egregious because Jenkins lied to the SEC staff to try to escape detection."

The SEC's complaint also alleges that Jenkins made up so-called confidential client accounts, purportedly based in Switzerland, and repeatedly claimed the accounts contained more than $1 billion in assets that she managed.[3] From at least 2003 to 2009, falsehoods concerning the confidential accounts were communicated in brochures, in meetings, in submissions to online databases that prospective clients used to select money managers, and in SEC filings.

Even as Locke Capital Management began to take on clients in late 2006, the assets under management of its real clients never amounted to more than a very small portion of the billion-plus dollars that Jenkins claimed to manage. "This brazen web of lies to investors constituted a serious breach of fiduciary duty," said David Bergers, director of the SEC's Boston Regional Office.[4]

Besides the invented client and assets under management, the SEC's complaint alleges several other lies Jenkins and her firm told to investors. These include misrepresenting Locke's performance for years in which Locke had no clients and deceiving clients about the makeup of the firm, including the number, identity, and role of its employees.

According to David Scheer's report in Bloomberg.com, "Locke intends to contest the action brought by the SEC," said Edmund "Ned" Searby, a Cleveland attorney representing Jenkins and her company.[5] The agency's case focuses on the accuracy of the firm's marketing, and "we do not understand that there is any issue with client funds or securities being missing, or misappropriated."[6] The company "has significantly outperformed the applicable indexes through remarkably difficult recent times in the market," Searby added.[7] "Locke's investors have fared better than they would have in the average fund."

The case has not yet been resolved.

In the two odd cases discussed in this chapter, the first case involved criminal charges for sophisticated theft from the government through filing of fraudulent tax returns seeking refunds that were then diverted to the perpetrators. The second case is in more of a gray area, and was filed civilly. In the SEC's view, Locke illegally lured investors by claiming to have a large but fictitious client. The goal was to lure other clients on that basis, making the marketing material materially misleading. However the case turns out, it underscores the importance of transparency, full disclosure, and accuracy in all information related to the investment process, and emphasizes that integrity and trust are essential for markets to operate properly.

Afterword

What Does the
Future Hold?

The Ethics of the Fathers—"Pirkei Avot" (Chapter 5, Mishna 21) teaches what Rabbi Yehuda Ben Teimah said: "*ben shishim lezikna*" which literally translates as "at [age] sixty, one [becomes] an elder."[1] This is generally understood as an allusion to someone of 60 attaining the age of wisdom, based on the *Sifra*, where we find: "[the initial letters of] He who has acquired wisdom" (*Zeh shKaNah chokmah*) spell out the word ZKN (an elder).[2] So on the strength of that, and in the hope that I have indeed acquired a little wisdom over the past 60 years, permit me to foresee the following trends.

Knee-Jerk Regulation and More Big Government

Dr. Frenkel's sage advice to Congress notwithstanding, Congress and the Obama administration will show that they are "doing something" by spending more money for more bureaucrats and piling on more burdensome regulation rather than intelligently and properly enforcing the rules already on the books using expert staff with substantial private-sector experience.

Just as the O.P.M. Leasing scandal improved the auditing of physical inventory, and the AOL, Computer Associates, Enron, and WorldCom scandals tightened audit standards related to revenue recognition, Madoff and other Ponzi scandals will ensure that auditors check that securities supposed to be in investment accounts are really there.

Anyone taking money from the public will need to be audited by a peer-reviewed Public Company Accounting Oversight Board (PCAOB) regulated auditor.[3] Auditors will not be able to rely solely on third-party confirmations, but will need to be satisfied that cash and securities are really on deposit at custodial institutions.

Whereas Madoff was audited by a non–peer-reviewed auditor, this will no longer be allowed for anyone taking an investor's money. And that is a good thing.

More Regulation and Decrease in Popularity of Hedge Funds

On the same note, the economic pendulum has been struck hard by the projectile of governmental meddling. It will trace a wide arc to the left, and it will be some years before the projectile's energy will be dissipated, in accordance with the rule of physics that when the projectile is fired, its momentum is transferred to the pendulum and its velocity can be determined from the height to which the pendulum rises. This projectile was fired very hard. So, the days of laissez-faire regulation are over for a while, and the government will err on the side of too much regulation, until the pendulum ultimately swings the other way.

In closing, the question that must be posed is the one asked by Terence Gourvish, director of the London School of Economics' Business History Group, namely, "Is financial fraud inevitable?"[4] Gourvish thinks so. "People aren't bothered when boom times are rolling, but when they need their money again, that's what catches out the crooks," he said.[5]

Greed: Not a Sufficient Explanation

So does greed inevitably cause bubbles? Greed is a factor, but doesn't explain everything.

It was widely reported that the bank robber Willie Sutton replied to a reporter's inquiry as to why he robbed banks by saying, "Because that's where the money is."[6] However, he denied ever saying so. In a 1976 book he co-authored, *Where the Money Was: The Memoirs of a Bank Robber*, he wrote, "The credit belongs to some enterprising reporter who apparently felt a need to fill out his copy. . . . I can't even remember where I first read it. It just seemed to appear one day, and then it was everywhere."[7]

According to Snopes.com, "the earliest print sighting of the coined phrase 'because that's where the money is' dates to March 15, 1952, when it appeared in *Redlands Daily Facts*, a Southern California news-paper."[8] So what actually motivated Sutton to hold up banks? Sutton wrote: "Why did I rob banks? Because I enjoyed it. I loved it. I was more alive when I was inside a bank, robbing it, than at any other time in my life. I enjoyed everything about it so much that one or two weeks later I'd be out looking for the next job. But to me the money was the chips, that's all."[9]

Insider Trading Must Continue to Be Restricted

The allegations of insider trading that we have discussed, includ-ing those involving the Galleon Group and Mark Cuban, have shone a spotlight on illegal insider trading, and have sparked much debate. Some[10] have suggested that insider trading laws are hypocritical. Others[11] have argued that the laws are unenforceable and should be abolished. I'm a Ralph Waldo Emerson ("The less government we have the better") Jeffersonian, and I disagree with that proposition. I'm not, however, in favor of abolishing restrictions on insider trading, as markets simply cannot function properly when material information is not disseminated to the public in a timely fashion. We have seen that insider trading dates back to the dawn of the seventeenth century, going back to the Amsterdam Stock Exchange, which was founded in 1602. Not long afterward, Isaac Le Maire was banned from naked short selling (a form of market manipulation).

We have also seen that one of the all-time largest cases of rumor-mongering and trading on inside information was pulled off in 1815, when London financier Nathan Rothschild led British investors to believe that the Duke of Wellington had lost to Napoleon at the Battle of Waterloo and Rothschild swiftly bought up the entire market in government bonds, thereby acquiring a dominant holding in England's debt for pennies on the pound, building the great House of Rothschild through massive trading on inside information.

The bargain you make when you accept the public's money to grow your business is that you agree to disseminate adequate, timely, accurate, and nonmisleading information. A corollary to that bargain is that you may not trade when you possess inside information that hasn't been disseminated to the public.

It's true that, as we noted in the beginning of the book, we all have a little bit (or a lot) of larceny within us, and we only buy or sell stocks because we think we know more than the next guy (after all, for every buyer, there has to be a seller).

However, there is a great difference between a *belief* that is based on analysis and expectations, and *certain knowledge*.

Consider the games of blackjack and poker. If you have a good memory and can figure probabilities in your head, you may have a long-term advantage over someone who doesn't. That's hugely different from rigging the outcome by loading the dice, secretly marking the cards, or bribing the dealer to stack the deck.

Certainly, there are not always bright lines to distinguish the legal from the illegal, but that does not suggest that we ought throw out the baby with the bathwater.

It is inarguable that securities laws play a vital role in capital formation and economic growth. Abuses of the free-market system, whether they be fraud, improper insider trading, market manipulation, pump-and-dump scams, or whatever, not only unjustly enrich a few at the expense of the many, but they also hinder economic growth. Many countries have discovered that while a wild and woolly, loosely regulated stock market offered an initial advantage to a few, to achieve real growth, they needed to enforce the transparency and fairness that bring the trust that is essential for markets to function properly.

Of course, regulation is not perfect, and some will always break the rules and escape getting caught. That is no reason, however, for abrogating the rules and making for a free-for-all. As Voltaire said, "The perfect is the enemy of the good."

Closing Thought

So at the end of the day, is it just human nature?

This question brings me back to my saintly grandmother Rachel Leah Horowitz, whose story you read in Chapter 2. She was a very practical lady, who not only disliked and stayed away from *luftgescheften* (air business), but also understood the adage that "if it's too good to be true, it probably is." Unfortunately, many others think they are so clever that they can sneak in, get their unfair share, and sneak out. Sadly, it's not so. There's no such thing as a free lunch![12]

Notes

Introduction

1. Flavius Josephus (trans. William Whiston), *The Antiquities of the Jews*, book X1, chap. 8, p. 1041, www.swcs.com.au/uploads/Josephus_The_Antiquities_ of_the_Jews.pdf (accessed February 2, 2010).

2. "Tamid," Babylonian Talmud, 32b, http://halakhah.com/pdf/kodoshim/ Tamid.pdf (accessed February 1, 2010).

3. Jon Cohen, *Shots in the Dark: The Wayward Search for an AIDS Vaccine* (New York: W.W. Norton, 2001).

4. *The American Heritage Dictionary of the English Language*, 4th ed. (Boston: Houghton Mifflin, 2000; updated 2009).

5. Tom Cahill, "Madoff's 19th Century Forerunner Shows Flaws of Rule," Bloomberg.com, March 20, 2009, www.bloomberg.com/apps/news?pid= newsarchive&sid=aXSszo3IlHiU (accessed February 2, 2010).

6. Goldwin Smith, *Lectures and Essays* (New York: Bibliolife, 2009).

7. As quoted in Howard Silverstone and Howard R. Davia, *Fraud 101: Techniques and Strategies for Detection* (New York: John Wiley & Sons, 2005), 87.

Chapter 1: Selling Air—Why Now?

1. For more information on the terms *recession* and *depression*, see http://economics .about.com/cs/businesscycles/a/depressions.htm.

2. It was best translated into English by Hillel Halkin.

3. Ecclesiastes 1:9, *King James Bible* (Oxford: Oxford University Press, 2000).

4. Joseph Penso de la Vega, *Confusion of Confusions* (New York: Sonsbeek Publishers, 2006), 55.

5. Shamim Adam, "Global Financial Assets Lost 50 Trillion Last Year, ADB Reports," Bloomberg.com, March 9, 2009, www.infowars.com/ global-financial-assets-lost-50-trillion-last-year/.

6. Ibid.

7. Ibid.

8. Ibid.

9. "The SEC Charges Goldman Sachs with Fraud in Connection with the Structuring and Marketing of a Synthetic CDO," Securities and Exchange Commission, Litigation Release No. 21489, April 16, 2010, Securities and Exchange Commission v. Goldman, Sachs & Co. and Fabrice Tourre, 10 Civ. 322, www.sec.gov/litigation/litreleases/2010/lr21489.htm.

10. Ayn Rand, *Atlas Shrugged* (New York: Random House, 1957; Signet, 1996), 32.

11. "One Must Think of the Final Result," January 3, 2001, http://1boringoldman .com/index.php/2009/01/03/one-must-think-of-the-final-result/ (accessed February 2, 2010).

12. "Stanford Caught Out—at Long Last," *Financial Times*, February 20, 2009, www.ft.com/cms/s/0/c7a2183e-ff88-11dd-b3f8-000077b07658,dwp_ uuid=74411c86-fe74-11dd-b19a-000077b07658.html?nclick_check=1 (accessed February 2, 2010).

13. Ibid.

Chapter 2: Crash Postmortem—How Greed, Hubris, and Lack of Supervision Did Investors In

1. Tunku Varadarajan. "'Nationalize' the Banks," *Wall Street Journal*, February 21, 2009, http://online.wsj.com/article/SB123517380343437079.html (accessed February 2, 2010).

2. J. P. Morgan quote and information about his life can be found at www .barrypopik.com/index.php/new_york_city/entry/it_will_fluctuate_j_ pierpont_morgan/.

3. Alison Leighn Cowan, "Market Turmoil: Bitter Lessons Seen in Plunge," *New York Times*, October 22, 1987. Reviewed online at www.nytimes .com/1987/10/22/business/market-turmoil-bitter-lessons-seen-in-plunge .html?pagewanted=all on February 21, 2010.

4. Heidi Moore, "The Real Credit Crunch Culprit: Drexel Burnham Lambert?" Deal Journal, a *Wall Street Journal* blog, accessed at http://blogs.wsj.com/

deals/2008/04/04/the-real-credit-crunch-culprit-drexel-burnham-lambert
-fault/tab/article/ on February 17, 2010.

5. Ibid.

6. Ibid.

7. Andrew Ross Sorkin, "Don't Blame Milken for the Mortgage Crisis,"
DealBook, http://dealbook.blogs.nytimes.com/2008/04/29/dont-blame-milken
-for-the-mortgage-crisis/ (accessed May 20, 2010).

8. Andrew Ross Sorkin, *Too Big to Fail: The Inside Story of How Wall Street and
Washington Fought to Save the Financial System—and Themselves* (New York:
Viking, 2009).

9. Evan Newmark, "Mean Street: The Stock Market Stinks—That's Why
I'm Buying It," *The Wall Street Journal*, February 1, 2010, http://blogs.wsj
.com/deals/2010/02/01/mean-street-the-stock-market-stinks-thats-why
-im-buying-it/ (accessed February 1, 2010).

10. Megan Barnett, "Daily Brief: On Madoff: The Scholar, the Regulator, and
the Trader," *Portfolio.com*, posted February 26, 2009, www.portfolio.com/
views/blogs/daily-brief/2009/02/26/on-madoff-the-scholar-the-regulator
-and-the-trader/ (accessed February 20, 2010).

11. Ibid. (accessed February 2, 2010).

12. Ibid.

13. Ibid.

Chapter 3: Why We Do It—Bubbles and Fraud

1. Mr. Blodget cites www.businessinsider.com/henry-blodget.

2. Ibid.

3. Sigmund Freud (trans. James Strachey), Civilization and Its Discontents
(New York: W.W. Norton & Company, 1989), 56–57. Also available on-
line with a different translation as Sigmund Freud, Civilization and Its
Discontents, translated from the German by Joan Riviere (W.W. Norton &
Company, 2005). (accessed at www.writing.upenn.edu/~afi lreis/50s/freud-
civ.html on February 20 , 2010).

4. Virginia Postrel, "Pop Psychology," *The Atlantic*, December 2008, www
.theatlantic.com/doc/200812/financial-bubbles (accessed February 2, 2010).

5. Rabbi Jonathan Mishkin, *New World Order Part 1*, www.vbm-torah.org/
archive/intparsha/bereishit/02-59noach1.doc (accessed on February 20, 2010).

6. Ibid.

7. Ibid.

8. Robert L. Heilbroner, *The Worldly Philosophers: The Lives, Times, and Ideas of the Great Economic Thinkers*, 7th ed. (New York: Touchstone, 1999).

9. Sir Winston Churchill, Hansard, November 11, 1947. Quoted in Evsey D. Domar, *Capitalism, Socialism, and Serfdom: Essays by Evsey D. Domar* (Cambridge: Cambridge University Press, 1989), xiii.

10. Sam Antar, "White Collar Fraud," posted October 10, 2008, at http://whitecollarfraud.blogspot.com/2008/10/crisis-of-confidence-some-small-steps.html (accessed February 20, 2010).

11. See Charles P. Kindleberger, *Manias, Panics, and Crashes: A History of Financial Crises* (Wiley Investment Classics) (New York: Palgrave Macmillan, 2001), 76.

Chapter 4: Securities Fraud—Its Long and Storied Past

1. George Santayana, *The Life of Reason or the Phases of Human Progress* (New York: Charles Scribner's Sons, 1920), 284 (available online at http://goo.gl/4W8R).

2. Herbert H. Rowan, *The Low Countries in Early Modern Times* (New York: Harper & Row, 1972), 55.

3. Geoffrey Cotterell, *Amsterdam: The Life of a City* (New York: Little, Brown, 1972), 131.

4. Jean-Baptiste Alphonse Karr, *Les Guêpes*, January 1849, vi.

5. *Daughters of the American Revolution Magazine*, vol. 105 (1971), issues 1–10, 858.

6. Richard O'Connor, *The Oil Barons: Men of Greed and Grandeur* (New York: Little, Brown, 1971), 47.

7. Princess Grace Irish Library (Monaco) Electronic Irish Records Dataset, www.pgil-eirdata.org/html/pgil_datasets/index.htm (accessed February 21, 2010).

8. George Robb, *White-Collar Crime in Modern England: Financial Fraud and Business Morality 1845–1929* (Cambridge: Cambridge University Press, 1992).

9. James O'Shea, *Prince of Swindlers: John Sadleir, M.P., 1813–1856* (New York: Geography Publications, 1999).

10. The term *Ponzi scheme* is often loosely used to refer to any system of unfunded liabilities. For example, some say that the national debt, or the Social Security system, or Medicare "is a Ponzi scheme."

11. Ponzi's biography is available as *Ponzi's Scheme: The True Story of a Financial Legend* by Mitchell Zuckoff (New York: Random House, 2005).

12. Ibid.

Chapter 5: The Perils of Greed—It's All for the Easy Money

1. See A Cockren, "History of Alchemy," www.alchemylab.com/history_of_ alchemy.htm (accessed April 14, 2010).

2. See www.albany.edu/sourcebook/ (accessed April 14, 2010).

3. "American Greed—Case File: Sholam Weiss," www.cnbc.com/id/35058489 (accessed April 14, 2010)

4. Homicide: Legal Aspects—Penalties, http://law.jrank.org/pages/1330/ Homicide-Legal-Aspects-Penalties.html (accessed April 14, 2010).

5. Luke Mullins, "The Collar—A White-Collar Sentence of 330 Years," *U.S. News and World Report*, May 7, 2008, www.usnews.com/money/blogs/ the-collar/2008/05/07/a-white-collar-sentence-of-330-years (accessed April 14, 2010).

6. "Operator Of Mx Factors Sentenced To 100 Years In Prison For Ponzi Scheme That Cost Victims $39 Million," Los Angeles Legal News, September 30, 2009, www.lalegalnews.com/operator-of-mx-factors-sentenced-to-100 -years-in-prison-for-ponzi-scheme-that-cost-victims-39-million/ (accessed April 14, 2010).

7. Alex Berenson, "Ex-Executive Agrees to Pay $800 Million in Restitution," *New York Times*, April 13, 2007, www.nytimes.com/2007/04/13/technology/ 13compute.html (accessed February 14, 2010).

8. Alex Prud'homme, *The Cell Game: Sam Waksal's Fast Money and False Promises— and the Fate of ImClone's Cancer Drug*, (New York: HarperBusiness, 2004).

9. "Lilly to Acquire ImClone Systems in a $6.5 Billion Transaction," Eli Lilly and Company Press Release, October 6, 2008, newsroom.lilly.com/releasedetail .cfm?releaseid=338523 (accessed April 14, 2010).

10. "Macau vs. Vegas: Where Would You Rather Play Blackjack?" Casino Gambling Rules, http://casinogamblingrules.com/casinos/macau-vs-vegas -where-would-you-rather-play-blackjack (accessed April 14, 2010).

Chapter 6: The Elements of Financial Fraud—A Case Study with "Crazy Eddie" Antar

1. Judge Harold A. Ackerman in his opinion issued in the civil case *Securities and Exchange Commission vs. Sam M. Antar et al.* (93-3988), July 15, 1998 (see Litigation Release No. 15814, July 16, 1998, www.sec.gov/litigation /litreleases/lr15814.txt); opinion available at www.whitecollarfraud.com/ files/19832592.pdf (accessed February 20, 2010).

2. E-mail from Larry Weiss to Walter Reisman dated March 22, 2009. JGE is discussed in "What's the story, Jerry?" available at www.barrypopik.com/index.

php/new_york_city/entry/whats_the_story_jerry_jge_forget_about_it_tops_
appliance_city/ (accessed April 14, 2010).

3. Sam E. Antar, "Making a Strong Case for Sarbanes-Oxley," MarketWatch.
com, October 11, 2006, www.marketwatch.com/story/a-reformed-crooks
-view-of-sarbanes-oxley (accessed February 2, 2010).

4. Joseph T. Wells, *Frankensteins of Fraud*, chap. 8, "The Antar Complex,"
accessed at web site of the Association of Certified Fraud Examiners, www
.frankensteinsoffraud.com/pages/chapter1.html, on February 20, 2010.

5. Sam Antar on his web site, www.whitecollarfraud.com/1410602.html (accessed
February 20, 2010).

6. Sam E. Antar, "Crazy Eddie Fraud Summary," www.whitecollarfraud.com/
947660.html (accessed February 2, 2010).

7. Testimony of Sam Antar, as recounted on his blog, www.whitecollarfraud
.com/Frequently_Asked_Questions.html (accessed February 20, 2010).

8. Testimony of Sam Antar, www.whitecollarfraud.com/947660.html (accessed
February 20, 2010).

9. Ibid.

10. Testimony of Sam Antar, www.whitecollarfraud.com/Frequently_Asked_
Questions.html (accessed February 20, 2010).

Chapter 7: "Other People's Money"—The O.P.M. Leasing Fraud

1. It was discussed at length in a *New York Times Magazine* article by Stuart
Taylor Jr. entitled "Ethics and the Law: A Case History" (January 9, 1983),
www.nytimes.com/1983/01/09/magazine/new-york-times-magazine
-january-9-1983.html.

2. Peter Evans, *Ari: The Life and Times of Aristotle Onassis*, (New York: Summit
Books, 1986).

Chapter 8: Smaller-Company Fraud—The "ISC" Story

1. Not its real name, but the story is true. All other names in this chapter are
likewise fictitious.

2. The trustee's commission of what is sold is 25 percent of the first $5,000, plus
10 percent of any amount over $5,000, but less than $50,000, plus 5 percent
of any amount over $50,000 and under $1,000,000, and 3 percent of any
amount above $1,000,000. Section 503(b)(4) of the Bankruptcy Code allows
"reasonable compensation for professional services rendered by an attorney
or an accountant of an entity whose expense is allowable under paragraph (3)
of this subsection. . . ."

3. *Rosh Hashanah, Babylonian Talmud* (New York: Masorah Publishing Company, 1944), 16b.

4. See Committee on Uniform Security Identification Procedures (CUSIP), https://www.cusip.com/static/html/webpage/welcome.html (accessed February 2, 2010).

5. Elmer Wheeler, *Tested Sentences That Sell* (Prentice-Hall, Inc., 1949).

Chapter 9: Selling Long and Short—But Mostly Short

1. Edwin Lefèvre, *Reminiscences of a Stock Operator*, www.stockvision.org/books/Edwin_LeFevre-Reminiscences_of_a_Stock_Operator-EN.pdf (accessed February 2, 2010).

2. For more information, see the Securities and Exchange Commission site at www.sec.gov/spotlight/keyregshoissues.htm (accessed February 20, 2010).

3. Securities and Exchange Commission, Division of Market Regulation, "Key Points about Regulation SHO," www.sec.gov/spotlight/keyregshoissues.htm (accessed on February 20, 2010).

4. See the Securities and Exchange Commission site for more information, /www.sec.gov/litigation/admin/2008/34-57961.pdf (accessed February 2, 2010).

5. See the Securities and Exchange Commission site for more information, www.sec.gov/answers/shortsalevolume.htm (accessed February 2, 2010).

6. *SEC News Digest*, issue 2007-113, June 13, 2007, available at www.sec.gov/news/digest/2007/dig061307.txt (accessed February 21, 2009).

7. Nina Mehta, "SEC May Reinstate Uptick Rule," *Traders Magazine.com*, www.tradersmagazine.com/news/102225-1.html (accessed February 21, 2010).

8. Charles R. Schwab, "Restore the Uptick Rule, Restore Confidence," *Wall Street Journal*, December 9, 2008, A17, http://online.wsj.com/article/SB122878208553589809.html (accessed February 21, 2010).

9. See the Securities and Exchange Commission site for more information, www.sec.gov/rules/proposed/2009/34-60509.pdf (accessed February 2, 2010).

Chapter 10: Market Manipulation—Improper Short Selling and Other Abuses

1. Quoted by Mike Nickerson, *Life, Money and Illusion: Living on Earth as If We Want to Stay*, rev. ed. (Philadelphia: New Society Publishers, 2009), quotes Ivan Boesky, Commencement Speech, University of California–Berkeley, School of Business Administration, 1985, 126. http://law.jrank.org/pages/12165/Boesky-Ivan.html#ixzz0gBwCo9ko. (accessed April 14, 2010).

Read more: Connie Bruck, *The Predators' Ball* (Penguin, New York, 1989) and James B. Stewart, *Den of Thieves 4th edition* (Simon & Schuster, New York, 1991) and "Ivan Boesky - A Golden Opportunity, White-collar Crime, Michael Milken, The Junk Bond King, The Symbol Of Greed" (http://law .jrank.org/pages/12165/Boesky-Ivan.html)

2. The rules are summarized in an SEC press release entitled "SEC Issues New Rules to Protect Investors Against Naked Short Selling Abuses," www.sec .gov/news/press/2008/2008-204.htm (accessed February 2, 2010).

3. The case is *TASER International v. Morgan Stanley*, No. 2008-EV-004739-B. Complaint was assigned LexisNexis Transaction ID: 19976955 (May 27, 2008) and may be downloaded at www.dailyreportonline.com/Editorial/ PDF/PDF%20Archive/Taser-complaint.pdf (accessed February 20, 2010).

4. Gregg Land, "Short-Selling Sparks RICO Suit Against Financial Giants," *Fulton County Daily Report*, May 15, 2009, accessed at http://www.law.com/ jsp/article.jsp?id=1202430726911 on February 21, 2010.

5. "Lawsuit Filed Against Major Financial Institutions Alleging a Conspiracy to Engage in Illegal Naked Short Selling of TASER International Inc. and to Create, Loan and Sell Counterfeit Shares of TASER Stock," MarketWatch. com, May 28, 2008. Quoted in www.rgm.com/articles/taser.html (accessed February 21, 2010).

6. Gary Weiss, *Wall Street versus America: The Rampant Greed and Dishonesty That Imperil Your Investments* (New York: Portfolio, 2006); Gary Weiss, *Born to Steal: When the Mafia Hit Wall Street* (New York: Warner Books, 2003).

7. See Taser International, Filing on Form 10-K, Notes to Financial Statement, "Other Litigation," available at www.sec.gov/Archives/edgar/data/1069183/ 000095015309000201/p14088e10vk.htm#113 (accessed February 21, 2010).

8. Gary Weiss, "Taser Shareholders Blame the Boogeyman," May 29, 2008, accessed at http://garyweiss.blogspot.com/2008_05_01_archive.html on February 21, 2010.

9. Pierre Paulden and Caroline Salas, "Goldman Targeted by Investor Complaints of Naked Short-Selling," Bloomberg.com, November 17, 2008, www.bloomberg.com/apps/news?pid=20601009&sid=as3PwfEfBlhk (accessed February 21, 2010).

10. Ibid.

11. Ibid.

12. Ibid.

13. Bryan Burrough, "Bringing Down Bear Stearns," *Vanity Fair*, August 2008, www.vanityfair.com/politics/features/2008/08/bear_stearns200808 (accessed February 21, 2010).

14. Ibid.

15. Ibid. The fall of Bear Stearns is also chronicled in *Street Fighters: The Last 72 Hours of Bear Stearns, the Toughest Firm on Wall Street*, by Kate Kelly (New York: Portfolio, 2010).

16. Chairman Cox Letter to Basel Committee in Support of New Guidance on Liquidity Management, 2008-03-20, www.sec.gov/news/press/2008/2008 -48_letter.pdf" (accessed April 16, 2008).

17. The fall of Lehman is discussed in detail in *The Murder of Lehman Brothers: An Insider's Look at the Global Meltdown* (New York: Brick Tower Press, 2009) by Joseph Tibman (a pseudonym for a senior former Lehman executive).

18. Benjamin Weiser and Ben White, "In Crisis, Prosecutors Put Aside Turf Wars," *New York Times*, October 31, 2008, query.nytimes.com/gst/fullpage. html?res=9F04E7DF103EF932A05753C1A96E9C8B63 (accessed April 15, 2010).

19. Benjamin Weiser and Ben White, "In Crisis, Prosecutors Put Aside Turf Wars," *New York Times*, October 31, 2008, http://query.nytimes.com/gst/fullpage .html?res=9F04E7DF103EF932A05753C1A96E9C8B63&scp=1&sq=I n%20Crisis,%20Prosecutors%20Put%20Aside%20Turf%20Wars&st=cse (accessed February 21, 2010).

Chapter 11: PIPEs—Investing Unfairly

1. Lawrence Delevingne, "IPO 2009: Testing the Waters," *CNNMoney*, February 5, 2009, http://money.cnn.com/2009/02/05/magazines/fortune/ investor_daily.fortune/ (accessed February 21, 2010).

2. Matthew Goldstein, "Another Hedge Fund Discloses PIPEs Probe," TheStreet.com, December 1, 2005, www.thestreet.com/story/10255157/ another-hedge-fund-discloses-pipes-probe.html (accessed February 21, 2010).

3. Not the company's real name.

4. Not its real name.

5. FBI Seattle Press Release, "Bellevue Woman Sentenced to Over Seven Years in Prison for 'Pump and Dump' Securities Scheme Involving More Than 3,000 Victims," August 7, 2009, available at http://seattle.fbi.gov/dojpressrel/ pressrel09/se080709.htm (accessed February 21, 2010).

6. SEC Administrative Proceeding, File No. 3-13413, "In the Matter of Jeanne M. Rowzee," www.sec.gov/litigation/admin/2009/34-59604.pdf (accessed February 21, 2010).

7. "SEC Charges Bogus PIPE Promoters in $52 Million Ponzi Scheme," Press Release 2008-202, www.sec.gov/news/press/2008/2008-202.htm (accessed February 21, 2010).

8. FBI Los Angeles Press Release, "Operator of MX Factors Sentenced to 100 Years in Prison for Ponzi Scheme That Cost Victims $39 Million," September 28, 2009, http://losangeles.fbi.gov/dojpressrel/pressrel09/la092809.htm (accessed February 21, 2010).

Chapter 12: Promotion Fraud—Pump and Dump

1. "Beverage Creations (BVRG) Initiates Trading as It Introduces Its Patented Water/Oxygen Product into the Multi-Billion Dollar Sports Drink Industry," Press release dated January 30, 2008, www.thefreelibrary.com/B everage+Creations+(BVRG)+Announces:+3-Time+World+Champion,+ Chad . . .-a0174279380 (accessed February 21, 2010).

2. Northern District of Texas, Civil Action No. 3:08-CV-0438-B, www .sec.gov/litigation/complaints/2009/comp20990-amended.pdf (accessed February 21, 2010).

3. Ibid.

4. Ibid.

5. "Civil Action No. 3:OS-CV-0438-B, "Securities and Exchange Commission, December 22, 2008, www.sec.gov/litigation/complaints/2008/comp20838 .pdf (accessed February 2, 2010).

6. *Securities and Exchange Commission v. Ryan M. Reynolds et al.*, Case No. 3-08 CV-438-B (N.D. Tex.), "SEC Sues Three Stock Promoters and Their Minnesota-Based Entities for Registration and Fraud Violations," www.sec .gov/litigation/litreleases/2008/lr20838.htm (accessed February 21, 2010).

7. SEC Litigation Release No. 21220, September 23, 2009, "SEC Sues Air Travel Company, Its President and Others Involved in Pump and Dump Scheme," *Securities and Exchange Commission v. ConnectAJet.com, Inc., et al.*, Case No. 3-09 CV-01742-B (N.D. Tex.), www.sec.gov/litigation/litreleases/2009/lr21220 .htm (accessed February 21, 2010).

8. Northern District of Texas, Case 3:09-cv-01742-B, www.sec.gov/litigation/complaints/2009/comp21220.pdf.

9. WNP Consulting, LLC, "Knowledge Is Power! Alchemy Creative Is Pleased to Announce the Engagement of Jane Swift as an Advisor to the Company (Representing Bill and Melinda Gates' Personal Investment)," www .wnpconsulting.com/AlchemyRelease.html (accessed February 21, 2010).

10. George Keizer, "Pump-and-Dump Spam Nets Scammers $20 Million," Computerworld, September 10, 2007, www.computerworld.com/s/article/ 9035158/Pump_and_dump_spam_nets_scammers_20_million.

11. "SEC and U.S. Attorney Charge Repeat Stock Promoter and Penny Stock Trader with Illegal IPOs and Pump-and-Dump Manipulation Schemes,"

Release 2007-173, September 6, 2007, www.sec.gov/news/press/2007/2007
-173.htm (accessed February 21, 2010).

12. "Spanish Police Arrest Six over Massive '£420m London Stock Exchange
Fraud,'" January 28, 2009, www.dailymail.co.uk/news/worldnews/article
-1130402/Spanish-police-arrest-massive-420m-London-Stock-Exchange
-fraud.html#ixzz0gD1L8SSf (accessed February 21, 2010).

13. Ibid.

14. Ibid.

Chapter 13: Leaks, Front-Running, and Insider Trading—Test Yourself

1. Details of this case can be found at "SEC Files Insider Trading Charges Against
Mark Cuban," Securities and Exchange Commission, www.sec.gov/news/
press/2008/2008-273.htm (accessed February 2, 2010).

2. Northern District of Texas, Dallas Division, Case 3-08CV2050-D, November
17, 2008. www.sec.gov/litigation/complaints/2008/comp20810.pdf (accessed
February 21, 2010).

3. For more details on this case, see "Federal Court Dismisses SEC Insider
Trading Charges Against Mark Cuban," JD Supra, www.jdsupra.com/
post/documentViewer.aspx?fid=6e18d2b1-2e27-459b-ad5f-406f149cf67c
(accessed February 2, 2010).

4. Lynnley Browning, "Breathless Pitches for Penny Stocks, Now in Newspapers," New York Times, September 5, 2007.

5. Ibid.

6. Ibid.

7. Ibid.

8. For more information, see the Securities and Exchange Commission report
"SEC Charges Seattle Attorney and Accomplices with Orchestrating Stock
Dumping Scheme," July 19, 2009, www.sec.gov/litigation/litreleases/2009/
lr21126.htm (accessed February 2, 2010).

9. Ibid.

10. Western District of Washington, Case No. CV-09-0960 RAJ (WD Wa. filed
July 13, 2009), www.sec.gov/litigation/complaints/2009/comp21126.pdf
(accessed February 21, 2010).

11. Ibid.

12. Ibid.

13. Browning, "Breathless Pitches."

14. "BioStem, Inc.(BTEM.OB) to Acquire $190 Million Revenue Stream Through Merger," Market Wires Press Release, March 22, 2007, www.biospace.com/news_story.aspx?NewsEntityId=49958 (accessed February 21, 2010).

15. Ibid.

16. Eastern District of New York, Case 1:04-cv-02343-NGG-CLP, June 7, 2004, https://ecf.nyed.uscourts.gov/doc1/12311232590 (access requires PACER subsciption).

Chapter 14: Fictitious Volume—A Pump-and-Dump Scam with Intrigue

1. Adam Wills, "Spinka Grand Rabbi, Four Others Plead Guilty," *JewishJournal.com*, March 30, 2009. www.jewishjournal.com/breaking_news/article/spinka_grand_rabbi_four_others_plead_guilty_20090804/ (accessed February 2, 2010); FBI Los Angeles, "New York Rabbi Sentenced to Two Years in Federal Prison in Scheme to Defraud Federal Tax Authorities," December 21, 2009, http://losangeles.fbi.gov/dojpressrel/pressrel09/la122109.htm (accessed February 21, 2010).

Chapter 15: Parachute into Prison—*U.S. v. Schrenker*

1. "Would-Be Fugitive Marcus Schrenker Thoroughly Humiliated at Sentencing," *New York Post*, August 2, 2009; "Would-Be Fugitive Marcus Schrenker Thoroughly Humiliated at Sentencing," Daily Intel, http://nymag.com/daily/intel/2009/08/would_be_escape_artist_marcus.html#ixzz0gDzKobiY. (retrieved February 21, 2010); "Timeline: Marcus Schrenker Plane Hoax Mystery," *FoxNews.com*, www.foxnews.com/story/0,2933,479883,00.html (accessed February 21, 2010); Steve Huff, "Marcus Schrenker's Fake-Out," True Crime Report, www.truecrimereport.com/2009/01/marc_schrenkers_fake-out.php.

2. Andrea Beaumont, "Pilot Pleads Guilty in Plane Crash," *ABC News*, June 5, 2009, http://abcnews.go.com/Business/story?id=7760353&page=1 (accessed February 2, 2010).

Chapter 16: Affinity Group Fraud—Scamming Your Own Community

1. "Affinity Fraud: How to Avoid Investment Scams That Target Groups," www.sec.gov/investor/pubs/affinity.htm (accessed February 21, 2010).

2. O. T. Seville, "Profiles in Crime: The Jews of the Otisville Prison Camp" (unpublished).

3. Matthew Purdy, "The Man with Two Faces: In an Orthodox Jewish World of Honor, a Fraud Case Shocks," *New York Times*, June 16, 1996, www.nytimes

.com/1996/06/16/nyregion/the-man-with-two-faces-in-an-orthodox
-jewish-world-of-honor-a-fraud-case-shocks.html?pagewanted=1 (accessed
February 2, 2010).

4. Ibid. (accessed February 21, 2010).

5. "SEC Halts $23 Million Ponzi Scheme and Affinity Fraud Targeting Haitian-
American Investors," Securities and Exchange Commission, December 30, 2008,
www.404.gov/news/press/2008/2008-306.htm (accessed February 2, 2010).

6. Ibid.

7. "SEC Halts Ponzi Scheme Targeting Deaf Investors," Release 2009-30, February
19, 2009, www.sec.gov/news/press/2009/2009-30.htm (accessed February 21,
2010).

8. District of Hawaii, Case No. CV09-00068, February 18, 2009, www.sec.gov/
litigation/complaints/2009/comp20906.pdf (accessed February 21, 2010).

Chapter 17: Twentieth-Century Ponzi Schemes—Larger and Longer-Lasting Scams

1. "Statement of Tamar Frankel, Professor of Law, Boston University Law
School, Before the Committee on Financial Services of the U.S. House of
Representatives," U.S. House of Representatives, January 5, 2009, www
.house.gov/apps/list/hearing/financialsvcs_dem/frankel010509.pdf (accessed
February 2, 2010).

2. Ibid.

3. Ibid.

4. "Former CFO of Allied Deals, Inc. Sentenced After Cooperating in
Investigation and Prosecution of $683 Million Ponzi Scheme," New York
Department of Justice, June 17, 2008, http://newyork.fbi.gov/dojpressrel/
pressrel08/ponzischemesentence061708.htm (accessed February 2, 2010).

5. Ibid.

6. Ibid.

7. U.S. Attorney, Southern District of New York, Press Release, "Former CFO
of Allied Deals, Inc. Sentenced for $683 Million Ponzi Scheme," June 7,
2008, www.justice.gov/usao/nys/pressreleases/June08/anandallieddealssen
-tencingpr.pdf (accessed February 21, 2010).

Chapter 18: Hit Charade—Lou Pearlman

1. "Lou Pearlman—Biography," www.netglimse.com/celebs/pages/lou_pearl
-man/index.shtml (accessed February 22, 2010).

2. Dave Scheiber, "The Starmaker," *St. Petersburg Times*, October 23, 2000,
www.sptimes.com/News/102300/Floridian/The_starmaker.shtml (accessed
February 22, 2010).

3. Helen Huntley, "Unmasking Lou Pearlman," *St. Petersburg Times*, June 3, 2007, www.sptimes.com/2007/06/03/Business/Unmasking_Lou_Pearlma. shtml (accessed February 22, 2010).

4. Travis Reid, "Boy Band Mogul Pearlman Faces Allegations of Fraud," *Ocala Star-Banner*, November 7, 2006, 6B (reproduced at http://news.google.com/ newspapers?nid=1356&dat=20061107&id=AGk0AAAAIBAJ&sjid=qgkEAA AAIBAJ&pg=4992,3853812, accessed February 22, 2010).

5. "Lawsuits against Boy-Band Impresario Lou Pearlman Grow to $130 Million," February 2, 2007, www.loupearlman.org/History/Lawsuits-against-boy -band-impresario-Lou-Pearlman-grow-to-130-million.html (accessed February 22, 2007).

6. http://tripatlas.com/Lou_Pearlman#ref_text_35 (accessed February 22, 2010).

7. Ibid.

8. Tyler Gray, *The Hit Charade: Lou Pearlman, Boy Bands, and the Biggest Ponzi Scheme in U.S. History* (New York: HarperCollins, 2008).

Chapter 19: Hedge Fund Ponzi Fraud—Hedge Funds Are for Big Boys

1. Southern District of New York, Verified Complaint 05 CIV, 7722, September 1, 2005, www.azag.gov/victims_rights/Bayou/SDNY%20Bayou %20Civil%20Complaint.pdf (accessed February 22, 2010).

2. Thom Weidlich and David Glovin, "Bayou's Israel Gets 20-Year Term for Hedge-Fund Fraud (Update 5)," Bloomberg.com, www.bloomberg .com/apps/news?pid=20601087&sid=aiA5inzy9bBo (accessed February 22, 2010).

3. "Samuel Israel III," *New York Times*, http://topics.nytimes.com/topics/ reference/ timestopics/people/i/samuel_israel_iii/index.html (accessed February 22, 2010).

4. Nelson D. Schwartz and Abha Bhattarai, "The Search for a Missing Trader Goes Global," *New York Times*, June 14, 2008, www.nytimes.com/2008/06/14/ business/14bayou.html?n=Top/Reference/Times%20Topics/People/S/ Stowe,%20Stacey (accessed February 22, 2010); Southern District of New York, Case 1:05-cr-01039-CM, Document 66, Filed 04/18/2008, http:// graphics8.nytimes.com/packages/pdf/business/2008/06/14Bayou-doc1.pdf (accessed February 22, 2010).

5. Ibid.

6. Schwartz and Bhattarai, "Search for Missing Trader" (accessed February 2, 2010).

7. Gretchen Morgenson, "A Fib Here, a Scandal There," *New York Times*, September 18, 2005, www.nytimes.com/2005/09/18/business/yourmoney/ 18gret.html (accessed February 22, 2010). C.R.D. records can be publicly accessed through the FINRA web site, www.finra.org/index.htm.

8. Ibid.

9. Ibid.

10. Ibid.

11. Ibid.

12. Ibid.

13. Ibid.

14. "Grim Clues as Bayou Founder Goes Missing," *New York Times*, June 10, 2008, http://dealbook.blogs.nytimes.com/2008/06/10/possible-suicide -of-fund-manager-investigated/ (accessed February 22, 2010).

15. May be downloaded at www.nysb.uscourts.gov/opinions/ash/150925_22_ opinion.pdf (accessed February 22, 2010).

16. Southern District of New York, Case No. 08 Civ. 07104, www.sec .gov/litigation/complaints/2008/comp20678.pdf (accessed February 22, 2010).

17. Ibid.

18. Ibid.

19. Ibid.

20. Jacob Zamansky, "WexTrust Capital Investigation Eerily Similar to Peter Dawson's Long Island Fraud," August 15, 2008, www.zamansky.com/ blog/2008/08/wextrust-capital-joseph-shereshevsky.html (accessed Feburary 2, 2010).

21. Ianthe Jeanne Dugan, "The Rabbi, the Do-Gooder, the Lost $100 Million," *Wall Street Journal*, August 15, 2008, http://online.wsj.com/article/ SB121875802247042717.html (accessed February 22, 2010).

22. Ibid.

23. "SEC Charges Defendants in $255 Million Ponzi-Type Scheme Involving Wextrust Capital, LLC and Other Wextrust Entities," SEC Press Release 2008-173, www.sec.gov/news/press/2008/2008-173.htm (accessed February 22, 2010).

24. "Former CEO of Wextrust Capital Pleads Guilty in Manhattan Federal Court to Conspiracy and Securities Fraud," United States Attorney Southern District of New York Press Release, April 13, 2010, www.justice.gov/usao/ nys/pressreleases/April10/byersstevenwextrustpleapr.pdf (accessed May 3, 2010).

Chapter 20: Madoff and the World's Largest Ponzi Scheme— The Mother of All Ponzi Schemes

1. Jan Larsen and Paul Hinton, "SEC Settlements in Ponzi Scheme Cases: Putting Madoff and Stanford in Context," NERA Economic Consulting, March 13, 2009, http://www.nera.com/image/PUB_Ponzi_Schemes3_0309_final.pdf (accessed May 22, 2010).

2 The case is Southern District of New York, No. 08 MAG 2735. The complaint may be downloaded at www.slideshare.net/hblodget/bernie-madoff-indictment-presentation (accessed February 22, 2010).

3. Christopher Dela Cruz, "Bernard Madoff Goes Directly to Jail after Pleading Guilty for Bilking Investors," Star-Ledger, March 12, 2009, www.nj.com/news/index.ssf/2009/03/madoff_apologizes_in_court_for.html (accessed February 22, 2010).

4. Judy Woodruff, "Madoff Pleads Guilty to Massive Wall Street Fraud," PBS Newshour, March 12, 2009, www.pbs.org/newshour/bb/law/jan-june09/madoff_03-12.html (accessed February 22, 2010).

5. Madoff's allocution is available at www.slideshare.net/LegalDocs/findlaw-madoff-guilty-plea-allocution (accessed February 22, 2010).

6. Ashby Jones, "From the Madoff Hearing: Jail-Bound Bernie in His Own Words," Wall Street Journal, March 12, 2009, http://blogs.wsj.com/law/2009/03/12/from-the-madoff-hearing-jail-bound-bernie-in-his-own-words (accessed February 22, 2010).

7. Ibid.

8. Ibid.

9. Robert Frank and Amir Efrati, "'Evil' Madoff Gets 150 Years in Epic Fraud," Wall Street Journal, June 30, 2009, http://online.wsj.com/article/SB124604151653862301.html (accessed February 22, 2010).

10. Ibid.

11. Dianna B. Henriques, "Madoff in Partial Settlement with S.E.C.," New York Times, www.nytimes.com/2009/02/10/business/10madoff.htm l (accessed February 22, 2010).

12. Southern District of New York, Case No. 1:09-cr-00 213-DC Document 38 Filed March 10, 2009. Information may be downloaded at www.justice.gov/usao/nys/madoff/20090310criminalinfo.pdf (accessed February 22, 2010).

13. Ibid.

14. Ibid.

15. Ibid.

16. Ibid.

17. U.S. Bankruptcy Court for the Southern District of New York, Case No. Adv. Pro. No. 08–1789 (BRL), Trustee's First Interim Report for the Period December 11, 2008 through June 30, 2009, www.madofftrustee.com/documents/TrusteeInterimReport_090709.pdf (accessed February 22, 2010).

18. Andy Borowitz, "Bin Laden Latest Madoff Casualty," *Borowitz Report*, December 27, 2008, www.borowitzreport.com/2008/12/27/bin-laden-latest-madoff-casualty/ (accessed February 22, 2010).

19. Ibid.

20. Laurence Leamer, "Is Bernie Madoff's Life in Danger?" *Huffington Post*, January 12, 2009, www.huffingtonpost.com/laurence-leamer/is-bernard-madoffs-life-i_b_157261.html (accessed February 22, 2010).

21. Stephanie Strom, "Wall Street Fraud Leaves Charities Reeling," *New York Times*, December 16, 2008, www.nytimes.com/2008/12/16/business/worldbusiness/16iht-16charities.18710774.html (accessed February 22, 2010).

22. Randall Smith, "Ex-Merrill Executives Got Burned by Madoff," *Wall Street Journal*, January 30, 2009, http://online.wsj.com/article/SB123327579767931341.html (accessed February 22, 2010).

23. Claudio Gatti and Dinna B. Henriques, "JPMorgan Exited Madoff-Linked Funds Last Fall," *New York Times*, January 28, 2009, www.nytimes.com/2009/01/29/business/29madoff.html (accessed February 22, 2010).

24. Susan Thompson, "Bernard Madoff Has 'Blood on His Hands' over William Foxton Suicide," *Times Online*, February 12, 2009, http://business.times-online.co.uk/tol/business/industry_sectors/banking_and_finance/article5720211.ece (accessed February 22, 2010).

25. Ibid.

26. Ibid.

27. Ibid.

28. Megan Barnett, "Wiesel Lost 'Everything' to Madoff," *Portfolio.com*, February 26, 2009, www.portfolio.com/executives/2009/02/26/Elie-Wiesel-and-Bernard-Madoff/ (accessed February 22, 2010).

29. Ibid.

30. Ibid.

31. Ibid.

32. Ibid.

33. Ibid.

34. Ibid.

35. Ibid.

36. Ibid.

37. Ibid.

38. Ibid.

39. Ibid.

40. Ibid.

41. "The Madoff Panel Transcript," *Portfolio.com*, February 26, 2009, www.port
-folio.com/executives/2009/02/26/Wiesel-and-Madoff-Transcript/ (accessed
February 22, 2010).

Chapter 21: How Madoff Got Away with It—Who Helped Plot in the Mother of All Ponzi Schemes; Who Can Be Made to Pay?

1. Jason Zweig, "How Bernie Madoff Made Smart Folks Look Dumb,"
Wall Street Journal, December 13, 2008, http://online.wsj.com/article/
SB122912266389002855.html (accessed February 22, 2010).

2. Dara Horn, "Right on the Money," Jbooks: The Online Jewish Book
Community, www.jbooks.com/interviews/index/IP_Horn_Aleichem.htm
(accessed February 22, 2010).

3. Ibid.

4. Ibid.

5. Harry Markopolos, "The World's Largest Hedge Fund Is a Fraud,"
Submission to SEC, November 7, 2005, http://online.wsj.com/documents/
Madoff_SECdocs_20081217.pdf (accessed February 22, 2010).

6. Gregory Z. Zuckerman, "Fees, Even Returns and Auditor All Raised Flags,"
Wall Street Journal, December 13, 2008, http://online.wsj.com/article/
SB122910977401502369.html (accessed February 22, 2010).

7. Ibid.

8. Ibid.

9. Cassell Bryan-Low, "Inside a Swiss Bank, Madoff Warnings," *Wall Street Journal*,
January 14, 2009, http://online.wsj.com/article/SB123188437723478727.html
(accessed February 22, 2010). See also Southern District Court of New York,
Case No. 09 Civ 6043, Farrell et al v. Union Bancaire Privee et al, a class action
suit filed against UBP, (accessed February 22, 2010).

10. Leslie Wayne and Zachery Kouwe, "Imprisoned Felon Was Advisor to
Madoff Investor," *New York Times*, February 13, 2009, www.nytimes.com/
2009/02/14/business/14merkin.html (accessed February 22, 2010).

11. Ibid.

12. "The Monster Mensch," *New York*, February 22, 2009, http://nymag.com/
news/businessfinance/54703/index5.html (accessed February 22, 2010).

13. Charles A. Bowsher et al., Report of the 2009 Special Review Committee on
Finra's Examination Program in Light of the Stanford and Madoff Schemes,

September 2009, www.scribd.com/doc/20843329/Finra-Internal-Report (accessed February 22, 2010).

14. Ibid.

15. Statement from FINRA Chairman and CEO Richard G. Ketchum on the Report of the Special Review Committee of the FINRA Board of Governors, October 2, 2009, www.finra.org/Newsroom/NewsReleases/2009/P120086 (accessed February 22, 2010).

16. Kara Scannell, "Madoff Chasers Dug for Years, to No Avail," *Wall Street Journal*, January 5, 2009, http://online.wsj.com/article/SB123111743915052731.html (accessed February 22, 2010).

17. Ibid.

18. Ibid.

19. Ibid.

20. Joanna Chung, "Finra Probed 19 Madoff Complaints," *Financial Times*, January 14, 2009, www.ft.com/cms/s/0/362a6262-e282-11dd-b1dd-0000779fd2ac.html (accessed February 22, 2010).

21. "Live Blog of the House's Hearing on Madoff," DealBook blog of the *New York Times*, February 4, 2009, http://dealbook.blogs.nytimes.com/2009/02/04/live-blogging-the-houses-madoff-hearing/ (accessed February 22, 2010).

22. Report of Investigation, U.S. SEC Office of Inspector General, Case No. OIG-509, Investigation of Failure of the SEC to Uncover Bernard Madoff's Ponzi Scheme, August 31, 2009, www.sec.gov/news/studies/2009/oig-509-exec-summary.pdf (accessed February 22, 2010).

23. Tom Lauricella et al., "Madoff Used U.K. Office in Cash Ploy, Filing Says," *Wall Street Journal*, March 12, 2009, http://online.wsj.com/article/SB123681392137901653.html (accessed February 22, 2010).

24. Cassell Bryan-Low, "U.K. Could Charge More Than Just Madoff," *Wall Street Journal*, March 28, 2009.

25. Ibid.

26. Ibid.

27. Lauricella et al., "Madoff Used U.K. Office."

28. Ibid.

29. Ibid.

30. Ibid.

31. Ibid.

32. Ibid.

33. Ibid.

34. Ibid.

35. Ibid.

36. Cassell Bryan-Low, "U.K. Expanding Its Madoff Probe," *Wall Street Journal*, March 5, 2009, http://online.wsj.com/article/SB123621328150235043.html (accessed February 22, 2010).

37. Ibid.

38. Ibid.

39. Madoff's allocution is available at www.slideshare.net/LegalDocs/findlaw-madoff-guilty-plea-allocution (accessed February 22, 2010).

40. Beth Healy, "Madoff Creditors Get First Report," *Boston Globe*, February 21, 2009, www.boston.com/business/articles/2009/02/21/madoff_creditors_get_first_report/ (accessed February 22, 2010).

41. Southern District of New York, Case No. 09-CV-7085, August 11, 2009. Complaint can be downloaded at www.sec.gov/litigation/complaints/2009/comp21174.pdf (accessed February 22, 2010).

42. "Madoff Lieutenant a Point Man for Prosecutors: Report," Reuters, January 21, 2009, www.reuters.com/article/idUSTRE50K1C520090121 (accessed February 23, 2010) and Aaron Lucchetti, et. al, "Madoff's Point Man is Cast in Same Role for Prosecutors," January 21, 2010, online.wsj.com/article/SB123249539137500157.html (accessed April 17, 2010).

43. David Voreacos et al., "Madoff's 'Street-Smart' Aide DiPascali Was Investors' Go-To Guy," Bloomberg.com, www.bloomberg.com/apps/news?pid=20601109&sid=ag7.rlaGZLw (accessed February 23, 2010).

44. United States Attorney Southern District of New York, "Frank DiPascali, Jr., Former Employee at Bernard L. Madoff Investment Securities LLC, Pleads Guilty to Ten-Count Criminal Information," press release, August 11, 2009, www.dol.gov/ebsa/pdf/cepr081109.pdf (accessed February 23, 2010).

45. The Court Transcript, including the Allocution of Frank DiPascali before Judge Richard J. Sullivan on August 11, 2009, may be downloaded at www.scribd.com/doc/18550615/Frank-DiPascali-81109-Guilty-Plea-Court-Transcript- (accessed February 23, 2010).

46. Ibid.

47. Ibid.

48. Ibid.

49. Kara Scannell and Amir Efrati, "Madoff Case Has SEC Working Backward," *Wall Street Journal*, January 23, 2009, www.look.ca/en/files/Newspaper_ad_Globe_and_Mail_23012009.pdf (accessed February 23, 2010).

50. Jason Szep, "Did Middleman Know about Madoff Losses Beforehand?" Reuters, February 6, 2009, www.reuters.com/article/idUSN0537547520090206 (accessed February 23, 2010).

51. Ibid.

52. Ibid.

53. Ibid.

54. "SEC Charges Madoff Auditors with Fraud," SEC Litigation Release No. 20959, March 18, 2009, Accounting and Auditing Enforcement Release No. 2992, March 18, 2009, www.sec.gov/litigation/litreleases/2009/lr20959.htm (accessed February 23, 2010).

55. Southern District of New York, Case No. 09-cv-2467, March 18, 2009, www.sec.gov/litigation/complaints/2009/comp20959.pdf (accessed February 23, 2010).

56. Southern District of New York, Case No. 1:09-cr-00700-AKH, March 17, 2009, sealed complaint, www.slideshare.net/LegalDocs/findlaw-madoff-accountant-david-friehlings-criminal-charges.

57. "SEC Charges Madoff Auditors with Fraud," SEC Litigation Release No. 20959, March 18, 2009, Accounting and Auditing Enforcement Release No. 2992, March 18, 2009, www.sec.gov/litigation/litreleases/2009/lr20959.htm (accessed February 23, 2010).

58. Aaron Smith, "Madoff Accountant Out on $2.5 Million Bond," *CNNMoney*, March 19, 2009, http://money.cnn.com/2009/03/18/news/companies/madoff_jail_appeal/index.htm (accessed February 23, 2010).

59. William K. Rashbaum and Diana B. Henriques, "Accountant for Madoff Is Arrested and Charged with Securities Fraud," *New York Times*, March 18, 2009, www.nytimes.com/2009/03/19/business/19madoff.html (accessed February 23, 2010).

60. Ibid.

61. District of New York, Case No. 1:09-cr-00700-AKH, July 17, 2009, Information, https://ecf.nysd.uscourts.gov/doc1/12716613489 (accessed February 23, 2010).

62. Ibid.

63. Commonwealth of Massachusetts, Office of the Secretary, Docket No. E-2009-0015, Consolidated Order, www.sec.state.ma.us/sct/sctcohmad/cohmad_consolidated_order.pdf (accessed February 23, 2010).

64. Commonwealth of Massachusetts, Office of the Secretary, Docket No. E-2009-0015, complaint, www.sec.state.ma.us/sct/sctcohmad/cohmad_complaint.pdf (accessed February 23, 2010).

65. "Medici's Kohn Says Did Not Get Madoff Payments," Reuters, February 12, 2009, http://uk.reuters.com/article/idUKLC60093820090212 (accessed February 23, 2009).

66. David Crawford, "Madoff Kickbacks Alleged in Austria," *Wall Street Journal*, July 3, 2009, http://online.wsj.com/article/SB124655465632586957.html (accessed February 23, 2010).

67. Ibid.

68. Ibid.

69. Ibid.

70. Ibid.

71. Ibid.

72. Ibid.

73. Ibid.

74. Southern District of New York, Bankruptcy Court, *Irving H. Picard v. Herald Fund SPC and HSBC Bank Plc and HSBC Securities Services (Luxembourg) SA* (08-01789), July 13, 2009, http://www.madofftrustee.com/CourtFilings -Download.aspx?Docket=271 (accessed February 23, 2010).

75. Southern District of New York, Bankruptcy Court, *Irving H. Picard v. Fairfield Sentry* (08-01789), May 18, 2009, www.scribd.com/doc/15600919/ Madoff-Trustees-Lawsuit-Against-Fairfield-Greenwich (accessed February 23, 2010).

76. Thomas Zambitto, "Judge Puts Off Bernie Madoff Sentencing Two Weeks," *Daily News*, May 15, 2009, www.nydailynews.com/money/2009/05/15/2009 -05-15_judge_puts_off_bernie_madoff_sentencing_two_weeks.html (accessed February 23, 2010).

77. Amir Efrati, "Fairfeld Hit with Lawsuit over Madoff," *Wall Street Journal*, May 19, 2009, http://online.wsj.com/article/SB124268427496031983.html (accessed February 23, 2010).

78. Ibid.

79. Ibid.

80. Ibid.

81. Southern District of New York, Bankruptcy Court, Case No. 08-01789 (BRL), *Picard v. Chais et al.*, http://graphics8.nytimes.com/packages/images/ nytint/docs/madoff-lawsuit-against-stanley-chais/original.pdf (accessed February 23, 2010); *Picard v. Harley International (Cayman) Ltd.*, 09-01187, and *Picard v. Picower*, 09-01197, U.S. Bankruptcy Court, Southern District of New York (Manhattan), www.madoff.com/CourtFilings-Download.aspx? Docket=277 (accessed February 23, 2010).

82. Ibid.

83. Amir Efrati, "Madoff Victims Investigated," *Wall Street Journal*, May 18, 2009, http://online.wsj.com/article/SB124261271530929129.html (accessed February 23, 2010).

84. Ibid.

85. Ibid.

86. Ibid.

87. "Picower's Wife Seeks Madoff Deal after Filing of Will," *Bloomberg News*, via *Los Angeles Times*, November 11, 2009, http://articles.latimes.com/2009/nov/11/business/fi-picower11 (accessed February 23, 2010).

88. Efrati, "Madoff Victims Investigated."

89. Christopher Scinta and David Glovin, "Madoff Trustee Seeks $150 Million from Gibraltar Bank," Bloomberg.com, April 9, 2009, www.bloomberg.com/apps/news?pid=20601103&sid=aw6heihseIMg&refer=us (accessed February 23, 2010).

90. Ibid.

91. Amir Efrati, "Judge Freezes Assets of Madoff's Family," *Wall Street Journal*, April 1, 2009, http://online.wsj.com/article/SB123851832507274247.html (accessed February 23, 2010).

92. Southern District of New York, Bankruptcy Court, *Picard v. Peter B. Madoff et al.*, October 2, 2009, www.madoff.com/CourtFilings-Download.aspx?Docket=291 (accessed February 23, 2010).

93. Grant McCool, "Judge to Hear Potential Conflict in Madoff," March 3, 2009, www.reuters.com/article/idUSTRE5226SH20090303 (accessed February 23, 2010).

94. Ibid.

Chapter 22: Madoff Plea and Its Aftermath—Governments Go after Merkin, Kohn, and Maybe Others in the Mother of All Ponzi Schemes

1. Barry Ritholtz, "Why Might a Madoff Plea Deal Take Place?" Big Picture, January 13, 2009, www.ritholtz.com/blog/2009/01/why-might-a-madoff-plea-deal-take-place/ (accessed February 23, 2010).

2. Grant McCool, "More Charges May Lie Ahead for Madoff," Reuters, March 12, 2009, www.reuters.com/article/idUSTRE52B6DK20090312 (accessed February 23, 2010).

3. Peter J. Henning, "Madoff's Future: Where the Case Is Likely to Go," *New York Times*, DealBook, March 11, 2009, http://dealbook.blogs.nytimes.com/2009/03/11/madoffs-future-where-the-case-is-likely-to-go/ (accessed February 23, 2010).

4. Ibid.

5. Ibid.

6. Bruce Golding, "Bernie Pal in Plea Play," *New York Post*, July 18, 2009 http://www.nypost.com/p/news/regional/bernie_pal_in_plea_play_zUdm-1nqS5RDRN1pCwTqJ6H (accessed February 23, 2010).

7. David Scheer and Jesse Westbrook, "Madoff 'Tragedy' Said to Have Escaped Scrutiny by SEC," Bloomberg.com, December 15, 2009, www.bloomberg.com/apps/news?pid=20601170&sid=a3T.FJ8oI5hI (accessed February 23, 2010).

8. Ibid.

9. Lecture, University of Lille (December 7, 1854).

10. Peter J. Henning, "Once Again, Seeing the Shadow of Madoff," *New York Times* DealBook, February 8, 2010, http://dealbook.blogs.nytimes.com/2010/02/08/once-again-seeing-the-shadow-of-madoff/ (accessed February 24, 2010).

11. TBRNews.org, www.tbrnews.org/aboutus.htm (accessed February 23, 2010).

12. "The Voice of the White House," December 31, 2008, www.tbrnews.org/Archives/a2906.htm (accessed February 23, 2010).

13. Lucinda Franks, "Feds Zero In on Bernie's Inner Circle," Daily Beast, March 16, 2009, www.thedailybeast.com/blogs-and-stories/2009-03-16/feds-zero-in-on-bernies-inner-circle/full/ (accessed February 24, 2010).

14. Ibid.

15. Ibid.

16. Lucinda Franks, "Source: Madoff Indictments Imminent," Daily Beast, August 17, 2009, www.thedailybeast.com/blogs-and-stories/2009-08-17/sources-madoff-indictments-imminent/ (accessed February 24, 2010).

17. Bernard L. Madoff Investment Securities LLC Liquidation Proceeding, Irving H. Picard, Trustee, "Claims Processing Status," www.madoff.com/Status.aspx (accessed February 24, 2010).

18. Peter Robison et al., "Merkin Intimidated Co-Op Board While Building Funds Madoff Lost," Bloomberg.com, January 9, 2009, www.bloomberg.com/apps/news?pid=20601087&sid=aYQaNaSbUS2Q (accessed February 24, 2010).

19. Ibid.

20. Ibid.

21. Ibid.

22. Ibid.

23. Patricia Hurtaldo, "Zuckerman Sues Merkin over $40 Million Madoff Loss," Bloomberg.com, April 6, 2009, www.bloomberg.com/apps/news?pid=20601087&sid=aLkekcV4uaxo (accessed February 24, 2010).

24. Liz Rappaport, "Merkin to Put Funds in Receivership," *Wall Street Journal*, May 20, 2009, http://online.wsj.com/article/SB124274106281334617.html (accessed February 24, 2010).

25. Amir Efrati, "Merkin Says His Clients Knew about His Madoff Investments," *Wall Street Journal*, July 3, 2009, http://online.wsj.com/article/SB124656803752088361.html (accessed February 24, 2010).

26. Ibid.

27. Southern District of New York Bankruptcy Court, Case No. 08-01789 (BRL), *Picard v. J. Ezra Merkin et al.*, complaint, May 6, 2009, http://online.wsj.com/public/resources/documents/20090507merkincomplaint.pdf (accessed February 24, 2010).

28. Steve Fishman, "The Monster Mensch," *New York*, February 22, 2009, http://nymag.com/news/businessfinance/54703/ (accessed February 24, 2010).

29. Southern District of New York Bankruptcy Court, Case No. 08-01789 (BRL), *Picard v. J. Ezra Merkin et al.*, complaint, May 6, 2009, http://online.wsj.com/public/resources/documents/20090507merkincomplaint.pdf (accessed February 24, 2010).

30. Hurtaldo, "Zuckerman Sues Merkin."

31. Ibid.

32. Leslie Wayne and Zachery Kouwe, "Imprisoned Felon Was Advisor to Madoff Investor," *New York Times*, February 13, 2009, www.nytimes.com/2009/02/14/business/14merkin.html (accessed February 24, 2010).

33. Vicky Ward, "Greenwich Mean Time," *Vanity Fair*, April 2009, www.vanityfair.com/style/features/2009/04/noel200904 (accessed February 24, 2010).

34. Southern District of New York Bankruptcy Court, Case No. 08-01789 (BRL), *Picard v. J. Ezra Merkin et al.*, complaint, May 6, 2009, http://online.wsj.com/public/resources/documents/20090507merkincomplaint.pdf (accessed February 24, 2010).

35. Daphne Merkin, "If Looks Could Steal," *New York Times*, March 21, 2009, www.nytimes.com/2009/03/22/opinion/22merkin.html (accessed February 24, 2010).

36. Ibid.

37. Ibid.

38. Sheryl Weinstein, *Madoff's Other Secret: Love, Money, Bernie, and Me* (New York: St. Martin's Press, 2009).

39. Robert Frank and Charles Forelle, "Sonja Kohn Denies Receiving Madoff Payments," *Wall Street Journal*, February 13, 2009, http://online.wsj.com/article/SB123456507552385937.html (accessed February 24, 2010).

40. David Crawford et al., "Vienna Banker in Spotlight as Madoff Fallout Spreads," *Wall Street Journal*, January 16, 2009, http://online.wsj.com/article/SB123206919264588423.html (accessed February 24, 2010).

41. Haig Simonian and Eric Frey, "Profile: Bank Medici's Sonja Kohn," *Financial Times*, January 7, 2008, www.ft.com/cms/s/0/d9d58eba-dcfa-11dd-a2a 9-000077b07658.html (accessed February 24, 2010); "Austria's Bank Medici, Owned by Jewess, Sonja Kohn, Loses $2.1 Billion in Maddoff [sic] Investment," http://zionistgoldreport.wordpress.com/2008/12/17/

austrias-bank-medici-owned-by-jewess-sonja-kohn-loses-21-billion-in
-maddoff-investment/. Posted December 17, 2008.The blog has since been
terminated for violation of WordPress's Terms of Service. Google cached
a copy that may be viewed at http://74.125.93.132/search?q=cache:
lTvXYqW7rXgJ:zionistgoldreport.wordpress.com/2008/12/17/austrias
-bank-medici-owned-by-jewess-sonja-kohn-loses-21-billion-in-maddoff
-investment/+zionistgoldreport+Kohn&cd=1&hl=en&ct=clnk&gl=us.

42. Ian Moley, "Madoff's Little Helper Makes $2.1 Billion Disappear,"
WhiteCivilRights.com, January 26, 2009, www.whitecivilrights.com/?
p=1649#more-1649 (accessed February 24, 2010).

43. Southern District of New York, Civil Action No. 09-cv-00289-RMB, Class
Action (Document 1), January 12, 2009, http://cryptome.org/madoff/
repex-001.pdf (accessed February 24, 2010).

44. David Crawford et al., "Vienna Banker in Spotlight as Madoff Fallout
Spreads," *Wall Street Journal*, January 16, 2009, http://online.wsj.com/article/
SB123206919264588423.html (accessed February 24, 2010).

45. Ibid.

46. Ibid.

47. Nelson D. Schwartz and Julia Werdigier, "Austria's 'Woman on Wall St.' and
Madoff," *New York Times*, January 6, 2009, www.nytimes.com/2009/01/07/
business/07medici.html?pagewanted=all (accessed February 24, 2010).

48. Joanna Chung and Brooke Masters, "Madoff's Wife Took $15.5m Ahead
of His Arrest," *Financial Times*, February 12, 2009, www.ft.com/cms/s/0/
05d78dbc-f8a6-11dd-aae8-000077b07658.html (accessed February 24, 2010).

49. Simonian and Frey, "Profile: Bank Medici's Sonja Kohn."

50. Anthony Weiss, "Madoff Scandal Sends Sheytl-Wearing Banker into Hiding,"
Jewish Daily Forward, January 7, 2009, http://blogs.forward.com/bintel
-blog/14872/ (accessed February 24, 2010).

51. Henry Blodget, "Madoff Feeder Bank Medici Probed Criminally in
Vienna," *Business Insider*, March 1, 2009, www.businessinsider.com/madoff
-feeder-bank-medici-probed-criminally-in-vienna-2009-3 (accessed February
24, 2010).

52. "Bank Medici Denies $5–8 bln Flow to Madoff Scheme," Reuters, May 28,
2009, www.reuters.com/article/idUSLS98042220090528 (accessed February
24, 2010).

53. Ibid.

54. Michael Peel and Eric Frey, "UK Fraud Agency Launches Medici Inquiry,"
Financial Times, June 29, 2009, www.ft.com/cms/s/0/5b4b5ca0-64d1-11de
-a13f-00144feabdc0.html (accessed February 24, 2010).

55. Ibid.

Chapter 23: Mopping up after Madoff—Lawyers Feast on Madoff Feeders in the Mother of All Ponzi Schemes

1. "Madoff Sought, Got Cash in Days Before Arrest," *SmartMoney*, February 7, 2009, www.smartmoney.com/breaking-news/smw/?story=20090107105536 (accessed February 24, 2010).

2. Richard Johnson et al., "Madoff Pal's Wife Strikes Back," Page Six, *New York Post*, February 21, 2009, www.nypost.com/p/pagesix/item_ GkaXbCT8S0ljiGrEG6lSPK (accessed February 24, 2010).

3. Ibid.

4. Ibid.

5. Southern District of New York, Case No. 09 cv 5680, June 22, 2009, www .sec.gov/litigation/complaints/2009/comp21095.pdf (accessed February 24, 2010).

6. Ibid.

7. David Glovin, "Cohmad's Jaffe Seeks Dismissal of SEC, Picard Counts," Bloomberg.com, August 21, 2009, www.bloomberg.com/apps/news?pid=2 0601103&sid=a81_r.GbN1_4 (accessed February 24, 2010).

8. Ibid.

9. Ibid.

10. Ibid.

11. Ibid.

12. Dismissal order, dated February 1, 2010, may be downloaded at www .scribd.com/doc/26281088/Dismissal-Order-in-S-E-C-v-Cohmad (accessed February 24, 2010).

13. Ian Urbina, "A Palm Beach Enclave, Stunned by an Inside Job," *New York Times*, December 14, 2008, www.nytimes.com/2008/12/15/business/15palm .html (accessed February 24, 2010).

14. Vicky Ward, "Greenwich Mean Time," *Vanity Fair*, April 2009, www .vanityfair.com/style/features/2009/04/noel200904 (accessed February 24, 2010).

15. Julia Werdigier, "Santander Offer Pressures Rivals to Match It," *New York Times*, January 28, 2009, www.nytimes.com/2009/01/29/business/world business/29santander.html.

16. Ibid.

17. Jose de Cordoba and Thomas Catan, "A Spanish Bank's Madoff Redress," *Wall Street Journal*, January 28, 2009, online.wsj.com/article/SB123307162647119559 .html (accessed February 24, 2010).

18. Ibid.

19. Bill Alpert, "Santander Heaps Insult on Madoff Injury," *Barron's*, February 23, 2009, online.barrons.com/article/SB123518108981938483.html (accessed February 24, 2010).

20. Tom Cahill, "Madoff 'Red Flags' Could Have Been Raised by Software," Bloomberg.com, www.bloomberg.com/apps/news?pid=20601109&sid=ag7CfzPDNpiM&refer=exclusive (accessed February 24, 2010).

21. Ibid.

22. Ibid.

23. Press Release of Irving H. Picard, "Trustee Announces Settlement of $235 Million," May 26, 2009, www.madoff.com/News-Download .aspx?PressRelease=14 (accessed February 24, 2010).

24. Jonathan Wheatley, "Madoff Victims Emerge at Safra," *Financial Times*, February 17, 2009, www.ft.com/cms/s/0/1a36be84-fcea-11dd-a103-000077b07658.html (accessed February 24, 2010).

25. Ibid.

26. Ibid.

27. Ibid.

28. Antonio Regalado, "Bank to Cover Some Madoff Losses," *Wall Street Journal*, March 10, 2009, http://online.wsj.com/article/SB123665403576179839.html (accessed February 24, 2010).

29. Ibid.

30. Peggy Hollinger et al., "UBS Starts to Pay Madoff-Hit Investors," *Financial Times*, January 16, 2009, www.ft.com/cms/s/0/0b6da8ce-e406-11dd-8274 -0000779fd2ac.html (accessed February 24, 2010).

31. Stanley Pignal and Brooke Masters, "UBS under Regulatory Fire over Madoff Feeder Fund," *Financial Times*, February 26, 2009, www.ft.com/cms/s/0/ 685d2d76-03a4-11de-b405-000077b07658.html (accessed February 24, 2010).

32. Ibid.

33. Ibid.

34. Hollinger et al., "UBS Starts to Pay."

35. Ibid.

36. Ibid.

37. Stephanie Bodoni, "UBS, HSBC Have Duty to Madoff Investors, Frieden Says," Bloomberg.com, June 5, 2009, www.bloomberg.com/apps/news?pid= 20601087&sid=a8KUxW1cXdvU (accessed February 24, 2010).

38. Allison Hoffman, "Madoff Investors Want Payback," *Jerusalem Post*, March 1, 2009 www.jpost.com/servlet/Satellite?cid=1235410740529&pagename=JPo st/JPArticle/ShowFull.

39. Nelson D. Schartz and Julia Werdigier, "From Behind the Curtain, Madoff Drew in Victims," *New York Times*, January 16, 2009, www.nytimes.com/2009/01/16/business/worldbusiness/16iht-medici.4.19438677.html (accessed February 24, 2010).

40. Southern District of New York, U.S. Bankruptcy Court, Case No. 08 -01789 (BRL), complaint, May 18, 2009, www.madoff.com/CourtFilings -Download.aspx?Docket=278 (accessed February 24, 2010).

41. Cynthia Cotts, "Fairfield Greenwich's Madoff Investment Triggers Suit," Bloomberg.com, December 22, 2008, www.bloomberg.com/apps/news?pid =20601127&sid=aCVH_C9vsCEs&refer=law (accessed February 24, 2010).

42. Ibid.; the case is *Pasha and Julia Anwar v. Fairfield Greenwich*, 603769/2008, New York Supreme Court (Manhattan).

43. http://online.wsj.com/article/SB125244800864593735.html.

44. Victor Mallet, "Lawyers Plan Global Action on Madoff," *Financial Times*, January 27, 2009, www.ft.com/cms/s/0/cf8da916-ec12-11dd-8838-0000779fd2ac.html (accessed February 24, 2010).

45. Ibid.

46. Ibid.

47. Regalado, "Bank to Cover Some Madoff Losses."

48. Ibid.

49. Ibid.

50. Ianthe Jeanne Dugan and David Crawford, "Accounting Firms That Missed Fraud at Madoff May Be Liable," *Wall Street Journal*, February 18, 2009, http://online.wsj.com/article/SB123491638561904323.html?mod=testMod (accessed February 24, 2010).

51. Ibid.

52. Ibid.

53. Thom Weidlich, "Madoff Feeder Sues Own Auditors for Not Finding Fraud," February 2, 2009, www.bloomberg.com/apps/news?pid=20601087&sid=avo W3gb0yUsY (accessed February 24, 2010). The case is *Maxam Absolute Return Fund LP v. McGladrey & Pullen LLP*, Connecticut Superior Court.

54. Miles Costello and Christine Seib, "Madoff's Clients at the Heart of UK Establishment," *Times Online*, February 5, 2009, http://business.timesonline.co.uk/tol/business/industry_sectors/banking_and_finance/article5669316.ece (accessed February 24, 2010) (accessed February 24, 2010).

55. Southern District of Florida, Miami Division, Case No. 1:09-cv-20215 -PCH, Document 156, complaint, October 21, 2009, www.labaton.com/en/cases/upload/156-2009-10-21-CONSOLIDATED-AMENDED -CLASS-ACTION-COMPLAINT.pdf (accessed February 24, 2010).

56. Dugan and Crawford, "Accounting Firms That Missed Fraud."

57. Ibid.

58. Ibid.

59. Lynnley Browning, "I.R.S. Plans a Deduction for Madoff Victims," *New York Times*, March 17, 2009, www.nytimes.com/2009/03/18/business/18madoff. html (accessed February 24, 2010).

60. "Ponzi Scheme Published Guidance," Internal Revenue Service, March 31, 2009, www.irs.gov/pub/irs-drop/rr-09-09.pdf and www.irs.gov/pub/irs-drop/ rp-09-20.pdf (accessed February 24, 2010).

61. Jane J. Kim and Tom Herman, "Madoff Victims Turn to IRS to Get Relief," *Wall Street Journal*, February 18, 2009, http://online.wsj.com/article/ SB123492015025305063.html (accessed February 24, 2010).

62. Charles E. Schumer, "Schumer Unveils Comprehensive Madoff Investors' Tax Bill of Rights—Aims to Provide Expanded Tax and Retirement Relief to Small Investors Who Invested All and Have Nothing Left Because of Convicted Scam Artist," press release, December 7, 2009, http://schumer.senate.gov/ new_website/record.cfm?id=320506 (accessed February 24, 2010).

63. Curt Anderson, "Ponzi Schemes' Collapses Nearly Quadrupled in '09,'" Associated Press, December 29, 2009, reprinted in Law.com, www.law.com/ jsp/article.jsp?id=1202437299784 (accessed February 24, 2010).

64. "Statement Regarding Madoff Investigation, " RSEC Release 208-297, December 16, 2008, www.sec.gov/news/press/2008/2008-297.htm (accessed February 24, 2010).

65. "Re: The Vast Amount That We Don't Know about the Madoff Matter," Velvel on National Affairs, July 8, 2009, http://velvelonnationalaffairs.blogs -pot.com/2009/07/re-vast-amount-that-we-dont-know-about.html (accessed February 24, 2010).

Chapter 24: Other Recent Ponzi Schemes—Madoff was a Crook but He Had No Monopoly on Recent Ponzi Schemes

1. Jason Szep, "U.S. Regulator Probing 'Rampant Ponzimonium,'" Reuters, March 20, 2009, www.reuters.com/article/idUSTRE52J48B20090320 (accessed February 24, 2010).

2. "SEC Charges Joseph S. Forte for Conducting Multi-Million Dollar Ponzi Scheme," SEC Release 2009-5, January 8, 2009, www.sec.gov/news/ press/2009/2009-5.htm (accessed February 24, 2010).

3. Ibid.

4. Ibid.

5. Jeff Blumenthal, "Forte Sentenced to 15 Years for Ponzi Scheme," *Philadelphia Business Journal*, November 24, 2009, http://philadelphia.bizjournals .com/philadelphia/stories/2009/11/23/daily18.html (accessed February 24, 2010).

6. "SEC Charges CRE Capital Corporation and James G. Ossie with Conducting Multi-Million Dollar Ponzi Scheme," SEC Release 2009-6, January 15, 2009, www.sec.gov/news/press/2009/2009-6.htm (accessed February 24, 2010).

7. *Securities and Exchange Commission v. Arthur Nadel, et al.*, U.S. District Court for the Middle District of Florida, Civil Action No. 8:09-CV-00087-RAL -TBM filed January 21, 2009 (accessed February 24, 2010).

8. Michael Peltier, "FBI Joins Search for Missing Florida Money Manager," Reuters, January 18, 2009, www.reuters.com/article/idUSTRE50G0JZ20090118 (accessed February 24, 2010).

9. Ibid.

10. John Hielscher et al., "Nadel's Note Reveals Guilt, Fear," *Sarasota Herald -Tribune*, January 21, 2009, www.heraldtribune.com/article/20090121/ ARTICLE/901210342 (accessed February 24, 2010).

11. Michael Pollick, "Nonprofits Lose Out When Donor Goes Missing," *Sarasota Herald-Tribune*, January 19, 2009, www.heraldtribune.com/article/20090119/ ARTICLE/901190356 (accessed February 24, 2010).

12. Ibid.

13. Caroline Waxler, "Details Emerge about Florida Ponzi Runner Art Nadel," *Business Insider*, January 17, 2009, www.businessinsider.com/2009/1/details -emerge-about-the-florida-ponzi-runner-art-nadel (accessed February 24, 2010).

14. Middle District of Florida, Tampa Division, Case No. 8:09cv00087- T26 (TBM), complaint, January 21, 2009, www.sec.gov/litigation/com -plaints/2009/comp20858.pdf.

15. Ibid.

16. "Hedge Fund Manager Pleads Guilty to Securities Fraud," *New York Times*, February 24, 2010, www.nytimes.com/2010/02/25/business/25fraud. html (accessed February 24, 2010); "Former Hedge Fund Manager Arthur G. Nadel Pleads Guilty in Manhattan Federal Court to a Massive Ponzi Scheme," FBI New York, Press Release, February 24, 2010, http://newyork. fbi.gov/dojpressrel/pressrel10/nyfo022410a.htm (accessed same day).

17. *Securities and Exchange Commission v. Neil V. Moody and Christopher D. Moody* (U.S. District Court for the Middle District of Florida, Civil Action No. 8:10-CV-0053-T-33TBM), SEC Litigation Release No. 21372, January

12, 2010, www.sec.gov/litigation/litreleases/2010/lr21372.htm (accessed February 24, 2010).

18. Case No. 1:09-cr-00059-1, Northern District of Illinois. "Frank A. Castaldi Charged with Allegedly Swindling More Than 450 Investors in $77 Million Ponzi-Scheme," U.S. Attorney, Northern District of Illinois, Press Release, July 22, 2009, www.justice.gov/usao/iln/pr/chicago/2009/pr0722_02.pdf (accessed February 25, 2010).

19. *Securities and Exchange Commission v. Rod Cameron Stringer, individually and d/b/a RCS Hedge Fund*, Civil Action No. 5-09CV0009-C (U.S.D.C./N.D. Texas, Lubbock Division), (accessed February 25, 2010).

20. "Lamesa, Texas, Man, Who Ran Fraudulent Investment Scheme, Sentenced to 10 Years in Federal Prison, without Parole, " U.S. Attorney James T. Jacks, Northern District of Texas, Press Release, October 2, 2009, www .justice.gov/usao/txn/PressRel09/stringer_sen_pr.html (accessed February 25, 2010).

21. Oren Yaniv et al., "Prosecutors: Nicholas Cosmo, L.I.'s 'Bernie Madoff,' Spent Ill-Gotten Gains on Fancy Hotels, Jewelry," *Daily News*, January 28, 2009, www.nydailynews.com/money/2009/01/27/2009-01-27_prosecutors_nicholas_ cosmo_lis_bernie_ma.html#ixzz0gY8k0dng (accessed February 25, 2010).

22. "President of Long Island Investment Firms Charged in $370 Million Fraud Scheme," FBI New York, Press Release, January 27, 2009, http://newyork. fbi.gov/dojpressrel/pressrel09/nyfo012709a.htm (accessed February 25, 2010).

23. Patricia Hurtado et al., "Cosmo Surrenders, Faces Mail-Fraud Charge in Alleged Scheme," Bloomberg.com, January 27, 2009, www.bloomberg .com/apps/news?pid=20601087&sid=aF5DS2S.OGrA&refer=home (accessed February 25, 2010).

24. Ibid.

25. "CFTC Charges Nicholas Cosmo and Agape Companies with Defrauding Customers of Tens of Millions of Dollars in Commodity Futures Trading Scheme," CTFC Press Release, January 27, 2009, www.cftc.gov/newsroom/ enforcementpressreleases/2009/pr5606-09.html (accessed February 25, 2010).

26. Aarhi Sivaraman, "NY Financier Cosmo Held on Ponzi Scheme Charge," Reuters, January 27, 2009, www.reuters.com/article/idUSTRE50Q0EQ2009 0127 (accessed February 25, 2010).

27. Chris Hansen, "Nicholas Cosmo: A Madoff in the Making?" Transcript, MSNBC, May 10, 2009, www.msnbc.msn.com/id/30648858#storyContin ued (accessed February 25, 2010).

28. "SEC Charges Two New York Residents for Misappropriating More Than $500 Million in Investment Scheme," SEC Release 2009-35, February 25,

2009, www.sec.gov/news/press/2009/2009-35.htm (accessed February 25, 2010).

29. Steve Stecklow et al., "Pair Lived Large on Fraud, U.S. Says," *Wall Street Journal*, February 29, 2009, http://online.wsj.com/article/SB123558626099474177.html (accessed February 25, 2010).

30. Ibid.

31. Lisa W. Foderado, "Westchester's Horse Country Image Rides into the Sunset," December 23, 1989, www.nytimes.com/1989/12/23/nyregion/westchester-s-horse-country-image-rides-into-the-sunset.html (accessed February 25, 2010).

32. Ianthe Jeanne Dugan, "A Small New York Town Grapples with Alleged Fraud," February 28, 2009, http://online.wsj.com/article/SB123578179781497969.html (accessed February 25, 2010).

33. Ibid.

34. Steve Stecklow et al., "Pair Lived Large on Fraud, U.S. Says," *Wall Street Journal*, February 29, 2009, http://online.wsj.com/article/SB123558626099474177.html (accessed February 25, 2010).

35. David Glovin, "Ex-WG Compliance Chief Duffy Pleads Guilty in Fraud," Bloomberg.com, July 21, 2009, www.bloomberg.com/apps/news?pid=20601103&sid=aBB54VFyLv9Q (accessed February 25, 2010). The SEC case is *SEC v. Duffy*, 09-cv-6458, U.S. District Court, Southern District of New York (Manhattan). The criminal case is *U.S. v. Duffy*, U.S. District Court, Southern District of New York (Manhattan).

36. FBI New York, "Former BDO Seidman Partner Pleads Guilty to Investment Fraud and Tax Shelter Charges," Press Release, July 30, 2009, http://newyork.fbi.gov/dojpressrel/pressrel09/nyfo073009.htm. David Glovin, "Ex-BDO Seidman's Mark Bloom Pleads Guilty in Hedge Fund Fraud," Bloomberg.com, July 31, 2009, www.bloomberg.com/apps/news?pid=20601014&sid=a3AKj.bZC5KM (accessed February 25, 2010).

37. Megan V. Winslow, "FBI Arrests Hedge Fund Manager James M. Nicholson," *Palm Beach Daily News*, February 27, 2009.

38. "U.S. Complaint against James Nicholson," www.scribd.com/doc/12817245/US-Complaint-Against-James-Nicholson (accessed February 25, 2010).

39. Andrew W. Tangel, "Saddle River Man Pleads Guilty in Ponzi Scheme," NorthJersey.com, December 14, 2009.

40. "*SEC v. William L. Walters*, United States District Court for the District of Colorado, Civil Action No. 09-cv-00337-REB-MEH," SEC, Litigation Release No. 20904, February 18, 2009, www.sec.gov/litigation/litre-leases/2009/lr20904.htm (accessed February 25, 2010).

41. Szep, "U.S. Regulator Probing 'Rampant Ponzimonium'" (accessed February 25, 2010).

Chapter 25: Stanford Group—Massive $7 Billion, Multinational Fraud Comes to Light

1. Nico Hines, "Profile: Alex Dalmady, the Internet Whistleblower on Allen Stanford's Alleged Fraud," *Times Online*, February 18, 2009, www.timesonline.co.uk/tol/news/world/us_and_americas/article5761474.ece (accessed February 25, 2010).

2. Ibid

3. Robert Cookson et al., "SEC Alerted about Stanford in 2003," *Financial Times*, February 27, 2009, www.ft.com/cms/s/0/148817be-043b-11de-845b-000077b07658.html (accessed February 25, 2010).

4. Ibid.

5. Ibid.

6. "SEC Statement on the Case against R. Allen Stanford," SEC Release 2009-32, February 19, 2009, www.sec.gov/news/press/2009/2009-32.htm (accessed February 25, 2010).

7. "SEC Charges R. Allen Stanford, Stanford International Bank for Multi-Billion Dollar Investment Scheme," SEC Release 2009-26, February 27, 2009, www.sec.gov/news/press/2009/2009-26.htm (accessed February 25, 2010).

8. Ibid.

9. Devlin Barrett, "Texas Billionaire Stanford Indicted in Alleged $7B Fraud Scheme," Associated Press, reprinted in Law.com, June 19, 2009, www.law.com/jsp/article.jsp?id=1202431602838 (accessed February 25, 2010).

10. Clifford Krauss, "Texas Financier and Antiguan Official Charged with Fraud," *New York Times*, June 19, 2009, www.nytimes.com/2009/06/20/business/20stanford.html (accessed February 25, 2010).

11. Ibid.

12. "Stanford Indicted for Alleged Ponzi Scheme; Justice Dept: Empire a Pyramid Scheme Built on Lies, Bluster and Bribery," Associated Press, reprinted by MSNBC, June 19, 2009, www.msnbc.msn.com/id/31439494/ns/business-us_business/ (accessed February 25, 2010).

13. Ibid.

14. Hendy Blodger, "SEC Blasted for Blowing Another $8 Billion Fraud," *Business Insider*, www.businessinsider.com/sec-blasted-for-blowing-another-8-billion-fraud-2009-2 (accessed February 25, 2010).

15. Ibid.

16. Kaja Whitehouse, "Damon: 'I Can't Pay Bills Right Now,'" *New York Post*, February 20, 2009, www.nypost.com/p/sports/yankees/item_GcqPM3BXTL4SJIqaLDFmLK (accessed February 25, 2010).

17. Ibid.

18. Ibid.

19. Benedict Mander et al., "Venezuela, Peru and Mexico Act," *Financial Times*, February 19, 2009, www.ft.com/cms/s/0/73a04c1e-febc-11dd-b19a-000077b07658.html (accessed February 25, 2005).

20. "What's the Problem?" Skeptical CPA, March 11, 2009, http://skeptical-texascpa.blogspot.com/2009/03/whats-problem.html (accessed February 25, 2010).

21. Glenn R. Simpson et al., "Madoff Case Led SEC to Intensify Stanford Probe," *Wall Street Journal*, http://online.wsj.com/article/SB123500982598918793.html (accessed February 25, 2010).

22. SEC complaint may be downloaded at www.sec.gov/litigation/complaints/2009/comp20901.pdf (accessed February 25, 2010).

23. Ibid.

24. Ibid.

25. Jesse Westbrook and Ian Katz, "Finra's Stanford Probe Raises Questions on Oversight," Bloomberg.com, February 18, 2009, www.bloomberg.com/apps/news?pid=20601087&sid=ahaUscXNr5wY&refer=home (accessed February 25, 2010).

26. Zach Lowe, "Stanford Financial Scandal and Whistleblowing Rules for Lawyers," Law.com, February 19, 2009, www.law.com/jsp/law/LawArticleFriendly.jsp?id=1202428390098 (accessed February 25, 2010).

27. Joe Weisenthal, "Check Out Stanford's $10k FINRA Fine," *Business Insider*, February 19, 2009, www.businessinsider.com/check-out-stanfords-10k-finra-fine-2009-2 (accessed February 25, 2010) (FINRA Case #2005002203701).

28. Lowe, "Stanford Financial Scandal."

29. Justin Rood and Brian Ross, "Charges against Stanford a Long Time Coming, Offshore Banking Experts Say," *ABC News*, February 19, 2009, http://abcnews.go.com/Blotter/story?id=6907429&page=1 (accessed February 25, 2010).

30. "Sir Allen May Have Been Laundering Drug Money for Mexican Cartel: Report," *Financial Week*, February 19, 2009, www.financialweek.com/article/20090219/REUTERS/902199997/1028 (accessed February 25, 2010).

31. Stephen Labaton and Charlie Savage, "S.E.C. Fines Didn't Avert Stanford Group Case," *New York Times*, February 18, 2009, www.nytimes.com/2009/02/19/business/19stanford.html (accessed February 25, 2010).

32. Ibid.

33. Ibid.

34. Ibid.

35. Rood and Ross, "Charges against Stanford."

36. Ibid.

37. Ibid.

38. "Report from the Special Review Committee," Financial Industry Regulatory Authority, www.finra.org/AboutFINRA/Leadership/Committees/P120076 (accessed February 25, 2010).

39. Ibid.

40. Ibid.

41. Michael Crittenden and Kara Scannell, "Report Says SEC Missed Many Shots at Stanford," *Wall Street Journal*, April 17, 2010, http://online.wsj.com/article/SB10001424052702303491304575188220570802084.html (accessed April 17, 2010).

42. Report of Investigation, US Securities and Exchange Commission, Office of Inspector General, Case No. OIG-526, Investigation of the SEC's Response to Concerns, *Regarding Robert Allen Stanford's Alleged Ponzi Scheme, March 31, 2010,* http://www.sec.gov/news/studies/2010/oig-526.pdf (accessed April 17, 2010).

43. Southern District of Texas, Houston Division, Criminal N0. H-09-335, Plea Agreement, August 27, 2009, http://blogs.chron.com/stanford/Davis%20Plea%20Filed%20Version.pdf (accessed February 25, 2010).

Chapter 26: Ultimate *Chutzpah*—The Strange Tale of Marc Dreier, Esq.

1. Alison Leigh Cowan et al., "Lawyer Seen as Bold Enough to Cheat the Best," *New York Times*, December 13, 2008, www.nytimes.com/2008/12/14/nyregion/14lawyer.html (accessed February 25, 2010).

2. Ibid.

3. Ibid.

4. Ann Woolner, "Chutzpah Spree by Accused Lawyer Nets $380 Million," Bloomberg.com, December 26, 2009, www.bloomberg.com/apps/news?pid=20601039&refer=columnist_woolner&sid=aU2wrsZKcjOA (accessed February 26, 2010).

5. Ibid.

6. Ibid.

7. Ibid.

8. Robert Kolker, "The Impersonator," *New York*, April 3, 2009, http://nymag .com/news/features/55863/ (accessed February 25, 2010).

9. Ibid.

10. Bob Van Voris, "Dreier Pleads Guilty to Fraud; Faces Life in Prison," Bloomberg.com, www.bloomberg.com/apps/news?pid=20601127&sid=aE7 dadsp.B.o (accessed February 25, 2010).

11. David Glovin, "Lawyer Marc Dreier Is Sentenced to 20 Years for Fraud," Bloomberg.com, July 13, 2009, www.bloomberg.com/apps/news?pid=2060 1087&sid=a8OstHJoK_JY (accessed February 25, 2010).

12. David Glovin, "Lawyer Dreier-Linked Ex-Broker Kovachev Pleads Guilty," Bloomberg.com, November 2, 2009, www.bloomberg.com/apps/news?pid= newsarchive&sid=aj4kN4rVuDD4 (accessed February 25, 2010).

13. Bryan Burrough, "Marc Dreier's Crime of Destiny," *Vanity Fair*, August 2008, www.vanityfair.com/business/features/2009/11/marc-dreier200911 (accessed May 20, 2010).

Chapter 27: Detecting Fraudulent Financial Schemes— How Much to Regulate? How Much to Verify?

1. "Ronald Reagan on Homeland Security," OnTheIssues.org, www.ontheissues .org/Celeb/Ronald_Reagan_Homeland_Security.htm (accessed February 25, 2010), quoting Edmund Morris, *Dutch: A Memoir of Ronald Reagan* (Modern Library, reprint edition, 2000).

2. James Mackintosh, "Fund Plans Third-Party Checks," *Financial Times*, March 1, 2009, www.ft.com/cms/s/0/8e96480a-0698-11de-ab0f-000077b07658 .html?dbk.

3. Erin Arvedlund, "Innocence Lost," *Portfolio.com*, December 17, 2008, www .portfolio.com/news-markets/top-5/2008/12/17/madoff-barrons/ (accessed February 25, 2010).

4. Kara Scannell, "Perjury Charges Being Considered," *Wall Street Journal*, January 28, 2009, http://online.wsj.com/article/SB123306961806319721 .html (accessed February 25, 2010).

5. U.S. Senate Committee on Banking, Housing and Urban Affairs, Concerning Investigations and Examinations by the Securities and Exchange Commission and Issues Raised by the Bernard L. Madoff Investment Securities Matter, Testimony of Linda Chatman Thomsen, January 27, 2009, http://banking.senate.gov/public/_files/ThomsenSECTestimony12709.pdf (accessed February 25, 2010).

6. Elisse B. Walter, "Testimony Concerning Securities Law Enforcement in the Current Financial Crisis," March 20, 2009, www.sec.gov/news/testimony

/2009/ts032009ebw.htmandwww.sec.gov/news/testimony/2009/ts032009ebw
.htm (accessed February 25, 2010).

7. "Schumer, Schapiro push for SEC self-funding," *InvestmentNews,* April 15, 2010, http://www.investmentnews.com/article/20100415/FREE/100419924 (accessed April 17, 2010).

8. John Dizard, "Two Easy Ways to Spot the Investment Con," *Financial Times,* March 1, 2009, www.ft.com/cms/s/0/0c31c740-050d-11de-8166 -000077b07658.html (accessed February 25, 2010).

9. Ibid.

10. Ibid.

11. Ibid.

12. Tom Cahill, "Madoff's 19th Century Forerunner Shows Flaws of Rules," Bloomberg.com, March 20, 2009, www.bloomberg.com/apps/news?pid=n ewsarchive&sid=aXSszo3IlHiU (accessed February 25, 2010).

13. "Wiesel Lost 'Everything' to Madoff," *Portfolio.com,* February 26, 2009, www.portfolio.com/executives/2009/02/26/Elie-Wiesel-and-Bernard -Madoff/ (accessed February 25, 2010).

14. Ibid.

15. Ibid.

16. Ibid.

17. Barbara Kiviat, "How to Fix the Credit-Ratings Agencies," *Time,* March 23, 2009, www.time.com/time/business/article/0,8599,1886880,00.html (accessed February 25, 2010).

18. "Written Testimony of Harry Markopolos," U.S. House Committee on Financial Services, February 4, 2009, http://online.wsj.com/public/resources/ documents/MarkopolosTestimony20090203.pdf (accessed February 25, 2010).

19. Ibid.

20. Ibid.

21. Liz Moyer, "Madoff Claims Another Victim," *Forbes.com,* February 9, 2009, www.forbes.com/2009/02/09/bernard-madoff-sec-business-wall-street_ 0209_thomsen.html (accessed February 25, 2009).

22. "Written Testimony of Harry Markopolos," U.S. House Committee on Financial Services, *Wall Street Journal,* February 4, 2009, http://online.wsj .com/public/resources/documents/MarkopolosTestimony20090203.pdf (accessed February 25, 2010).

23. Ibid.

24. Ibid.

25. Ibid.

26. Ibid.

27. Ibid.

28. Ibid.

29. Bradley Block, "Madoff, Merkin and the Epidemiology of Fraud," *Huffington Post*, January 7, 2009, www.huffingtonpost.com/bradley-w-bloch/madoff-merkin-and-the-epi_b_155795.html (accessed February 25, 2010).

30. Mary L. Schapiro, "Speech by SEC Chairman," Address to Practising Law Institute's "SEC Speaks in 2009" Program, February 6, 2009, www.sec.gov/news/speech/2009/spch020609mls.htm (accessed February 25, 2010).

31. Stephen Labaton, "S.E.C. Chief Pursues Tougher Enforcement," *New York Times*, February 22, 2009, www.nytimes.com/2009/02/23/business/23schapiro.html (accessed February 25, 2010).

32. Ibid.

33. David H. Kotz, "Securities and Exchange Commission Office of Inspector General, Semiannual Report to Congress, April 1, 2009–September 30, 2009," www.sec-oig.gov/Reports/Semiannual/2009/semifall09.pdf (accessed February 26, 2010).

34. Ibid.

35. Ibid.

36. Ibid.

37. Kevin Drawbaugh, "Wrapup 1—Obama Pushes Reform to Restore Investor Confidence," Reuters, June 17, 2009, www.reuters.com/article/idUSN1733076620090617 (accessed February 26, 2010).

38. "Economists React: Regulatory Overhaul, Sensible or Burdensome?" Real Time Economics—Economic Insight and Analysis from the *Wall Street Journal*," June 17, 2009, quoting Douglas J. Elliott, "Reviewing the Administration's Financial Reform Proposals," Brookings, June 17, 2009, www.brookings.edu/papers/2009/0617_financial_reform_elliott.aspx (accessed February 25, 2010).

39. "Economists React: Regulatory Overhaul, Sensible or Burdensome?" Real Time Economics—Economic Insight and Analysis from the *Wall Street Journal*," June 17, 2009, http://blogs.wsj.com/economics/2009/06/17/economists-react-regulatory-overhaul-sensible-or-burdensome/tab/article/ (accessed February 26, 2010).

Chapter 28: Fraudulent Offerings—A Short Look

1. SEC v. Transnational Fund, Inc., et al., http://www.sec.gov/litigation/complaints/2007/comp20294.pdf (accessed 5/20/10).

Chapter 29: Auction Rate Securities —A $330 Billion Fraud?

1. "St. Louis Couples Angry at Stifel Nicolaus over Auction Rate Securities," *St. Louis Post-Dispatch* via Acquire Media NewsEdge, January 11, 2009, http://it.tmcnet.com/news/2009/01/11/3905215.htm (accessed February 25, 2010).

2. Ibid.

3. Ibid.

4. "ARC and ARP Securities: How Wall Street Brokerage Firms May Have Defrauded Their Clients Out of Billions Overnight" (undated), www.stock -broker-fraud.com/lawyer-attorney-1284530.html (accessed February 25, 2010).

5. Ibid.

6. Christopher Condon, "Pimco's Auction-Rate Holders Fail to Get Satisfaction," Bloomberg.com, May 30, 2009, www.bloomberg.com/apps/news?pid=20601 110&sid=a3Qh75M3UpDw (accessed February 25, 2010).

7. Shefali Anand, "Pimco's Auction-Preferred Shift," *Wall Street Journal*, March 2, 2009, http://online.wsj.com/article/SB123595319810605265.html (accessed February 25, 2010).

8. Ibid.

9. Ibid.

10. Patricia Hurtado and David Scheer, "Ex-Credit Suisse Brokers Accused of Subprime Fraud, Sued by SEC," Bloomberg.com, September 3, 2009, www .bloomberg.com/apps/news?pid=20601103&sid=aacj9vBCee8c&refer=news (accessed February 26, 2010).

11. The case is *U.S. v. Julian Tzolov and Eric Butler*, 08-CR-370, filed in the Eastern District of New York.

12. "Two Former Credit Suisse Brokers Indicted for Securities Fraud, Wire Fraud, and Conspiracy in Connection with a Fraudulent Scheme to Sell Mortgage-Backed Collateralized Debt Obligations," U.S. Attorney's Office, Eastern District of New York, Press Release, September 3, 2008, www.justice .gov/usao/nye/pr/2008/2008sep03.html (accessed February 26, 2010).

13. Chad Bray, "Credit Suisse Ex-Broker Pleads Not Guilty," *Wall Street Journal*, September 8, 2008, http://online.wsj.com/article/SB122084230788909213. html.

14. Ibid.

15. Chad Bray, "Ex-Broker Pleads in Auction-Rate Case," *Wall Street Journal*, July 23, 2009, http://online.wsj.com/article/SB124827298693672193.html (accessed February 26, 2010).

16. Patricia Hurtado, "Ex-Credit Suisse Broker Butler Gets Five-Year Prison Sentence," Bloomberg.com, January 23, 2010, www.bloomberg.com/apps/news?pid=20601108&sid=ao3g1KEa21x4 (accessed February 26, 2010).

17. Lindsay Fortado and Linda Sandler, "Credit Suisse Sued over Auction-Rate Securities," Bloomberg.com, August 7, 2009, www.bloomberg.com/apps/news?pid=20601085&refer=europe&sid=akpqvlVoMq.I (accessed February 25, 2010).

18. Ibid.

19. For the FINRA award, see http://finraawardsonline.finra.org/turing.aspx?doc=41723 (accessed February 26, 2010).

Chapter 30: $132 Million Tax-Free Exchange Fraud — Section 1031

1. Larry O'Dell, "Miami Man Convicted of Bilking 600 People of $126M," *ABC News*, March 19, 2009, http://abcnews.go.com/US/wireStory?id=7122786 (accessed February 26, 2010).

2. Ibid.

3. Erik Larson, "Con Man Edward Okun Gets 100 Years for Fraud Scheme," Bloomberg.com, August 4, 2009, www.bloomberg.com/apps/news?pid=20601103&sid=aXb9Rat_AfYQ (accessed February 26, 2010).

Chapter 31: Not Smart—The Smart Online Trading Scam

1. SEC, "Order of Suspension of Trading," File 500-1, January 17, 2006, www.sec.gov/litigation/suspensions/34-53129-o.pdf (accessed February 26, 2010).

2. Cited in class action suit filed in Middle District of North Carolina, Durham Division, Case No. 07-cv-00785-WO-PTS, http://securities.stanford.edu/1038/SOLN_01/200898_r01c_07785.pdf (accessed February 26, 2010).

3. Martha Graybow, "Update 3—Smart Online Chief, Brokers Accused of Stock Fraud," Reuters, September 11, 2007, www.reuters.com/article/idUSN1143199920070911 (accessed February 26, 2010); FBI New York, "Smart Online CEO and Two Others Found Guilty of Manipulation of Company Stock," July 2, 2009, http://newyork.fbi.gov/dojpressrel/press-rel09/nyfo070209.htm (accessed February 26, 2010).

4. Ibid.

5. Smart Online, Inc., Form 10-Q for the Quarterly Period Ended September 30, 2009, www.sec.gov/Archives/edgar/data/1113513/000114420409059721/v166630_10q.htm (accessed February 26, 2010).

6. Smart Online, Inc. Report on Form 10-K, April 15, 2010, http://www.sec
   .gov/Archives/edgar/data/1113513/000114420410020625/v181173_10k.htm
   (accessed April 17, 2010).

7. David Glovin, "Smart Online's Ex-Chief Nouri Gets 8 Years for Fraud
   (Update1)," *Business Week* (May 20, 2010), http://www.businessweek.com/
   news/2010-05-20/smart-online-s-ex-chief-nouri-gets-8-years-for-fraud
   -update1-.html (accessed 5/20/2010)

Chapter 32: Boiler Rooms—Where the Heat Rises

1. Ben Younger, writer and director, *Boiler Room* (New Line Cinema, 2000).

2. Nick Paumgarten, "Gekko's Little Goons: Backstage with the Real Boiler
   Room Boys," *New York Observer*, January 30, 2000, www.observer.com/
   node/42516 (accessed February 26, 2010).

3. Warren Meyer, "A Peak [*sic*] Inside the Boiler Room," Coyote Blog,
   November 13, 2008, www.coyoteblog.com/coyote_blog/2008/11/a-peak
   -inside-the-boiler-room.html (accessed February 26, 2010).

4. Ibid.

5. *People v. Cohen*, 2004 NYSlipOp 01687, March 11, 2004, http://pub.bna
   .com/cl/01687.pdf (accessed February 26, 2010).

Chapter 33: Accounting Frauds—With Examples

1. "SEC Charges Eight Former Executives of AOL Time Warner for the
   Company's Accounting Fraud," Litigation Release No. 20586, May 19,
   2008, Accounting and Auditing Enforcement Release No. 2829, May 19,
   2008; *SEC v. John Michael Kelly, Steven E. Rindner, Joseph A. Ripp, and
   Mark Wovsaniker*, Civil Action No. 08 CV 4612 (S.D.N.Y.); *SEC v. David
   M. Colburn, Eric L. Keller, James F. MacGuidwin, and Jay B. Rappaport*,
   Civil Action No. 08 CV 4611 (S.D.N.Y.), www.sec.gov/litigation/litre
   -leases/2008/lr20586.htm. Complaint may be accessed at www.sec.gov/liti
   -gation/complaints/2008/comp20586_kelly.pdf (accessed February 25, 2010).

2. Ibid.

3. Ibid.

4. Ibid.

5. Tim Arango, "From a Whistle-Blower to a Target," *New York Times*, June 9,
   2009, www.nytimes.com/2008/06/09/business/media/09aol.html (accessed
   February 26, 2010).

6. SEC v John Michael Kelly, Steven E. Rinder, Joseph A. Ripp, and Mark
   Wvosaniker, (1:08-cv-04612-CM-GWG), http://www.sec.gov/litigation/
   complaints/2008/comp20586_kelly.pdf (accessed April 17, 2010).

7. Alex Berenson, "3 Plead Guilty in Computer Associates Case," *New York Times*, April 9, 2004, www.nytimes.com/2004/04/09/business/3-plead -guilty-in-computer-associates-case.html (accessed February 26, 2010).

8. Ibid.

9. The general counsel is referred to as "Executive A" in the SEC complaint against David Kaplan (04 Civ. 1465 (I.L.G.) in the Eastern District of New York, www .sec.gov/litigation/complaints/comp18665a.htm (accessed February 26, 2010).

Chapter 34: Stock Option Frauds—Alchemy That Benefits Insiders

1. Werner Menges, "Kobi Disputes 'Money Laundering' Claim," *The Namibian*, March 17, 2008, www.namibian.com.na/index.php?id=28&tx_ttnews [tt_news]=48507&no_cache=1 (accessed February 26, 2010).

2. Ibid.

3. Ibid.

4. For further information, see SEC Litigation Release Nos. 19796 (August 9, 2006), 19878 (October 24, 2006), 19964 (January 10, 2007), and 21090 (June 18, 2009).

5. Werner Menges, "Kobi Wins Appeal on Extradition Act," *The Namibian*, April 12, 2010, www.namibian.com.na/news/full-story/archive/2010/april/ article/kobi-wins-appeal-on-extradition-act/ (accessed April 17, 2010).

Chapter 35: Odd and Unusual Financial Frauds—Not Your Everyday Fraud

1. District of Rhode Island, Case No. CA-09-100, March 9, 2009, www.sec.gov/ litigation/complaints/2009/comp20936.pdf.

2. "SEC Charges Investment Adviser for Inventing a Billion-Dollar Client to Lure New Investors," SEC Press Release, 2009-51, March 9, 2009, http:// www.sec.gov/news/press/2009/2009-51.htm (accessed February 26, 2010).

3. Ibid.

4. Ibid.

5. David Schees, "Money Manager Concocted $1.2 Billion Client, SEC Says," Bloomberg.com, March 9, 2009, www.bloomberg.com/apps/news?pid=206 01110&sid=aTNBxgiOtjlI (accessed February 26, 2010).

6. Ibid.

7. Ibid.

Afterword: What Does the Future Hold?

1. Herbert Danby, ed., *The Mishnah* (Oxford: Oxford University Press, 1933), 458.

2. Eisik Hirsch Weiss, ed., *Sifra Debe Rav hu' Sefer Torat Kohanim on Leviticus*, vol. II, (Vienna, 1862; reprint, New York: Om Publishing Company, 1946); photo offset of Vienna: Jacob Hakohen Schlossberg, 1881/2), 91a.

3. Securities and Exchange Commission, Release No. 34-60497, File No. PCAOB-2008-04), August 13, 2009; Public Company Accounting Oversight Board, Order Approving Proposed Rules on Annual and Special Reporting by Registered Public Accounting Firms, www.sec.gov/rules/pcaob/2009/34-60497.pdf, 2–3 (accessed February 20, 2010).

4. Tom Cahill, "Madoff's 19th Century Forerunner Shows Flaws of Rules (Update 1)," Bloomberg.com, March 20, 2008 www.bloomberg.com/apps/news?pid=20601170&refer=special_report&sid=aBj2XKSxQ138 (accessed February 20, 2010).

5. Ibid.

6. Willie Sutton and Edward Lin, *Where the Money Was: The Memoirs of a Bank Robber* (New York: Viking, 1976; reprint, New York: Broadway, 2004).

7. Ibid.

8. Barbara and David P. Mikkelson, www.snopes.com/quotes/sutton.asp (accessed February 20, 2010).

9. Willie Sutton and Edward Lin, *Where the Money Was: The Memoirs of a Bank Robber,*(New York: Viking, 1976).10. Terry Mitchell, "The Hypocrisy of Insider Trading," http://blog.vici.ro/2010/02/14/the-hypocrisy-of-insider-trading-laws-terry-mitchell/ (accessed February 25, 2010).

11. Larry Elder, "Legalize Insider Trading," *Capitalism*, September 24, 2004, www.capmag.com/article.asp?ID=3933 (accessed February 26, 2010).

12. For the history of the saying "There's no such thing as a free lunch," see the late William Safire's column, "On Language: Words Out in the Cold," *New York Times*, February 14, 1993, www.nytimes.com/1993/02/14/magazine/on-language-words-out-in-the-cold.html (accessed February 26, 2010). According to Safire, its present usage as an economic lesson seems to date back to Mayor Fiorello LaGuardia, who announced at his inauguration, "E finita la cuccagna!" ("No more free lunch!"), promising an end to graft.

About the Author

David E. Y. Sarna has over 35 years of experience as a management consultant and as an executive of high-technology companies, and is managing director of Hendon, Stamford Hill & Company, Inc. (HSH). He has experience in detecting and avoiding financial fraud. His popular blog, GreedWatcher.com, covers financial greed, including securities fraud, money laundering, insider trading, Ponzi schemes, pump-and-dump scams, and related white-collar crime.

Sarna has been involved in several start-up companies, primarily in the areas of technology, biotechnology, and medical devices. He has been a director of publicly traded companies specializing in computer technology and has served as chairman of audit and compensation committees, as well as in an advisory position to the boards of directors of public, private, and not-for-profit organizations. Prior to founding HSH, Sarna served on the advisory board of Hudson Venture Partners, a New York venture capitalist.

Sarna was chairman, chief executive officer, and a director of ObjectSoft Corporation, a publicly traded company that he founded in 1990, and Image Business Systems Corporation (IBS), a software company specializing in document image processing that he founded in 1988 as a spin-off of International Systems Services Corporation. IBS's flagship product, ImageSystem, was the first large-scale client-server software for document image processing. IBM and Warburg Pincus were major investors in IBS. Both ObjectSoft Corporation and IBS were listed on the NASDAQ.

Prior to founding Image Business Systems Corporation, Sarna was executive vice president and a co-founder of International Systems Services Corporation (ISS), a management consulting firm. There, he architected ISS Three, a computer capacity planning tool that ISS successfully marketed and ultimately sold to UCCEL Corporation, now part of Computer Associates. ISS was also successfully sold to a public company.

Earlier in his career, Sarna was employed by Price Waterhouse & Company as a management consultant, and worked for Honeywell, Inc. and IBM in engineering and sales capacities.

Sarna holds a BA degree cum laude with honors from Brandeis University and did his graduate work in computer science at the Technion—Israel Institute of Technology.

He is a certified systems professional, certified computer programmer, and certified data processing auditor. He is the co-author, with G. J. Febish, of *PC Magazine Windows Rapid Application Development* (published by Ziff-Davis Press in 1994), which was translated into several languages; four other books; and over 120 articles published in professional magazines. His book *Implementing and Developing Cloud Computing Applications* will be published by Auerbach Press in 2010. His writing has appeared in publications as diverse as the *Washington Post*, the *Jerusalem Post*, and *Datamation*. He also holds several patents in the fields of bar coding and kiosk technologies.

Sarna has been honored by the Computer Measurement Group, Inc., by IBM, and by Microsoft Corporation, where he was a founding regional director of the Microsoft Developers Network.

He is a popular speaker and has appeared on television many times, including multiple national appearances on the Fox Network, CNN, and MSNBC.

He has been a board member, director, and executive officer of the Ramaz School, and has been on the board of Yavneh Academy, both not-for-profit schools.

Sarna is married, has three adult children, and lives in suburban New York.

Further Reading

The notes to each chapter provide detailed references for the sources cited. Here, I provide suggested topical reading from books that I have found especially worthwhile.

Anne Goldgar's *Tulipmania: Money, Honor, and Knowledge in the Dutch Golden Age* (University of Chicago Press, 2007) is a meticulous account and cultural history of the 1630 tulipmania in the Netherlands. For more information about other early cases of greed, I recommend *White-Collar Crime in Modern England: Financial Fraud and Business Morality 1845–1929* (Cambridge University Press, 1992). I also like *Prince of Swindlers: John Sadleir, M.P. 1813–1856* by James O'Shea (Dublin, Ireland: Geography Publications, 1999), *Manias, Panics, and Crashes: A History of Financial Crises*, by Charles Kindleberger (New York: John Wiley & Sons, 2000); and *Extraordinary Popular Delusions and the Madness of Crowds*, by Charles Mackay (available at www.gutenberg.org/etext/636 as a text file or at http://tinyurl.com/aewvq7 as a PDF). Edwin Lefèvre gives an engaging account of early stock fraud and short-selling in *Reminiscences of a Stock Operator, Annotated Edition* (Hoboken, NJ: John Wiley & Sons, 2009), available at http://www.wiley.com/WileyCDA/WileyTitle/productCd-0470481595.html

You might also like this early history of the Rothschilds: *The Rothschilds: The Financial Rulers of Nations* by John Reeves (Chicago: A. C. McClurg, 1887), available at www.archive.org/details/rothschildsfinan00reevuoft. Other robber barons are featured in Richard O'Connor's, *The Oil Barons:*

Men of Greed and Grandeur (New York: Little Brown & Company, 1971). In *The Great Crash, 1929* (New York: Penguin Books, 1954), John Kenneth Galbraith, one of only a handful of honorees to be twice awarded the Presidential Medal of Freedom, provides us with a good understanding of the nature of bubbles. If you'd like more details on Charles Ponzi, I recommend *Ponzi's Scheme: The True Story of a Financial Legend* by Mitchell Zuckoff (New York: Random House, 2005).

For more modern tales of greed and avarice, I suggest starting with the antics of Crazy Eddie and the Antar family as showcased in *Frankensteins of Fraud: the 20th Century's Top Ten White-Collar Criminals*, by Joseph T. Wells (Aurora, Colorado: Obsidian Publishing, 2000). *OPM: Other People's Money*, by Michael A. Lechter (New York: Warner Books, 2005), tells the tale of Mordechai Weissman and the O.P.M. fraud in great detail.

Fraud detection is well-covered by Howard Silverstone and Howard R. Davia in *Fraud 101: Techniques and Strategies for Detection* (Hoboken, NJ: John Wiley & Sons, 2005). (Apparently the SEC staffers dealing with Madoff never read it.)

Connie Bruck's *The Predators' Ball* (New York: Penguin Books, 1989) and James B. Stewart's *Den of Thieves, Fourth Edition* (New York: Simon & Schuster, 1991) provide detailed accounts of the "junk bond, Ivan Boesky and Michael Milken (Drexel Burham)" era on Wall Street. Tom Wolfe's *The Bonfire of the Vanities* (New York: Dial Press, 1987), and Michael Lewis' *Liar's Poker: Rising Through the Wreckage on Wall Street* (New York: W.W. Norton & Company, 1989), provide memorable and engaging accounts of the events leading to the October 1987 stock market crash.

Joseph Tibman's, *The Murder of Lehman Brothers: An Insider's Look at the Global Meltdown* (New York: Brick Tower Press, 2009), reveals that what killed Lehman (as much as anything) was Richard S. Fuld's emasculation of the risk management function, which serves investment banks as a moral compass. *Street Fighters: The Last 72 Hours of Bear Stearns, the Toughest Firm on Wall Street*, by Kate Kelly (New York: Portfolio, 2010) is a similar look at the demise of Bear Stearns, with perhaps a little more information than you care to know.

In *The Hit Charade: Lou Pearlman, Boy Bands, and the Biggest Ponzi Scheme in U.S. History* (New York: HarperCollins, 2008), Tyler Gray weaves together a fascinating behind-the-scenes story of the greed and desperation of this boy–band mogul and monumental scam artist as he unravels Pearlman's 20-year-long Ponzi scheme.

The definitive books about Madoff and his accomplices, the charges leveled against Goldman Sachs, and the 25,000 investors scammed by Allen Stanford's fraud, however, have yet to be written. Their stories are still unfolding, and the rush-to-press books published to date are not worth reading (trust me on this, I've read quite a few).

HistoryofGreedBook.com is a web site maintained by the author that keeps up with the latest occurrences of financial fraud and greed. You will also find links to SEC and other government fraud-watchers on the site.

Index